# Max Weber

# MODERNITY AND SOCIETY

**General Editor:** *Ira J. Cohen*

*Modernity and Society* is a series of readers edited by the most eminent scholars working in social theory today. The series makes a distinctive and important contribution to the field of sociology by offering one-volume overviews that explore the founding visions of modernity originating in the classic texts. In addition, the volumes look at how ideas have been reconstructed and carried in new directions by social theorists throughout the twentieth century. Each reader builds a bridge from classical selections to modern texts to make sense of the fundamental social forces and historical dynamics of the twentieth century and beyond.

1 *Marx and Modernity: Key Readings and Commentary*, edited by Robert J. Antonio
2 *Emile Durkheim: Sociologist of Modernity*, edited by Mustafa Emirbayer
3 *Max Weber: Readings and Commentary on Modernity*, edited by Stephen Kalberg
4 *Modernity and Society*, edited by Ira J. Cohen

# Max Weber

## READINGS AND COMMENTARY ON MODERNITY

*Edited by*
Stephen Kalberg

*Series Editor*
Ira J. Cohen

**Blackwell** Publishing

BLACKWELL PUBLISHING
350 Main Street, Malden, MA 02148-5020, USA
9600 Garsington Road, Oxford OX4 2DQ, UK
550 Swanston Street, Carlton, V ictoria 3053, Australia

First published 2005 by Blackwell Publishing Ltd

4    2007

*Library of Congress Cataloging-in-Publication Data*

Max Weber : readings and commentary on modernity /
edited by Stephen Kalberg.
p. cm. – (Modernity and society ; 3)
Includes bibliographical references and index.
ISBN 978-0-631-21489-2 (hardback); ISBN 978-0-631-21490-8 (paperback)
1. Weber, Max, 1864-1920.   2. Sociology—Germany—History.   3. Sociology—
History.  4. Civilization, Modern—Philosophy.   I. Title: readings and commentary
on modernity.   II. Weber, Max, 1864-1920.   III. Kalberg, Stephen.   IV. Series.

HM477.G3M39 2005
301'092—dc22

2004052974

A catalogue record for this title is available from the British Library.

Set in 10/12pt Book Antiqua
by Graphicraft Ltd, Hong Kong
Printed and bound in India
by Replika Press Pvt. Ltd

The publisher's policy is to use permanent paper from mills that operate a
sustainable forestry policy, and which has been manufactured from pulp processed
using acid-free and elementary chlorine-free practices. Furthermore, the publisher
ensures that the text paper and cover board used have met acceptable environmental
accreditation standards.

For further information on
Blackwell Publishing, visit our website:
www.blackwellpublishing.com

# Contents

| | |
|---|---|
| *General Editor's Foreword* | *xi* |
| *Chronology of Max Weber's Life* | *xv* |
| *Glossary* | *xxi* |
| *Acknowledgments* | *xxxi* |

**Introduction – Max Weber: The Confrontation with Modernity**   **1**
Stephen Kalberg

| | |
|---|---|
| Max Weber: The Man | 7 |
| Foundational Features of Weber's Interpretive Understanding Sociology | 8 |
| Research Strategies and Procedures | 14 |
| The Vision of "Society" | 19 |
| Weber's Multicausality | 22 |
| Modern Western Rationalism I: Weber's Model | 27 |
| Modern Western Rationalism II: Empirical Variation | 30 |
| Fears about the Future and Proposals for Social Change | 34 |
| Weber on Modernity and Weber's Sociology: An Assessment | 37 |
| Notes | 41 |

| | | | |
|---|---|---|---|
| **PART I** | **THE UNIQUENESS OF THE WEST** | | 49 |
| | *Introduction* | | 49 |
| | **1** | **The "Rationalism" of Western Civilization** | 53 |
| | | From "Prefatory Remarks" to Collected Essays on the Sociology of Religion | 53 |
| | | From *The Religion of India* | 64 |
| | | From *Economy and Society* | 65 |

PART II     THE UNIQUENESS AND ORIGINS OF THE MODERN WESTERN
            WORK ETHIC                                              69
            *Introduction*                                         69

        2   The Religious Origins of the Vocational
            Calling: The Protestant Ethic and the Spirit of
            Capitalism                                             75
            From *The Protestant Ethic and the Spirit of
            Capitalism*                                            75
            From "Discussion Contributions"                       107
            From "On the Psychological Physics of
            Industrial Work"                                      108

        3   Continuous Ethical Discipline                         111
            From "The Protestant Sects and the Spirit of
            Capitalism"                                           111

PART III    THE ECONOMY, THE WORKPLACE, AND THE SPECIALIZED
            NATURE OF WORK IN THE MODERN EPOCH                    121
            *Introduction*                                        121

        4   Market and Planned Economies: Modern
            Capitalism's Substantive Conditions                  125
            From *Economy and Society*                            125

        5   The Separation of the Worker from the Means
            of Production, the Spread of Officialdom, and
            Organizational Discipline in the Factory             130
            From "Socialism"                                      130
            From "A Research Strategy for the Study of
            Occupational Careers and Mobility Patterns"          134
            From *Economy and Society*                            135

        6   The "Specialist" and the "Cultivated Man":
            Certificates and the Origin of Ideas in Science      137
            From *Economy and Society*                            137
            From "Science as a Vocation"                          139

        7   Old and New Civilizations: Contrasting
            Rural Social Structures in Germany and the
            United States                                         142
            From "Capitalism and Rural Society in Germany"        142

PART IV    STRATIFICATION AND INEQUALITY                    147
           *Introduction*                                   147

     8    The Distribution of Power Within the Group:
           Class, Status, Party                             151
           From *Economy and Society*                       151

     9    Germany as a Nation of Commoners                  163
           From "National Character and the Junkers"        163

     10   The Counterbalancing of Economic and
           Social Inequality by Universal Suffrage          168
           From "Suffrage and Democracy in Germany"         168

PART V     AUTHORITY IN THE MODERN EPOCH                    173
           *Introduction*                                   173

     11   Power and Authority: When and Why Do
           People Obey?                                     179
           From *Economy and Society*                       179

     12   The Bureaucracy I: External Form, Technical
           Superiority, Ethos, and Inequality               194
           From *Economy and Society*                       194
           From "The Social Psychology of the World
           Religions"                                       198
           From *Economy and Society*                       198

     13   The Bureaucracy II: The Impact upon
           Society                                          209
           From *Economy and Society*                       209

     14   Past and Present: Charismatic Authority and
           its Routinization                                217
           From "The Social Psychology of the World
           Religions"                                       217
           From *Economy and Society*                       218
           From "The Social Psychology of the World
           Religions"                                       220

PART VI　　The Nation, the Modern State, and Modern Law　　221
　　　　　　*Introduction*　　221

　　15　The Nation: A Sentiment of Solidarity and the
　　　　　"National" Idea　　225
　　　　　From *Economy and Society*　　225

　　16　The State, its Basic Functions, and the
　　　　　Economic Foundations of Imperialism　　230
　　　　　From *Economy and Society*　　230

　　17　From Particularistic Law to Formal Legal
　　　　　Equality and the Rights of Individuals　　238
　　　　　From *Economy and Society*　　238

PART VII　The Circumscription of Ethical Action Today and
　　　　　Weber's Response　　245
　　　　　*Introduction*　　245

　　18　The Antagonism of the Economy and Political
　　　　　Domains to Ethical Action　　251
　　　　　From *Economy and Society*　　251
　　　　　From "Religious Rejections of the World and
　　　　　Their Directions"　　253

　　19　A "Casing of Bondage" and the Rule
　　　　　of Functionaries: The Call for Political
　　　　　Leadership, Strong Parliaments, and an Ethic
　　　　　of Responsibility　　255
　　　　　From *Economy and Society*　　255
　　　　　From "Politics as a Vocation"　　257
　　　　　From *Economy and Society*　　260
　　　　　From "Suffrage and Democracy in Germany"　　262
　　　　　From "Politics as a Vocation"　　265

PART VIII　The Political Culture of American Democracy:
　　　　　The Influence of the "Sect Spirit"　　273
　　　　　*Introduction*　　273

　　20　The Autonomy of the Individual in the
　　　　　Sect and the Ability to Form Democratic
　　　　　Communities: Tolerance and Freedom
　　　　　of Conscience　　277

From *The Protestant Ethic and the Spirit of Capitalism* 277

From *Economy and Society* 280

From *The Protestant Ethic and the Spirit of Capitalism* 280

From *Economy and Society* 282

From "'Churches' and 'Sects' in North America" 284

From *Economy and Society* 287

From "'Churches' and 'Sects' in North America" 287

From *The Protestant Ethic and the Spirit of Capitalism* 288

PART IX  ON "RACE," THE COMPLEXITY OF THE CONCEPT OF ETHNICITY, AND HEREDITY 291
Introduction 291

21  On "Race" Membership, Common Ethnicity, the "Ethnic Group," and Heredity 297

From *Economy and Society* 297

From "Comment on the Lecture by Alfred Ploetz" 306

From "Prefatory Remarks" to Collected Essays on the Sociology of Religion 314

PART X  THE MEANING, VALUE, AND VALUE-FREEDOM OF SCIENCE: "SCIENCE AS A VOCATION" AND OTHER WRITINGS 315
Introduction 315

22  The Meaning and Value of Science: Disenchantment, "Progress," and Civilized Man's Meaninglessness 321

From "Science as a Vocation" 321

23  Ethical Neutrality in the Classroom and the Usefulness and Limits of an Empirical Science 328

From "Science as a Vocation" 328

From "Debate Commentary" 335

**24  The Opposition of Salvation Religions to
    Science and Modern Culture**                    337
    From "Science as a Vocation"                     337
    From "Religious Rejections of the World and
    Their Directions"                                340

PART XI    MODERN READINGS                           345
           *Introduction*                            345

**25  Private Authority and Work Habits: England
    and Russia**                                     347
    Reinhard Bendix

**26  The Data Protection Act: A Case of
    Rationalization**                                353
    Martin Albrow

**27  The McDonaldization of Society**               357
    George Ritzer

**28  Hitler's Charisma**                            361
    Luciano Cavalli

**29  The Routinization of Charisma: Rituals of
    Confession within Communities of *Virtuosi***    363
    Hans-Georg Riegl

**30  The Political Culture of American Democracy:
    The Enduring Influence of Religion**             367
    Seymour Martin Lipset

*Bibliography*                                       377

*Author Index*                                       383

*Subject Index*                                      385

# General Editor's Foreword

In 1919, less than a year before he died, Max Weber observed in "Science as a Vocation":

> In science each of us knows that what he has accomplished will be antiquated in ten, twenty, fifty years. That is the fate to which science is subjected; it is the very *meaning* of scientific work ... Every scientific "fulfillment" raises new questions: it *asks* to be "surpassed" and outdated. Whoever wishes to serve science has to resign himself to this fact.

For the most part, Weber was right. In history, sociology, anthropology, and political science, brilliant answers to once compelling questions stand lifeless and unopened on library shelves as if stricken by a kind of scholarly *rigor mortis*. They were not done in by their own shortcomings but rather by neglect. Scholars simply moved on.

Perhaps Weber would have been amused by the irony that his own works have so far successfully avoided the fate for which he allowed no exceptions. Today, more than 80 years after he declared, unequivocally, that all scientific questions grow outdated, the questions Weber posed are more relevant than ever. And even though this is also true of other classical social theorists, Weber's questions survive in a special way. Unlike Adam Smith, Karl Marx, Emile Durkheim, and other classical theorists, readers do not need any interpretive filter to separate the enduring significance of Weber's questions from an untenable philosophy of history, an anachronistic ideology, outdated pivotal concepts, or polemical engagements with long-forgotten intellectual foes. The same can be said of only a few other thinkers: Alexis de Tocqueville and Georg Simmel immediately come to mind. But what makes Weber's works invaluable for social theory today is that he introduced an entire agenda of questions about the nature and origin of modern Western civilization, inaugurated with the advent of modern capitalism, bureaucratic forms of administration, science and scientific technology, and systematically codified and administered bodies of formal law.

That Weber ultimately was motivated by a broad agenda of questions regarding modernity at large can be difficult for many readers to bear in mind. For many sociologists and political scientists, Weber is first and foremost the author of ideal types of bureaucracy, the three forms of legitimate domination, class, status, and party, and so on. For historically minded readers he is best known for his signature work, *The Protestant Ethic and the Spirit of Capitalism*. Considered individually, as they often are, each of these works sparkles like a burnished stone in its own theoretical setting. There is no need to deny the brilliance of Weber's concepts and historical investigations taken individually. Weber's own intellectual methods and the piecemeal manner in which his works are organized encourage us to focus first on one item and then on another. But no one can claim to be familiar with Weber's thought until she or he perceives that, for all of the different topics he addressed, there are greater themes embedded in his work.

So what, then, are the great themes of Weber's works? I can think of no one better qualified to summarize the questions Weber put to modernity than Stephen Kalberg, an internationally respected scholar who brings more than 25 years of scholarly dedication to Weber's *œuvre* to the production of this volume. In the course of his lucid yet comprehensive Introduction Kalberg provides a fine summary of the questions that framed Weber's concern with modernity at large:

> What defines the particularity of the West? What is the fate in the industrial society of ethical action, the unique individual, and the personality unified by a constellation of noble values, compassion and the notion of a personal calling? How can dynamic and open societies be sustained despite the necessity, if high standards of living are to be maintained widely, to organize work comprehensively in bureaucracies? Do values or means–end calculations of advantage now predominately orient action? How can societies be organized in a manner that nourishes individualism and individual rights? What are the parameters of social change in the West? (p. 37)

How does Weber pursue these questions? As mentioned above, Weber does not provide answers with broad strokes of the theoretical brush. He resolutely refuses to sacrifice the contingencies of individual historical sequences of events for the sake of even the most profound general insights into modernity at large. Even his famous ideal types, though they make no empirical claims of any kind, never even hint at grand generalizations. Instead, they stay close enough to historical situations to enable sociologists and historians to compare and contrast them with historically and culturally specific facts.

But, then, what is Weber's deeper understanding of modernity? What are the "value-relevant interests," to adopt Weber's own methodological term, that permit us to read his works as motivated by the agenda summarized by Kalberg? Weber's deepest concerns stem from the insight that a unique constellation of rationalities characteristic of the modern West has undermined and supplanted most traditional ways of life and religious beliefs. These traditions and beliefs, in all other cultures, both in the pre-modern West and in other civilizations, instilled and supported moral meanings in the great events and daily routines of their day. In pre-modern cultures life and death made sense. People understood their place in the cosmos and the significance of their actions. But in Western modernity, Weber believes that the rationalities of capitalism, the formal legal system, bureaucratic administration, and scientific knowledge become differentiated into individual spheres. The rationalities in all of these societal domains conspire, each in its own way, to replace traditions and religious beliefs with morally hollow rules, regulations, and forms of knowledge.

Only in rare instances did Weber drop his restrictions to permit readers a glimpse of the passion that generated the interests that motivated his works. One such passage appears in the midst of a set of reflections included in his collection of studies on *The Economic Ethics of the World Religions*. In this essay known as "Religious Rejections of the World and Their Directions," Weber observes that today:

> [C]ulture's every step forward seems condemned to lead to an ever-more devastating senselessness. The advancement of culture . . . seems to become a senseless hustle in the service of worthless, moreover self-contradictory and mutually antagonistic ends. . . .
> . . . Culture becomes ever more senseless as a locus of imperfection, of injustice, of suffering, of futility. . . . Viewed from a purely ethical point of view, the world has to appear fragmentary and devalued in all those instances when judged in light of the religious postulate of the divine meaning of existence.

In the full force of this passage it is impossible to deny Weber's passionate objection to the erosion of ethical meaning from Western modernity at large. But again, Weber's genius lies not in his passion but in his scholarship. The art of reading Weber is to read his individual scholarly contributions for themselves, but to bear in mind while doing so that a single author concerned with the fate of the meaning of life in modernity was the author of them all.

But is Weber as entirely bleak and despairing of the culture of modernity as he appears in the preceding passage? Perhaps not. Both in Stephen Kalberg's Introduction and in several of his selections from Weber's writings, he invites us to consider that perhaps Weber found glimmers of more promising developments for modernity in his observations on the United States, which Weber visited and where he traveled extensively in 1904. Though one essay on the United States, "The Protestant Sects and the Spirit of Capitalism" is well known, few scholars previously have sought to balance Weber's negative reactions to Western modernity at large with his more positive reactions to the social, economic, and cultural ways of life in the USA. I suspect that Kalberg's use of Weber's writings on the United States to temper his harsher assessments of modernity may provoke some controversy. But there can be no doubt that Weber's views on the USA need to be considered more carefully by readers than has hitherto been the case. It is remarkable indeed how many of Weber's best-known works take the USA into account.

Be that as it may, Kalberg, in this volume, offers a splendid introduction to Weber's thought. A century after *The Protestant Ethic and the Spirit of Capitalism* was published, and 80 years after Weber proposed that it was the fate of all scientific works to fade from current interests, his work remains a vital force in contemporary intellectual life and a fertile source of new ideas. In Stephen Kalberg's exceptional collection, readers from a multitude of backgrounds will find on the one hand wise and reliable guidance and, on the other hand, the secure editorial judgement that make it possible to discover the vitality of Weber's thought for themselves.

*Ira J. Cohen*

# Chronology of Max Weber's Life

| | |
|---|---|
| April 21, 1864 | Born in Erfurt, Thuringia; eldest of six children. |
| 1866 | The child becomes ill with meningitis; sister Anna dies in infancy. |
| 1868 | Brother Alfred, who will become a prominent economist and sociologist, is born. |
| 1869 | The family moves to Berlin. |
| 1872–82 | Attends the Königliche Kaiserin-Augusta-Gymnasium (elite German high school) in the Berlin suburb of Charlottenburg. |
| 1876 | Four-year-old sister Helene dies. |
| 1877–81 | School papers on ancient history and letters on Homer, Herodotus, Virgil, Cicero, Goethe, Kant, Hegel, and Schopenhauer. |
| 1882 | Attends the University of Heidelberg; joins the Allemannia dueling fraternity; studies law, economic history, philosophy, and history of late Antiquity. |
| 1883–84 | One year of military service in Strasburg; occasional attendance at the University of Strasburg. |
| 1884–85 | Continuation of studies, now at the University of Berlin. |
| 1885 | Officers training in Strasburg; studies in Berlin for the bar exam. |
| 1885–86 | Completion of law studies at the University of Göttingen. |
| 1886 | Passes the bar exam in Berlin; returns to parental home and remains there (except for military duty) until 1893; studies commercial law and ancient rural history. |
| 1887–88 | Military service in Strasbourg and Posen. |
| 1889 | Doctoral dissertation on the development of joint liability in medieval trading companies. |
| 1890 | Participates with mother in the first Evangelical Social Congress. |

| | |
|---|---|
| 1891 | Finishes his second academic dissertation (on the agrarian history of Rome), thus becoming qualified to teach at a German university (*Habilitation*). |
| 1891–92 | Study of farmworkers in East Elbia region (East and West Prussia); publication in 1892. |
| 1893 | Engagement to Marianne Schnitger in March; marriage in September; wedding trip to London; moves out of parental home; substitutes for his teacher Levin Goldschmidt at the University of Berlin; Associate Professor of Commercial and German Law. |
| 1894 | Military exercises in Posen (spring); appointed Professor of Economics, University of Freiburg; moves to Freiburg (fall); participates in the Evangelical Social Congress in Frankfurt (report on farmworkers); publishes study on the stock exchange. |
| 1895 | Second trip to England, Scotland, and Ireland (August–October); inaugural academic lecture, University of Freiburg. |
| 1896 | Participates in Evangelical Social Congress; appointed Professor of Economics at the University of Heidelberg. |
| 1897 | Declines to run for election to the Reichstag; father dies in summer; trip to Spain in fall. |
| 1897–1903 | Prolonged incapacity. |
| 1898 | Travel to Geneva; first sanatorium visit (Lake Constance); further breakdown at Christmas. |
| 1899 | Excused from teaching in the spring semester; resumes teaching in the fall but suffers another breakdown; offers his resignation to the University of Heidelberg (declined); trip to Venice. |
| 1900 | Leaves Heidelberg in July; sanatorium residence until November (Urach); fall and winter in Corsica. |
| 1901 | Resides in Rome and southern Italy in spring; summer in Switzerland; fall and winter in Rome. |
| 1902 | Lives in Florence; again submits his resignation; returns in April to Heidelberg and begins to write on social science methodology questions; travels in winter to the French Riviera; reads Georg Simmel's *Philosophy of Money*. |
| 1903 | Trips to Rome, Holland, Belgium and northern Germany; resigns his position at the University of Heidelberg and becomes *Honorarprofessor*; publishes "Roscher and Knies" (1973a) and begins intense work on *The Protestant Ethic and the Spirit of Capitalism* (PE; 2002b). |
| 1904 | August–December travels widely in the United States; publication of half of *PE* in November and " 'Objectivity' |

in Social Science and Social Policy" (1949b), both in a journal Weber begins to co-edit, *Archive for Social Sciences and Social Policy*.

1905     Publication of second half of *PE* in *Archive* in spring; debates with the economist Schmoller on value-judgments; studies Russian before breakfast.

1906     Attends the Social Democracy Party Convention; travels to southern Italy in the fall; publication of " 'Churches' and 'Sects' in North America" (1985) and "The Prospects for Liberal Democracy in Tsarist Russia" (1978).

1907     Relapse of illness; travels to Italy, Holland, and western Germany; publishes a further essay on methodology questions (1977).

1908     Trip to Provence and Florence in spring; travel to Westphalia in the fall to study the psycho-physics of work in his relatives' textile factory (1995); publication of *The Agrarian Sociology of Ancient Civilizations* (1976a); attacks in a newspaper article the practice in German universities of refusing to promote Social Democrats.

1909     Travel in southern Germany in spring; summer in the Black Forest after a relapse; attends meeting of the Association for Welfare Politics in Vienna; attacks bureaucratization together with brother Alfred; co-founds the German Sociological Association; assumes editorial leadership of the multi-volume *Outline of Social Economics*, a task that eventually leads to *Economy and Society* (*E&S*; 1968a).

1910     Trips to Berlin, Italy, and England; Georg Lukács and Ernst Bloch begin regular visits to Weber's home; the poet Stefan George attends the *jour fixe* twice; speaks against "race biology" at the first German Sociological Association Convention.

1911     Travels to Italy in the spring and Munich and Paris in the summer; criticisms of higher education policies in Germany and fraternity practices in schools of business lead to intense newspaper controversies; begins his Economic Ethics of the World Religions (EEWR) series and continues work on *E&S*.

1912     Spring in Provence; trips to Bayreuth for the Richard Wagner Festival with Marianne and the pianist Mina Tobler, and to further regions in Bavaria in summer; defends a value-free definition of the nation at the German Sociological Association conference in Berlin; resigns from the Association.

| | |
|---|---|
| 1913 | Italy in spring and fall (Ascona, Assisi, Siena, Perugia, Rome); residence for several months in the counter-culture community in Ascona; publishes an early version of *E&S*'s "Basic Concepts" (Chapter 1); continues to work on *E&S*. |
| 1914 | Travels in spring to Ascona and Zurich to defend Frieda Gross in a child custody case; after outbreak of war in August commissioned as reserve officer to establish and manage nine military hospitals around Heidelberg; participation in further debates on value-judgments. |
| 1915 | Youngest brother Karl dies on the Russian Front; returns to research on EEWR; political activity in Berlin against German annexation policy; honorably retired in fall as hospital administrator. |
| 1916 | Trip to East Prussia with sister Lili in spring to visit Karl's grave; further trips to Vienna and Budapest; summer travel to Lake Constance; first public lecture in Germany given in nineteen years; newspaper articles opposing intensified German submarine warfare against English and American ships; participates in a study group focussing on the Polish problem and the creation of a European-wide free trade zone and economic community; publishes *The Religion of China* (1951) and *The Religion of India* (1958) in the *Archive*. |
| 1917 | *Ancient Judaism* (1952) published in the *Archive*; lectures in Munich on science as a vocation (see 1946d); extensive advocacy in newspapers for electoral and parliamentary reform, and argues against censorship; alienates, despite adulation, younger generation at conferences in May and October at Lauenstein Castle in Thuringia; professorship (Economics) offered by the University of Vienna; reads Stefan George's poetry while vacationing in summer in western Germany; publishes essay on value-judgments (1949a). |
| 1918 | Begins teaching after a nineteen-year hiatus; two courses in Vienna offered in the university's largest lecture hall: "A Positive Critique of the Materialist View of History" and "Sociology of the State"; twenty-fifth wedding anniversary; supports a British-style constitutional monarchy for Germany; member of the founding committee of a new liberal party (the German Democratic Party); gives several election campaign speeches; encourages the Kaiser to abdicate; fails to gain a seat in the Constitutional Convention. |

1919      Continues speeches on behalf of the German Democratic Party and is elected to its executive committee; lectures in Munich on "Politics as a Vocation" (1946b); member of the German peace delegation to Versailles charged with drafting a reply to the Allies' war guilt memorandum; in May tries to persuade General Ludendorff in Berlin to voluntarily surrender to the Allies; appointed Professor of Economics at the University of Munich; lecture courses on "General Categories in Sociology" in spring/summer and "Outline of a Universal Social and Economic History" (see 1961) in fall/winter; moves to Munich; farewell party in Heidelberg; mother dies in October.

1920      Writes "Prefatory Remarks" (2002a) to *Collected Essays on the Sociology of Religion*; revises first volume (*PE*, "Sects," 1946e, 1946c, *Religion of China*) of this three-volume project; Part I of *E&S* goes to press; "Political Science" and "Socialism" lecture courses offered in Munich; suicide of youngest sister in April; marriage crisis leads to practical separation; flu develops into pneumonia at the beginning of June; dies on June 14 in Munich.

# Glossary

Italics indicate a cross-reference to another entry in this Glossary.

**Adventure capitalism (promoter, colonial).** This type of capitalism has appeared universally. Since the dawn of history, entrepreneurs and speculators have financed wars, piracy, construction projects, shipping, plantations using forced labor, political parties, and mercenaries. These money-making enterprises are of a purely speculative nature and often involve wars and violent activities. Loans of every sort are offered.

**Affinity (elective, inner; *Wahlverwandtschaft, innere Verwandtschaft*).** A notion taken from Goethe that implies an internal connection between two different phenomena rooted in a shared feature and/or a clear historical linkage (for example, between certain religious beliefs and a vocational calling). The causal relationship is not strong enough to be designated "determining."

**Ascetic Protestantism.** This generic term refers to the Calvinist, Pietist, Methodist, Quaker, Baptist, and Mennonite churches and sects. Weber compares and contrasts the vocational callings of these faiths to each other and to that of Lutheran Protestantism. He discovers the origins of a *"spirit of capitalism"* in their teachings and practices.

**Asceticism.** An extreme taming, channeling, sublimating, and organizing of the believer's spontaneous human drives and wants (the *status naturae*) by a set of values. Western asceticism grounded a "methodical-rational organization of life" in values in two "directions": ascetic Protestantism did so *in* the world ("this-worldly asceticism") and medieval Catholic monks, living sequestered in monasteries, did so *outside* the world ("other-worldly asceticism").

**Authority (domination, rulership; *Herrschaft*).** Why do people obey commands? To Weber, in contrast to sheer *power*, authority implies that persons attribute, for a variety of reasons, legitimacy to the commands. Hence, a voluntary element is characteristic; that is, a belief, in the end, that the authority is justified. Weber identifies three types of authority: *traditional* (patriarchalism, feudalism, patrimonialism), *charismatic*, and *rational-legal* (bureaucratic).

**Bureaucratic authority (rational-legal).** Authority resides in a position in an organization, and the rights it grants to incumbents, rather than in persons or traditions. Hence, obedience to authority rests upon a belief in the appropriate enactment of impersonal statutes and regulations. Attached to "the office," authority remains even though people come and go. Historically unusual, this type of authority has largely been found in the West in the past 200 years.

**Calling (religious calling; vocational calling; *Beruf*).** Originally denoted a task given by God; hence it must be honored and performed diligently. The calling introduced a demarcated and respected realm of work into the Protestant believer's life in the sixteenth and seventeenth centuries in the West. Despite a vast comparative-historical search, Weber found this definition of "calling" only in Protestantism (originally in Luther). In secularized form – "service" to a profession and to a community – it continues even to some extent today.

**Capitalism.** Capitalism has existed in all the world's civilizations. It involves the expectation of profit and peaceful opportunities for acquisition. A calculation of earnings in money terms occurs – at the beginning (starting balance) and end of the project (concluding balance), and in respect to the utility of all potential transactions. The origins of profits and losses are ascertained.

**Carrier (social carriers; *Träger*).** Patterned social action oriented to values, traditions, interests, and ideas becomes important as a causal force, according to Weber, only when "carried" by demarcated and influential groupings (e.g., classes, status groups, organizations). *Sects* and churches, for example, served as indispensable carriers of the *Protestant ethic*. All manner of ideas have appeared in all cultures, yet only those that acquire cohesive social carriers have an impact. Visible throughout Weber's writings, this concept separates his sociology unequivocally from all Idealist views of history.

**Charismatic authority.** See *authority*. Obedience results from a belief in and devotion to the extraordinary sanctity and heroism of an individual person who is viewed as exceptional. This type of authority opposes all existing values, customs, laws, rules, and traditions.

**Disenchantment of the world (*Entzauberung*).** This famous phrase refers, on the one hand, to a development within the domain of religion from ritual and magic to "other-worldly salvation religions" in which paths to salvation completely devoid of magic (Puritanism) are formulated (see

*The Protestant Ethic*), and, on the other, to a broad historical development in the West according to which knowledge of the universe is less and less understood by reference to supernatural forces and salvation doctrines, and more and more by reference to empirical observation and the experimental method of the natural sciences (see "Science as a Vocation", 1946d).

**Economic ethic (work ethic)**: See *traditional economic ethic* and *modern economic ethic*.

**Economic Ethics of the World Religions**. In this three-volume work, Weber investigated the extent to which Confucianism, Taoism, Hinduism, Buddhism, Jainism, ancient Judaism, ancient Christianity, medieval Catholicism, Lutheranism, and *ascetic Protestantism* introduced an *economic ethic*. He wanted to know, if a religion did so, whether the ethic was more *traditional* or *modern*.

**Economic form**. In contrast to an *economic ethic*, an economic form refers to the way in which a company is organized and managed; that is, the relationship of employers to workers, the type of accounting, the movement of capital, etc. (all of which can occur according to a *traditional* or *modern economic ethic*).

**Ethic of conviction** (*Gesinnungsethik*). Adherence to an ethical position in an absolute manner; that is, regardless of the possible negative consequences that might result from doing so. (Luther: "Here I stand, for I can do no other.") Good intent alone is central. Opposed to the *ethic of responsibility*.

**Ethic of responsibility** (*Verantwortungsethik*). An account is given to oneself of the foreseeable results of an action, and responsibility for them is accepted. Conceivably, the planned action might be abandoned if assessment of its outcome reveals negative consequences. Opposed to the *ethic of conviction*.

**Ethical action**. Rooted in values and containing a strong "obligatory" element, Weber sees ethical action as weakened and circumscribed in the modern era to the extent that *practical*, *theoretical*, and *formal rationality* expand.

**Ethnic group**. Weber contends that this concept is of little utility to a social science that seeks to explain how social action arises and becomes patterned so that groups are formed. Many other social factors are generally more important. Weber counsels caution and circumspection. See *race*.

**Formal rationality**. Central to "*modern Western rationalism*" and *bureaucratic authority*. Omnipresent in *modern capitalism*, *modern law*, and the modern state, this type of rationality implies decision-making "without regard to persons"; that is, by reference to sets of universally applied rules, laws, statutes, and regulations.

**Frame of mind (*Gesinnung*).** The temperament or disposition that Weber sees as specific to a group of people. The term refers to essential features (in the sense of an *ideal type*) of Calvinists, Catholics, Lutherans, adventure capitalists, feudal aristocrats, old commerce-oriented (patrician) families, the middle class, etc. Each group possesses its own temper or outlook. In some groups the frame of mind may be more weighted toward values (and even ethical values, as in the religious groups); in others, it tends more toward endowing interests (adventure capitalists) or traditions (peasants) with greater meaning.

**Honoratiores (notables).** With the development of the economy, only the wealthy (landowners, patrician merchants) will possess the time and resources to fulfill administrative tasks. Hence, direct democracy will likely turn into rule by notables. The bureaucratic functionary generally carries out tasks in a manner *technically* superior (precision, speed, knowledge of the files, etc.) to the avocational and honorific service of honoratiores.

**Ideal type.** Weber's major methodological tool. This heuristic concept seeks to capture the essential *subjective meaning* in a group from the point of view of the theme under investigation (such as the *economic ethics* of different religions). Once formed, ideal types serve as standards against which particular empirical cases can be "measured" and then defined. They are central also in establishing causality. Ideal types constitute Weber's level of analysis rather than historical narrative or global concepts (society, modernization).

**Individual autonomy.** Weber is worried that, in a modern world in which impersonal political, economic, and legal orders dominate, and large-scale bureaucracies characterized by rigid hierarchies, specialized tasks, conformist pressures, and routine work are ubiquitous, individual autonomy and ethical responsibility will be eroded.

**Interpretive understanding (*Verstehen*).** This is the term Weber uses to describe his own methodology. He wishes to understand the patterned actions of people in demarcated groups by reconstructing the milieu of values, traditions, interests, and emotions (see *social action*) within which they live, and thereby to comprehend how *subjective meaning* is formulated.

**Location (*Ort*).** Integral to his methodology of interpretive understanding, Weber perpetually "locates" particular ideas, economies, values, interests, salvation-striving, types of authority and law, power, social honor, etc., within complex social contexts.

**Middle class (*bürgerlich, das Bürgertum*).** *The Protestant Ethic* offers an analysis of the religious origins of the ethos and frame of mind of a new class that elevated steady and constant work to the center of life. Composed of both employers and workers, this middle class was the *carrier* of a set of values oriented to economic activity and "earning a living" that distinguished it significantly from the destitute urban poor, feudal nobles, patrician old-family capitalists, and adventure capitalists. Weber seeks to offer an explanation for the origin of this set of values and to argue that they played a role in calling forth *modern capitalism*.

**Modern capitalism (middle-class industrial capitalism).** Arose in the West in the seventeenth and eighteenth centuries. A rational (systematic) organization of (free) labor, a methodical pursuit of profit, an intense orientation to market opportunities, a *modern economic ethic*, and industrial companies and factories characterize this type of capitalism.

**Modern capitalism's substantive conditions.** To Weber, modern markets do not develop out of the "natural propensity" discovered by Adam Smith to "truck, barter, and exchange." Nor do they arise from the rational choices of individuals. Rather, many "substantive conditions" must have developed beforehand, such as rational modes of accounting and administration, enacted formal law "rationally interpreted and applied" by jurists, the concept of the citizen, advanced science and technology, a modern economic ethic, the separation of the household from the industrial company, and the absence of strict market monopolies.

**Modern (rational) economic ethic.** See *spirit of capitalism*

**Modern law.** Characterized by formal legal equality and a rootedness in documents (such as a constitution) and judicial precedent rather than sacred traditions or charismatic persons, modern law is enacted and implemented by specialists (legislators, judges). The impersonal execution of laws, by reference to systematic and universally applied procedures, is taken as an ideal.

**Modern science.** Although highly technologically advanced, modern science, unlike science in Antiquity, the Middle Ages, and the seventeenth century in the West, is characterized by an incapacity to offer a justification for its own foundations. Hence, it fails to assist us to find an answer to Tolstoi's question: "How we should live?" Fearing yet another "caste of specialists" that would intrude upon the individual's autonomy, now in the name of science, Weber wishes to limit its legitimate goals to insight, clarity, and knowledge.

**Modern Western rationalism.** Weber's term for the modern West; also referred to as the "modern Occident." Through wide-ranging comparisons to the ancient and medieval civilizations of China, India, and the West, he wishes to identify the modern West's unique features. Prominent are the *formal*, *practical*, and *theoretical types of rationality*.

**Nation**. An "entirely ambiguous" concept, according to Weber. Rejecting common language, religious creed, and "common blood" as definitive features of nations, he instead emphasizes a "sentiment of solidarity," rooted in values.

**National character**. Explanation of differences between groups by reference to national character was widespread in Weber's time. Because it failed to acknowledge the influence of religious, historical, economic, political, social, etc. forces, Weber thoroughly rejected this explanation.

**Notables**. See *honoratiores*.

**Objectivity**. Social scientists never approach empirical reality in an "objective" manner, Weber argues; rather, they bring to it sets of questions and interests related to their *values* ("value-relevant"). Hence, every approach to "the data" is "perspectival" – all the more as every epoch defines in its own way, in accord with its predominant concerns and currents of thought, certain aspects of empirical reality as "culturally significant." And even though new fashions, themes, and concerns render heretofore occluded aspects of social reality visible, other aspects, by the same token, always remain in the shadows. See *value-freedom*.

**Organization of life; organized life**. Weber's term, *Lebensführung*, implies a conscious directing, or leading, of life. Although for him the organized life is generally "internally" rooted in a set of values, this is not always the case; the practical-rational *Lebensführung* is anchored by interests, or "externally." This term in Weber's writings stands opposed to the undirected life that simply, like a natural event, flows on in time without guidance. It was necessary for the Puritans in particular, as *ascetic Protestants*, to organize their lives methodically according to their values.

**Ossification**. Dominated by extreme bureaucratization, ossified – or closed and stagnant – societies are ones in which social and political hierarchies become massive and rigid. Opposite of societal dynamism. Weber argues that ossified societies will not allow conflicts to surface over interests and ideals – and these are indispensable if political leadership and a sense of ethical responsibility are to develop and be sustained. He fears that such stagnant societies *may* be on the horizon in the West.

**Power**. In direct contrast to *authority*, power, in Weber's classic definition, implies sheer coercion, or "the likelihood that one person in a social relationship will be able, even despite resistance, to carry out his own will".

**Practical rationality**. The random flow of daily interests is here central, and the individual's adaptation – through means–end rational calculations – to them. Contrasts directly with substantive rationality, according to which the random flow of interests is confronted and ordered by an orientation of action to values.

**Predestination (doctrine of)**. Prominent especially among Calvinists. God has willed a few to be saved; most people are condemned. His reasons are unknowable and no human activity can change one's "predestination status." The logical consequence of belief in this doctrine was fatalism and despair among the devout. Revisions by theologians and ministers led to "the Protestant ethic."

**Protestant ethic**. The source of the *spirit of capitalism*. Sixteenth- and seventeenth-century interpretations of the Calvinist doctrine of *predestination* eventually led to a situation in which believers could experience "psychological rewards" *vis-à-vis* their salvation status once they oriented their activities to methodical work, economic competition, profit, and the attainment of wealth.

**Providential (sanctifying)**. Rendering with religious (salvation) significance an activity heretofore purely utilitarian (work, for example).

**Puritans**. Weber's general term for the ascetic Protestant churches and sects of England and North America: the Calvinists (later Presbyterians), Methodists, Baptists, Quakers, and Mennonites. All Puritans organized their lives around work and a this-worldly, morally rigorous asceticism. Hence, Puritanism, Weber argues, provides a consistent foundation for the idea of a vocational calling found in "the Protestant ethic." Remarkably, because oriented to salvation in the next life rather than this-worldly goods or interests, the intense activity of Puritans was *in* the world but not *of* the world.

**Race**. Weber opposes the notion that reference to innate and inheritable qualities can be helpful in sociological analysis. "Racial theories" anchored in notions of inherited instincts, he argues, are hypothetical and methodologically weak. *Social action* that appears to be oriented to race is, on closer inspection, Weber holds, actually a consequence of the juxtaposition of other (e.g., economic, political, social) forces. See *ethnic group*.

**Rational**. An adjective that denotes a systematic, rigorous, disciplined element to action.

**Rationalism of Western civilization**. This term implies the predominance, in a civilization, of systematic work, a modern economic ethic, cities characterized by the presence of autonomous governing units, modern law, bureaucratic authority, impersonal judiciary codes and civil servants to implement them, a modern bureaucratic state, modern science, advanced technology, etc. It does not imply the "superiority" of the West.

**Rationalization of action**. A systematization of action, even to the point of a "methodical-rational" organization of life. Ascetic Protestant believers "rationalized" their activities in the most rigorous fashion. Under modern capitalism today external coercion alone (rather than belief and religious values), emanating from the demands of the workplace and modern capitalism itself, calls forth rationalized activity and the *organized life*.

**Sect**. As opposed to a church, an exclusive and tightly-knit group that admits new members only once specific criteria have been fulfilled. Membership implies both "good character" and a monitoring of behavior to ensure compliance with high moral standards.

**Social action (meaningful action)**. Weber's sociology seeks "to offer an interpretive understanding of social action." Unlike "reactive" or "imitative" action, social action implies a subjectively meaningful component that "takes account of the behavior of others." This aspect can be understood by the researcher. Weber identifies (as *ideal types*) four "types of social action": affectual, traditional, means–end rational, and value-rational. Among other major goals, *Economy and Society* seeks to chart out the social contexts that call forth meaningful action in a variety of *societal domains*.

**Societal domains (orders, arenas, realms, spheres;** *gesellschaftliche Ordnungen*). *Social action* arises, to Weber, mainly within the law, the economy, authority, religion, status groups, and "universal organizations" (family, clan, and traditional neighborhood) domains. Each constitutes a demarcated realm characterized by definable constellations of subjective meaning. His comparative-historical analyses are organized around these spheres (and their various manifestations in different civilizational settings), and the different themes, dilemmas, and problematics typical of each, rather than "society," institutions, or the individual's "rational choices." In certain epochs, such as our own, some domains may fall into relationships of irreconcilable antagonism (e.g. the rational economy and the religious ethos of brotherhood and compassion).

**Specialists**. People who develop only one talent or ability. This occurs, Weber emphasizes following Goethe, to the detriment of other talents or abilities. In contrast to the "cultivated" person who possesses *Bildung* – a broad and deep education and a wide range of experience – that integrates and unifies the personality.

**Spirit of capitalism**. Represented by Benjamin Franklin, the spirit of capitalism constitutes a secularized legacy of the *Protestant ethic*. It refers to a methodical orientation toward profit, competition, work "as an absolute end in itself," and a perceived duty to increase one's wealth (yet the avoidance of its enjoyment). Weber insists that its origin cannot be located in economic interests; rather, a set of religious values and the quest for certainty of salvation constitute the source of this *frame of mind: the Protestant ethic*. As an important causal factor, among many others, this "spirit" played a part in giving birth to *modern capitalism*.

**The state**. An organization that monopolizes the legitimate use of force within specified territorial boundaries. Its laws, statutes, and legal procedures must be conceptualized as possessing autonomy, even *vis-à-vis* a modern capitalist economy.

**Status (status groups)**. Status groups appear where social action is patterned and oriented to social honor, social esteem, and a shared style of life and consumption patterns. Inequality arises not only from property ownership, Weber holds, but also from status differences.

**Subjective meaning**. Weber's sociology never aspires to establish that which is objectively valid. Rather, it seeks to understand the subjective meaningfulness of particular patterned action by persons in specific groups (e.g., churches, sects, bureaucracies, status groups, etc.). Throughout his sociology, Weber seeks to understand how people view their own behavior and how they justify it to themselves, or lend it "meaning" (no matter how odd it may appear to the observer). He wishes in *The Protestant Ethic*, for example, to understand why, for ascetic Protestants, continuous hard work constitutes a subjectively meaningful endeavor. *Ideal types* capture subjective meaning.

**Substantive rationality**. A constellation of values. If regular social action is oriented to it, people are uprooted from the random flow of interests typical of everyday life. Weber fears that the dominance under *modern Western rationalism* of formal, theoretical, and practical rationality will weaken all substantive rationalities.

**Testify (*bewähren*)**. To testify is a central notion for all ascetic Protestants. It indicates a striving for salvation that implies both an outward demonstration of faith visible to others (one's conduct, demeanor, and bearing) and a psychological element: the devout understand that their very strength to "prove" their belief through perpetual righteous conduct emanates from God – and hence feel an inner confidence regarding their salvation status.

**Theoretical rationality**. The mastering of reality, which is undertaken alike by theologians in search of greater doctrinal consistency and modern-day scientists, here occurs through systematic thought and conceptual schemes. Reality is confronted cognitively rather than through values, interests, or traditions, although the confrontation for theologians, unlike for modern scientists, ultimately aims to introduce new values.

**Traditional authority**. See *authority*. Obedience results from an established belief in the sanctity of immemorial traditions and the legitimacy of those exercising rulership under them (for example, clan patriarchs). This type of authority has been far more widespread throughout history than either *charismatic* or *bureaucratic authority*. Unlike the latter, under traditional authority a personal bond between ruler and ruled exists, which implies that an ethical appeal can be made directly to the ruler in the event of abuse.

**Traditional economic ethic (economic traditionalism).** A *frame of mind* in respect to work. Work is viewed as a necessary evil and only one arena of life, no more important than the arenas of leisure, family, and friends. "Traditional needs" are implied; when fulfilled, then work ceases. This frame of mind stands in opposition to the development of modern capitalism. (In Weber's time "traditionalism" referred to the conduct of activities in an accustomed, habitual fashion.)

**Types of rationality.** See *formal rationality, practical rationality, substantive rationality,* and *theoretical rationality*.

**Value-freedom, freedom from values (*Wertfreiheit*).** Weber insisted that all social science research must be "value-free." Once investigators have selected their theme of inquiry (see *objectivity*), personal values, preferences, and prejudices must not be allowed to interfere with the collection of empirical data and its evaluation. An intermixing of the researcher's values with those of the actors being studied must be avoided. This axiom also implied a strict division between that which *exists* (the question for scientific analysis) and that which *should be* (the realm of personal values and preferences). Social scientists must strive, also in the classroom, to uphold this ideal.

**Value-judgment.** The insertion of one's personal values (whether rooted in political, religious, or philosophical positions) into the lecture hall or the collection and evaluation of empirical data. See *value-freedom* and *objectivity*.

**Vocational calling.** See *calling*.

# *Acknowledgments*

The editor and publisher gratefully acknowledge the permission granted to reproduce the copyright material in this book:

Albrow, Martin, "The Data Protection Act: A Case of Rationalization," in *Rationalization and Modernity*, eds Scott Lash and Sam Whimster (London: Allen & Unwin, 1987), pp. 173–5, 179–80, 182. Reprinted by permission of the author.

Bendix, Reinhard, "Private Authority and Work Habits: England and Russia," in *Nation-Building and Citizenship* (Berkeley, CA: University of California Press, 1977; original edition John Wiley & Sons, Inc. 1964), pp.181–6, 189–93.

Cavalli, Luciano, "Hitler's Charisma," in *Rationalization and Modernity*, eds Scott Lash and Sam Whimster (London: Allen & Unwin, 1987), pp. 326–9.

Lipset, Seymour Martin, "The Political Culture of American Democracy: The Enduring Influence of Religion," in *The First New Nation: The United States in Historical and Comparative Perspective* (New York: W.W. Norton & Co., 1979), pp. xxxvi–xxxviii, 153–6, 158–65, 169. © Seymour Martin Lipset, 1963, 1979. Reprinted by permission of the author.

Riegl, Hans-Georg, "The Routinization of Charisma: Rituals of Confession within Communities of Virtuosi," *Totalitarian Movements and Political Religions* 1, 1 (Winter 2000): 16–18, 22–3, 26–9. Reprinted by permission of Taylor & Francis Ltd, http://www.tandf.co.uk/journals

Ritzer, George, *The McDonaldization of Society* (Thousand Oaks, CA: Pine Forge Press, 2000), pp. 47–8, 50–6. © 2000 by Sage Publications. Reprinted by permission of Sage Publications.

Weber, Max, " 'Churches' and 'Sects' in North America," trans. Colin Loader, *Sociological Theory* 3 (Spring 1985): 8, 10, 10–11. Reprinted by permission of Colin Loader and the American Sociological Association.

Weber, Max, *Economy and Society: An Outline of Interpretive Sociology*, eds Guenther Roth and Claus Wittich, trans. Ephraim Fischoff, Ferdinand Kolegar, Talcott Parsons, Max Rheinstein, Guenther Roth, and Claus Wittich

(Berkeley, CA: University of California Press, 1978), pp. 29–30, 85–6, 109–11, 161–2, 212–13, 215–16, 223, 224, 225, 243–4, 246, 385–95, 585, 635–7, 657–8, 667–8, 695–6, 698–9, 811–14, 883, 908–9, 910–20, 922–6, 926–39, 941–54, 956–8, 958–9, 960–1, 963, 973–5, 979–80, 980–4, 983–6, 987–9, 989–93, 994, 998–1000, 1000–2, 1149–50, 1156, 1186–7, 1206–10, 1394–5, 1401–4, 1409, 1417, 1420, 1426–8. © 1978 The Regents of the University of California. Reprinted by permission of the publisher.

Weber, Max, *Max Weber*, ed. J. E. T. Eldridge, trans. D. Hÿtch (London: Nelson, 1972), pp. 154–5, 197–9, 200–2, 203–4, 209. Reprinted by permission of J. E. T. Eldridge.

Weber, Max, "National Character and the Junkers," in *From Max Weber: Essays in Sociology*, eds and trans. Hans H. Gerth and C. Wright Mills (New York: Oxford University Press, 1946), pp. 386–8, 390–3. © 1946, 1958, 1973 by H. H. Gerth and C. Wright Mills. Reprinted by permission of Oxford University Press.

Weber, Max, "On the Psychological Physics of Industrial Work," in *Studienausgabe der Max Weber – Gesamtausgabe Band 1/11: Zur Psychophysik der industriellen Arbeit – Schriften und Reden, 1908–12*, ed. Wolfgang Schluchter (Tubingen: Mohr Verlag, 1998) pp. 109–11, trans. Stephen Kalberg. Reprinted by permission of Mohr Siebeck e.K. Tübingen.

Weber, Max, "Political Groups," in *Wirtschaft und Gesellschaft: Grundriss der verstehenden Soziologie* [*Economy and Society: An Outline of Interpretive Sociology*], ed. Johannes Winckelmann (Tübingen: Mohr Verlag, [1922] 1976), p. 516, trans. Stephen Kalberg. Reprinted by permission of Mohr Siebeck e.K. Tübingen.

Weber, Max, "Political Organizations and the State," in *Wirtschaft und Gesellschaft* (*Economy and Society*), ed. Johannes Winckelmann (Tübingen: Mohr Verlag, [1922] 1976), pp. 29–30, trans. Stephen Kalberg. Reprinted by permission of Mohr Siebeck e.K. Tübingen.

Weber, Max, "Politics as a Vocation," in *From Max Weber: Essays in Sociology*, ed. and trans. Hans H. Gerth and C. Wright Mills (New York: Oxford University Press, 1946), pp. 95, 114–17, 120–8. © 1946, 1958, 1973 by Hans H. Gerth and C. Wright Mills. Reprinted by permission of Oxford University Press.

Weber, Max, "Power and Domination," in *Wirtschaft und Gesellschaft.* [*Economy and Society*], ed. Johannes Winckelmann (Tübingen: Mohr Verlag, [1922] 1976), pp. 28–9, trans. Stephen Kalberg. Reprinted by permission of Mohr Siebeck e.K. Tübingen.

Weber, Max, "Religious Rejections of the World and Their Directions," in *From Max Weber: Essays in Sociology*, eds and trans. Hans H. Gerth and C. Wright Mills (New York: Oxford University Press, 1946), pp. 333–5, 350–3, 355–7. © 1946, 1958, 1973 by Hans H. Gerth and C. Wright Mills. Reprinted by permission of Oxford University Press.

Weber, Max, "Science as a Vocation" in *From Max Weber: Essays in Sociology*, eds and trans. Hans H. Gerth and C. Wright Mills (New York: Oxford University Press, 1946), pp. 134–6, 138–45, 145–53, 153–6. © 1946, 1958, 1973 by Hans H. Gerth and C. Wright Mills. Reprinted by permission of Oxford University Press.

Weber, Max, "Suffrage and Democracy in Germany," (1917) in *Studien-ausgabe der Max Weber – Gesamtausgabe Band 1/15: Zur Politik im Weltkrieg – Schriften und Reden 1914–1918*, ed. Wolfgang Mommsen (Tübingen: Mohr Verlag, 1988), pp. 170–2, 186–9, trans. Stephen Kalberg. Reprinted by permission of Mohr Siebeck e.K. Tübingen.

Weber, Max, *The Protestant Ethic and the Spirit of Capitalism*, 3rd edn, trans. Stephen Kalberg (Los Angeles: Roxbury Publishing, 2002), pp. 14–16, 26–7, 35–7, 48–50, 100–1, 103–25, 149–60, 163–4, 195–6, 210–12, 222, 255–7. Reprinted by permission of the publisher.

Weber, Max, "The Protestant Sects and the Spirit of Capitalism," in *The Protestant Ethic and the Spirit of Capitalism*, 3rd edn trans. Hans H. Gerth and C. Wright Mills (Los Angeles: Roxbury Publishing, 2002), pp. 127, 128–31, 132–4, 134–5, 137–8, 144–6, 146–7. The English text previously published in *From Max Weber: Essays in Sociology*, eds and trans. H. H. Gerth and C. Wright Mills (New York: Oxford University Press, 1946) © 1946, 1958, 1973 by H. H. Gerth and C. Wright Mills. Reprinted by permission of Oxford University Press.

Weber, Max, *The Religion of India: The Sociology of Hinduism and Buddhism*, eds and trans. Hans H. Gerth and Don Martindale (New York: The Free Press of Glencoe, 1958), pp. 342–3.

Weber, Max, "The Social Psychology of the World Religions," in *From Max Weber: Essays in Sociology*, eds and trans. Hans H. Gerth and C. Wright Mills (New York: Oxford University Press, 1946), pp. 295–6, 297, 299. © 1946, 1958, 1973. Reprinted by permission of Oxford University Press.

Every effort has been made to trace copyright holders and to obtain their permission for the use of copyright material. The publisher apologizes for any errors or omissions in the above list and would be grateful if notified of any corrections that should be incorporated in future reprints or editions of this book.

# Max Weber: The Confrontation with Modernity

## Stephen Kalberg

Every single important activity and ultimately life as a whole, if it is not to be permitted to run on as an event in nature but is instead to be consciously guided, is a series of ultimate decisions through which the soul – as in Plato – *chooses* its own fate; that is, the meaning of its activity and existence. (Weber, 1949a, p. 18; emphasis in original)

The professional bureaucrat is chained to his activity in his entire economic and ideological existence. In the great majority of cases he is only a small cog in a ceaselessly moving mechanism which prescribes to him an essentially fixed route of march. The official is entrusted with specialized tasks, and normally the mechanism cannot be put into motion or arrested by him, but only from the very top. The individual bureaucrat is, above all, forged to the common interest of all the functionaries in the perpetuation of the apparatus and the persistence of its rationally exercised domination. (Weber, 1968a, p. 988)

[We are] *cultural beings* endowed with the capacity and will to take a deliberate stand toward the world and to lend it meaning. (Weber, 1949b, p. 81; trans. altered; emphasis in original)

Only one thing is indisputable: no matter how it is constituted, every arena of societal relationships must without exception and in the last analysis also be examined, if one wishes to *evaluate* it, in light of the optimal opportunities it offers – owing to various external and internal (motivational) operating forces – to *certain types of persons* to rise to positions of authority. (Weber, 1949b, p. 27; trans. altered; emphasis in original)

Of the three major founders of modern sociology, Max Weber spans the widest horizon. He pursued an extraordinarily broad and deep comparative agenda even by the ambitious standards of scholarship in his day.

His empirical studies investigated ancient and medieval China and India, yet also each century of the West's 2,600-year development. He explored, for example, the prophecy of ancient Israel, the medieval origins of Western music, and the salvation doctrines of Buddhism, Hinduism, ancient Judaism, early Christianity, medieval Catholicism, Lutheranism, and Calvinism. He conducted in-depth research as well on the decline of the Roman Empire, the origins of notions of citizenship in the West in the cities of the Middle Ages, the accounting practices of medieval trading companies, the caste system in India, and the possibilities for democracy in Russia.

Several large themes unite Weber's breathtaking works. He attempted to *understand* the ways in which people in various groupings, in light of varieties of social configurations, attributed meaning on a regular basis to certain activities and not to others. How do people in different social settings create meaning in their lives? He wanted to know in particular how they do so by reference to values. And which values? Weber attempted to examine these questions impartially even though at times the behavior of social groups across the globe appeared to him, from the point of view of his own preferences, odd and even bizarre.

He especially sought to demarcate and define clearly, through comparisons across civilizations and epochs, the "causal origins" and present-day direction of a world transforming itself rapidly before his eyes. How did the modern West arise? In what direction was it moving and with what consequences for "how we live today"? Weber saw a slow-paced, agrarian society of feudal estates and firm social hierarchies just a few miles outside his home in Heidelberg, yet discovered in London and Berlin industrial capitalism, impersonal and fast-paced relationships, democratic forms of governance, and widespread secularism. Trained as a comparative economic historian, he scrutinized other societies and epochs for clues. Perhaps certain patterns characterized all epochs undergoing rapid social change.

Emile Durkheim (1858–1918), Karl Marx (1818–83), and Max Weber (1864–1920) stood between the industrial and feudal eras. All these founders of modern Sociology looked back to a familiar age in its final hours and ahead to a new, only partially visible era inexorably approaching. What kind of world was now bursting forth at breakneck speed and, Weber wished also to know, what "type of person" would dwell in it? How shall we live with dignity in this new era of "modern Western rationalism" and how can ethical values be preserved? What parameters characterize the social changes taking place all around us? How, Marx asked, as the mechanized wheels of modern capitalism steamrolled all in the working class into "false consciousness," could those qualities distinct to the human species – creative action and thought – be retained? How would individuals in the industrialized and secular era, Durkheim queried, deprived of a common "collective conscience," acquire firm bearings and avoid self-interested egocentrism? All the founders were worried.

Weber, influenced no less than Marx by the literary works of the German Romantics Goethe (1749–1832) and Schiller (1759–1805), perceived the Western world's autonomous individual as especially threatened. Both Marx and Weber asked, amidst modern capitalism's instrumental calculations and impersonal exchange relationships, how compassion, creativity, and ethical action could continue to exist. Yet Weber broadened out considerably the Marxian nightmare vision: the standardization of activity demanded by the assembly line. Workers were not alone in performing monotonous, repetitive, and alienated tasks, he argued; rather, *all* who labored in the industrial society's large-scale organizations – bureaucracies – shared this demeaning fate. How could employees, in light of task specialization, the narrow delineation of competencies typical in the mega-organization, and its regulations and firmly hierarchical and unalterable chain of command, avoid becoming passive, risk-averse, and security-seeking? Cautious and conformist functionaries incapable of cultivating expansive hopes and an "ethic of responsibility," he feared, would become dominant. How could a genuine autonomy of individuals, and an orientation to noble values and ideals in general, be sustained?

Although he shared a concern with a variety of themes eloquently addressed by Marx, Weber's vision of our epoch departed fundamentally from that of his great predecessor. He never entertained the hope that a politicized working class would, once capitalism's "internal contradictions" had been exposed, inevitably "throw off its chains" and lead the way to a more humane and egalitarian society organized around a socialist economy. And, in spite of his worries, Weber identified a number of positive features in the "cosmos" dominated by capitalism. Market competition, he argued, called forth a degree of societal dynamism potentially capable of weakening the thrust toward bureaucratization. Moreover, socialism would introduce – to regulate the economy – a "caste" of functionaries and yet another large bureaucracy, he feared. A further sapping of society's dynamism, even an accelerated drift toward a closed "ossification," might be the outcome.

Unconvinced of the proletarian revolution's immanence, Weber lived fully and actively within the world of industrial capitalism, rejecting as futile and utopian all calls for its overthrow. Instead, and despite pessimistic statements regarding the modern predicament, in many ways he welcomed the new era, in particular the personal liberties it awarded to autonomous individuals. Throughout his life he remained a peripatetic activist in support of strong and contending political parties, the constitutional division of powers, an ethic of responsibility for politicians, constitutional guarantees of civil liberties, and an extension of suffrage. He argued vigorously that democracy would be possible only where strong parliaments existed, which he saw as a training ground for the political leaders of the "plebiscitory leadership democracy" he advocated (1968b: 1409–14). And, in order to check the power of bureaucracies, he sought to erect various mechanisms that would sustain pluralistic, competing interest groupings. Unlike many in his day in Germany, he opposed all attempts to turn the historical clock back to a presumably pristine and more humane past era. To him: "After all, it is a gross deception to believe that without the achievements of the age of the 'Rights of Man' any one of us (including the most conservative) can go on living his life" (Weber, 1968b: 1403). Nonetheless, at the same time Weber scorned the naïve optimism of American and British Social Darwinists who hailed the dawning of modern capitalism as evidence of progress and synonymous with a new age of egalitarianism.

His ambivalence was palpable. While favoring the high standards of living and national wealth produced only by capitalist, bureaucratized, and urban societies, he lamented the inevitable placing of individuals, performing repetitive and uncreative tasks, into large-scale organizations – whose massive power, he knew, could scarcely be monitored and restricted by democratic political processes. Weber wanted open and dynamic societies in which noble values, competing hard against each other, would force choices and command loyalties. Activity would then be oriented toward a higher plane and firmly directed "from within." The aimless "flow of life" in response to instrumental calculations of advantage typical of the marketplace, and external circumstances in general, would be challenged and circumscribed by value-based ideals and ethical action of a broad scope. The autonomous individual would be sustained. Were these hopes unrealistic?

Unease burdened Weber. Unlike Marx, who foresaw better days ahead, or Durkheim, who believed that reform movements would banish social disintegration and anomie by binding people more closely to one another in firm communities, Weber seemed to see little likelihood that individuals oriented to expansive ethical values would prevail. Nevertheless, he continued to the end his engagement on the stage of German politics, marshaling his relentless and piercing ammunition in innumerable speeches and newspaper articles, directing it against nearly all major classes and groupings.

Despite his deep awareness of worrisome overarching trends, Weber charted out how modern societies, if each is examined closely, were far from monolithic. They varied significantly and some seemed to offer more favorable social configurations than others. Unlike Marx or Durkheim, Weber developed finely-tuned concepts and procedures capable of isolating and defining the particular pathways taken by the United States, England, France, and Germany into industrialism and, in the twentieth century, the unique contours of each nation. Might one society's constellation offer greater potential to call forth individuals directed by ethical values and hence endowed with dignity? And could lessons then be drawn?

In full command of a vast empirical palette of knowledge, Weber formulated comparative concepts and rigorous theories that have contributed massively to sociology's intellectual capital. To this day his direct impact is visible in a variety of the discipline's sub-areas, including political sociology, sociological theory, comparative-historical sociology, urban sociology, stratification, the sociology of religion, and the sociology of developing countries. As a theorist of the state, his influence on political scientists and political economists remains strong. Historians recognize him as a profound commentator upon nineteenth- and early twentieth-century Germany.

This volume aims to convey the enduring analytic power and expansive capacity of his sociology to conceptualize and comprehend the modern world's unique features, fundamental contours, and pivotal dilemmas and tensions. Weber's full-steam ahead confrontation with the central problems of our age led him, remarkably, as noted, to systematic investigations that span the centuries and move with complete sovereignty across the civilizations of the East and West. Through these comparative studies he wished to isolate the uniqueness of the modern West and to explain the causes of its unusual development. All speak directly or indirectly to modern Western rationalism's problems now, and even to others that will perhaps become evident on the horizons of the not-too-distant future.

A selection of Weber's most pivotal writings on the nature of social action and social groupings in the modern epoch is presented in this volume. Some have been newly translated; a few appear for the first time in English translation. My aim has been to offer at least a sampling of the many modernity themes addressed by Weber. He explores and conceptualizes, from a distinct vantage point, issues that remain at the center of social science debates even today.

The readings in this volume span a wide variety of topics. Weber describes the unique features of Western societies and explains how a systematic orientation to work originated by reference to a "Protestant ethic" (Parts I–II). He examines the effects of formal and substantive rationality in market and planned economies, and offers the classical description of the organized nature of labor in industrial societies and its location in large-scale bureaucracies characterized by a division of labor, specialization of tasks, an hierarchical chain of command, and impartial hiring and promotion procedures (Part III). After providing an explanation of the origins of stratification and inequality in Part IV, he discusses the form of legitimate authority distinct today in contrast to earlier periods, and charts its expansion into all fields (Part V). The "nation" is then defined in Part VI, and the modern state and modern law are explored. Furthermore,

Weber investigates how ethical action is circumscribed in an epoch dominated by the free market and the laws of the bureaucratized state (Part VII), and emphasizes the importance of societal dynamism and political leadership if action oriented to values is to be cultivated and sustained. Parts VIII and IX then address the unique contours of the American political culture, the influence of "ethnicity" and "race" (Weber's inverted commas) upon our behavior, and the question of whether heredity possesses a causal impact. Finally, Part X scrutinizes modern social science and seeks to assess its legitimacy, value, and major tasks today. A brief synopsis of major themes introduces the readings in each Part.

This volume's final Part turns to several works by distinguished recent scholars who utilize Weber's concepts and theories in their own research. These chapters demonstrate that his voice remains vigorous, compelling, and far-reaching 100 years after the publication of his most celebrated masterpiece, *The Protestant Ethic and the Spirit of Capitalism* (*PE*). Weber's penetrating insights are manifest in more contemporary form on every page of Part XI.

Our attention in this Introduction must now turn to the major features of Weber's complex sociology and, intertwined closely with it, his view of modernity. The orientation of his sociology to "interpretive understanding," the subjective meaning of actors, and "four types of social action" are first examined. His adherence to "value-freedom" is also scrutinized, as is the way in which, according to him, social scientists select topics for research by reference to their values. Weber's research strategies and procedures are then explored. His fundamental tool – the ideal type – is discussed; how it is formed and used, as a model, in research captures our attention. "Societal domains" (e.g., the law, authority, economy, and religion spheres), which offer mechanisms to "locate" social action, are defined.

Weber's rejection of organic holism anchors the discussion of his vision of society. Rooted in ideal types and societal domains rather than "society," his sociology articulates a conceptual framework capable of assessing whether central domains unfold in parallel as social change occurs and the degree to which societies vary across a closed–open spectrum. This section also draws attention to a fundamental axiom: to Weber, the past always penetrates significantly into the present. The wide-ranging multicausality typical of his mode of research is then investigated in some detail. The groups that "carry" patterned social action are particularly noted, as are values.

Weber's modernity model – modern Western rationalism – is demarcated after this overview of his sociology's major components. Its major elements – "formal," "practical," and "theoretical" rationality – are first examined. An exercise that "applies Weber" illustrates the capacity to serve of this model as a standard, or "yardstick," against which particular empirical cases can be compared and "measured." The unique contours of two modern nations, Germany and the United States, are isolated in this exercise.

This examination of the many ways Weber's sociology confronts modern themes and dilemmas then addresses his view of the future of Western societies and his proposals on behalf of social reform. Finally, the extent to which his writings provide an adequate understanding of our era is evaluated. Does this giant among Sociology's founders assist us even today to understand the modern experience? Weber's biography must be briefly outlined before turning to these themes.

## Max Weber: The Man[1]

Born in Erfurt, Germany, into a distinguished and cosmopolitan family of entrepreneurs, scholars, politicians, and strong and devout women, Max Weber spent his younger years in Berlin. His excellent school required a strenuous regimen of study. An exceptional student, he developed a precocious love of learning and a particular fondness for philosophy, literature, and ancient and medieval history. His teenage letters comment upon, among many others, the merits of Goethe, Kant, Hegel, Spinoza, and Schopenhauer. They also convey, as the eldest of six children, a concern for his overburdened mother. Although influenced strongly by his work-obsessed father, a mover and shaker for three decades in the city government of Berlin and the state government of Prussia, he deplored his patriarchal ways and insensitive treatment of his wife.

Weber studied economic history, law, and philosophy at the universities of Heidelberg, Strasbourg, Berlin, and Göttingen. His letters convey a keen awareness of the varying quality of instruction in his lectures and seminars, as well as rather free-wheeling spending habits. He became in Berlin the protégé of the legal historian Levin Goldschmidt and the Roman historian Theodor Mommsen, and was appointed at an unusually young age in 1893 to a position in the Humboldt University Law School in Berlin. In quick succession appointments to the Economics departments (*Nationalökonomie*) of the universities in Freiburg and Heidelberg (1896) followed. At the age of 33, having recently married a distant cousin, Marianne Schnitger, Weber evicted his father, who had mistreated his mother, from their home. The father's death soon afterwards apparently served as the catalyst for a paralyzing mental illness that endured for more than five years. During much of this time Weber passively pondered the fate of people living in the new world of secularism, urbanism, and capitalism.

A three-month visit to the United States in the fall of 1904 played a part in his recovery. Journeying with his wife across much of the East,

South, and Midwest, he gained an appreciation of America's dynamism, energy, and uniqueness, as well as the self-reliance and distrust of authority widespread in the United States. *The Protestant Ethic and the Spirit of Capitalism* (henceforth *PE*), his most famous work, was completed soon after his return to Germany. Although unable to teach until 1918, Weber began once again to publish on a broad array of topics.

His interest in the "ascetic Protestantism" of the American Quaker, Methodist, Presbyterian, and Baptist churches derived in part from the religiosity of his mother, Helene, and her sister, Ida Baumgarten. As Christian social activists and admirers of American Unitarianism, the pious sisters transmitted to the young Weber a heightened sensitivity to moral questions, an appreciation of the ways in which the life of dignity must be guided by ethical standards, and a respect for the worth and uniqueness of every person. His wife Marianne reaffirmed these values, although they opposed the lessons taught by Max's father: the necessity to avoid "naïve idealism," to confront the ways of the world in a pragmatic – even amoral – fashion, and to avoid personal sacrifice.

Weber waged impassioned battles throughout his life on behalf of ethical positions and scolded relentlessly all who lacked a rigorous sense of justice and social responsibility. As his student, Paul Honigsheim, reports, he became a man possessed whenever threats to the autonomy of the individual were discussed (see Honigsheim, 1968, pp. 6, 43) – whether of mothers seeking custody of their children, women students at German universities, or bohemian social outcasts and political rebels. Not surprisingly, his concerns for the fate of the German nation and the future of Western civilization led him perpetually into the arena of politics. Vigorously opposed to the definition of this realm as one of *Realpolitik*, "sober realism," and wheeling and dealing, he called out vehemently for politicians to act by reference to a stern moral code: an ethic of responsibility.[2]

## Foundational Features of Weber's Interpretive Understanding Sociology: Its Aim and the Centrality of Subjective Meaning, the Four Types of Social Action, and Value-Freedom and Value-Relevance[3]

Weber's approach to empirical research proved unique. He abjured, on the one hand, a focus upon singular causal forces, and sought to offer multidimensional analyses that evaluated the varying weight of an array of factors. On the other, he attempted to understand the great variety of ways in which people, acting in reference to delineated social contexts, endow certain action-orientations in a patterned manner with meaning, even to such an extent that groups are formed. How, in particular, do they do so by reference to values, he asked? Foundational features of Weber's sociology must now be outlined.

Many of the pivotal axioms of his methodology remain central to sociology even today. Only a few of its major aspects can be examined: its aim, concepts of interpretive understanding and subjective meaning, and "four types of social action" are first discussed; Weber's principles of value-freedom and value-relevance are then addressed.

### The aim of Weber's sociology, interpretive understanding, subjective meaning, and the four types of social action

Commentaries upon Weber's works have frequently failed to note that he orients his research to discrete problems and the causal analysis of specific cases and developments. He proposes that the causal explanation of this "historical individual" should serve as sociology's primary aim:

> We wish to understand the reality that surrounds our lives, in which we are placed, *in its characteristic uniqueness*. We wish to understand on the one hand its context (*Zusammenhang*) and the cultural *significance* of its particular manifestations in their contemporary form, and on the other the causes of it becoming historically so and not otherwise. (1949b, p. 72b; trans. altered; emphasis in original; see also p. 69)

> The aim should . . . be . . . to identify and define the *individuality* of each development, the characteristics which made the one conclude in a manner different from that of the other. This done, one can then determine the causes which led to these differences. (1976a, p. 385; emphasis in original; see also 1968a, p. 10)

Hence, Weber strongly opposed the numerous positivist schools of thought in his day that sought, following the method offered by the natural sciences, to define a set of general laws of history and social change and then to explain all specific cases and developments by deduction. He forcefully rejected the position that the social sciences should aim "to construct a closed system of concepts which can encompass and classify reality in some definitive manner and from which it can be deduced again" (1949b, p. 84), and expressed his firm opposition to the view that laws themselves comprise causal explanations. Because concrete realities, individual cases and developments, and subjective meaning cannot be deduced from them, laws are incapable of providing the knowledge of reality sufficient to offer causal explanations. To Weber, individual cases can be explained causally only by "other equally individual configurations" (1949b, pp. 75–6; see Kalberg, 1994, pp. 81–4; see below, pp. 14–27).

At the core of his sociology stands the attempt by sociologists to "understand interpretively" (*verstehen*) the ways in which people view their own "social action." This "subjectively meaningful action" constitutes the researcher's concern rather than merely reactive or imitative behavior (as occurs, for example, when people in a crowd expect rain and open their umbrellas simultaneously). Social action, he insists, involves *both* a "meaningful orientation of behavior to that of others" *and* the individual's interpretive, or reflective, aspect (1968a, pp. 22–4). People are social, but not only social. They are endowed with the capacity actively to interpret situations, interactions, and relationships by reference to values, beliefs, interests, emotions, power, authority, law, customs, conventions, habits, ideas, etc.

> Sociology . . . is a science that offers an interpretive understanding of social action and, in doing so, provides a causal explanation of its course and its effects. We shall speak of "action" insofar as the acting individual attaches a subjective *meaning* to his behavior – be it overt or covert, omission or acquiescence. Action is "social" insofar as its subjective meaning takes account of the behavior *of others* and is thereby oriented in its course. (1968a, p. 4; emphasis in original; trans. altered)[4]

The centrality of social, or meaningful, action separates Weber's sociology fundamentally from all behaviorist, structuralist, and positivist schools.

Sociologists can understand the meaningfulness of others' action either through "rational understanding," which involves an intellectual grasp of the meaning actors attribute to their actions, or through "intuitive," or "empathic," understanding, which refers to the comprehension of "the emotional context in which the action [takes] place" (1968a, p. 5). Thus, for example, the motivation behind the orientation of civil servants to impersonal statutes and laws can be understood by the sociologist, as can the motivation behind the orientation of good friends to one another. To the extent that this occurs, a *causal* explanation of action, Weber argues, is provided. Because it attends alone to external activity, stimulus–response behaviorism neglects the issues foremost to Weber: the *diverse* possible motives behind an observable activity, the manner in which the subjective meaningfulness of the act varies accordingly, and the significant differences that follow in respect to action.[5]

Social action can be best conceptualized as involving one of "four types of meaningful action": means–end rational, value-rational, affectual, or traditional action. Each type refers to the ideal-typical (see below) motivational orientations of actors.

Weber defines action as *means–end* rational (*zweckrational*) "when the end, the means, and the secondary results are all rationally taken into account and weighed."[6] Similarly, people possess the capacity to act *value-rationally*, even though this type of action has appeared empirically in its pure form only rarely. It exists when social action is:

> determined by a conscious belief in the value for its own sake of some ethical, aesthetic, religious, or other form of behavior, independently of its prospects of success ... Value-rational action always involves "commands" or "demands" which, in the actor's opinion, are binding (*verbindlich*) on him. (1968a, pp. 24–5)

Notions of honor involve values, as do salvation doctrines. In addition, "determined by the actor's specific affects and feeling states," *affectual* action, which involves an emotional attachment, must be distinguished clearly from value-rational and means–end rational action. *Traditional* action, "determined by ingrained habituation" and age-old customs, and often merely a routine reaction to common stimuli, stands on the borderline of subjectively meaningful action. Taken together, these constructs – the "types of social action" – establish an analytic base that assists conceptualization of empirical action. Rational action in reference to interests constitutes, to Weber, only one possible way of orienting action (see 1968a, pp. 24–6).[7]

Each type of meaningful action can be found in all epochs and all civilizations. The social action of even "primitive" peoples may be means–end rational and value-rational (see, e.g., 1968a, pp. 400, 422–6), and modern man is not endowed with a greater inherent capacity for either type of action than his ancestors. However, as a result of identifiable social forces, some epochs may tend predominantly to call forth a particular type of action. Weber is convinced that sociologists can understand even the ways in which the social action of people living in radically different cultures is subjectively meaningful. Assuming that, as a result of intensive study, researchers have succeeded in becoming thoroughly familiar with a particular social context and thus capable of imagining themselves "into" it, an assessment can be made of the extent to which actions approximate one of the types of social action. The subjective meaningfulness of the motives for these actions – whether means–end rational, value-rational, traditional, or affectual – then become *understandable*.[8] Weber's "interpretive sociology" in this manner seeks to assist sociologists to comprehend – and hence explain causally – social action in terms of the actor's *own* intentions.[9]

This foundational emphasis upon a pluralism of motives distinguishes Weber's sociology unequivocally from all schools of behaviorism, all approaches that place social structures at the forefront (such as, for example, those rooted in Durkheim's "social facts" or Marx's classes), and all positivist approaches that endow norms, roles, and rules with centrality and a determining power over people. Even when social action seems tightly bonded to a social structure, a heterogeneity of motives must be recognized; within a single "external form" a great array of motives is both analytically and empirically possible, Weber argues – *and* significant to the sociologist. The subjective meaningfulness of action varies even within the firm organizational structure of the political or religious sect. Yet just this reasoning leads him to a conundrum: for what subjective reasons do people orient their social action *in common* so that patterns of action, social relationships, and demarcated groupings are formulated? This question assumes a great urgency, for Weber is convinced that the absence of such orientations – toward, for example, the state, bureaucratic organizations, traditions, and values – means that "structures" cease to exist. The state, for example, in the end is *nothing more* than the patterned action-orientations and social relationships of its politicians, judges, police, civil servants, etc.[10]

Far from formal methodological postulates only, these foundational positions directly anchor Weber's empirical studies. The investigation of the subjective meaning of action stood at the very center of his famous "Protestant ethic thesis," for example. Why is it meaningful among members of a particular group, when a eudaemonistic outlook on life would seem preferable, to place methodical, systematic work at the center of their life? Weber engaged throughout his comparative-historical sociology in a massive empirical effort to understand the subjective meaning of "the other" on its own terms, or "from within," whether that of the Confucian scholar, the Buddhist monk, the Hindu Brahmin, the prophets of the Old Testament, feudal rulers, monarchs and kings, or functionaries in bureaucracies. For what subjective reasons do people conclude that authority is legitimate and render obedience to it? Weber wished to understand the diverse ways in which people subjectively "make sense" of their activities. He argued that sociologists should attempt to do so even when the subjective "meaning-complexes" they discover seem strange or odd to them.

### Value-freedom and value-relevance

Hence, Weber's sociology never seeks to discover "an objectively 'correct' meaning or one which is 'true' in some metaphysical sense" (1968a, p. 4).[11] Moreover, neither empathy toward nor hostility against the actors under investigation is appropriate, he proclaims, for the social scientist. In respect to the research process, researchers are obligated to set aside their ideological preferences, personal values, likes, and dislikes as much as humanly possible and to make every effort to remain fair and impartial. Clear standards of inquiry, as well as an unbiased observation, measurement, comparison, and evaluation of the sources, must be the prescriptive

ideal. Even if the habits, values, and practices of the groups under investigation are discovered to be repulsive, social scientists must strive to uphold
this ideal.

To maintain such an "objective," and "value-free" (*wertfrei*) posture in
respect to the gathering and evaluation of data, Weber knew well, is not an
easy task. We are all "cultural beings," and hence values remain inextri-
cably intertwined with our thinking and action; a thin line separates "facts"
from "values", and values intrude even into our modes of observation.
Indeed, modern Western science itself *arose* as a consequence of a series
of specific historical and cultural developments (pp. 321–7). Nonetheless, the social scientist must make a concerted effort to distinguish
empirically based arguments and conclusions from normative – or value-
based – positions. The latter should be eliminated as much as possible.

However, in regard to a foundational aspect of the research process,
values remain appropriately central, Weber insists: they orient the *selection* of topics. Far from being "objective" in some metaphysical or predetermined sense, our choice – unavoidably so, for him – is directly related
to our values (*Wertbezogenheit*) and our interests. A sociologist, for example,
who strongly believes that people of different ethnic groupings should
be treated equally, may well decide – as a result of *this value ideal* – to
study how civil rights movements have assisted heretofore excluded
groupings to acquire basic rights. Values are here correctly central.

Yet Weber argues forcefully that researchers must strive to exclude values
in respect to the overall task of the social sciences: all value-judgments
that pronounce, in the name of science, a particular activity or way of
life as noble or base, ultimately rational or irrational, provincial or
cosmopolitan, must be avoided. The social sciences cannot – and should
not – help us to decide with certainty which values are superior. Those
of the Sermon on the Mount cannot be proven scientifically superior to
those of India's Rig Vedas. Nor can social scientists argue that specific
values *should* guide our lives. Science provides knowledge, insight, and
clarity, and informs us regarding the various effects of employing a
certain means to reach a specified goal and nothing more. It must never
be utilized in order to "prove" the correctness of political views or
allowed to take responsibility for the individual's decisions (pp. 328–34;
1949a, pp. 18–19).

> We know of no ideals that can be demonstrated scientifically. Undoubtedly,
> the task of pulling them out of one's own breast is all the more difficult
> in an epoch in which culture has otherwise become so subjective. But we
> simply have no fool's paradise and no streets paved with gold to promise,
> either in this world or the next, either in thought or in action. It is the stigma
> of our human dignity that the peace of our souls can never be as great as
> the peace of those who dream of such a paradise. (1909, p. 420)

Weber pronounced such an ethos of "value-freedom" as indispensable to the definition of sociology – if it wished to be a social science rather than a political endeavor:

> Science today is a "vocation" organized in special disciplines in the service of self-clarification and knowledge of interrelated facts. It is not the gift of grace of seers and prophets dispensing sacred values and revelations, nor does it partake of the contemplation of sages and philosophers about the meaning of the universe. (pp. 334–5)

How does the sociologist best proceed to ascertain subjective meaning in the groups under investigation, to establish the causes for patterned action, and to do so in an unbiased fashion? An answer to this question requires a brief discussion of Weber's *ideal-typical* mode of analysis and his basic research strategies and procedures.

## Research Strategies and Procedures: Ideal Types, Model-Building, Societal Domains, and the "Locating" of Social Action

Although Weber takes the meaningful action of individuals as his basic unit of analysis, his interpretive sociology never views social life as an "endless drift" of solitary and unconnected action-orientations. The diverse ways in which people engage in social action *in concert*, rather than the action of the isolated individual, capture his attention. Indeed, he defines the sociological enterprise as oriented to the investigation of the subjective meaning of people in delimited groups – that is, the identification of *regularities of social action*:

> There can be observed, within the realm of social action, actual empirical regularities; that is, courses of action that are repeated by the actor or (possibly also: simultaneously) occur among numerous actors because the subjective *meaning* is typically *meant* to be the same. Sociological investigation is concerned with these *typical* modes of action. (1968a, p. 29; emphasis in original; trans. altered)

This patterned social action results not only from an orientation to values, but also to traditional and even affectual and means–end rational action, he argues. The various ways in which merely imitative and reactive behavior is *uprooted* from its random flow and transformed into *meaning*-based regularities anchored in one of the four types of social action constitute a fundamental theme in his sociology of interpretive under-standing and particularly in his monumental analytic treatise, *Economy and Society* (*E&S*).[12]

## Capturing patterned subjective meaning: ideal types

Weber's major heuristic concept – the ideal type – "documents" these regularities of meaningful action. Each of these *research tools* charts the patterned action-orientations of groupings of individuals and the social relationships of people oriented to each other – and nothing more. For example, his ideal type "the Puritan" identifies the regular action of these believers (an orientation toward methodical work and an ascetic style of life). Thus, Weber's sociology, in seeking to capture through the formation of ideal types the patterned action of people in groups, steers away from a focus upon isolated action – such as one's "rational choices" – on the one hand, and society, societal evolution, social differentiation, "the question of social order," and the influence of social structures, on the other. This level of analysis prevails throughout Weber's texts rather than either detailed historical narrative or global concepts. How are ideal types formed?

These research tools never summarize or classify social action. Instead, they are formulated, first, through a conscious exaggeration of the *essential* features of empirical patterns of social action of interest to the sociologist and, second, through a synthesis of these characteristic action-orientations into an internally unified and logically rigorous concept:

> An ideal type is formed by the one-sided *accentuation of one or more* points of view and by the synthesis of a great many diffuse, discrete, more or less present and occasionally absent *concrete individual* phenomena, which are arranged according to those one-sidedly emphasized viewpoints into a unified *analytical* construct. In its conceptual purity, this construct cannot be found empirically anywhere in reality. (1949b, p. 90; emphasis in original)

While inductive procedures from empirical observations are first followed, deductive procedures then guide the logical ordering of the separate patterns of action into a unified and precise construct. Nonetheless, the anchoring of ideal types empirically precludes their understanding as "abstract" or "reified" concepts (see 1949a, pp. 42–5; 1949b, pp. 92–107; 1968a, pp. 19–22).

Above all, according to Weber, ideal types serve *to assist* empirical, cause-oriented inquiry rather than "replicate" or directly comprehend the external world (an impossible task, owing to the unending flow of events, the infinite diversity and complexity of even a particular social phenomenon, and sociologists' "perspectival" angle upon reality, given their demarcated research theme and the overarching presuppositions of the particular epoch and culture within which they live) or to articulate an ideal, hoped-for development. Thus, the "Puritan" portrays accurately the subjective meaning of neither a particular Puritan nor all Puritans. And this ideal type also never implies praise for Puritanism. The same holds for ideal types of bureaucratic functionaries, prophets, intellectuals, charismatic leaders, and prostitutes. As he notes: "Concepts are primarily analytical instruments for the intellectual mastery of the empirically given and can be only that" (1949b, p. 106; trans. altered).

Once formed as clear constructs that capture regular action-orientations and social relationships, ideal types anchor Weber's sociology in a fundamental fashion: they enable the precise definition of the empirical social action under investigation. As a logical concept, the ideal type establishes clear points of reference – or standards – against which empirical regularities of meaningful action of interest to the researcher can be compared and "measured." In other words, the main features and distinctiveness of particular cases – the state bureaucracy *vis-à-vis* the bureaucracy in private industry – can be defined through an assessment of their approximation to or deviation from this constructed "yardstick." Hence: "Ideal types such as Christianity . . . are of great value for research and of high systematic value for expository purposes when they are used as conceptual instruments for *comparison* and the *measurement* of reality. They are indispensable for this purpose" (1949b, p. 97; emphasis in original; see also pp. 90–3; 1949a, p. 43).[13]

### *Ideal types as models: the centrality of model-building in Weber's sociology*

When Weber forms, in his three-volume analytic treatise, *E&S*, an ideal type of the prophet, the manager in a bureaucracy, the market or natural economy, the feudal aristocrat, the peasant, or the intellectual, for example, he is in each case, as noted, conceptualizing patterned orientations of social action and social relationships by people in groups. The ideal type "bureaucratic functionary" identifies orientations held in common toward work, punctuality, reliability, specialized tasks, and an hierarchical chain of command; and the "charismatic leader" outlines emotional orientations of an audience toward persons viewed as possessing extraordinary qualities. Importantly, each ideal type implies that patterned social action involves a degree of endurance and firmness. Indeed, the regular action-orientations demarcated by ideal types can be understood as, depending upon the push and pull of the configuration of action-orientations within their milieu, potentially asserting an autonomous (*eigengesetzliche*) influence empirically. Hence, these constructs isolate and define causal forces. That is, every ideal type not only facilitates – as a yardstick – a conceptual grasp upon otherwise diffuse empirical realities, but also formulates causal hypotheses regarding empirical patterned action-orientations and social relationships – and these can be tested through in-depth investigation. Finally, many of Weber's ideal types chart a path of development. Specialists can investigate, in reference to these "developmental models" (*Entwicklungsformen*), whether the particular grouping under investigation empirically follows the hypothesized course (1949b, p. 103). These models, such as "the routinization of charisma" (pp. 217–20), are found throughout his sociology (see Kalberg, 1994, pp. 92–142).

A strongly theoretical dimension – a model-building capacity – is injected by ideal types in this manner into the very core of Weber's sociology of interpretive understanding. He emphasizes that, unlike the discipline of history, sociology *must* include a rigorous theoretical framing – through such models – of the problem under investigation (see 1968a, pp. 19–20). Indeed, the arrays of models in *E&S* that conceptualize patterned, meaningful action[14] draw Weber's sociology of interpretive understanding *away* from an exclusive focus upon delineated social problems and historical narrative. Nonetheless, as noted, the empirical grounding of his models distinguishes his sociology from all schools anchored in broad, diffuse generalizations (society) and long-range, overarching developments (differentiation, modernization, evolution).

According to Weber, unique to sociology is always a back and forth movement between conceptualization – the formulation of models as theoretical frameworks – and the detailed investigation of empirical social groupings, whether cases or developments. If the goal of offering causal explanations for the appearance of particular groups (the Calvinist, the Hindu Brahmin, the civil servant, the spirit of capitalism, etc.) is to be realized, *both* empirical particularity and conceptual generalization are indispensable (see Kalberg, 1994, pp. 92–5, 98).[15]

## "Locating" social action: societal domains

Weber is convinced that the crystallization of social action from mere reactive and imitative action, and then its patterning, are related to social contexts and hence are not random. However, he is also persuaded that this crystallization is inadequately comprehended by reference to familiar concepts, such as "class" or "social fact." Least of all can patterned social action be said to arise out of Hegelian ideas or immanent, evolutionary forces. *E&S* aims, among other major tasks, to explain the origin of patterned meaningful action and social relationships, and to specify *where* such regularities are likely to arise. A central theoretical cornerstone for his sociology has been laid to the extent that he succeeds in *E&S* in *locating*, analytically, patterned social action. This task must be pursued if his interpretive sociology – again, an understanding by the researcher of the subjective meaning people in diverse groups attribute to their patterned social action – is to constitute more than an empty, formalistic enterprise.

Based on massive comparative-historical research, Weber argues in *E&S* that social action and social relationships crystallize on a regular basis not only in the groups captured by the numerous ideal types formulated in this treatise, but also in a number of "societal domains" (*gesellschaftliche Ordnungen*): the economy, rulership, religion, law, status groups, and "universal organizations" (family, clan, and traditional neighborhood) arenas.[16] To him, people are "placed into various societal domains, each of which is governed by different laws" (1946b, p. 123). *E&S* undertakes the huge task of delimiting the major realms, which can be identified according to indigenous themes, dilemmas, and sets of questions, within which social action significantly congeals. For example, a focus upon explanations for suffering, misfortune, and misery distinguishes the sphere of religion, while the arena of rulership concerns the reasons why people attribute legitimacy to authority (as opposed to sheer power) and their motives for rendering obedience. The status groups domain involves social honor and defined styles of life. Analytic boundaries for each realm are established in this manner.

*E&S* traces out how action in the various spheres, with a certain likelihood, becomes uprooted from its random and reactive, imitative flow and acquires a meaningful component, thereby becoming social action. For example, in respect to economic activity, action becomes social action "if it takes account of the behavior of someone else . . . [and] in so far as the actor assumes that others will respect his actual control over economic goods" (1968a, p. 22; see also p. 341); and action oriented to status becomes social action wherever a specific way of leading a life is acknowledged and restrictions on social intercourse become effective (pp. 151–8). *Here*, with societal domains, a further major heuristic tool for the interpretive sociologist's research is discovered. In Weber's terminology, each sphere is a realm of subjective meaning (*Sinnbereich*) within which patterned social action – that is, social groupings – may arise.

In fulfilling the pivotal task of conceptualizing *where* empirical patterns of social action are likely to appear, *E&S* renders also a related contribution. Its ideal types and societal domains, by locating significant social action contextually on a wide-ranging, comparative-historical scale, assist sociologists to understand how a vast variety of action *can become* subjectively meaningful to people. This treatise serves as a bulwark in this manner against any tendency researchers may have to explore meaningful action solely from the vantage point of their *own* assumptions. Doing so increases the likelihood, Weber is convinced, that "unusual action" will be interpreted incorrectly – namely, as odd, irrational, and incomprehensible rather than as subjectively meaningful.

In sum, by locating patterns of subjective meaning, the numerous ideal types and societal domains in *E&S* facilitate comprehension of how values, interests, emotions, and traditions in many empirical settings may actually take action out of its imitative or reactive flow and endow it with meaning, thereby establishing, as Weber contends, the foundation for social groupings and social relationships (see Kalberg 1994, pp. 30–46). By assisting an understanding of the putatively "irrational" actions of others as indeed meaningful, this analytic treatise *expands* the imaginations of sociologists. For example, the ideal type "missionary prophet" enables "we moderns" to comprehend the ways in which this charismatic figure, who views the cosmos as internally unified by God's commandments and intentions (1968a, pp. 450–1), attributes meaning to his actions – however "irrational" they may appear from the point of view of today's scientific and secularized presuppositions. And "the Calvinist," in situating the faithful within a religious context dominated by the doctrine of Predestination and certain revisions of it (see below), assists understanding of why systematic and continuous work constitutes a meaningful activity to these devout believers.

## The Vision of "Society": Ideal Types, Societal Domains, Open Models, and the Interweaving of Past and Present

Grounded in subjective meaning, four types of action, ideal types, and societal domains, Weber's sociology of interpretive understanding stands in the most strict opposition to all approaches that view societies as quasi-organic, holistic units and their separate "parts" as components fully integrated into a larger "system." All such positivist schools of thought comprehend the larger collectivity within which the individual acts as an objectivity structure, and social action and interaction as merely particularistic expressions of this "whole."

The degree of societal integration and unity postulated by organic theories is questionable to Weber. He sees fragmentation, tension, open conflict, and the exercise of power as frequent, and considers the clearly formed society with delineated boundaries as a hypothetical case only. A high risk of reification arises, he contends, if organic theories are utilized *other than* as a means of facilitating preliminary conceptualization. "Society" and the "organic whole" would then be perceived as the fundamental unit of analysis rather than the individual's subjective meaning, and people would be incorrectly understood as primarily the "socialized products" of societal forces (1968a, pp. 14–15). Weber argues instead that, always standing apart from their societies to some degree and capable of *interpreting* their social milieux, people bestow subjective meaning upon certain aspects of it and may initiate independent action: "[We are] *cultural* beings endowed with the capacity and will to take a deliberate stand toward the world and to lend it *meaning (Sinn)*" (1949b, p. 81; trans. altered; emphasis in original).

He opposes positivist approaches and organic holism in a further significant way. Because his multiple ideal types and analytically independent societal domains imply a vision of society as constructed alone from the innumerable patterns of action and social relationships by people in arrays of delimited groupings, his sociology readily conceptualizes a broad variety of societal configurations. They range across a spectrum from those characterized by stagnant, all-encompassing tradition to others in which continuous movement and flux reign. Ideal types and societal domains, as heuristic constructs that document regularities of social action, "interact" – at times (depending on arrays of empirical causal forces) coalescing, even into wide-ranging alliances, and at other times (depending on arrays of empirical causal forces) opposing one another in relationships of antagonism and shifting conflict.

The extent to which multiple alliances across groups are actually formed empirically, even coalitions that call forth societal "equilibrium" and an overarching "societal unity," or the degree to which social action in demarcated groupings flows in opposed directions so that enduring conflict and societal fragmentation prevail – all this remains to Weber a subject exclusively for investigation. Rooted in open-ended models, no general axioms or presuppositions regarding inevitable antagonisms across groups (and even "class conflict") or a "drift toward" coalitions and "social order" underlie his sociology. Whether a "normative integration" or disintegration takes place over longer historical periods is perceived by Weber exclusively to be a question for case-by-case research. Comprised of distinct configurations of groupings, as captured by ideal types and societal domains, "societies" – more closed or more open, dynamic, and even fragmented – can be located on an *analytic* continuum only.

Thus, Weber's sociology strictly opposes holistic modes of analysis that view societies, for example, as "traditional" or "modern." These schools reify historical disjunctions to an unwarranted degree, downplay the varying paths taken by different nations into the modern world, and inappropriately homogenize both "traditional" and "modern" societies. By abjuring global dichotomies and formulating a vast array of precise analytic tools that represent patterns of subjective meaning and their open-ended interactions, his procedures and research strategies are well suited to convey historical development as empirically occurring across a broad range of directions and as taking place in a more uneven OR more linear fashion.

This focus in Weber's sociology upon the patterned action of people in social relationships and groups, as captured by ideal types, forcefully takes cognizance of an intimate interweaving of past and present. The patterns of social action in some groupings, as demarcated by ideal types, can quickly be acknowledged as living on, indeed, as placing an "autonomous" thrust into motion on the basis of their indigenous problematics. The vision of social life that flows out of a sociology rooted in ideal types captures the "survival" of arrays of regularities of action from the past. Long-standing customs, conventions, laws, relationships of domination, and values, for example, his sociology recognizes, may survive for millennia and permeate even the central core of the present in multiple, though often obscure and scarcely visible ways. Even the abrupt appearance of "the new" – even the extraordinary power of charismatic leadership – never fully ruptures ties to the past, he holds.[17] Similarly, Weber's construct "societal domains" also captures a close interweaving of past and present. As manifest through its ideal types,[18] each societal sphere (religion, economy, law, etc.) implies the potential of empirical causal viability – that is, an empirical unfolding at its own tempo and in a manner not necessarily parallel with the other spheres.[19] His open-ended societal domains emphasize that some patterns of social action may endure, even penetrating deeply into subsequent epochs (often in scarcely visible, even clandestine ways), while others prove fleeting and without a significant causal impact.[20]

Endowing open-ended models with a central place, Weber's sociology reveals that the pathway to modernity can neither be characterized as an inevitable evolutionary development – and least of all one anchored alone in a Protestant work ethic (see below) – nor as a unilinear "march of rationalization." Indeed, the societal domains neither articulate nor disconfirm empirically-rooted linkages of any sort across their ideal types. And the stages of any developmental model constructed from ideal types, Weber argues, should never be viewed either as capturing the course of history or as "effective forces" – and surely not as depicting a "lawful" and universal tendency for all history to pass through a succession of invariable stages (1949b, pp. 102–3).[21] As little as his sociology as a whole, *E&S* can never be understood as tracing a linear historical expansion of means–end rational and value-rational action, or as depicting a general societal evolution characterized by a substitution of universalistic for particularistic values.[22]

Whether the course of history in a particular epoch or civilization followed the analytic path demarcated by a particular developmental model, or deviated from it, always remains an issue for detailed empirical investigation by specialists, especially historians, according to Weber (1949b, p. 103). Modern societies are best understood as particular mixtures of past and present, he contends, rather than as the product of a unilinear evolutionary unfolding in which the present "replaces" the past. Despite vast structural transformations (bureaucratization, urbanization, and the rise of modern capitalism), some patterns of action endure, he notes repeatedly, and to varying degrees in different nations (pp. 30–4), interweaving with the present.

These foundational procedures and research strategies in Weber's sociology lead to the conclusion that each particular modern society, and its unique developmental pathway into the present, must be examined separately (Kalberg, 1994: 81–4). How did the routes taken by Germany, England, France, and the United States vary? How do these nations diverge today? Nonetheless, Weber *does* formulate a modernity *model*: "modern Western rationalism." Before turning to this important construct, however, one further pivotal component in his sociology of interpretive understanding must be examined briefly: its multicausality.

## Weber's Multicausality: Social Carriers and Values

The search for a single guiding hand, whether that of a monotheistic God, Adam Smith's laws of the market, Hegel's spirit, or Karl Marx's class conflict as the "engine of history," remained anathema to Weber. He perceived all such overarching forces as residuals of now-antiquated world views permeated by religious and quasi-religious ideas (see Kalberg, 2003a, pp. 134–8). Indeed, Weber's adamant refusal to define the "stages of historical development" (Marx) or "evolutionary progress" as a point of departure for his causal explanations paved the way for the focus of his sociology upon empirical reality, interpretive understanding, subjective meaning, ideal types, and societal domains. As importantly, it also provided the underlying precondition for his embrace of radically *multicausal* modes of explanation. Having abandoned reference to all forms of "necessity" in order to explain social change, Weber placed, as causal forces, the actions and beliefs of people at the forefront.

As noted, each ideal type implies the empirical likelihood of regular action-orientations with a degree of endurance and firmness, or an "autonomy," and a resistance to random and competing action-orientations. As also discussed, each societal domain in *E&S* articulates a clearly bounded and independent realm *vis-à-vis* other spheres: the status group, universal organizations, religion, law, authority, and economy realms. In introducing his chapters in *E&S* on traditional and charismatic authority, for example, Weber summarizes his aims as involving not only an evaluation of the extent to which the "developmental chances" of each type can be said to be subject to "economic, political or any other external determinants," but also an assessment of the degree to which the types of authority follow "an 'autonomous' logic inherent in their technical structure" (1968a, p. 1002). He insists that this "logic" must be conceptualized as capable even of exerting an independent effect upon economic factors (1968a, pp. 578, 654–5, 1002). A "bounded group," crystallizing as its "social carrier," constitutes the empirical precondition for this to take place (see below).

Hence, even while remaining cognizant of the frequent centrality of economic factors, Weber emphasizes that multicausal approaches must be pursued (see, e.g., pp. 45 (n. 27), 50, 62–3; 1968a, p. 341). By insisting upon the autonomous potential of patterned action-orientations in each societal domain, he argues that questions of causality cannot be addressed by reference primarily to economic forces, material interests, or *any* single sphere: "The connections between the economy and the societal domains are dealt with [in *E&S*] more fully than is usually the case. This is done deliberately so that the autonomy of these domains *vis-à-vis* the economy is made manifest" (1914, p. vii). Hence, Weber's orientation to an array of societal spheres implies a principled and broad multicausality; his sociology opposes the elevation of a particular domain or ideal type to a position of general causal priority. At the analytic level, no "superiority" of action-orientations indigenous to any particular ideal type or societal realm arises.[23]

This attention to the analytic autonomy of ideal types and societal spheres poses an urgent question: *on what basis* do regular action-orientations and social relationships outlined by these constructs *empirically* acquire prominence and influence social action, indeed, even across epochs? *Why* do some patterns of social action endure across the ages? Why do others call forth social change? Reference to the role of charismatic leadership in his sociology offers only an incomplete picture as concerns Weber's analysis of change. His answers turn this exploration of his practiced sociology away from his constructs – ideal types and societal domains – and toward a variety of demarcated causal forces enumerated in his texts.

Historical events, social carriers, power, values, and ideas also comprise for Weber, throughout his works and in many ways, pivotal causal forces. Only the manner in which social carriers and values constitute causal factors in his sociology can be examined here.[24]

## Social carriers

Weber is convinced that regular action of every imaginable variety has arisen in every epoch and civilization. Yet only *certain* traditional, affectual, value-rational, and means–end rational patterns of meaningful action acquire strong exponents and become important aspects of the social fabric. Hence, his sociology characteristically attends to whether powerful and cohesive groupings appear as social carriers, for only then can the influence of regular action range across decades and even centuries. The question of "within what *carrier* grouping action occurs" remains fundamental to him. Status groups, classes, and organizations serve as the most prominent bearers of patterned action. As Weber notes: "Unless the concept 'autonomy' is to lack all precision, its definition presupposes the existence of a bounded group of people which, though membership may fluctuate, is determinable" (1968a, p. 699; trans. altered). *PE*, for example, rather than exclusively focussing on ideas and values, explores ideas

and values *in reference to* the churches, sects, organizations, and strata that
bear them.

He defines a wide variety of carrier groups in *E&S*. Regularities of social
action in some groupings can be recognized as firm, and carriers can be
seen to be powerful in some cases; others fail to carry action forcefully
and prove fleeting. Patterned action may fade and then later, owing to
an alteration of *contextual* action-orientations, acquire carriers and become
reinvigorated, influential, and long-lasting. At times coalitions of carriers
are formed; at other times carriers stand clearly antagonistic to one another
(see Kalberg, 1994, pp. 58–62).

A great continuity of social carriers across epochs has been characteristic in some civilizations. The patrimonial bureaucracy and literati
stratum in China, for example, remained the central carriers of patterned
action oriented to Confucian teachings for more than two thousand
years. In India, the Brahmins carried Hinduism for more than a millen-
nium. In Japan, "the greatest weight in social affairs was carried by a
stratum of professional warriors . . . Practical life situations were governed
by a code of chivalry and education for knighthood" (1958, p. 275).
Without powerful carriers, ideas, values, and interests could not move
history, nor could other ideas, values, interests, and traditions uphold a
status quo. Only values as a causal force can be explored here.

## *Values:* The Protestant Ethic and the Spirit of Capitalism

A renowned classic, *PE* is Weber's both best-known and most accessible
work. Its thesis regarding the role played by values in the development
of modern capitalism set off an intense debate that has continued to this
day. This study also constitutes his first attempt to isolate the uniqueness
of the modern West and to define its causal origins.

Weber sought to understand certain origins of modern capitalism
in this classic.[25] For him, a specific "frame of mind" (*Gesinnung*) – an
eighteenth-century "spirit of capitalism" – was, among other factors (see
below, pp. 85–106), causally important. Religious roots anchored this
"spirit," namely, the doctrines of the ascetic Protestant sects and churches
of the sixteenth and seventeenth centuries.[26] Puritanism's Predestination
doctrine, according to which it has been forever decreed by God that a very
few are saved and all others are condemned, and no earthly "good works"
can change this decree, introduced among believers a deep anxiety. Some
theologians and ministers – the "Puritan divines" – gradually formulated
new interpretations that allowed the devout *to believe* they were among
the saved – and here the "psychological rewards" at the origin of a
systematic work ethic can be located. First, simply to praise His majesty,
the faithful knew that God expected the devout to create abundance

and wealth throughout His earthly kingdom. Hence, if only to attain this goal, it became clear that God ordained all should work. Moreover, God "willed" that the faithful work methodically, for labor in a calling (*Beruf*) was "pleasing to Him": it counteracted egocentric wishes and tamed creaturely desires (both of which distracted the devout from their appropriate focus on God and His commandments). For their part, the devout knew that hard work dispelled doubt and anxiety regarding one's salvation status and provided regularity to the believer's life. Furthermore, the faithful came to believe that their unusually intense devotion, capacity for righteous conduct, and energy to work hard must have its source in God – for He is omnipotent.

In this manner faith, conduct, and intense work *testified* to believers and their communities that God's divine powers were active – and this majestic Deity would not "operate within" and assist just anyone. If the faithful sought to uphold His commandments and to work in a methodical manner, and discovered an ability to do so, a *sign* of God's favor had been given to them, it could be concluded. They were – or so they could convince themselves – among the predestined elect. Work now directly became "providential"; it acquired a religious value.

Finally, systematic labor became sanctified in a further manner. In light of God's desire for an earthly kingdom of abundance to serve His glory, the devout could logically conclude that the actual production of wealth by people for a community was a positive sign from God. In effect, personal riches, which were received exclusively through the favor of an omnipotent and omniscient God, became important *evidence* in the eyes of the sincere believer of religious virtue and one's salvation status – and they were valued in this sense alone rather than for their own sake. In this manner, wealth now also, as had work in a calling, acquired a positive *religious* significance; it lost its traditionally suspect character, as particularly apparent in Catholicism, and became sanctified as a sign that indicated one's salvation. Moreover, the continuous reinvestment of one's wealth, rather than its squandering on worldly pleasures, proved a further effective means to create God's kingdom of abundance – and hence great success, which *must* have come from God's hand, also became sanctified. To Weber, with this "Protestant ethic," the ascetic, "other-worldly" organization of life by medieval monks in monasteries became transformed into an "inner-worldly asceticism" that *organized* the believer's life comprehensively and methodically around work in a calling.

An "ethos" originated in this manner. Carried by ascetic Protestantism, including above all Calvinist sects and churches, this ethic spread throughout several New England, Dutch, and English communities in the sixteenth and seventeenth centuries. Both the disciplined, hard labor in a calling and the wealth that followed from a steadfast adherence to religious values marked a person as "chosen." One century later, in

Benjamin Franklin's America, this "Protestant ethic" had spread beyond churches and sects and, as a secularized "spirit of capitalism," into entire communities. *PE* investigates its causal origins in this way. The subjective meaning, patterned social action, and social relationships of believers in groups, which crystallized out of religious sources and values rather than social structures, rational choices, economic interests, domination and power, class-based interests, evolutionary progress, or Hegel's ideas, remain central throughout Weber's argument. To him, the spirit of capitalism gave an important – although in the end imprecise – push to the development of modern capitalism.

In charting this monumental shift away from a traditional economic ethic – that is, a *religion*-based cause of modern capitalism – Weber never sought to substitute an "idealist" for a "materialist" explanation. Rather, he aimed only to isolate the heretofore neglected cultural side in order to emphasize that a comprehensive explanation of modern capitalism's origins must include consideration of the "economic ethic" as well as the "economic form." Sociological analysis must not, Weber insists, focus exclusively upon material interests, power, and structural forces to the neglect of cultural values. Yet sociologists must also reject a focus alone upon such "ideal" forces. "*Both* sides" must be given their due (see 2002b, p. 125).

The origin in Weber's sociology of patterned social action and social relationships spans a far-reaching spectrum. His empirical investigations across a vast palette of themes, epochs, and civilizations yield a clear conclusion in this respect: rather than a causal "resting point," he found only continuous movement across a broad array of, above all, political, economic, religious, legal, social strata, and familial groupings. Each set of patterned actions might acquire a cohesive social carrier and become a significant causal force (see, e.g., 1968a, p. 341).[27] Frequent conflict – involving political, economic, and rulership interests, power and the sheer strength of tradition-oriented action – accompanies social life, according to Weber. And the motivations behind patterned action also vary widely.

Weber never views causal forces either in isolation or as located within and subordinate to evolutionary, modernization, or differentiation processes. Rather, cause always implies to him a deep *embeddedness of action in constellations* of patterned action-orientations and social relationships. Even charismatic leaders who move history by the sheer force of their personalities do so in Weber's interpretive sociology only if supported by facilitating *contexts* of regular social action; even mighty missionary prophets were normally dependent upon the existence of a "certain minimum of intellectual culture" (1968a, p. 486). In all cases, empirical investigation is necessary. Do, for example, the values of a particular salvation doctrine acquire powerful carriers and prevail over patterned social action oriented to, for example, material interests, social honor, traditions,

power, authority, or laws? Sociologists cannot formulate *a priori* generalities that assume the dominance of a single set of action-orientations.

Having investigated the foundational features of Weber's interpretive
sociology, and his research strategies and procedures, vision of "society,"
and multicausality, his general view of modernity can now be addressed.
His modernity model first captures our attention: "modern Western
rationalism." It starkly reveals his concern regarding the fate of ethical
action, compassion, and the autonomous individual in our era.

## Modern Western Rationalism I: Weber's Model

Modern Western rationalism constitutes a distinct model in Weber's
sociology, as do "Chinese rationalism" and the "rationalism of India."
Formulated as an ideal type that accentuates a unique essence, it can be
utilized as a standard against which particular Western nations, as well
as the rationalism of China and India, can be compared. Part I first summarizes the major aspects of modern Western rationalism; its central
formal, practical, and theoretical "types of rationality" are defined. Weber's
model is then "applied," namely, to Germany and the United States.
This exercise offers an illustration of its analytic capacity to demarcate
the important ways in which modern societies often categorized under a
global concept – for example, the "industrial society," the "secular society"
– are in fact quite different.

*Formal* rationality appeared in a nearly omnipresent manner, Weber
argued, in the bureaucracies of the industrial society. In its major societal
domains – law, the economy, and the state – decision-making occurs by
reference to sets of universally applied rules, laws, statutes, and regulations and "without regard to persons". In this ideal type, favoritism is
precluded in respect as well to hiring, promotion, and certification; an
adherence to the dictates of abstract procedures holds sway over all
concerns for distinctions in respect to status or personality. The "logical-
formal" law of our day is implemented by trained jurists who insure
that "only unambiguous general characteristics of the case are taken
into account in terms of purely processual and legal factors" (1968a,
pp. 656–7), and formal rationality increases in the economy domain to
the degree that all technically possible calculations within the "laws of
the market" are carried out. Those who would seek to acquire a mortgage are treated by a bank's specialists in reference alone to impersonal
criteria: credit reports, savings, monthly income, etc. (pp. 251–4; 1968a,
pp. 346, 600; 1946c, p. 331).[28]

Weber sees a different type of rationality as dominant in daily life in the
industrial epoch: *practical* rationality. The individual's egoistic interests
and merely adaptive capacities come to the fore in this ideal type, and

pragmatic, calculating – means–end rational – strategies are typically employed in order to master the common obstacles of everyday life in the most expedient manner. As a consequence of their normal activities, all business-oriented strata in particular exhibit a strong tendency to order their ways of life in a self-interested, practical rational manner (see 2002b, p. 37; 1946e, pp. 279, 284, 293).

Finally, Weber understands modern societies as pervaded by *theoretical* rationality; their new world view – science – cultivates this type of rationality. An abstract confrontation with empirical reality is here typical; rigorous experiments, precise concepts, and logical deduction and induction become the tools to address and master reality. Whereas theologians, ministers, and priests in earlier epochs adjusted and refined inconsistencies in religious doctrines through theoretical rationalization processes, the same systematic, cognitive search for explanations takes place today – yet now alone in reference to an *empirical* reality. In both cases, reality is mastered through systematic thought and conceptual schemes. Religion becomes, because requiring a step beyond – "a leap of faith" – that which can be observed, defined as "irrational" to the same degree that a scientific world view ascends to a dominating position (pp. 337–42; 1946c, pp. 350, 355).[29]

What are the consequences that follow from the dominance in modern Western rationalism of formal, practical, and theoretical rationality? These types of rationality stand in opposition to constellations of values (substantive rationality) and traditions from the past. Moreover, all types are incapable of calling forth and giving sustenance to new sets of expansive and noble values, Weber contends. The present-day functionary in a bureaucracy orients his or her action alone to duty, caution, security, conformity, order, reliability, and punctuality. Laws and regulations must be implemented above all according to procedures of formal correctness and precedent rather than by reference to overarching values: justice, freedom, and equality. The practical rationality of daily life is characterized by the calculation of interests and advantage. And the scientist of today is engaged in an enterprise that calls to the fore, as the locus of "truth," empirical observation, description, and abstract synthesizing. Knowledge, insight, clarity, and the "tools and the training for thought" result from satisfactory scientific work rather than values (see 1946d, pp. 150–1; 1949a, pp. 18–19). Weber asks what domains "carry" and cultivate compassion, a brotherhood ethic, binding values, personal liberties, individual autonomy, ethical responsibility, charity, and the unified personality wherever this model holds sway. He searches but finds none. On the contrary, now unconstrained by constellations of noble values, the formal, practical, and theoretical types of rationality develop more and more unhindered.

Weber sees that clear consequences result from the absence of a religious world view under modern Western rationalism. When firmly entrenched and carried by powerful strata, classes, and organizations, these ethical universes and their salvation doctrines – as coherent constellations of values that address fundamental questions concerning the ultimate meaning of life – placed psychological rewards upon action that uprooted the devout believer from activities anchored in practical rationality. A "sublimation" of means–end rational action to value-rational action had occurred.

Yet world views declined in the West precisely at a time when the "worldly realms" became differentiated as distinct, according to Weber. Uniquely, because no longer circumscribed by the values cultivated and carried by religious organizations, they now "follow their own laws," whether those of the market, the state's pragmatism and power considerations, or the bureaucracy's statutes and regulations. This fateful conjuncture of forces raises the urgent question of whether, under the modern Western rationalism model, influential social groupings remain to shoulder the task of carrying social action and relationships oriented to the values of compassion, brotherhood, and ethical action. Intimate and familial bonds, because anchored in deeply personal and blood ties, retain such values. However, owing to a weakening of the salvation doctrines of religious world views and their carrier strata and organizations, the penetration of religious values *into the worldly realms* – where formal, theoretical, and practical rationality otherwise reign – has become less comprehensive. The West's 2,000-year journey, Weber argues, characterized by the societal-wide influence of the Judeo-Christian world view's value constellation, appears to be coming to a close (pp. 321–7).

Moreover, according to the modern Western rationalism model, "material goods [have] acquired an increasing and, in the end, inescapable power over people" (2002b, p. 124) and the "interests of daily life" have become empowered to such an extent that they consistently manipulate and exploit values. A clear *disjunction* between value ideals held dear, on the one hand, and the practical rational flow of life, on the other, is disappearing. Without values as obligatory standards, the "pragmatic approach to life" more and more reigns, pushing aside not only general ethical ideals and even all notions of ethical responsibility, but also the autonomous and integrated – or unified – personality "directed from within" on the basis of beliefs and values (see 1949a, p. 18; 1946c, pp. 327–57). Instrumental action and an uninterrupted, directionless flow of activity, rather than a set of vibrant ethical values ultimately endowed with legitimacy by religious world views, more and more hold sway under modern Western rationalism. The life methodically *directed* toward a set of internally coherent ideals appears less and less frequently and becomes less and less possible.

Modern Western rationalism unequivocally implies the loss of the traditional ethical universe and the expansion of a cold and harsh aspect.

Non-binding relationships increasingly rise to the forefront in this impersonal "cosmos." Once firmly grounded and given direction by a "devotion to a cause" – a calling – rooted ultimately in coherent and meaningful configurations of values, social relationships outside the familial and friendship bonds of intimacy are largely adrift, blowing back and forth according to momentary interests, strategic calculations, cognitive processes, power, rulership orientations, and interpretations of statutes and laws (see pp. 337–40; 1946c, pp. 327–40).

## Modern Western Rationalism II: Empirical Variation

Modern Western rationalism must be understood as an ideal type, namely, as a conceptual device useful as an orientational tool against which particular cases – nations – can be compared. As a standard, this model enables isolation of their particularity and "measurement" of the precise manner in which they vary from the construct and from each other. On the other hand, similarity can also be defined. Empirical investigation is required in order to assess the extent to which a given case conforms to or deviates from this model.

Weber is convinced that nations developing toward modernity followed unique pathways, and significant differences remained in place even in the modern era. All historical visions that discover in the West a linear evolutionary route, "increasing differentiation," or a "march of rationalization" stand opposed to Weber's fine-grained methodological and comparative-historical writings attentive to variation.[30]

Each Western religious grouping, for example, Weber repeatedly emphasizes, formulated a distinct "economic ethos"; significant sociological consequences followed depending upon whether a nation had been primarily influenced by Puritanism, Lutheranism, or Catholicism. And European Continental Law diverged distinctly from English Common Law, as did the German state from the American, French, and English states. Formal rationality's clear triumph cannot be assumed empirically. Its reach varied, as did the extent of its circumscription by constellations of values and the sheer strength in general of practical and theoretical types of rationality. Case-by-case investigation is necessary. To Weber, "modernity" is far from monolithic.

The foundational features, research strategies and procedures, vision of "society," and multicausality that constitute Weber's interpretive sociology as discussed above provide the operating axioms empowered to identify the uniqueness of specific modern cases and developments: ideal types, open-ended societal domains, social carrier groupings, and a principled interlocking of the present with the past. In conjunction with these constituent elements of his sociology, Weber's modern Western rationalism model can now be applied to two particular cases. Its analytic power to demarcate specificity can then be assessed.

In incomplete form in a variety of scattered texts, Weber charted out the divergent routes followed into modernity by Germany and the United States, and their continuing significant variation despite modern-day industrialism's homogenizing constraints. The analytic strength of the modern Western rationalism model can be illustrated by a brief summary of the ways in which it captures important aspects of their diverging pathways into modernity and significant aspects in which they vary even today.[31]

## *The United States*

Weber's research led him to conclude that the ascetic Protestant doctrines in the United States and their carrier sects and churches combined to inject an ethical aspect powerfully into the formal rationality of the marketplace. Devout businessmen came to understand their commercial dealings by reference to a set of religious values rather than by reference alone to the utilitarian calculations of the free market. For sincere believers, standards of honesty, fair play, social trust, and candor became binding *even* upon economic action. A direct confrontation with and penetration of the means–end rational action at the foundation of both formal and practical rationality took place. As this occurred, practical rational and formal rational orientations of action, according to Weber, became transformed into "practical-ethical" action.

These religion-influenced patterns of economic action became considerably weaker as industrialism and large cities developed and the grip of ascetic Protestantism over Americans became weaker. However, a banishing of the past never fully occurred, Weber contends. Although now carried also by families, neighborhoods, and civic associations, rather than by congregations alone, the values of this inner-worldly asceticism remained viable in many regions. They endured and, in the form of secular *ideals* of fair play, social trust, honesty, and equal opportunity, became "public ideals" and "civic ethics" in a "civic arena." In other words, and despite empirical abuse and violation on a regular basis, they became behavioral standards that perpetually reinvigorated *hopes* for ethical action in economic and political relationships, thereby empowering citizens to act – on occasion and at times decisively – on behalf of their fulfillment.[32] These integrating, civic values are visible even today, albeit in far less intense manifestations.[33]

The strong salience of civic ideals implied a specific consequence. Assisted by strong legacies left by the central social role played by the ascetic Protestant churches and sects in the early American religious ethos, as well as its emphasis upon personal liberties and the limited tasks of governance generally, ethical action became located beyond its accustomed home in private sphere relationships (the family, the extended family, and friendship relationships), yet fully disassociated from secular political authorities and the state (see below, pp. 284–6). In other words, with inestimable consequences, ethical action became *diffused* across American society's political and economic arenas in innumerable quasi-sect organizations: *civic associations*.[34] "Political-ethical" ideals now ubiquitously challenged utilitarian and interest-oriented calculations – that is, the formal and practical rationality postulated by the modern Western rationalism model as common to the political and economic domains. At times, civic values empirically permeated and altered these spheres, thereby establishing a specifically American version of social solidarity. The state and its laws constituted distant, secondary and tertiary mechanisms of societal integration.

Hence, influenced by substantive rationality – a particular religious tradition's constellation of values – the American case circumscribed the prominence of the formal and practical types of rationality in the modern Western rationalism model.[35] Quite different political and economic cultures characterized Germany in Weber's time, a nation in which civil servant functionaries and the state's laws largely encompassed – even monopolized – *all* understandings of the public domain (see Weber 1946b, pp. 103, 111–14; 1968b, pp. 1381–469; 1994: 80–129). Weber's model defines its unique contours.

## Germany

Political-ethical activity was located differently in Germany than in the United States. Its Lutheranism and lay Catholicism lacked the inner-worldly asceticism, Weber argues, that placed a set of values *rigorously* at the forefront of the believer's life and, moreover, *vigorously and intensively* thrust these values into the routine activity of the devout in a manner that directly confronted the massive instrumental relationships of the political and economic spheres (see Weber, 2002b, pp. 44–6, 58; Mommsen, 1974: 81–4). Rather, with urbanization, secularization, and the unfolding of modern capitalism in the nineteenth century, the "traditional economic ethics" of Catholicism and Lutheranism – as well as quasi-feudal, particularistic, and hierarchical conventions, customs, and rituals anchored in rulership relationships from the distant past – penetrated these domains.

These patterned orientations of action failed to restrain, to the same extent as in the United States, the interest-based and calculating relationships that became more widespread with the growth of modern capitalism's formal rationality. Hence, especially in light of wide-ranging secularization,[36]

Germans concluded that the full resources of a strong state must be mobilized for this circumscription to become effective. A "strong state" tradition was also called forth by the widespread view in Germany that a state-assisted economy would strengthen the nation's ability to compete with its powerful economic and political rivals. Accordingly, the state and its laws became understood as major carriers of social trust, fair play, and "civic ethics" rather than churches, sects, and civic associations, as in the United States. The ethical obligations of the German state involved the construction of a comprehensive legal code and its universal implementation, a guarantee of formal equality before the law, and the management and restriction of the capitalist economy on behalf of an array of social equity, social welfare, and solidarity measures.[37]

Far more than occurred in the United States, political-ethical action in Germany took the state as its major point of reference. Deviation from the modern Western rationalism model is again apparent, as well as from the American case: whereas a broad array of civic associations that articulated ethical ideals and a civic sphere in tension with divisive instrumental and purely utilitarian relationships constituted the diffuse and extended "political" and "economic" arenas characteristic of the United States, the state fulfilled this purpose in Germany.[38] Although in decidedly different ways, apparent in both cases is a constriction of the prominent role played by formal rationality in the modern Western rationalism model.

This brief comparison of the political and economic cultures of two nations to the modern Western rationalism model must suffice to convey the manner in which Weber's sociology captures significant differences in modernizing and modern Western nations. The German and American cases illustrate his opposition to all views of the pathways into modernity as linear and all understandings of modernity as monolithic. Different nations followed different routes and retain singular features in the present despite numerous structural organizational constraints indigenous to industrialism. A demarcation of these variations emerges from the power of Weber's sociology to combine large-scale model-building ("modern Western rationalism") with ideal types, open-ended societal domains, social carrier groupings, and an emphasis upon both the multicausality of patterned social action and the intertwining of the present closely with the past.

Weber's interpretive sociology, owing to its conceptualization of the diverse ways ideal types may empirically fall either into coalitions or stand antagonistic to one another, and of the various societal domains as empirically either unfolding in terms of "their own laws" or as merging together, strictly opposes all schools that view societies as "modern" or "traditional." Rather, to Weber, they are constituted from *configurations* of features – which may be in flux and relationships of tension or more stable and in wide-ranging coalition relationships. Only empirical investigations can draw conclusions in this respect.

## Fears about the Future and Proposals for Social Change

Weber worried, on the one hand, that the bureaucracy's formal rationality would expand into more and more societal domains with enormous consequences,[39] and, on the other, that constellations of values – substantive rationalities – would become too weak to circumscribe either formal or practical rationality. As industrial societies become comprehensively bureaucratized, they will become more and more closed, stagnant, and ossified, he predicted, suffocating alike the orientation of persons to values and individual freedoms. Drawing upon conclusions arrived at from his sweeping comparative studies, Weber became convinced that values die out whenever denied their means of sustenance: strong social carriers *and* vigorous competition between groupings cultivating different values. As people defend their values against criticism and develop loyalties, values become viable. They then increasingly guide action and form the foundation for a sense of dignity, ethical responsibility, initiative-taking, and leadership.

Only particular societies nourish values to the point where they become binding, Weber insists, indeed, even at times despite opposing material interests – namely, *dynamic and open* societies in which pluralistic values *struggle against* one another. A greater likelihood exists in these societies that people will become "responsible" in reference to a set of values and hence able to pursue ethical action. Yet Weber feared that the contending societal domains indispensable for this flourishing of competing values and a realm of freedom were losing their distinct boundaries in the modern epoch and merging. Societies would become more closed to the extent this occurred, and leaders – defending values – would fade from the social landscape. Driven increasingly by the managerial rule of technical efficiency, the modern West appeared to be headed toward ossification (see pp. 255–7).

In this nightmare vision of the distant future, the domination of bureaucracies calls forth a caste of functionaries and civil servants who monopolize power; "A fettering [of] every individual to his job . . . his class . . . and maybe to his occupation" then occurs, as well as the imposition upon the ruled of a "status order" tied to the bureaucracy (p. 256). To the same extent opportunities for the development of genuine entrepreneurs and political leaders vanish in this rigidly stratified society "as austerely rational as a machine." If the "inescapable power" of the bureaucracy's functionaries reigns, a "pacifism of social impotence," a loss of all societal dynamism, and thorough societal stagnation will result.

Devoid of brotherhood, compassion, and heroic ethical action, this possible future becomes dominated by the impersonal and cautious values of the functionary, the calculation of interests and advantage, and the mighty, inexorable expansion of instrumental rationality. In possession of specialized knowledge and capable of concentrating power, the bureaucracy's functionaries, in this vision, more and more intrude into domains of policy-making appropriately ones of open political debate and conflict between interest groups and political parties. Weber fears that, as this occurs, the few remaining legacies of public sphere ideals will disappear. Ossification will then proceed and a closed, rigid, and inward-looking society devoid of noble ideals, pluralistic and competing values, and public sphere ethical action will come into being. The frame of mind of the bureaucratic functionary – risk-averse, cautious, petty, and pro-pounding the bureaucracy's values – will become dominant.

Weber insists that ideals, ethical action, and noble values must not become simply dead legacies from the past, devoid of a social grounding in the present. To him, the dominance of instrumental calculations will offer neither dignity to people as unique and responsible individuals nor prevent the rule of force. Massive conformity will result and individual autonomy will disappear. How, then, would the orientation of action to values endure? How would it be possible "to save *any remnants* of 'individual' freedom of movement"? Will only "narrow specialists without mind" and "pleasure-seekers without heart" populate the future (p. 103)?

What types of activity will be available to confront these future dangers and dilemmas? Weber's answers to this question opposed those of Friedrich Nietzsche; his insistence that social action is embedded within contexts prevented Weber from placing faith in prophets and great "supermen." Moreover, he argued that secularism, industrialism, urbanism, and the Enlightenment had already empowered "the people" with rights to such an extent that Nietzsche's call for authoritarian heroes went too far, for they would inevitably circumscribe the open, public space indispensable if individuals are to acquire personal liberties, possess ethically-based choices, and defend values. Would future individuals, cast adrift from all directing and obligatory values and traditions, and now forced to locate meaning by reference to their "own demons," become either opportunistic actors or psychologically paralyzed? Weber rejected the loud calls in his time for "a romantic irrational heroism which sacrifices itself amidst the delirium of self-decomposition" (Salomon, 1935, p. 384). He criticized, as noted, all hopes that a politicized proletariat would usher in a more just society as unrealistic. Would configurations of *binding* values capable of anchoring ethical decisions remain? Would "personalities" – people oriented to and *unified* by values – survive?

## Proposals for social change

Weber's opposition is evident to the many American and English social thinkers of his generation who upheld an optimistic faith in the unending progress of civilization. However, he also cannot be characterized as a dour pessimist.[40] Nor was he a seeker after an idealized past, as his frequently used phrase – "disenchantment (*Entzauberung*) of the world" (see below, pp. 321–7) – has implied to many; his sociological analyses convinced him that this route remained closed. If truly a cultural pessimist or romantic, Weber would have withdrawn into fatalism and passivity, and perhaps even joined one of Germany's many "cults of irrationality." Instead, he mocked the Romantics as delusional and scorned such cults.

He wished to see a constellation of values and ideals in place that would both effectively orient action and offer dignity to individuals. As a self-conscious defender of Western traditions, he placed individual autonomy, responsibility, personal liberties, the unified personality, ethical action, brotherhood, compassion, and charity on a pedestal. How, in light of the advance of formal, practical, and theoretical rationalization in all industrial nations, could the bleak future scenario outlined above be avoided?

Weber's personal response was clear: critique and activism. A life-long player on the stage of German politics, he proved combative and indefatigable. He condemned Bismarck for crushing all independent leadership; the German monarchy for blatant incompetence and dilettantism; the bourgeoisie for its weak class consciousness and unwillingness to struggle for political power against the state bureaucracy; the agrarian aristocrats for their militarism, their authoritarianism, their attempts to deny citizenship rights to the working class, and their inability to place the nation's interests above their own concerns for material gain; and the German civil servants for their slavish conformity, obsessive adherence to rules and regulations, meekness, and general unwillingness to take responsibility for their decisions. Weber seemed to admire only the German workers, yet he criticized them as well: while appreciating their competence and notion of duty, he lamented their general passivity in the face of authority (especially compared to their counterparts in France).

In pivotal ways Weber welcomed the modern world, especially the freedoms and rights it bestowed upon individuals. Rather than the fatalism and despair so prominent among his contemporaries in Germany, particularly Nietzsche and Georg Simmel, his position mixed skepticism with appreciation. If competing domains prevail, industrial societies, he believed, would then offer an opportunity for the development of the autonomous individual guided by ethical values. *This* individual would be capable of circumscribing the instrumental rationality that characterized the life guided by practical rationality.[41]

## Weber on Modernity and Weber's Sociology: An Assessment

Important questions about the modern world drove Weber's sociology of interpretive understanding. What defines the particularity of the West? What is the fate in the industrial society of ethical action, the unique individual, and the personality unified by a constellation of noble values, compassion, and the notion of a personal calling? How can dynamic and open societies be sustained despite the necessity, if high standards of living are to be maintained widely, to organize work comprehensively in bureaucracies? Do values or means–end calculations of advantage now predominantly orient action? How can societies be organized in a manner that nourishes individualism and individual rights? What are the parameters of social change in the West? Today our scholarship seldom poses questions of such magnitude. Perhaps their formulation, in this accentuated form, is possible only by theorists writing on the cusp of modernity.

Weber's attention to the important place in modern societies of formal, practical, and theoretical rationality, and the potential threat they pose to compassion, brotherhood, individual autonomy, and a public realm of individual liberties, may appear too bleak today, especially to people living in nations characterized by democratic forms of governance, strong civic values, and a securely institutionalized pluralism of competing groupings. The possible future outlined in his political and social-philosophical writings – massive bureaucratization, the reign of a cold, instrumental rationality in the public realms of work and politics, and societal ossification – has not become reality. Modern societies have experienced waves of populist protest against bureaucratization, retained more dynamism than Weber foresaw as likely, and repeatedly rejuvenated ethical debates. A closed caste of powerful and prestigious functionaries has not generally eviscerated political debate and introduced societal stagnation, as Weber believed might occur (see Kalberg, 2001a, pp. 190–3).

Fortunately, Weber "translated" his wide-ranging concerns regarding the modern West into clear and cogent concepts, research strategies, modes of analysis, models, and methodological axioms. Thus, his writings today are understood as formulating a *Weberian sociology* rather than simply a set of insightful commentaries upon and concerns about the rapidly changing era in which he lived. He created a distinct and rigorous approach that combined empirical description with theoretical generalization.

Distinguished by its staggering comparative and historical breadth, and its cognizance of the extreme complexity of societies and causal questions, his interpretive sociology investigates the social action and relationships of people in groups by reference to values, traditions, interests, and emotions. It seeks to offer causal analyses of unique cases and developments, and proceeds by reference to ideal types, societal domains, social contexts, and the exploration of subjective meaning. His studies emphasize the ineluctable intertwining of the past with the present and assert that the subject of his sociology – meaningful action – may crystallize and replace merely imitative and reactive action in a broad spectrum of realms: religious belief, economic and political interests, legitimate authority and legal statute, family loyalties, and the social honor of status groups all may give rise to social action. To Weber, all these "directions" for meaningful action imply causal significance. Power, historical events, competition, conflict, and technology must also be recognized as viable causes of action. In all cases, however, social carriers must congeal for new patterns of meaningful action to become effective. While some societies may become, Weber acknowledges, as a result of multiple, identifiable patterns of action, more closed or even ossified in certain epochs, he scorns organic holism, retains ideal types as his level of analysis throughout his sociology, repeatedly calls attention to both coalitions and antagonisms across constellations of ideal types, and takes omnipresent conflict and power for granted. Captured in precise forms by ideal types, regularities of social action arise ubiquitously on the basis of values, traditions, interests, and even emotions.

Moreover, Weber is convinced that people repeatedly view authority as legitimate and render obedience, yet they also overthrow established ruling groups from time to time – only then to erect further authorities. Social change is inevitable, even though it never follows an evolutionary or lawful pathway. And it cannot be comprehended by reference *alone* to material or ideal factors, and least of all to transcendent forces, mysterious causes, or "ultimate" determinants. While material interests possess a strong grip upon everyday activities, people are also capable of orienting their action to values, conventions, customs, habits, and emotions – even when doing so flies in the face of their economic well-being. Meaning is formulated in a vast variety of ways, though internally consistent sets of values that address overarching questions – world views – have congealed in the major civilizations to set the "tracks" within which meaningful action becomes defined, acquires continuity, and is then altered (see 1946e, p. 280). Sociologists, in studying social relationships, groups, organizations, epochs, themes, and civilizations of interest to them, take as their task the interpretive understanding of meaningful action. However, they also seek to comprehend the social dynamics that give birth to and sustain specific patterns of meaningful action, and the further patterns of social action that lead to their transformation.

Weber's sociology poses a variety of demarcated questions and provides innumerable concepts and procedures that facilitate identification of modernity's unique aspects, assist conceptualization of its parameters, and offer insight into its internal workings and major dilemmas. It defines even today arrays of delimited research topics that can be empirically investigated. Are the social carriers of ethical action, in a particular society, powerful? Do politicians uphold an ethic of responsibility or act in reference alone to instrumental-rational considerations? Does a strong state oriented to solidarity values effectively constrain the impersonal laws of the market, or do value-based economic and civic ethics tend to do so? Or neither? Does a "civil service mentality" intrude significantly into public life? Have the notions "service to an ideal" and "vocation" disappeared today? As a far-reaching model, modern Western rationalism unveils and articulates pivotal aspects and underlying dimensions characteristic of all modern societies.

Although impressive in many ways, Weber's ambitious approach is not without its weaknesses. Several criticisms cut to the core of his sociology. Many have faulted his orientation to subjective meaning, questioning the viability of an approach that takes motives as pivotal. A number of more recent sociologists insist that interaction, creativity, identity formation, and narrative accounts must constitute the fundamental level of analysis. Moreover, while subjective meaning rooted in means–end rational action may be identifiable, further critics contend that value-based subjective meaning will always remain amorphous and problematic. Indeed, some have questioned whether an analytic armament that includes traditions and values is at all necessary for sociologists; people act, they argue, exclusively by reference, on the one hand, to pragmatic interests and, on the other, to external constraints and power.

Not surprisingly, organic holists have attacked Weber's elevation of ideal types and subjective meaning to the center of his methodology and lamented the absence of their major explanatory concept – "society" – and his indifference to "the problem of social order." Many of these same commentators have viewed his definition of sociology's aim – to offer causal explanations of unique cases and developments – as exceedingly modest. In rejecting his view of theory as an endeavor in the service of heuristic ends only and hence as always provisional, and his value-relevance axiom, they seek to establish a sociology empowered to articulate the general "laws of social life," to offer predictions about the future, and, in the name of science, to assist policy-makers and confront injustice.

The strengths and weaknesses of Weber's rich sociology will undoubtedly be debated for many years to come. Even as an array of his writings continues to be widely discussed, the opposition by many schools to the core features of his approach will endure. Nonetheless, as the microchip and globalization revolutions reach into the twenty-first century and continue to bring diverse nations into direct contact, a place remains for a wide-ranging, comparative-historical sociology anchored in ideal types and societal domains, oriented to the establishment of causality, and seeking to understand how people near and far endow their activity with subjective meaning.

### A Note on Weber's Way of Writing, the Translations, and this Reader's Particular Juxtaposition of Texts

Weber's texts are often difficult to decipher. In part, external features account for this problem. Long and expansive sentences abound and declarative statements are repeatedly qualified; single sentences weave together many themes – to the point of exhausting the reader. The heroic work of Weber's many translators, who have broken up his lengthy sentences and paragraphs, added subheadings, and written clarifying endnotes, has not alleviated this problem.

However, a further reason exists for the difficulty of Weber's texts. Because of his conviction that comparisons with other civilizations and epochs alone allows an understanding of modernity, he writes on our era in a far more comparative and historical manner than do sociologists today. Few of us today are accustomed to comparative analysis of such breadth and scope. Indeed, Weber emphasizes that the major contours and uniqueness of *any* given epoch or civilization can be isolated and defined clearly only through comparisons. Even in his texts explicitly on modernity, cross-epoch and cross-civilizational comparisons abound to such an extent that they often seem to convey an interest in the other civilization and epoch as such, and in the capacity of the comparison itself to offer insight. These impressions, however, testify to the existence of a different mode of scholarship in Weber's day rather than a turning away from the important central tasks evident throughout his works: the isolation of the major contours of the modern West and a multicausal explanation for its uniqueness.

Several features have been introduced to facilitate a better comprehension of Weber's texts. First, the introductions to each Part offer an overview glance of major themes; when unusually complex, a summary of his central arguments is provided. Second, the introductions often cross-reference related themes. Third, explanatory endnotes (followed by [sk]) and in-text bracketed clarifications have been added. Fourth, all translations have been checked line-by-line. On behalf of standardization and consistency, some terminological changes have been made (although see n. 1, p. 177 on the translation of *Herrschaft*). Further occasional alterations have been undertaken to ensure clarity, accuracy, and ease of comprehension. "Revised by Stephen Kalberg" or "Slightly revised by Stephen Kalberg" indicates those selections that have been altered. Approximately 30 pages are new translations by the editor. Fifth, a glossary of major Weberian terms has been included which refers both to Weber's writings on modernity and to his sociology in general.

Finally, it must be emphasized that this volume frequently presents excerpts from larger texts and generally omits his endnotes. Access for *everyone* to Weber's major themes on modernity, it is hoped, will be facilitated by this Reader's particular juxtaposition of writings. However, and although it is further hoped that interpreters of Weber's works will find this volume valuable as a helpful guide through the maze of his ideas on modernity, reference to the complete original text is indispensable. A note immediately preceding each reading identifies its source. The bibliography lists Weber's major texts in German and English, as well as an array of major commentaries.

## Acknowledgments

I am grateful to my colleagues and friends Robert J. Antonio, Jane Fair Bestor, Guenther Roth, Ilana Silber, and David Swartz for indispensable assistance throughout the preparation of this volume. The generous support of Ira Cohen and Ken Provencher, the Blackwell development editor, is also acknowledged with gratitude. Many thanks also to Ann Dean for producing a thorough index, to Kelvin Matthews for securing permissions, and to Susan Dunsmore for excellent copy-editing.

NOTES

1. This section, as well as major parts of the remainder of this Introduction, draw freely upon Kalberg, 2003a.
2. A number of studies examine Weber's life. See the Bibliography.
3. This and the following three sections address foundational methodological features of Weber's complex sociology. Although perhaps somewhat dry to readers exclusively interested in Weber's sociology of modernity, this brief scrutiny is indispensable – for these features underpin his understanding both of modernity and its origins. The exploration of Weber's interpretation of modernity commences below (pp. 27ff.).
4. Following Weber, I will be using the terms "meaningful action" and "social action" (and action-orientations) synonymously. Despite his emphasis upon the *capacity* of the human species to bestow subjective meaning upon action, Weber nonetheless argues that this often does not occur:

   > In the great majority of cases *actual* action goes on in a state of inarticulate half-consciousness or actual unconsciousness of its "subjective meaning." Actors are more likely to "feel" this meaning in a vague sense than to "know" it or explicitly to "make themselves" aware of it. In most cases action is governed by impulse or habit; the subjective meaning of the action (whether rational or irrational) is only occasionally elevated into consciousness. This occurs in the uniform action of large numbers only in the case of a few individuals. Meaningful action that

is actually effective – that is, when the meaning is fully conscious and apparent – is in empirical reality a marginal case. Every sociological or historical investigation that analyzes empirical reality must acknowledge this situation. However, sociology should not, for this reason, hesitate to construct its *concepts* through a classification of possible "subjective meanings"; in other words, as if action consciously oriented to meaning actually occurs. (1968a, pp. 21–2; trans. altered; emphasis in original)

For this reason, as well as his stress upon *four* types of action (see below), Weber cannot be understood simply as a "rationalist" thinker or "rational choice" theorist, as some recent commentators have asserted.

5.  Weber succinctly notes the indispensability of interpreting the meaning of an action:

[T]he simple relating [of occurrences] to a strict *rule* . . . even one in the end empirically observed, proves inadequate [to establish causality] in the case of the interpretation of human "action." Rather, we require that the interpretation of action refer back to the "meaning" of action. If this "meaning" (we will leave aside for the time being the problems behind this concept) is in the particular case directly evident and ascertainable, it is of no concern whether a "rule" can be *formulated* that encompasses this case. On the other hand, the formulation of such a rule, even one characterized by strict lawfulness, can never lead to the replacement of the task of "meaningful" interpretation by simple mention of the rule. Even more, such "laws" *as such* "mean" to us nothing for the interpretation of "action."

Suppose a law exists that somehow manages to construct the most strict empirical-statistical proof in respect to a certain situation – namely, that all people subject to this law react always and everywhere in the same way and degree and that, regardless how often this situation is recreated experimentally, everyone will react the same every time. Hence, this law would literally indicate that this reaction can be "calculated." However, such a law would not take an "interpretation" [of social action] even one step further. This is the case for the simple reason that such a proof, standing alone, would not convey to us in the least an "understanding" of "why" this reaction ever occurred and, moreover, why it always occurred in the same way. As long as this understanding is absent, any possibility is precluded of "re-constituting" the motivation behind the action through "internal" imaginative thinking [on the part of the researcher]. *Without* this possibility, even the most comprehensive, empirical-statistical proof conceivable of a lawfully existing reaction would not suffice. The demands we place on the discipline of history and the (in this respect related) "social sciences" (for now we will fully leave aside . . . a discussion of the character of these demands) would *not*, in respect to the *quality* of knowledge we expect, be met. (1973b, pp. 69–70; trans. Stephen Kalberg)

6. Weber clarifies: "This involves a rational consideration of alternative means to the end, of the relations of the end to the secondary consequences, and finally of the relative importance of different possible ends" (1968a, p. 26).

7. He points out that his classification does not seek to exhaust all possibilities, "but only to formulate in conceptually pure form certain sociologically important types to which actual action is more or less closely approximated" (1968a, p. 26). Weber does not expect to discover *empirical* cases in which social action is oriented *only* to one of these types of action.

8. Motives for Weber are causes of action: "A motive is a complex of subjective meaning which seems to the actor himself or to the observer an adequate ground for the conduct in question" (1968a, p. 11).

9. Of the four types of social action, Weber found means–end rational action to be the most easily understandable by the sociologist (see 1968a, p. 5). In all cases, the interpretation of subjective meaning by the researcher must be based upon empirical evidence and rigorous procedures. Nonetheless, it may be quite difficult, Weber acknowledges, for the social scientist to understand certain action as subjectively meaningful. He notes that values "often cannot be understood completely" (1968a, p. 5). Yet this problem does not prevent him from formulating an ideal toward which researchers should strive. And, again, in-depth exploration of the contexts within which action occurs will, he argues, assist understanding. Finally, Weber notes:

> The more we ourselves are capable of such emotional reactions as anxiety, anger, ambition, envy, jealousy, love, enthusiasm, pride, vengefulness, loyalty, devotion, and appetites of all sorts, and to the "irrational" reactions that grow out of them, the more readily can we empathize with them. Even when such emotions are found in a degree of intensity of which the observer himself is completely incapable, he can still have a significant degree of emotional understanding of their meaning and can interpret intellectually their influence on the direction of action and the selection of means. (1968a, p. 6; trans. altered)

10. "For the subjective interpretation of action in sociological work these collectivities must be treated as *solely* the resultants and modes of organization of the particular acts of individual persons, since these alone can be treated as agents in a course of subjectively understandable action" (1968a, p. 13; emphasis in original).

11. This distinguishes the "empirical sciences of action," according to Weber, from jurisprudence, logic, ethics, and esthetics, all of which aim to ascertain "true" and "valid" meanings (see 1968a, p. 4).

12. This theme, which runs throughout *E&S*, is not adequately brought to light in the present translation (1968a; see, however, pp. 22–33). It is emphasized throughout this Introduction and in several Part introductions below (see pp. 147–50, 221–4, 291–6).

13. Weber makes this general point further in the chapter on rulership (*Herrschaft*) in Part I of *E&S*.

> Hence, the kind of terminology and classification set forth above has in no sense the aim – indeed, it could not have it – to be exhaustive or to confine the whole of historical reality in a rigid scheme. Its usefulness is derived from the fact that in a given case it is possible to distinguish what aspects of a given organized group can legitimately be identified as falling under or approximating one or another of these categories. (1968a, pp. 263–4; see also Kalberg, 1994, pp. 84–91)

14. *E&S* formulates also "dynamic" models and "contextual" models. See Kalberg, 1994, pp. 39–46, 95–102.
15. Weber's extremely complex causal methodology cannot be discussed here. See Kalberg, 1994, pp. 143–92.
16. For this reason, *E&S* is organized around these domains. The unfortunate title of this opus leaves the impression that his sociology is organized around a notion of "society." The title Weber gave to *E&S*'s major section – "The Economy and the Societal Domains and Powers" (pp. 311–1372) – points to the centrality of societal domains. "Domains," "realms," "spheres," and "arenas" will be used synonymously ("orders" also appear often in the *E&S* translation). See Kalberg, 1994, pp. 104, 149–51; 1997a, pp. 221–50; Schluchter, 1989, pp. 433–63.
17. "That which has been handed down from the past becomes everywhere the immediate precursor of that taken in the present as valid" (Weber 1968a, p. 29; trans. altered; see Kalberg, 1994, pp. 158–67, 187–9; 1997a, pp. 225–35).
18. An array of ideal types is connected analytically to each domain: the paths to salvation in the sphere of religion (through a savior, an institution, ritual, good works, mysticism, and asceticism), the types of law (primitive, traditional, natural, and logical formal), the stages of development in the economy (the agricultural and industrial organization of work; the natural, money, planned, market, and capitalist types of economies), the types of authority (charismatic, patriarchal, feudal, patrimonial, and bureaucratic), the types of universal organizations (the family and clan), and major status groups (such as intellectuals, civil servants, and feudal nobles).
19. Weber's rejection of the "parallel development of domains" position is apparent from the organization of *E&S* alone; however, it is evident even as early as *The Protestant Ethic*. He contested, in this classic work, Warner Sombart's view that the development of the fundamental feature of the modern economy – "economic rationalism" – could be explained by reference to a *general* historical advance of rationality, one that encompassed all societal domains in an overarching manner. See 2002b, pp. 35–7; Kalberg, 2002, pp. xxii–xxiii.
20. Two distinct modes of diachronic interaction, each of which charts the manner in which past patterned social action influences present regular action, reappear throughout Weber's causal analyses as well as his comparative-historical texts in general: "legacy" and "antecedent condition" interactions. See Kalberg, 1994, pp. 155–68.
21. For example, when viewed from the perspective of a change from substantive to formal rationality, the *types of legitimate rulership* can be arranged in a *developmental model* (*Entwicklungsform*) that moves from charismatic and

traditional to rational-legal rulership. However, this mode of conceptualization should not lead to the conclusion that such a transformation actually occurred empirically. This remains a question for research. See 1949b, pp. 101–3; Kalberg, 1994, pp. 117–42.

22. Of course, Weber sees *specific* empirical developments toward universalistic values (e.g., in the Greek *polis*, the medieval cities, the examination system in China, and the modern bureaucracy). However, no progressive, continuous and lawful evolutionary continuum from an ancient era of particularism to a modern epoch of universalism can be drawn from his sociological investigations. The frequent translation of Weber's term *Entwicklung* (development) as "evolution" has caused a great deal of confusion.

23. For example, the orientation of social action to the clan group implies, *analytically*, a causal weight equal to that of the orientation of social action to the modern capitalist economy. Similarly, the orientation of action to laws must be viewed, according to Weber, at the analytic level as the equal of the orientation of action to the economy. Law is particularly strong in the empirical case when it is strengthened by religion: "The dominance of law that has been stereotyped by religion constitutes one of the most significant limitations on the rationalization of the legal order and hence also on the rationalization of the economy" (1968a, p. 577).

24. For a more detailed discussion that includes Weber's view of the causal impact also of technology, historical events, geography, power, conflict, and competition, see Kalberg, 1994, pp. 50–78, 117–77; 1997a, pp. 225–35.

25. On Weber's crucial distinction between "capitalism" and "modern capitalism," see below, pp. 69–90.

26. The Baptists, Calvinists (Presbyterians), Methodists, and Quakers, above all. "Ascetic Protestantism" and "Puritanism" are used synonymously.

27. In commenting upon a paper at the first meeting of the German Sociological Association in 1910, Weber makes his position clear:

> I would like to protest the statement by one of the speakers that some one factor, be it technology or economy, can be the "ultimate," "final," or "true" cause of another. If we look at the causal lines, we see them proceeding quickly from technical to economic and political factors, and then quickly from political to religious and economic ones, etc. We find no resting point at any particular place. In my opinion, the not infrequently espoused view of historical materialism – that the "economic" is in some sense the "ultimate" point in the chain of causes – is completely finished as a scientific proposition. (1988a, p. 456; trans. Guenther Roth in 1968, p. lxiv; revised by S. Kalberg)

28. Weber is here formulating ideal types. He is well aware of the many ways in which rule-bound efficiency can be hampered by "red tape."

29. These "types of rationality" are discussed in greater detail by Levine (1985) and Kalberg (1980). Weber's fourth type of rationality – substantive rationality – implies a constellation of values toward which action is oriented.

30. Passages in Weber's political and social-philosophical essays (including "Science as a Vocation" (SV) [1946d], "Politics as a Vocation" (PV) [1946b], and "Parliament and Government in a Reconstructed Germany" [1968b]), and others from the concluding paragraphs of his books (see, e.g., 2002b, pp. 123–5), indeed, leave the impression that he does see a linear historical pathway. The secondary literature has emphasized these florid statements rather than the refined analyses offered in *E&S*.

31. The brief analysis here must be limited to a consideration of the manner in which the orientation of social action to *religious belief* rendered these two modern nations distinctly different. A fully Weberian analysis would have to incorporate differences in respect to the state, the types of law, the organization of the economy, etc. Nonetheless, it is hoped that this section can stand as an illustration of the way in which Weber's *sociology* of modernity – as opposed to his political-philosophical essays, some of which *do* see a linear march of rationalization – is oriented, on the one hand, to the modern Western rationalism model and, on the other, to cases that empirically deviate from this ideal type in different ways. The paragraphs that follow draw upon several previous studies (see Kalberg, 1997b, 2001a, 2001b, 2003b; see especially Weber, 1985, 2002c).

32. That ideals are not always upheld – indeed, only rarely – is self-evident to Weber. However, he is convinced that, under certain facilitating circumstances, they can and do guide action. Hence, they must not be eliminated from sociology's conceptual capital. See, for example, 1946c, p. 324; 1946e, p. 290.

33. Their strengthening, both as "business ethics" and "civic responsibility," is central to the Communitarian agenda today. See Etzioni, 1997, 1998. The organic holism of Parsonsian sociology remains unimaginable without this unifying cultural backdrop. Yet the generalization by Parsons of his sociology – as applicable universally – commits an error of parochialism.

34. Weber renders this point vividly when he notes that "exclusivities" rather than "atomized individuals" characterized American society. See below, pp. 284–8.

35. Of course, Weber well knew that corruption and a "spoils system" remained widespread in the America of the late nineteenth and early twentieth centuries, and that power and crass calculation frequently prevailed over public ethics. Indeed, he sees ethical action in reference to a public ethos at this time as the exception and the corrupt politics of city machines as unusually widespread (Weber 1946b, pp. 108–10; 1968b, p. 1401; 1978, pp. 281–2). Nonetheless, because they were deeply rooted in American religious history, civic virtues remained to him of significant sociological impact, even if now possessing mainly the power only of historical legacies penetrating into the present.

36. A far greater secularization existed in Europe in the nineteenth century than in the United States, as is the case today.

37. Hence, German Romanticism's ideals of universalism and inclusion became located in the state rather than in sects and churches. This development would have far-reaching effects upon the formation of Germany's political, intellectual, and social cultures.

38. Accordingly, bureaucratization of the state assumed, in comparison to the United States, in Germany a particularly developed form. Variation in respect to the extent of bureaucratization across the modern Western nations is apparent to Weber. Case-specific contextualization is necessary:

> One must in every individual historical case analyze the special direction in which bureaucratization develops. For this reason, it must remain an open question whether the *power* of bureaucracy is, without exception, increasing in the modern states in which it is spreading . . . Whether the power of bureaucracy as such increases cannot be decided *a priori*. (Weber 1968a, p. 991; trans. altered)

Even the social prestige of civil servants varies across nations:

> Usually the social esteem of the officials is especially low where the demand for expert administration and the hold of status conventions are weak. This is often the case in new settlements by virtue of the great economic opportunities and the great instability of their social stratification: witness the United States. (Weber 1968a, p. 960)

This being said, Weber fully expected that, with the growth of industrialism in the United States, bureaucratization would expand.

39. Even the United States, he believed, would move toward greater bureaucratization and become more like Europe. See, e.g., 1946b, pp. 106–14; Roth, 1985. Despite his emphasis upon the unique dynamism contributed by the Protestants sects and churches to the American political and economic cultures, Weber saw their impact as lessening with greater urbanization and industrialization. See Kalberg, 2001b, pp. 310–14.

40. Weber almost always uses qualifying expressions, multiple preconditions, and the subjunctive case when describing the future; the nightmare scenario *may* be on the horizon *if* configurations of forces come together.

41. For more details on Weber's proposals to slow down the wheels of bureaucratization, see Kalberg, 2003a, pp. 175–9.

# part 1

# The Uniqueness of the West

## Introduction

"Prefatory Remarks" ("PR"),[1] the major reading in this Part, demarcates succinctly and vividly the particularity of the West or, in Weber's terms, "the characteristic uniqueness of modern Western rationalism." Thus, this essay moves qualitatively beyond the focus of *The Protestant Ethic and the Spirit of Capitalism* (*PE*) upon the origin of a "spirit of capitalism" in the West. Moreover, unlike *PE*, it argues that a causal analysis of this particularity must focus not only upon orientations to salvation doctrines, but also upon economic, political, legal, and other patterns of action.

"PR" opens by noting the variety of ways in which the West proved distinct. A series of innovations in art, music, and architecture were unique, for example, as was a systematic science, a state based upon a "rationally enacted constitution and rationally enacted laws," parliaments composed of elected representatives and ministers obligated to adhere to parliamentary procedures, and "modern capitalism."

Weber's crucial distinction in "PR" between "capitalism" and "modern capitalism" must be singled out. The former has existed universally while the latter appeared only in the modern West. A "rational-capitalist organization of (legally) *free labor*," a relatively free market exchange, a "rational organization of industrial companies and their orientation to *market* opportunities," a separation of the business from the household, sophisticated bookkeeping, formally free labor, *and* a specific economic ethos distinguishes this "middle-class industrial" capitalism. Finally, modern capitalism requires a stable and calculable law and administration that "functions according to formal rules," hence enabling large-scale and future-oriented business transactions. The middle-class capitalist, unlike speculators, promoters, and financiers, or "adventure capitalists," was oriented systematically to profit and the industrial organization of free labor.

"PR" takes a strong stand on causal analysis. Although Weber stresses, as he had in *PE*, that the ways in which belief influences economic activity should always be kept in mind, he now addresses the "other side" of the causal equation: Economic Ethics of the World Religions (EEWR; see note 1) examines the influence of interests ("external forces") upon ideas ("internal forces") *as well as* the influence of ideas upon interests (see also 1961, pp. 312–14). However, the frequent search for a quick-and-easy causal formula must be abandoned:

> Religion nowhere creates certain economic conditions unless there are also present in the existing relationships and constellations of interests certain possibilities of, or even powerful drives toward, such an economic trans-formation. It is not possible to enunciate any general formula that will sum-marize the comparative substantive powers of the various factors involved in such a transformation or will summarize the manner of their accommo-dation to one another. (1968a, p. 577; see also p. 341; 1946d, pp. 267–70)

"PR" conveys EEWR's fundamental broadening of the *PE* study in just this manner. For example, a variety of non-religious obstacles to economic development in China are charted in EEWR, such as extremely strong clan ties and an absence of "a formally guaranteed law and a rational admin-istration and judiciary" (1951, p. 85; see pp. 91, 99–100), and in India, such as constraints placed by the caste system upon migration, the recruitment of labor, and credit (1958, pp. 52–3, 102–6, 111–17). Weber discovers as well, however, an entire host of conducive material forces that nonethe-less failed to bring about modern capitalism – such as, in China, freedom of trade, an increase in precious metals, population growth, occupational mobility, and the presence of a money economy (1951, pp. 12, 54–5, 99–100, 243). In the end, the many clusters of social action supportive of modern capitalism in China and India were outweighed by a series of opposing patterns of meaningful action. Nonetheless, Weber remained convinced that modern capitalism could be *adopted* by, and would flourish in, a number of Eastern civilizations. He even identified the forces that would allow this to occur (on Japan, see 1958, p. 275). Yet he insisted that adop-tion involved different processes than *his* main concern: the *origin* in a specific region only of a *new* economic ethos and a *new* type of economy.

The EEWR studies offer complex, multidimensional causal arguments. "PR" draws particular attention to "the fundamental significance of econ-omic factors," but also to "the capacity and disposition of persons to organ-ize their lives in a practical-rational manner" (pp. 62–3). In many societies magical and religious forces may have obstructed this mode of organiz-ing life. Moreover, the origin of the stable legal framework and stratum of professionally-trained jurists required by modern Western capitalism, Weber contends, cannot be found exclusively in economic interests, for "why then did capitalist interests not call forth this stratum of jurists and this type of law in China or India?" (p. 62). *Constellations* of forces must be scrutinized rather than single factors, "PR" asserts. In addition, their conjunctural interaction in delineated contexts must be charted out, as well as the ways in which, as a consequence, unique configurations are formulated (see Kalberg, 1994, pp. 98–102, 155–76, 189–92; 2002, pp. lix–lxi).

It is widely argued that Weber's research on China and India was oriented simply to the formulation of contrast cases to the West. However, these studies aim to accomplish much more. They investigate the *uniqueness* of "Chinese rationalism" and the "rationalism of India," and pursue explanations for the particular developmental routes followed by *each* great civilization. Importantly, EEWR seeks to offer a sociological analysis of the manner in which meaning is formulated in non-Western civilizations.

This chapter's second reading outlines, in abbreviated form, the distinctly Western "search for the individual self." In the third and fourth selections Weber argues that political and economic forces unique to the West have played a crucial role in the development of modern Western law. (See also, in general, 1961, pp. 275–8.)

NOTE

1. After writing *PE* in 1904 and 1905, and the two "sect essays" (2002c, 1985), Weber's research on the relationship between religious belief and economic activity became radically comparative. Around 1911 he began work on a series of studies on the economic ethics of Confucianism, Taoism, Hinduism, Buddhism, Jainism, and ancient Judaism. First published separately as articles in the journal *Archiv für Sozialwissenschaft und Sozialpolitik*, these investigations were prepared in 1919 and 1920 for publication in book form and were given the title Economic Ethics of the World Religions. The complete three-volume enterprise, which placed *PE* and "Sects" (2002c) at its beginning and included 1946c, 1946e, 1951, 1952, and 1958, was published after Weber's death in 1920 under the title *Collected Essays on the Sociology of Religion* (1972). Written late in 1919, "PR" is the general introduction to these volumes. It conveys the other prominent path, in addition to *E&S*, taken by Weber's sociology after *PE*.

# chapter 1

# The "Rationalism" of Western Civilization

From "Prefatory Remarks" to Collected Essays on the Sociology of Religion (1920/ 2002), in *The Protestant Ethic and the Spirit of Capitalism*, 3rd edn., trans. Stephen Kalberg (Los Angeles: Roxbury Publishing, 2002), pp. 149–60.

Any heir of modern European culture will, unavoidably and justifiably, address universal-historical[1] themes with a particular question in mind: What combination of circumstances led in the West, and only in the West, to the appearance of a variety of cultural phenomena that stand – at least as we like to imagine – in a historical line of development with *universal* significance and empirical validity?

*Science,* developed to the stage that we today recognize as "valid," exists only in the West. Empirical knowledge, reflection on the world and the problems of life, philosophical and theological wisdom of the deepest kind, extraordinarily refined knowledge and observation – all this has existed outside the West, above all in India, China, Babylon, and Egypt. Yet a fully developed systematic theology appeared only in Hellenic-influenced Christianity (even though some beginnings were apparent in Islam and a few sects in India). And despite empirical knowledge, Babylonian, and every other type of astronomy, lacked a mathematical foundation (rendering the development, in particular, of Babylonian astronomy all the more astonishing), which would be provided only later by the Greeks. A further product of the Hellenic mind, the idea of rational "proof," was absent from geometry in India. This mind also first created mechanics and physics. Moreover, although the natural sciences in India were quite well developed as concerns observation, they lacked the rational experiment, which was essentially a product of the Renaissance (although beginnings can be found in the ancient world). The modern laboratory was also missing in the natural sciences developed in India. For this reason, medicine in India, which was highly developed in terms of empirical technique, never acquired a biological and, especially, a biochemical foundation. A rational chemistry was absent from all regions outside the West.

The scholarly writing of history in China, which was very advanced, lacked the rigor of Thucydides [*ca.* 460–400 BCE].[2] Precursors of Machiavelli [1489–1527] existed in India, yet all Asian theorizing on the state omitted a systematic approach comparable to Aristotle's [384–322 BCE], as well as rational[3] concepts in general. A rational jurisprudence based on rigorous juridical models and modes of thinking of the type found in Roman law and the Western law indebted to it was absent outside the West, despite all beginnings in India (School of Mimamsa)[4] and the comprehensive codification of law in the Near East especially – and in spite of all the books on law written in India and elsewhere. A form of law similar to canon law cannot be found outside the West.

Similar conclusions must be drawn for art. The musical ear, apparently, was developed to a more refined degree among peoples outside the West than in the West to this day; or, at any rate, not less so. The most diverse sorts of polyphonic music have expanded across the globe, as did also the simultaneous playing of a number of instruments and singing in the higher pitches. All of the West's rational tone intervals were also widely calculated and known elsewhere. However, unique to the West were many musical innovations. Among them were rational, harmonic music (both counterpoint and harmony); formation of tone on the basis of three triads and the major third;[5] and the understanding of chromatics and enharmonics since the Renaissance harmonically and in rational form (rather than by reference to distance). Others were the orchestra with the string quartet as its core and the organization of ensembles of wind instruments; the bass accompaniment; and the system of musical notation (which made possible the composition and rehearsal of modern works of music and their very survival over time). Still other innovations were sonatas, symphonies, and operas (although organized music, onomatopoeia, chromatics, and alteration of tones have existed in the most diverse music as modes of expression). Finally, the West's basic instruments were the means for all this: the organ, piano, and violin.

[The situation is similar in architecture.] As a means of decoration, pointed arches existed outside the West, both in the ancient world and in Asia. Presumably, the juxtaposition of pointed arches and cross-arched vaults was not unknown in the Middle East. However, the rational utilization of the Gothic vault as a means to distribute thrust and to arch over variously formed spaces and, above all, as a principle of construction for large monumental buildings and as the foundation for a *style* that incorporated sculpture and painting, as was created in the Middle Ages – all this was missing outside the West. A solution to the weight problem introduced by domes was also lacking outside the West, even though the technical basis for its solution was taken from the Middle East. Every type of "classical" rationalization[6] of the entire art world – as occurred in painting through the rational use of both linear and spatial perspective – was also lacking outside the West, where it began with the Renaissance.

Printing existed in China. Yet a printed literature intended *only* to be printed and made possible exclusively through printing – "daily news-papers" and "periodicals," mainly – originated only in the West.

Universities of all possible types existed also outside the West (China and the Islamic world), even universities that look externally similar to those in the West, especially to Western academics. A rational and systematic organization into scientific disciplines, however, with trained and specialized professionals (*Fachmenschentum*), existed only in the West. This becomes especially evident if these disciplines are viewed from the vantage point of whether they attained the culturally dominant significance they have achieved in the West today.

Above all, the cornerstone of the modern state and modern economy – specialized *civil servants* – arose only in the West. Only precursors of this stratum appeared outside the West. It never became, in any sense, as constitutive for the social order as occurred in the West. The "civil servant," of course, even the civil servant who performs specialized tasks, appeared in various societies, even in ancient times. However, only in the modern West is our entire existence – the foundational political, technical, and economic conditions of our being – absolutely and inescapably bound up in the casing (*Gehäuse*) of an *organization* of specially trained civil servants. No nation and no epoch has come to know state civil servants in the way that they are known in the modern West, namely, as persons trained in technical, commercial, and above all, legal areas of knowledge who are the social carriers of the most important everyday functions of social life.

[And what about the state?] The organization of political and social groups on the basis of *status* has existed historically on a broad scale. Yet the *Ständestaat* in the Western sense – *rex et regnum* – has appeared only in the West.[7] Moreover, parliaments of periodically elected "represen-tatives," with demagogues and party leaders held responsible as "minis-ters" to parliamentary procedures, have come into existence only in the West. This remains the case even though "political parties," of course, in the sense of organizations oriented to the acquisition of political power and the exercise of influence on political policy, can be found throughout the world. The "state," in fact, as a political institution (*Anstalt*) operated according to a rationally enacted "constitution" and rationally enacted laws, and administered by civil servants possessing *specialized* arenas of competence and oriented to rules and "laws," has existed with these distinguishing features only in the West, even though rudimentary developments in these directions have crystallized elsewhere.

The same may be said of that most fateful power of our modern life: *capitalism*.

A "drive to acquire goods" has actually nothing whatsoever to do with capitalism, as little as has the "pursuit of profit," money, and the greatest possible gain. Such striving has been found, and is to this day, among waiters, physicians, chauffeurs, artists, prostitutes, corrupt civil servants, soldiers, thieves, crusaders, gambling casino customers, and beggars. One can say that this pursuit of profit exists among "all sorts and conditions of men" [Sir Walter Besant],[8] in all epochs and in all countries of the globe. It can be seen both in the past and in the present wherever the objective possibility for it somehow exists.

This naive manner of conceptualizing capitalism by reference to a "pursuit of gain" must be relegated to the kindergarten of cultural history methodology and abandoned once and for all. A fully unconstrained compulsion to acquire goods cannot be understood as synonymous with capitalism, and even less as its "spirit." On the contrary, capitalism *can* be identical with the *taming* of this irrational motivation, or at least with its rational tempering. Nonetheless, capitalism is distinguished by the striving for *profit*, indeed, profit is pursued in a rational, continuous manner in companies and firms, and then pursued *again and again*, as is *profitability*. There are no choices. If the entire economy is organized according to the rules of the open market, any company that fails to orient its activities toward the chance of attaining profit is condemned to bankruptcy.

Let us begin by *defining terms* in a manner more precise than often occurs. For us, a "capitalist" economic act involves first of all an expectation of profit based on the utilization of opportunities for *exchange*; that is, of (formally) *peaceful* opportunities for acquisition. Formal and actual acquisition through violence follows its own special laws and hence should best be placed, as much as one may recommend doing so, in a different category. Wherever capitalist acquisition is rationally pursued, action is oriented to *calculation* in terms of capital. What does this mean?

Such action is here oriented to a systematic utilization of skills or personal capacities on behalf of earnings in such a manner that, at the close of business transactions, the company's money *balances*, or "capital" (its earnings through transactions), exceed the estimated value of all production costs (and, in the case of a longer lasting company, *again and again* exceed costs). It is all the same whether goods entrusted to a traveling salesman are involved and he receives payment through barter, so that the closing calculation takes place in goods, or whether the assets of a large manufacturing corporation (such as buildings, machines, cash, basic materials, and partly or entirely manufactured goods) are weighed against its production costs. Decisive in both situations is that a *calculation* of earnings in money terms takes place, regardless of whether it is made on the basis of modern accounting methods or primitive, superficial procedures. Both at the beginning of the project and at the end there are specific calculations of balances. A starting balance is established and calculations are carried out before each separate transaction takes place; at every stage an instrumental assessment of the utility of potential transactions is calculated; and, finally, a concluding balance is calculated and the origin of "the profit" ascertained.

The beginning balance of the *commenda* transaction involves, for example, a designation of the amount of money agreed upon by both parties regarding what the relevant goods *should* be worth (assuming they have not already been given a monetary value). A final balance forms the estimate on the basis of which a distribution of profit and loss takes place. Calculation lies (as long as each case is rational) at the foundation of every single activity of the *commenda* partners. However, an actual exact accounting and appraisal may not exist, for on some occasions the transaction proceeds purely by reference to estimates or even on the basis of traditions and conventions. Indeed, such estimation appears in every form of capitalist enterprise even today wherever circumstances do not require more exact calculation. These points, however, relate only to the *degree* of rationality of capitalist acquisition.

Important for the formation of the *concept* of capitalism is only that economic action is decisively influenced by the *actual* orientation to a comparison of estimated monetary expenses with estimated monetary income, however primitive in form the comparison may be. Now in this sense we can see that, insofar as our documents on economies have reached into the distant past, "capitalism" and "capitalist" enterprises, at times with only a moderate degree of rationalization of capital accounting, have existed in *all* the world's civilizations. In other words, "capitalism" and "capitalist" enterprises have been found in China, India, Babylon, Egypt, the ancient Mediterranean, and medieval Europe, as well as in the modern West. Not only entirely isolated enterprises existed in these civilizations; rather, also businesses are found completely oriented to the continuous appearance of new companies and to a continuity of "operations." This remained the situation even though trade, over long periods, did not become perpetual, as it did in the West; instead, it assumed the character of a series of separate enterprises. A business context – the development of different "branches" for business – congealed only gradually and only slowly influenced the behavior of the *largescale* commercial traders. At any rate, the capitalist enterprise has been an enduring, highly universal, and ancient organization. Also capitalist businessmen, not only as occasional entrepreneurs but as persons oriented permanently to business, have been ancient, enduring, and highly universal figures.

The West, however, has given birth to types and forms of capitalism (as well as to directions for its unfolding) that have provided the foundation for the development of capitalism to an extent and significance unknown outside the West. Merchants have engaged in wholesale and retail trade, on a local as well as international scale, throughout the world. Businesses offering loans of every sort have existed widely, as have banks with the most diverse functions (although for the most part functions essentially similar to those of Western banks of the sixteenth century). Sea loans,[9] *commenda*, and *kommandit*[10] types of businesses and formal associations have been widespread. Wherever the financing of public institutions through *currency* has occurred,[11] financiers have appeared – in Babylon, ancient Greece, India, China, and ancient Rome. They have financed above all wars, piracy, and all types of shipping and construction projects; as entrepreneurs in colonies they have served the international policy goals of nations. In addition, these *adventure* capitalists have acquired plantations and operated them using slaves or (directly or indirectly) forced labor; they have leased land and the rights to use honorific titles; they have financed both the leaders of political parties standing for re-election and mercenaries for civil wars; and, finally, as "speculators" they have been involved in all sorts of money-raising opportunities.

This type of entrepreneur – the adventure capitalist – has existed throughout the world. With the exception of trade, credit, and banking businesses, his money-making endeavors have been mainly either of a purely irrational and speculative nature or of a violent character, such as the capture of booty. This has taken place either through warfare or the continuous fiscal exploitation of subjugated populations.

Promoter, adventure, colonial, and, as it exists in the West, modern finance capitalism can be characterized often, even today, in terms of these features. This becomes especially apparent whenever capitalism is oriented to warfare, although it holds even in periods of peace. Single (and only single) components of large-scale international commerce today, as in the past, approximate adventure capitalism.

However, in the *modern* era the West came to know an entirely different type of capitalism. Absent from all other regions of the globe, or existing only in preliminary developmental stages, this capitalism appeared side-by-side with adventure capitalism and took as its foundation the rational-capitalist[12] organization of (legally) *free labor*. With *coerced* labor, a certain degree of rational organization had been attained only on the plantations of antiquity and, to a very limited extent, on the ancient world's *ergasteria*.[13] An even lesser degree of rationality was reached in agricultural forced-labor enterprises generally, the workshops of medieval manors, and in manor-based cottage industries utilizing the labor of serfs at the dawning of the modern era. Outside the West, free labor has been found only occasionally. Even the existence of actual "cottage industries" has been documented with certainty only rarely outside the West. And the use of day laborers, which naturally can be found everywhere, did not lead to manufacturing and not at all to a rational, apprenticeship-style organization of skilled labor of the type practiced in the West's Middle Ages. This must be said despite a very few, very unusual exceptions, and even these diverged significantly from the modern Western organization of industrial work in companies (especially from those companies that, through support from the state, held market monopolies).

However, the rational organization of industrial companies and their orientation to *market* opportunities, rather than to political violence or to irrational speculation, does not constitute the only distinguishing mark of Western capitalism. The modern, rational organization of the capitalist industrial firm would not have been possible without two prior important developments: (1) the *separation of the household from the industrial company*, which absolutely dominates economic life today, and, connected closely to this development, (2) the appearance of rational *accounting*.

The spatial separation of the place of labor or sales from the place of residence can be also found elsewhere (in the Oriental bazaar and in the *ergasteria* of other cultures). Capitalist associations with accounting procedures separate from personal accounts existed in East Asia as well as in the Middle East and the ancient world. Nonetheless, compared to the modern situation in which company operations are fully independent, these examples show only very limited beginnings. This remained the case above all because the *internal* preconditions for independent business operation – rational *accounting* methods and a *legal* separation of company wealth from personal wealth – were either entirely absent or developed only to preliminary stages.[14] Instead, outside the West, industry-oriented endeavors tended to become simply one component of the feudal manor's *household* activities (the *oikos*). [Karl Johann] Rodbertus [1805–65] has already noted that all developments toward the *oikos* deviated distinctly from the route taken by capitalist activity in the West. Indeed, as he argues, and despite a number of apparent similarities, the *oikos* stood starkly in opposition to the Western pathway.

All these particular aspects of Western capitalism, however, in the end acquired their present-day significance as a result of their connection to the capitalist organization of *work*. Even what one is inclined to call "commercialization" – the development of stocks and bonds and the systematization, through stock markets, of speculation – must be seen as taking place in the context of a capitalist organization of labor. All this, even the development toward "commercialization," if it had been possible at all, would never have unfolded to anywhere near the same proportion and dimension if a capitalist-rational organization of work had been lacking. Hence, all of these new factors would never have significantly influenced the social structure and all those problems associated with it specific to the modern West. Exact calculation, the foundation for everything else, is possible only on the basis of *free* labor.

And as the world outside the modern West has not known the rational organization of work, it has also not known, and for this reason, rational *socialism*. Now, of course, just as history has experienced a full spectrum of types of economies, ranging from those, on the one hand, oriented to city development and city-organized food supply policies, mercantilism, the social welfare policies instituted by princes, the rationing of goods, a thorough regulation of the economy, and protectionism, and on the other hand to *laissez-faire* theories (also in China), the world has also known socialist and communist economies of the most diverse sorts. State socialist (in [ancient] Egypt) and cartel-monopolistic versions of socialism can be found, as can types of communism more rooted in (a) heterogeneous consumer organizations, (b) private sphere values of intimacy and the family, (c) religious values, and (d) military values. However (despite the existence everywhere at one time or another of guilds and brotherhood corporations, various legal distinctions between cities and provinces in the most diverse form, and cities that granted specific market advantages to particular groups), just as the concept of "citizen" is entirely missing except in the West and the concept of "bourgeoisie" is completely absent outside the modern West, so also the notion of a "proletariat" as a *class* is absent. Indeed, it could not appear outside the West precisely because a rational organization *of free labor* in *industrial enterprises* was lacking. "Class struggles" between strata of creditors and debtors, between those who owned land and those who did not (whether serfs or tenant sharecroppers), between persons with economic interests in commerce and consumers or owners of land – all these conflicts have existed for centuries in various constellations. Yet even the struggles typical in the West's medieval period between domestic industry entrepreneurs and their wage workers [the putting-out system] are found elsewhere only in a rudimentary form. The modern opposition between large-scale industrialists, as employers, and free workers paid a wage is completely lacking outside the West. And thus a situation of the type known to modern socialism also could not exist.

Hence, for us, as we investigate the universal history of civilizations, and even if we proceed by reference exclusively to issues directly related to the economy, the central problem in the end *cannot* be the unfolding of capitalist activity everywhere and the various forms it took. That is, our concern cannot be whether it appeared more as adventure capitalism, commercial capitalism, or a capitalism oriented to the opportunities for profit offered by war, politics, and state administration. Rather, the central problem must ultimately involve the origin of *middle class industrial* capitalism with its rational organization of *free labor*. Or, rendered in the terms of cultural history: The central problem must ultimately concern the origin of the Western middle class and its particular features. Of course, this theme is closely interwoven with the question of the origin of the capitalist organization of labor. Yet it is naturally not exactly the same – for the simple reason that a "middle class," in the sense of a stratum of people, existed before the development of this specifically Western capitalism anchored in the capitalist organization of labor. However, obviously this was the case *only* in the West.

Now evidently the capitalism specific to the modern West has been strongly influenced above all by advances in the realm of *technology*. The nature of the rationality of modern Western capitalism is today determined by the calculability of factors that are technically decisive. Indeed, these factors are the foundation for all more exact calculation. In turn this calculability is rooted fundamentally in the characteristic uniqueness of Western science, and especially in the natural sciences grounded in the exactness of mathematics and the controlled experiment.

The development of these sciences, and the technology that is based upon them, acquired – and continues to acquire – pivotal invigorating impulses from opportunities offered by capitalism. Market opportunities, that is, as rewards, are connected to the economic applications of these technologies. However, it must also be emphasized that the origin of Western science cannot be explained by the availability of such economic opportunities. Calculation, even with decimals, existed also in the algebra of India, where the decimal system was discovered. Yet in India it never led to modern calculation and accounting methods; this mode of calculation was first placed into *operation* only in the West's developing capitalism. Similarly, the origin of mathematics and physics was not determined by economic interests, yet the *technical* application of scientific knowledge was. Important for the quality of life of the broad population, this application was conditioned by economic rewards – and these crystallized precisely in the West. These rewards, however, flowed out of the particular character of the West's *social* order. It must then be asked: From *which* components of this unique social order did these rewards derive? Surely not all of its features have been of equal importance.

The rational structure of *law* and administration has undoubtedly been among the most central elements of this social order. This is the case for the simple reason that modern-rational industrial capitalism, just as it requires calculable technical means in order to organize work, also needs a calculable law and administration that function according to formal rules. Of course adventure capitalism and a trade-based capitalism oriented to speculation, as well as all types of capitalism determined by political considerations, can well exist without calculable law and administration.

However, a rational industrial firm – with fixed capital and reliable *calculation*, and operating in a private economy – is not possible without this type of law and administration.

Yet this type of law and administration, in *this* degree of legal-technical and formal perfection, was placed at the disposal of the economy and its development *only* in the West. Hence, one must ask: What was the source of this type of law in the West? Undoubtedly, in addition to other circumstances, *also* economic interests paved the way for the rule of a stratum of jurists who were professionally trained in rational law and who, in a disciplined and regular manner, practiced and administered law. This is evident from every investigation. Yet these economic interests were not the exclusive, or even the primary, causal forces in the rise of this stratum to importance. Moreover, economic interests did not of themselves *create* this type of law. Rather, entirely different powers were active in respect to this development. And why then did capitalist interests not call forth this stratum of jurists and this type of law in China or India? How did it happen that scientific, artistic, and economic development, as well as state-building, were not directed in China and India into those tracks of *rationalization* specific to the West?

The issue in all of the cases mentioned above evidently involves a characteristic aspect of a specifically formed "rationalism" of Western civilization. Now this word can be understood as implying a vast spectrum of matters. There is, for example, "rationalization" of mystical contemplation, that is, of a type of behavior that is specifically "irrational" if viewed from the perspective of other realms of life.[15] Similarly, there may be rationalization of the economy, technology, scientific work, education, warfare, administration, and the practice of law. One may further "rationalize" each one of these arenas from vantage points and goals of the most diverse sort and ultimate orientations. What may appear "rational" viewed from one angle may appear "irrational" when viewed from another.

Hence, we must note that rationalizations have occurred in the various arenas of life in highly varying ways and in all circles of cultural life.[16] It is necessary, in order to identify the ways in which the multiple rationalization paths have characteristically varied according to cultural and historical factors, to assess *which* arenas have been rationalized and in what directions. Again, important here above all are the special *characteristic features* of Western rationalism and, within this particular type of rationalism,[17] the characteristic features of modern Western rationalism. Our concern is to identify this uniqueness and to explain its origin.

Every such attempt at explanation, recognizing the fundamental significance of economic factors, must above all take account of these factors. However, the opposite line of causation should not be neglected if only because the origin of economic rationalism depends not only on an advanced development of technology and law but also on the capacity and disposition of persons to organize their lives in a practical-rational manner. Wherever magical and religious forces have inhibited the unfolding of this organized life, the development of an organized life oriented systematically toward *economic* activity has confronted broad-ranging internal resistance. Magical and religious powers, and the ethical notions of duty based on them, have been in the past among the most important formative influences upon the way life has been organized.

## NOTES

1. Stemming originally from the German polymath Johann Gottfried von Herder (1744–1803), "universal history" (*Universalgeschichte*) came to refer in the nineteenth century to a mode of German historiography that avoided specialist studies and instead attempted to offer a synthesizing portrait of an entire historical epoch or area of culture. The term does not imply "world history" [sk].
2. Thucydides of ancient Greece is best known for his history of the Peloponnesian War (431–404 BCE). Weber refers to his attempt to record events and occurrences as they empirically took place; hence he interviewed direct observers, avoided speculative interpretations and reference to supernatural forces ("the will of the gods"), and sought to offer an "objective" account. He was the first historian to do so [sk].
3. "Rational" here implies to Weber "rigor" and a "systematic aspect" (as also in the next paragraph and throughout). The term does not imply "better." See Kalberg, 1980, pp. 1145–79 [sk].
4. A religious-philosophical school in India that developed out of the pre-Hindu Vedas (seventh century BCE). It emphasized that salvation could be attained though the performance of certain ritualized good works [sk].
5. "Major third" (*harmonische Terz*) refers to the distance on the piano keyboard from note "c" to "e." Use of these notes together formed a harmonious sound that was used frequently in classical composition [sk].
6. "Rationalization" can be equated with "systematization." See the article cited in note 3 [sk].
7. The Western *Ständestaat* involved, uniquely, a precarious balancing of powers between the ruler, a cohesive aristocracy, and powerful municipally-based political actors. Hence, it implied temporary alliances and a rudimentary division of powers, an arrangement that was a precursor to the division of powers in the modern constitutional state. See *E&S*, pp. 1085–87 [sk].
8. Perhaps from the progressive English social critic, novelist, biographer, urban historian, and philanthropist, Sir Walter Besant (1836–1901) [sk].
9. The sea loan, which originated in Mediterranean antiquity and became used widely in the Western Middle Ages, was a response to the unusually high danger of shipping by sea and the attempt by borrowers (who had purchased the goods on credit) and creditors to distribute the risk of total loss: the

borrower agreed to pay to the creditor an extremely high interest rate (perhaps 30 percent) in exchange for which the creditor assumed liability for the goods in the event of loss. See Weber, 1927, pp. 204–06 [sk].

10. A type of company that limits liability for owners in respect to both damage caused by faulty products and injuries suffered by employees [sk].

11. In contrast to barter [sk].

12. Again, Weber is using "rational" in the sense of a systematic, organized, disciplined, and economically-efficient manner of organizing work [sk].

13. *Ergasteria* are shops, separate from the private residence, where workers perform their labor. They vary widely, from the bazaar, which combines the place of work and the place of sale, to the factory. Central in all cases is that an entrepreneur prescribes the conditions of work and pays wages. See Weber, 1927, pp. 119, 162 [sk].

14. Of course the contrast should not be understood as absolute. . . . [Weber notes several examples.]

15. By "other realms of life" Weber has in mind, for example, the arenas of the economy or politics. Because "activity in the world" is valued as worthwhile and meaningful in these realms, the mystic's withdrawal through contemplation is seen as meaningless, or "irrational." See *E&S*, pp. 541–51 [sk].

16. Weber's use of the expression "circles of cultural life" is not intended to refer to "high," "low," or "popular" culture. Instead, this term (*Kulturkreisen*) in his time refers to various arenas of life, such as the political, economic, religious, scientific, artistic, etc. [sk].

17. In the volumes that follow in the German edition, Weber will refer repeatedly to, for example, "Chinese rationalism," "the rationalism of India," and "the rationalism of the Middle Ages" [sk].

# Protection against the Western Search for the Individual Self

From *The Religion of India: The Sociology of Hinduism and Buddhism*, eds and trans. Hans H. Gerth and Don Martindale, slightly revised by Stephen Kalberg (New York: The Free Press of Glencoe, 1958), pp. 342–3.

Wherever an intellectual stratum attempted to establish the meaning of the world and the character of life and – after the failure of this unmediated rationalistic effort – to comprehend experience in its own terms, indirect rationalistic elements were taken into consideration. It was led in some manner to the style of the trans-worldly field of formless Indian mysticism. And where, on the other side, a status group of intellectuals rejected such world-fleeing efforts and, instead, consciously and intentionally pursued the charm and worth of the elegant gesture as the highest possible goal of inner-worldly consummation, it moved, in some manner, toward the Confucian ideal of cultivation.

Out of both these components, crossing and jostling one another, however, an essential part of all Asiatic intellectual culture was determined. The conception that through simple behavior addressed to the "demands of the day," one may achieve salvation – which lies at the basis of all the specifically Occidental significance of "personality" – is alien to Asia. This is as excluded from Asiatic thought as the pure factual rationalism of the West, which practically tries to discover the impersonal laws of the world.

They were, indeed, protected by the rigid ceremonial and hieratic stylization of their life conduct from the modern Occidental search for the individual self in contrast to all others – the attempt to take the self by the forelock and pull it out of the mud, forming it into a "personality." To Asia this was an effort as fruitless as the planned discovery of a particular artistic form of "style." Asia's partly purely mystical, partly purely inner-worldly aesthetic goal of self-discipline could take no other form than an emptying of experience of the real forces of experience. As a consequence of the fact that this lay remote from the interests and practical behavior of the "masses," they were left in undisturbed magical bondage.

. . . The appearance of [an ethic of everyday life] in the Occident, however – above all, in the Near East – with the extensive consequences borne with it, was conditioned by highly particular historical constellations without which, despite differences of natural conditions, development there could easily have taken the course typical of Asia, particularly of India.

# Western Law and the Modern Capitalist Enterprise

From *Economy and Society: An Outline of Interpretive Sociology*, eds and trans. Guenther Roth and Claus Wittich (Berkeley, CA: University of California Press, 1978), pp. 1394–5.

The "progress" toward the bureaucratic state, adjudicating and administering according to rationally established law and regulation, is nowadays very closely related to the modern capitalist development. The modern capitalist enterprise rests primarily on *calculation* and presupposes a legal and administrative system, whose functioning can be rationally predicted, at least in principle, by virtue of its fixed general norms, just like the expected performance of a machine. The modern capitalist enterprise cannot accept what is popularly called "*kadi*-justice": adjudication according to the judge's sense of equity in a given case or according to the other irrational means of law-finding that existed everywhere in the past and still exist in the Orient. The modern enterprise also finds incompatible the theocratic or patrimonial governments of Asia and of our own past, whose administrations operated in a patriarchal manner according to their own discretion and, for the rest, according to inviolably sacred but irrational tradition.

The fact that *kadi*-justice and the corresponding administration are so often venal, precisely because of their irrational character, permitted the development, and often the exuberant prosperity, of the capitalism of traders and government purveyors and of all the pre-rational types known for four thousand years, especially the capitalism of the adventurer and booty-seeker, who lived from politics, war and administration. However, the specific features of modern capitalism, in contrast to these ancient forms of capitalist acquisition, the strictly rational organization of work embedded in rational technology, nowhere developed in such irrationally constructed states, and could never have arisen within them because these modern organizations, with their fixed capital and precise calculations, are much too vulnerable to irrationalities of law and administration. They could arise only in such circumstances as: 1) In England, where the development of the law was practically in the hands of the lawyers who, in the service of their capitalist clients, invented suitable forms for the transaction of business, and from whose midst the judges were recruited who were strictly bound to precedent, that means, to calculable schemes; or 2) where the judge, as in the bureaucratic state with its rational laws, is more or less an automaton of paragraphs: the legal documents, together with the costs and fees, are dropped in at the top with the expectation that the judgment will emerge at the bottom together with more or less sound arguments – an apparatus, that is, whose functioning is by and large *calculable* or predictable.

From *Economy and Society: An Outline of Interpretive Sociology*, eds Guenther Roth and Claus Wittich, trans. Max Rheinstein (Berkeley, CA: University of California Press, 1978), p. 883.

Only the Occident has witnessed the fully developed administration of justice of the folk-community (*Dinggenossenschaft*) and the status-stereotyped form of patrimonialism; and only the Occident has witnessed the rise of the national economic system, whose agents first allied themselves with the princely powers to overcome the estates and then turned against them in revolution; and only the West has known "Natural Law," and with it the complete elimination of the system of personal laws and of the ancient maxim that special law prevails over general law. Nowhere else, finally, has there occurred any phenomenon resembling Roman law and anything like its reception. All these events have to a very large extent been caused by concrete political factors, which have only the remotest analogies elsewhere in the world. For this reason, the stage of law decisively shaped by trained legal specialists has not been fully reached anywhere outside of the Occident. Economic conditions have, as we have seen, everywhere played an important role, but they have nowhere been decisive alone and by themselves. To the extent that they contributed to the formation of the specifically modern features of present-day occidental law, the direction in which they worked has been by and large the following: To those who had interests in the commodity market, the rationalization and systematization of the law in general and, with certain reservations to be stated later, the increasing calculability of the functioning of the legal process in particular, constituted one of the most important conditions for the existence of economic enterprise intended to function with stability and, especially, of capitalistic enterprise, which cannot do without legal security. Special forms of transactions and special procedures, like the bill of exchange and the special procedure for its speedy collection, serve this need for the purely formal certainty of the guaranty of legal enforcement.

# part 2

# The Uniqueness and Origins of the Modern Western Work Ethic

## Introduction

A number of historians and economists in Weber's time emphasized the importance for economic development of technological innovations, the influx of precious metals, and population increases. Others were convinced that the greed, economic interests, and "desire for riches" of capitalists in general, but especially of great "economic supermen," had pushed the economy past the agrarian and feudal stages to mercantilism and modern capitalism. Disagreeing with all these explanations, evolutionists argued that the expansion of production, trade, banking, and commerce could best be understood as the clear manifestation of a general, societal-wide unfolding of progress.

None of these forces could offer, Weber insisted in his classic *PE*, an explanation for that which distinguished *modern* capitalism from capitalism as it had existed throughout the ages. *PE* addresses *one* component of modern capitalism: its "economic ethos" – more specifically, the *origins* of this economic ethos. Standing behind the rigorous organization of work, the methodical approach to labor, and the systematic pursuit of profit typical of this form of capitalism, this ethos was constituted from an "idea of the *duty* of the individual to increase his wealth, which is assumed to be a self-defined interest in itself" (p. 77); the notion that "labor [must be performed] as if it were an absolute end in itself" (2002b, p. 24); "the earning of more and more money, combined with the strict avoidance of all spontaneous enjoyment of it" (2002b, p. 17); the view that the "acquisition of money . . . is . . . the result and the expression of competence and proficiency in a calling" (2002b, p. 18); and "the frame of mind that . . . strives systematically and rationally *in a calling* for legitimate profit" (2002b, p. 26; emphasis in original). Embodied in these ideas, Weber contends, was a *spirit* of capitalism. A full understanding of the origins of modern capitalism, he argues vehemently, requires an identification of the sources of this "modern economic ethos" (pp. 75–8; 2002b, p. 18).

*PE* investigates the specific ancestry of this spirit, rather than the sources in general of either modern capitalism or capitalism. After citing numerous passages from Benjamin Franklin's *Autobiography*, whose values represent to Weber this frame of mind in a pure form, he asserts that he has here discovered an *ethos*, "the violation of [which] is treated not as foolishness but as forgetfulness of *duty*" (2002b, p. 77; emphasis in original). In seeking to unravel the sources of this new *set of values* and organized life, this "positive critique of historical materialism" rejects the view that capitalism's dominant class, in search of docile yet energetic workers, gave birth to this spirit. It opposes as well the argument that social structures – status groups or rulership organizations – stand at its origin. Instead, against strong opponents, Weber decided to examine the "idealist side." The realm of religious belief, he concluded after preliminary investigation, might yield particular insight. Previously neglected, its explanatory potential must be explored.

A set of work-oriented values heretofore scorned became of utmost centrality in the lives of Puritan believers. Not the desire for riches alone or the efficient adaptation to economic forces, but only work motivated "from within" by an "internally binding" set of religious values was empowered to introduce, Weber argues, a "systematization of . . . life organized around ethical principles" (2002b, p. 76) and a "planned regulation of one's own life" on behalf of work and the pursuit of wealth (2002b, p. 79; see also pp. 77–80). Only this ethically[1] *ordered way of life anchored in values* was endowed with the methodicalness and intensity requisite for an uprooting and banishing of the traditional economic ethic. *PE* traces the origin of this frame of mind back to the Puritan faithful in the sixteenth and seventeenth centuries in England and how, for them, a striving for salvation placed "psychological rewards" upon methodical work and entrepreneurial activity. Acknowledgment of this "Protestant ethic," which appeared a century later in secularized form as a "spirit of capitalism," must not be omitted, *PE* forcefully argues, from the array of causal forces that gave rise to modern capitalism.[2]

Surely Weber's Puritans, who worked methodically as a consequence of *otherworldly* considerations, would be appalled to see that their systematic labor and profit-seeking led, centuries later, to a degree of wealth threatening to their frugal and modest style of life oriented to God (pp. 98–9; 1968a, p. 1200). Moreover, their riches created a highly advanced technological cosmos anchored ultimately by the laws of science based on empirical observation rather than by the laws of God and methodical *ethical* action oriented to Him. A scientific world view, cultivated and developed by the modern capitalism that ascetic Protestantism helped to call into existence, opposes in principle – for it refuses to provide legitimacy to a "leap of faith" – all world views rooted in religion (pp. 337–40). Weber's writings frequently identify such unforeseen and paradoxical consequences in history.

PE's majestic concluding passages emphasize that those born into today's "powerful cosmos," where pragmatic necessities, sheer means–end calculations, and secularism reign, can scarcely imagine the actual contours of the religion-saturated world of the past. Even with the best of wills, "we moderns" can barely conceive of work in a vocation as motivated by that crucial query in the lives of the Puritan devout: "Am I among the saved?" The dominance today of radically different assumptions regarding typical motives for action, Weber believes, obscures our capacity to comprehend how activity was differently motivated in the distant past. Indeed, sociologists too often unknowingly impose present-day assumptions upon action in the past, he contends. For this reason, Weber calls for a sociology of interpretive understanding that seeks to comprehend, "from within," the subjective meaning of people. This can take place only through detailed investigation of *their* milieu of values, traditions, emotions, and interests.

Central passages from "The Protestant Sects in North America" ("Sects"; 2002c) comprise this Part's second major reading (Chapter 3). Informal in tone, it is built around Weber's perspicacious observations as he travels through the Midwest, the South, the Middle Atlantic states, and New England. Two early versions were written soon after his return to Germany and published in 1906. Weber significantly revised and expanded the essay in 1920.[3]

His delightful commentary should not be understood as providing merely fragmented "impressions of American life." Instead, Weber brings his audience up-to-date in respect to the fate of Puritan beliefs in the United States 250 years after their origin. Through this close-up view of American customs, conventions, and values, he hopes, first, to offer an analysis of how doctrinal-based ethical action is sustained through social dynamics and, second, to comment upon the unique social configuration dominant in American society. In doing so, he aims not least to confront stereotypes widespread in Germany.

"Sects" turns away from an analysis of the type of activity required of the sincere believer by ascetic Protestant doctrine to an explanation of how this behavior became cultivated in – even demanded by – the social group to which the devout belonged, namely, the *sect*. The particular social dynamic prevalent in this organization had the effect, Weber argues, of intensively "breeding" *ethical* qualities. In other words, his concern now centers upon how the religious belief of Puritans, anchored in the doctrine of Predestination and minister Baxter's revisions, were "put into practice." The Protestant sects did so in a remarkably effective manner, Weber insists, indeed to a degree that far more intensively penetrated the believer's entire being than occurred wherever churches carried religious belief.

Because membership in the sect was permitted only after an investigation into the moral conduct of candidates, sect members became widely recognized throughout the community as honest, respectable, decent, and upright. Rather than sincere beliefs alone, this "balloting" feature of the sect itself predisposed members (in order to protect their prestigious reputations and even their entire social existence) to take measures, if necessary, to insure the reputation of the sect. A monitoring of behavior became strict and continuous, and the sect offered assistance to members who fell on hard times. The benefit of such rigorous scrutiny was apparent: reputations for respectability were maintained, thereby guaranteeing acceptability and social prestige – yet also success in business. The entire community traded at sect-owned businesses, for here the rules of honesty and fair play, it was widely known, were upheld.

However, Weber sees the impact of this sect dynamic as extending even beyond the realm of economic activity and business success. A necessity, now within an all-encompassing, admonishing, and immediate social grouping, to demonstrate one's moral character – to "hold one's own"[4] – placed intense social pressure upon all sect members to abide by strict religious standards of good conduct. Indeed, proper behavior became indispensable, for it alone "testified" to – or "proved" – the sincerity of the believer's faith. The sect constitutes, Weber holds, for this reason, the strongest "breeding ground" for ethical action – which originates, he contends in "Sects," not only from religious doctrines. And moreover, owing to the salvation rewards placed upon business success by Puritan beliefs, the success of a sect member "testified to his worth" – to his state of grace. In turn, the wealth of sect members enhanced the sect's prestige within its community. And greater social prestige led to an intensification of the sect's monitoring activities and more social pressure upon members to conduct themselves strictly according to ethical standards.

An array of social constellations unique to American society flowed out of this "sect dynamic." Even in 1904 survivals and "derivatives" of the influence of the sects were visible to Weber, though largely in secular manifestations. To him, "no one doubts the decisive role of Puritanism for the American style of life" (2001, p. 104; trans. altered). Here we discover the second major theme in this essay. The sects proved extremely effective in diffusing and maintaining "the bourgeois capitalist business ethos among the broad strata of the middle classes" (p. 114). More generally, multiple legacies of the "sect spirit," Weber argues, form the sociological underpinnings in the United States of, for example, social trust, skeptical attitudes toward secular authority, the practice of self-governance, and the nimble capacity of Americans to form civic associations (see also 1968a, pp. 1204–6; pp. 277–90). Only the latter residual of the sect spirit can be addressed here.

Because sect membership implied honesty, respectability, and good character in general, these organizations served as "typical vehicles of social ascent" (p. 114). Weber observes that the pin in the suit lapel of members of businessmen's clubs – the Kiwanis, the Lions, the Rotary clubs, for example – conveyed acceptance by a selective group that cultivated standards of personal and civic behavior; hence membership constituted a "little badge" certifying personal integrity, social honor, and creditworthiness. Membership proved indispensable in many regions if one hoped to be fully accepted as honorable in one's community (see pp. 112–15, 284–7).

In this way the influence of ascetic Protestantism, manifest in 1904 as prestigious community norms of "involvement" and "service," contributed to the formation of diverse civic associations "between" the distant state and the individual standing alone. This achievement formed the historical foundation for American society's unique proclivity to create multitudes of such associations.[5] In turn, this capacity comprises a pivotal component in its political culture of participation and self-governance. Importantly, in this manner the sects forcefully extended *ethical* action beyond its traditional location – the private realm – into a public, or *civic*, arena (see Kalberg, 1997b, 2003b).

Thus, against stereotypes widespread in his time in Europe, Weber contends that American society cannot be accurately described as a "sandpile" of disconnected individuals adrift and anonymous, lost in states of anomie. Rather, in calling attention to the broad tendency among Americans to form associations, he emphatically called into question this common image of "modern society." Moreover, as a sociologist oriented to cases rather than to general "developmental laws" and to the influence of the past upon the present, he wished to demonstrate how the political and social cultures of modern nations vary as a consequence of specific historical legacies anchored in religion despite a common experience of urbanism, capitalism, and industrialism.

NOTES

1. Weber defines an "ethical" standard as:

> a specific type of value-rational belief among individuals which, as a consequence of this belief, imposes a normative element upon human

action that claims the quality of the "morally good" in the same way that action which claims the status of the "beautiful" is measured against aesthetic standards. (1968a, p. 36; trans. altered; emphasis in original)

Social action, Weber contends, can be influenced by an ethical standard even if "external" support for it is lacking and even, at times, in spite of opposing "external" forces.

2.  For a more detailed overview, see pp. 24–7 above and Kalberg, 2002, pp. xxviii–lv.
3.  The selections in this chapter are from the 1920 version (2002c). This version appeared in Weber's *Collected Essays on the Sociology of Religion* (1972) immediately after *PE*. Selections from the second publication in 1906 (1985) appear below (see pp. 277–90).
4.  Or, as we would say today in phrases without the least religious connotation, to "fend for oneself" and "prove one's mettle."
5.  Of course, Alexis deTocqueville had earlier emphasized exactly this developed capacity of American society. His explanation, however, for this proclivity to form associations (which opposes for him a tendency in the United States toward a "tyranny of the majority") varies distinctly from Weber's; Tocqueville refers to egalitarianism, commercial interests, and the interests of the individual, whereas Weber turns to the ascetic Protestant religious tradition. See Kalberg, 1997b.

# chapter 2

# The Religious Origins of the Vocational Calling

## THE PROTESTANT ETHIC AND THE SPIRIT OF CAPITALISM

## The Spirit of Capitalism

From *The Protestant Ethic and the Spirit of Capitalism*, 3rd edn, trans. Stephen Kalberg (Los Angeles: Roxbury Publishing, 2002), pp. 14–16.

... Our focus at the beginning should be only to provide a provisional *illustration* of the activity implied here by the term *spirit of capitalism*. Indeed, such an illustration is indispensable in order to attain our aim now of simply understanding the object of our investigation. On behalf of this purpose we turn to a document that contains the spirit of concern to us in near classical purity, and simultaneously offers the advantage of being detached from *all* direct connection to religious belief – hence, for our theme, of being "free of presuppositions."

Remember, that *time* is money. He that can earn ten shillings a day by his labor, and goes abroad, or sits idle, one half of that day, though he spends but sixpence during his diversion or idleness, ought not to reckon *that* the only expense; he has really spent, or rather thrown away, five shillings besides.

Remember, that *credit* is money. If a man lets his money lie in my hands after it is due, he gives me the interest, or so much as I can make of it during that time. This amounts to a considerable sum where a man has good and large credit, and makes good use of it.

Remember, that money is of the prolific, generating nature. Money can beget money, and its offspring can beget more, and so on. Five shillings turned is six, turned again it is seven and threepence, and so on, till it becomes a hundred pounds. The more there is of it, the more it produces every turning, so that the profits rise quicker and quicker. He that kills a breeding-sow, destroys all her offspring to the thousandth generation. He that murders a crown, destroys all that it might have produced, even scores of pounds. . . .

Remember this saying: *The good paymaster is lord of another man's purse.* He that is known to pay punctually and exactly to the time he promises, may at any time, and on any occasion, raise all the money his friends can spare. This is sometimes of great use. After industry and frugality, nothing contributes more to the raising of a young man in the world than punctuality and justice in all his dealings; therefore never keep borrowed money an hour beyond the time you promised, lest a disappointment shut up your friend's purse for ever.

The most trifling actions that affect a man's credit are to be regarded. The sound of your hammer at five in the morning, or eight at night, heard by a creditor, makes him easy six months longer; but if he sees you at a billiard-table, or hears your voice at a tavern, when you should be at work, he sends for his money the next day; demands it, before he can receive it, in a lump.

It shows, besides, that you are mindful of what you owe; it makes you appear a careful as well as an honest man, and that still increases your credit.

Beware of thinking all your own that you possess, and of living accordingly. It is a mistake that many people who have credit fall into. To prevent this, keep an exact account for some time, both of your expenses and your income. If you take the pains at first to mention particulars, it will have this good effect: you will discover how wonderfully small, trifling expenses mount up to large sums, and will discern what might have been, and may for the future be saved, without occasioning any great inconvenience.

For six pounds a year you may have the use of one hundred pounds, if you are a man of known prudence and honesty.

He that spends a groat a day idly, spends idly above six pounds a year, which is the price of using one hundred pounds.

He that wastes idly a groat's worth of his time per day, one day with another, wastes the privilege of using one hundred pounds each year.

He that idly loses five shillings' worth of time, loses five shillings, and might as prudently throw five shillings in the river.

He that loses five shillings, not only loses that sum, but all the advantage that might be made by turning it in dealing, which by the time that a young man becomes old, will amount to a comfortable bag of money.

It is *Benjamin Franklin* [1706–90] who preaches to us in these sentences. As the supposed catechism of a Yankee, Ferdinand Kürnberger satirizes these axioms in his brilliantly clever and venomous *Picture of American Culture.* That the spirit of capitalism is here manifest in Franklin's words, even in a manner characteristic for him, no one will doubt. It will not be argued here, however, that *all aspects* of what can be understood by this spirit is contained in them.

Let us dwell a moment upon a passage, the worldly wisdom of which is summarized thusly by Kürnberger: "They make tallow for candles out of cattle and money out of men." Remarkably, the real peculiarity in the "philosophy of avarice" contained in this maxim is the ideal of the *credit-worthy* man of honor and, above all, the idea of the *duty* of the individual to increase his wealth, which is assumed to be a self-defined interest in itself. Indeed, rather than simply a common-sense approach to life, a peculiar "ethic" is preached here: its violation is treated not simply as foolishness but as a sort of forgetfulness of *duty*. Above all, this distinction stands at the center of the matter. "Business savvy," which is found commonly enough, is here not *alone* taught; rather, an *ethos* is expressed in this maxim. Just *this* quality is of interest to us in this investigation.

A retired business partner of Jakob Fugger [1459–1525, an extremely wealthy German financier, export merchant, and philanthropist] once sought to convince him to retire. Yet his colleague's argument – that he had accumulated enough wealth and should allow others their chance – was rebuked by Fugger as "contemptible timidity." He "viewed matters differently," Fugger answered, and "wanted simply to make money as long as he could."

Obviously, the spirit of this statement must be *distinguished* from Franklin's. Fugger's entrepreneurial daring and personal, morally indifferent proclivities now take on the character, in Franklin, of an *ethically-oriented* maxim for the organization of life. The expression *spirit of capitalism* will be used here in just this specific manner – naturally the spirit of *modern* capitalism. That is, in light of the formulation of our theme, it must be evident that the Western European and American capitalism of the last few centuries constitutes our concern rather than the "capitalism" that has appeared in China, India, Babylon, the ancient world, and the Middle Ages. As we will see, *just that peculiar ethic was missing in all these cases.* . . .

# Capitalist Spirit and Capitalist Form

From *The Protestant Ethic and the Spirit of Capitalism*, 3rd edn, trans. Stephen Kalberg (Los Angeles: Roxbury Publishing, 2002), pp. 26–7.

. . . Rather than being in "lawful" dependency, the capitalist form of an economy and the spirit in which it is operated in fact exist generally in a less determinant relationship, namely, one of "adequacy" to each other. Nonetheless, if we provisionally employ the phrase *spirit of* (modern) *capitalism*[1] to refer to the particular frame of mind that, as in our example of Benjamin Franklin, strives systematically and rationally *in a calling* for legitimate profit, then we are doing so for historical reasons. We do so on the one hand because this frame of mind finds its most adequate form in the modern capitalist company and, on the other, because the capitalist company discovers in this frame of mind the motivating force – or spirit – most adequate to it.

Of course, it may happen that "spirit" and "form" do not come together at all. The "capitalist spirit" permeated Benjamin Franklin at a time when the organization of his publishing business did not vary from the older, traditional form typical in a handicraft shop. We shall also see that, on the threshold of the modern epoch, the capitalist entrepreneurs of the commercial aristocracy were by no means exclusively or predominantly the social carriers of that frame of mind here designated as the spirit of capitalism.[2] On the contrary, the upwardly mobile strata of the industrial middle classes were far more so. Similarly, in the nineteenth century, the classical representatives of this spirit were the Manchester or Rhineland-Westphalia upstart newcomers to wealth from modest circumstances, rather than the aristocratic gentlemen from Liverpool and Hamburg whose commercial fortunes were inherited from the distant past. Matters were not different even as early as the sixteenth century. The founders of the new *industries* of this period were predominantly upstart newcomers.

For example, surely a bank, a wholesale export company, a large retail concern, or, finally, a large cottage industry that produces goods in homes can be operated only in the form of a capitalist business. Nevertheless, all of these businesses could be managed according to a spirit of strict economic traditionalism. In fact, it is *impossible* to carry out the operations of a large bank of issue [federal reserve bank] in a different manner, and the foreign trade of entire epochs has been based upon monopolies and regulations rooted strictly in economic traditionalism. The revolution that brought the ancient economic traditionalism to an end is still in full motion in retail trade (we are not referring to the type of small-scale businesses that are today calling out for state subsidies), and it is just this transformation that destroyed the old forms of the cottage-industry system (to which the modern forms of work in the home are related only in form).

## NOTES

1.  We are referring here, of course, to that *modern* rational *business* that is unique to the West, rather than to the capitalism of usurers, purveyors of warfare, traders in offices, tax farmers, large merchants, and financial magnates.

This latter capitalism has, for 3,000 years, spread across the globe from China, India, Babylon, Greece, Rome, Florence, and into the present. See "Prefatory Remarks" [chapter 1 in this volume] [note added in 1920 edition].

2. The assumption (and this should be emphasized here) is by no means justified *a priori* that, on the one hand, the technique of the capitalist enterprise and, on the other, the spirit of "work as a vocational calling," which endows capitalism with its expansive energy, must have had their *original* sustaining roots in the same social groupings. Religious beliefs relate to social relationships in the same [imprecise] manner.

Historically, Calvinism was one of the social carriers of the socialization practices that gave rise to the "capitalist spirit." Yet, in the Netherlands, for example, those who possessed great fortunes were not predominately followers of the strictest Calvinism; rather, they were Arminians (for reasons that will be discussed later). In the Netherlands as well as elsewhere, the "typical" social carriers of the capitalist ethic and the Calvinist Church were persons from the upwardly mobile *middle* and *lower-middle* strata. The owners of businesses came out of these strata.

However, exactly this situation conforms very well with the thesis presented here. Persons who possessed great fortunes and large-scale merchants have existed in all epochs, yet a rational-capitalist organization of *industrial* work in a middle class first became known in the development that occurred between the Middle Ages and the modern period [note added in 1920 edition].

# The Spirit of Capitalism as One Part in a Larger Development?

From *The Protestant Ethic and the Spirit of Capitalism*, 3rd edn, trans. Stephen Kalberg (Los Angeles: Roxbury Publishing, 2002), pp. 35–7.

How then does it come about that activity which, in the most favorable case, is barely morally tolerable, becomes a "calling" in the manner practiced by Benjamin Franklin? How is it to be explained historically that in Florence, the center of capitalist development in the fourteenth and fifteenth centuries and the marketplace for money and capital for all of the great political powers, striving for profit was viewed as either morally questionable or at best tolerated? Yet in the business relationships found in small companies in rural Pennsylvania, where scarcely a trace of large-scale commerce could be found, where only the beginning stages of a banking system were evident, and where the economy was continuously threatened with collapse into sheer barter (as a result of a simple lack of money), the same striving for profit became viewed as legitimate.

Indeed, it became understood as the essence of a morally acceptable, even praiseworthy way of organizing and directing life.

To speak *here* of a "reflection" of "material" conditions in the "ideal superstructure" would be complete nonsense. Hence, our question: What set of ideas gave birth to the ordering of activity oriented purely to profit under the category of a "calling," to which the person felt an *obligation?* Just this set of ideas provided the ethical substructure and backbone for the "new style" employer's organized life.

Some have depicted economic rationalism as the basic characteristic of the modern economy in general (Sombart in particular, often in success-ful and effective discussions). Surely Sombart has done so correctly if "economic rationalism" refers to the increase in productivity that results from the organization of the production process according to *scientific* vantage points, hence the banishing of the situation in which gains were restricted owing to the naturally given "organic" limitations of people. This rationalization process in the arenas of technology and the economy undoubtedly also conditions an important part of the "ideals of life" in the modern, middle-class society in general. Work in the service of a rational production of material goods for the provision of humanity has without question always been hovering over the representatives of the capitalist spirit as a directing purpose of their life's labors. For example, one needs only to read about Franklin's efforts in Philadelphia in the ser-vice of community improvement to understand immediately this completely self-evident truth. Moreover, the joy and pride one feels in giving "work" to numerous people and in assisting the economic "flowering" (in the manner in which this term is associated, under capitalism, with popula-tion and trade figures) of one's hometown belongs obviously to the unique, and undoubtedly "idealistically" driven, satisfactions of the modern business establishment. And, likewise, the capitalist economy rationalizes on the basis of strictly *quantitative* calculations and is oriented to the sought-after economic success in a systematic and dispassionate manner. These operating principles are inherent in and fundamental to capitalism. They contrast directly with the situation of the peasant who lives from hand to mouth, to the guild craftsmen in the medieval epoch who main-tained market advantages rooted in old customs, and to the "adventure capitalist" who was oriented to political opportunities and irrational speculation.

Thus it appears that the development of the capitalist spirit can be most easily understood as one component part in a larger and overarch-ing development of rationalism as a whole. It appears further that this spirit should best be comprehended as derived from rationalism's basic position in respect to the ultimate problems of life. Hence, according to this interpretation, Protestantism would come into consideration historically only to the extent that it played a role as a "harbinger" of purely rationalistic views of life.

As soon as one seriously attempts to formulate the problem of the development of the spirit of capitalism in this way, however, it becomes clear that such a simple approach to this theme is inadequate. The reason is that the history of rationalism *by no means* charts out a progressive unfolding, according to which all the separate realms of life follow a *parallel* developmental line. The rationalization of private law, for example, if understood as the conceptual simplification and organization of the subject matter of the law, attained its heretofore highest form in the Roman law of later antiquity. It remained least rationalized, however, in some nations with the most highly rationalized economics. England offers an example. During the period of the development of [modern] capitalism in this nation, the power of large guilds of lawyers prevented the rebirth of Roman law. In contrast, rationalized Roman law has consistently remained dominant in the Catholic areas of southern Europe [where modern capitalism, compared to England, remained underdeveloped].

[Two more examples for the nonparallel development of the separate realms of life must suffice.] First, the purely secularized philosophy of the eighteenth century [the Enlightenment] surely was not based alone, or even primarily, in the highly developed capitalist nations. This philosophy of Voltaire [1694–1778] is even today the broad common inheritance of the upper and (what is more important practically) middle strata, especially in the nations of Roman Catholicism. Second, if one understands by the phrase *practical rationalism* that way of organizing life according to which the world's activities are consciously referred back to the practical interests of the *particular person,* and are judged from his or her specific vantage point,[1] then this style of life was typically unique primarily to *liberum arbitrium* [easygoing] peoples. Even today practical rationalism permeates the flesh and blood of the Italians and the French. And we have already convinced ourselves this is not the soil that primarily nourishes persons who relate to their "calling" as a task (as [modern] capitalism needs).

A simple sentence should stand at the center of every study that delves into "rationalism." It must not be forgotten that one can in fact "rationalize" life from a vast variety of ultimate vantage points. Moreover, one can do so in very different directions. "Rationalism" is a historical concept that contains within itself a world of contradictions.

Our task now is to investigate from whose spiritual child this matter-of-fact form of "rational" thinking and living grew. The idea of a "calling," and of the giving over of one's self to *work* in a calling, originated here. As noted, the entire notion of a "calling" must appear fully irrational from the vantage point of the person's pure self-interest in happiness. Yet the dedication to work in the manner of a "calling" has in the past constituted one of the characteristic components of our capitalist economic culture. It remains so even today. What interests us here is precisely the ancestral lineage of that *irrational* element which lies in this, as in every, conception of a "calling."[2]

## NOTES

1. On "practical rationalism" (and Weber's other types of rationalism), see Kalberg, 1980 [sk].
2. We will discover that the "birth of the calling" did not follow *logically* from ascetic Protestantism's doctrine of predestination. On the contrary, despair and bleakness followed logically from this doctrine. The revisions formulated by Richard Baxter, which concerned the pastoral care of believers, introduced the "calling" of significance to Weber or, more precisely, the notion of testifying to one's belief through conduct. These revisions could not be deduced rationally from the doctrine of predestination. See below, pp. 85–104 [sk].

# The Task of the Investigation

From *The Protestant Ethic and the Spirit of Capitalism*, 3rd edn, trans. Stephen Kalberg (Los Angeles: Roxbury Publishing, 2002), pp. 48–50.

Hence, in its modest manner, the following study might perhaps constitute a contribution to the illumination of the way in which "ideas" become generally effective in history. In order, however, to prevent misunderstandings at the outset in regard to the manner in which we are here asserting that purely ideal motives may become effective forces, a few further small clarifications on this theme may be permitted. These clarifications can serve as concluding comments to the introductory discussion.

It should be directly stated that studies such as this one are in no way concerned with the attempt to *evaluate* the substantive ideas of the Reformation [which, as we will see, stood at the origin of the spirit of capitalism], by reference to either social-political or religious vantage points. Instead our goals concern aspects of the Reformation that must appear to persons with a religious consciousness as peripheral and related to superficial matters only. After all, it is our task to investigate and to clarify the impact that religious motives had on that web of development in the direction of our modern, specifically "this-worldly"-oriented life and culture generally – a development that grew out of innumerable, fragmented historical forces. Thus we are in the end asking a question: Which characteristic features of our modern life and culture should be *attributed* to the influence of the Reformation? In other words, to what extent did the Reformation serve as a historical cause of these characteristic features?

In asking this question, on the one hand we must of course emancipate ourselves from the point of view that the Reformation can be "deduced" from economic transformations as a "developmental-historical necessity." Constellations of innumerable historical forces had to interact if the newly created churches were to endure. By no means can reference to a "law of economic development" or, more generally, to economic points of view of whatever sort, do justice to the complexity of these developments. Rather, political processes, in particular, had to interact with economic forces.

On the other hand, we shall not defend here two foolish and doctrinaire theses in any form: (1) that the capitalist spirit (in the still provisional use of this term utilized here) *could* have originated *only* as an expression of certain influences of the Reformation, and (2) that capitalism as an *economic system* was a creation of the Reformation. The latter position is rendered once and for all untenable by the simple fact that certain important *forms* of capitalist business companies are drastically older than the Reformation Instead, it should here be ascertained only whether, and to what extent, religious influences *co*-participated in the qualitative formation and quantitative expansion of this spirit across the globe. We wish further to assess which practical *aspects* of the *culture* upon which [modern] capitalism rests can be traced back to these religious influences.

In light of the immense confusion of the reciprocal influences among the material foundation, the forms of social and political organizations, and the various spiritual streams of the Reformation epoch, we can only proceed in the following manner. *First*, we will investigate whether (and in what ways) specific "elective affinities" (*Wahlverwandtschaften*) between certain forms of religious belief and a vocational ethic (*Berufsethik*) are discernible. Doing so will allow us, whenever possible, to illuminate the type of influence that the religious movement, as a consequence of these elective affinities, had upon the development of economic culture. In addition, the general *direction* of this influence upon economic culture, as a consequence of these elective affinities, can be clarified. Second, *only after* this influence has been satisfactorily established can an attempt be made to estimate to what degree the historical origin of the values and ideas of our modern life can be attributed to religious forces stemming from the Reformation, and to what degree to other forces.

# Testifying to Belief through Asceticism

From *The Protestant Ethic and the Spirit of Capitalism*, 3rd edn, trans. Stephen Kalberg (Los Angeles: Roxbury Publishing, 2002), pp. 100–1.

It is now our task to follow out the effect of the Puritan idea of a vocational calling on how people *acquire goods and earn a living*. We are now prepared to do so, having attempted to offer in this chapter a sketch of the way in which the religious anchoring of the calling idea developed. Although differences in details and variations in emphasis exist in the diverse communities of religious asceticism, the vantage points decisive for us have been present and manifest, in effective ways, in all of these groups.[1]

To recapitulate, decisive again and again for our investigation was the conception of the religious "state of grace." Reappearing in all the denominations as a particular status, this state of grace separated people from the depravity of physical desires and from "this-world." Although attained in a variety of ways depending upon the dogma of the particular denomination, possession of the state of grace could *not* be guaranteed through magical-sacramental means of any kind, through the relief found in confession, or through particular good works. Rather, it could be acquired only through a *testifying to belief*. Sincere belief became apparent in specifically formed conduct unmistakably different from the style of life of the "natural" human being. For the person testifying to belief there followed a *motivation* to *methodically supervise* his or her state of grace. An organizing and directing of life ensued and, in the process, its penetration by *asceticism*.

As we noted, this ascetic style of life implied a *rational* formation of the entire being (*Dasein*) and the complete orientation of this being toward God's Will. Moreover, this asceticism was *no longer opus supererogationis* [an achievement within the capability of only a few], but one expected of all who wished to become certain of their salvation. Finally, and of central importance, the special life of the saint – fully separate from the "natural" life of the wants and desires – could no longer play itself out in monastic communities set apart from the world. Rather, the devoutly religious must now live saintly lives *in* the world and amidst its mundane affairs. This *rationalization* of the organized and directed life – now in the world yet still oriented to the supernatural – was the effect of ascetic Protestantism's *concept of the calling*.

At its beginning, Christian asceticism had fled from the world into the realm of solitude in the cloister. In renouncing the world, however, monastic asceticism had in fact come to dominate the world through the church. Yet, in retreating to the cloister, asceticism left the course of daily life in the world by and large in its natural and untamed state. But now Christian asceticism slammed the gates of the cloister, entered into the hustle and bustle of life, and undertook a new task: to saturate mundane, *everyday* life with its methodicalness. In the process, it sought to reorganize practical life into a rational life *in* the world rather than, as earlier, in the monastery. Yet this rational life in the world was *not of* this world or *for* this world. In our further exposition we will attempt to convey the results of this dramatic turn.


NOTE

1.  The grounding of dogma, which varied widely, could be unified through a decisive interest in "testifying" to belief. The *ultimate* reason why this could occur is to be located in Christianity's religious-historical particular features in general. This reason is still to be discussed. [1920]


# Asceticism and the Spirit of Capitalism

From *The Protestant Ethic and the Spirit of Capitalism*, 3rd edn, trans. Stephen Kalberg (Los Angeles: Roxbury Publishing, 2002), pp. 103–25.

[This is the concluding chapter to *The Protestant Ethic and the Spirit of Capitalism*. In the immediately preceding chapter of this volume Weber had located "the Protestant ethic" (in varying degrees of intensity) in the salvation ethics of Calvinism, Pietism, Methodism, and the Baptizing sects (the Quakers, Mennonites, and Baptists). This chapter must be consulted if Weber's arguments are to be fully comprehended. His notes to this concluding chapter, which expand upon and document innumerable points, have for the most part been omitted here.

In order to comprehend the connections between the basic religious ideas of *ascetic Protestantism* and the maxims of everyday economic life, it is necessary above all to draw upon those theological texts that can be recognized as having crystallized out of the practice of pastoral care. In this [sixteenth- and seventeenth-century] epoch, everything depended upon one's relationship to the next life, and one's social position depended upon admission to the sacrament of communion. Moreover, through pastoral care, church discipline, and preaching, the clergy's influence grew to such an extent (as any glance in the collected *consilia, casus conscientiae,* and other church documents will indicate) that we today are *simply no longer* capable of comprehending its broad scope. Religious forces, as they became transmitted to populations through *these regular practices* of the clergy and became legitimate and accepted, were decisive for the formation of "national character."[1]

In contrast to later discussions in this chapter, we can *here* treat *ascetic Protestantism* as *a* unity. Because, however, English *Puritanism,* which grew out of Calvinism, provides the most consistent foundation for the *idea of a vocational calling,* we are placing one of its representatives at the center of our analysis (in accord with our previous procedures). *Richard Baxter* [1615–1691] is distinguished from many other literary representatives of the Puritan ethic on the one hand by his eminently practical and peace-loving position and on the other by the universal acknowledgment accorded his works, which have been repeatedly reprinted and translated.

Baxter was a Presbyterian and apologist for the Westminster Synod, although in terms of dogma he moved gradually away from an orthodox Calvinism (like so many of the best clergymen of his time). Because he was hostile to every revolution, all sectarianism, and even the fanatical zeal of the "saints," he opposed Cromwell's usurpation. Yet Baxter remained unusually tolerant of all extreme positions and impartial toward his opponents. His own projects were essentially oriented toward a practical advancement of the religious-moral life. On behalf of these endeavors he offered his services, as one of the most successful practitioners of pastoral care known to history, equally to Parliament, to Cromwell, and to the Restoration. He continued to do so until he departed from his pulpit, which took place before St. Bartholomew's Day.[2]

Baxter's *Christian Directory* [1673] is the most comprehensive compendium of Puritan moral theology. Moreover, it is oriented throughout to the practical issues he dealt with in his pastoral care. In order to offer appropriate comparisons, Spener's *Theological Considerations* [1712], as representative of German Pietism, Barclay's *Apology* [1701], as representative of the Quakers, and occasionally other representatives of the ascetic ethic will be referred to (generally in the endnotes, however, owing to space restrictions).

If we examine Baxter's *Saints' Everlasting Rest* [1651] or his *Christian Directory* or even related works by others, we are struck at first glance, in his judgments regarding wealth and its acquisition, by his emphasis on the New Testament ebionitic proclamations [which scorned wealth and idealized the poor]. Wealth as such is a serious danger and its temptations are constant. Moreover, in light of the over-riding significance of God's kingdom, the pursuit of wealth is seen as both senseless and morally suspect. Indeed, to Baxter, New Testament asceticism appeared oriented *against* every striving to acquire the products of this world in a far more pointed manner than Calvin, who never saw wealth among the clergy as a barrier to clerical effectiveness. On the contrary, according to Calvin wealth led to a thoroughly desirable increase of clerical prestige, and he allowed the clergy to acquire profit from their fortunes wherever it could be invested without causing difficulties. Yet in Puritan writings examples that condemn the pursuit of money and material goods can be accumulated without end. They can be contrasted with the ethical literature of the late medieval period, which was far less strict on this point. Moreover, the Puritan literature's suspicion of wealth was thoroughly serious. Its decisively ethical meaning and context, however, can be articulated only after somewhat closer scrutiny.

What is actually morally reprehensible is, namely, the *resting* upon one's possessions and the *enjoyment* of wealth. To do so results in idleness and indulging desires of the flesh and above all in the distraction of believers from their pursuit of the "saintly" life. Furthermore, the possession of goods is suspect *only because* it carries with it the danger of this resting. The "saint's everlasting rest" comes in the next world. On earth, in this life, in order to become certain of one's state of grace, a person must "work the works of Him who sent him, while it is day" [John 9:4]. According to the will of God, which has been clearly revealed, *only activity*, not idleness and enjoyment, serves to increase His glory.

Hence, of all the sins, *the wasting of time* constitutes the first and, in principle, the most serious. A single life offers an infinitely short and precious space of time to "make firm" one's own election. The loss of time through sociability, "idle talk," sumptuousness, and even through more sleep than is necessary for good health (six to eight hours at most) is absolutely morally reprehensible. Franklin's maxim – "time is money" – is not yet expressed by Baxter, yet this axiom holds in a certain spiritual sense. Because every hour not spent at work is an hour lost in service to God's greater glory, according to Baxter, time is infinitely valuable. Thus, inactive contemplation is without value and in the end explicitly condemned, at least if it occurs at the expense of work in a calling, for it pleases God *less* than the active implementation of His will in a calling. At any rate, Sundays exist for contemplation. For Baxter, it is always those who are idle in their vocational callings who have no time for God, even on the day of rest.

Accordingly, a sermon on the virtues of hard and continuous physical or mental *work* is continuously repeated, occasionally almost with passion, throughout Baxter's major treatise. Two motives come together here.

First, work is the tried and proven *mechanism* for the practice of *asceticism*. For this reason, work has been held in high esteem in the Catholic

Church from the beginning, in sharp contrast not only to the Middle East but also to almost all the regulations followed by non-Christian monks throughout the world. Indeed, work constitutes a particular defense mechanism against all those temptations summarized by the Puritan notion of the "unclean life." The part played by these temptations is by no means a small one. Sexual asceticism in Puritanism is different only in degree, and not in principle, from that in monastic practice. As a result of the Puritan conception of marriage, sexual asceticism is more comprehensive simply because, even in marriage, sexual intercourse is permitted *only* as a means, desired by God, to increase His glory through the fulfillment of His commandment: "be fruitful and multiply." Just as it is a bulwark against all religious doubt and unrestrained torment, the admonition "work hard in your calling" constitutes a prescription against all sexual temptations (as do a temperate diet, vegetarianism, and cold baths).

Second, in addition and above all, as ordained by God, the purpose of life *itself* involves work. [The Apostle] Paul's maxim applies to everyone without qualification: "if anyone will not work, let him not eat." An unwillingness to work is a sign that one is not among the saved.

The divergence of Puritanism from medieval Catholicism becomes clearly evident here. Thomas Aquinas also interpreted Paul's maxim. Work is simply a *naturali ratione* [naturally rational] necessity, according to him, in order to maintain the life of the individual and that of the community. Paul's maxim, however, ceases to hold wherever this aim is not relevant, for it offers simply a general prescription for all and fails to address each person's situation. That is, it does not pertain to those people who can, without working, live from their possessions. Similarly, contemplation as a spiritual form of activity in God's kingdom naturally takes priority over this maxim in its literal sense. In addition, according to popular theology, the highest form of monastic "productivity" was to be found in the increase of the *thesaurus ecclesiae* [the church's spiritual treasures] through prayer and choir service.

These violations of the ethical duty to work were, of course, abandoned by Baxter. In addition, and with great emphasis, he hardened his basic principle that even wealth does not free people from Paul's unconditional maxim. For Baxter even those with many possessions shall not eat without working. As God's commandment, this maxim remains in effect even if it is not necessary for people to work in order to fulfill their needs. The wealthy, just like the poor, must be obedient to this principle. Besides, God's providence reserves a calling for everyone without distinction. It is to be recognized by each person, and each person should work within his calling, according to Baxter. Moreover, this calling is not, as in Lutheranism, a fate to which believers must submit and reconcile themselves. Rather, it is God's command to each person to act on behalf of His honor.

This seemingly inconsequential nuance had broad-ranging psychological consequences. It went together with the Puritan understanding of the providential interpretation of the economic cosmos familiar to us from the Scholastics. Yet the Puritan outlook (*Anschauung*) constituted a further development of Scholasticism's ideas. Here we can once again, and most conveniently, make a connection to the thinking of Aquinas.

The notion of a societal division of labor and occupational stratification has been conceptualized, by Aquinas as well as others, as a direct manifestation of God's divine plan. The placement of people into this cosmos, however, follows *ex causis naturalibus* [from natural causes] and is random (or, in the terminology of the Scholastics, "contingent"). Luther, as we noted, viewed the placement of people in given status groups and occupations (which followed out of the objective historical order) as a direct manifestation of God's will. Thus, a person's abiding *persistence* in the position and circumscribed situation assigned to him by God constituted a religious duty. It was all the more so because the ways in which Lutheran piety connected the devout to the mundane "world" as given were, in general, from the beginning uncertain, and remained so. Ethical principles, in reference to which the world could be transformed, were not to be extracted from Luther's constellation of ideas (which never became fully severed from Paul's notions of indifference to the world). Hence, Lutherans had to take the world simply as it was. *This acceptance,* and only this acceptance, could become, in Lutheranism, endowed with a notion of religious duty.

The Puritan view nuanced the providential character of the interplay of societal forces with private economic interests in a different way. Here the providential purpose of occupational stratification can be recognized from its *fruits.* This view is consistent with the Puritan proclivity toward a pragmatic interpretation, and Baxter offers statements on this theme that remind one (on more than one occasion) immediately of Adam Smith's familiar deification of the division of labor.

Because the specialization of occupations makes it possible for workers to develop skills, it leads, Baxter argues, to a quantitative and qualitative increase in worker productivity and thus serves the "common best" [common good] (which is identical with the prosperity of the greatest possible number). So far, the motivation remains purely utilitarian and closely related to points of view already common in the secular literature of the period. But just at this point the characteristic Puritan element comes to the fore. Baxter places a discussion of the motivation involved at the center of his analysis:

> Outside of a firm calling, the workplace achievements of a person are only irregular and temporary. This person spends more time being lazy than actually working.

Moreover, Baxter's manner of concluding this discussion also reveals the Puritan dimension:

> And he (the worker with a vocational calling) will perform his work *in an orderly fashion* while others are stuck in situations of constant confusion; their businesses fail to operate according to time or place . . . Therefore a "certain calling" (or "stated calling" at other passages) is best for everyone.

Intermittent work, into which the common day laborer is forced, is often unavoidable, but it is always an unwanted, transitional condition. The systematic-methodical character required by this-worldly asceticism is simply lacking in the life "without a calling" (*Beruflosen*).

Also, according to the ethic of the Quakers, a person's vocational calling should involve a consistent, ascetic exercise of virtues. One's state of grace is *testified to* through the *conscientiousness* with which the believer, with care and methodicalness, pursues his calling. Rational work in a calling is demanded by God rather than work as such.

The Puritan idea of a calling continually emphasizes this methodical character of vocational asceticism rather than, as with Luther, the resignation to one's lot as irredeemably assigned by God.[3] Hence, for Puritanism the question of whether one may combine multiple callings is unequivocally answered affirmatively – if doing so proves beneficial to the common prosperity or to the individual and is not injurious to anyone, and if it does not lead to a situation in which one becomes "unfaithful" to one of the combined callings. Indeed, even the *change* of vocational callings is not at all viewed as reprehensible, if carried out in a responsible manner. On the contrary, when made for the purpose of securing a vocation more pleasing to God (that is, corresponding to the general rule here, to a more useful calling), then the initiative should be taken.

Most important, the usefulness of a vocational calling is assessed mainly in moral terms, as is its corresponding capacity to please God. A further criterion is closely bound to this moral dimension, namely, according to the degree of importance of the goods produced in the calling for the "community." A third criterion, one clearly the most important at the practical level, is also central in assessing a calling's usefulness: its economic *profitability* for the individual. For if his God whom the Puritan sees as acting in all arenas of life, reveals a chance for turning a profit to one of His faithful, He must do so with clear intentions in mind. Accordingly, the believer must follow this opportunity and exploit it:

> If God show you a way in which you *may*, in accordance with His laws, *acquire more profit* than in another way, without wrong to your soul or to any other and if you refuse this, choosing the less profitable course, *you then cross one of the purposes of your calling. You are refusing to be God's steward,*

and to accept His gifts, in order to be able to use them for Him when He requireth it. *You may labour, for God, to become rich*, though not for the flesh and sin.

Hence, wealth is only suspect when it tempts the devout in the direction of lazy restfulness and a sinful enjoyment of life. The striving for riches becomes suspect only if carried out with the end in mind of leading a carefree and merry life once wealth is acquired. If however, riches are attained within the dutiful performance of one's vocational calling, striving for them is not only morally permitted but expected.[4] This idea is explicitly expressed in the parable of the servant who was sentenced to hell because he failed to make the most of the opportunities entrusted to him. *Wishing* to be poor, it was frequently argued, signifies the same as wishing to be sick. Indeed, it would be abominable and detrimental to God's glory if poverty came to be viewed as sanctified. Furthermore, begging by those capable of working is not only sinful (as indolence) but also, according to the apostles, opposed to brotherly love.

Just as the endowment of the stable vocational calling with ascetic significance sheds an ethical glorification around the modern *specialized expert*, the providential interpretation of one's chances for profit glorified the *business*person. Asceticism on the one hand despises equally the refined nonchalance of the feudal noble and the parvenu-like ostentation of boasters. On the other hand, it shines a full beam of ethical approval upon the dispassionate, "self-made man" of the middle class. A common remark – "God blesseth his trade" – refers to these saints who have followed God's every decree with success. Moreover, the entire force of the *Old Testament God*, which required His disciples to become pious in *this* life, must have influenced the Puritans in the same direction. According to Baxter's advice, the devout must monitor and supervise their own state of grace through comparisons to the spiritual condition of biblical heroes. In doing so, they must "interpret" the words of the Bible as if they were reading "paragraphs of a law book."

Of course Old Testament scripture was not entirely clear. We noted that Luther first employed the concept of calling, in its *this-worldly* sense, in a translation of a passage from the Book of Jesus Sirach. According to its entire mood of devotion, however, and despite its Hellenic influences, this book belongs to those sections of the (expanded) Old Testament [the Apocrypha] that convey more traditional influences. Characteristically, Jesus Sirach appears to possess, even today, a special attraction for Lutheran German peasants and those broad streams of German Pietism more bound to Lutheranism.

In light of their harsh either-or distinction between the Divine and depraved human beings, the Puritans criticized the Apocrypha as uninspired. Among the canonical books, the Book of Job then became all the more central. On the one hand, it manifested a glorification of God's absolutely sovereign majesty, separate from all human standards, an idea highly congenial to Calvinist views. On the other, as breaks forth again in Job's concluding passages and combined with this idea of a majestic God, it presents a God who will, with certainty, bless His faithful – and will do so in this life, also in a material sense (as exclusively stated in this book). Though of secondary importance to Calvin, this promise proved important for Puritanism. At the same time, the Puritan interpretation abandoned all Near Eastern quietism, which came to the fore in some of the most devotional verses of Psalms and Proverbs. Similarly, in his discussion of a passage in the First Letter to the Corinthians, Baxter interpreted away its traditional overtones. Doing so proved essential for his concept of the calling. In light of these developments, the Puritans all the more placed an emphasis upon those Old Testament passages that praised *formal correctness in terms of religious law* in one's conduct as constituting a sign of God's approval.

[Further interpretations also moved in this direction.] The Puritans opposed the theory that the law of Moses had lost its legitimacy with the founding of Christianity. They argued instead that only those passages relating to Jewish ceremonial or historically conditioned statutes were invalid, and that otherwise this law, as an expression of *lex naturae* [natural law], had possessed its validity from eternity and therefore must be retained. This interpretation allowed on the one hand the elimination of statutes not easily adaptable to modern life, and on the other a powerful strengthening of a spirit of self-righteous and dispassionate legality suitable to Puritanism's this-worldly asceticism. Once in place, this development enabled numerous related features of Old Testament morality to flow freely into ascetic Protestantism.

Therefore, correctly understood, the repeated depiction of the basic ethical orientation of English Puritanism in particular, even by its contemporaries (as well as more recent writers), as "English Hebraism" is fully appropriate. Nevertheless, one should not think of this English Hebraism as the Palestinian Judaism from the period of the Old Testament's origin. Rather, one should recall the later Judaism that developed gradually under the influence of formal-legal and Talmudic learning over many centuries. Even then one must be extremely cautious regarding historical parallels. The mood of ancient Judaism, which was by and large oriented toward an appreciation of life's spontaneity as such, was far removed from the specific uniqueness of Puritanism.

Yet it should not be overlooked that Puritanism remained far distant as well from the economic ethic of medieval and modern Judaism in respect to features decisive for the development of the capitalist *ethos*. Judaism stood on the side of an "adventure" capitalism in which political or speculative motives were central. In a word, the economic ethic of Judaism was one of *pariah* capitalism. By contrast, Puritanism carried the ethos of a rational, middle-class *company* and the rational organization of *work*. It took from Judaism's ethic only that which proved adaptable to this framework. [1920]

To chart out the characterological consequences of the penetration of life by Old Testament norms would be impossible in the context of this sketch (however stimulating a task, although until now it has not been adequately undertaken even for Judaism itself). An analysis of the inner habitus of the Puritans in its entirety (*inneren Gesamthabitus*), in addition to the relationships already discussed, would also have to consider how it accompanied a grandiose rebirth of their belief in being the chosen people of God. Just as even the mild-mannered Baxter thanks God for allowing him to be born in England and in the true church, and not elsewhere, this thankfulness for one's own blamelessness (which was caused by God's grace) penetrated the mood of life of the Puritan middle class. It conditioned the formalistic, exacting, hard character of these representatives of the heroic epoch of capitalism.

We can now seek to clarify those aspects of the Puritan conception of the calling and promotion of an ascetic *organization of life* that must have *directly* influenced the development of the capitalist style of life.

As we have seen, asceticism turned with all its force mainly against the *spontaneous enjoyment* of existence and all the pleasures life had to offer. This aspect of asceticism was expressed most characteristically in the struggle over the *Book of Sports* [1637] which James I and Charles I raised to the level of law in order explicitly to confront Puritanism. Charles ordered the reading of this law from all pulpits. The fanatic opposition of the Puritans to the king's decree that, on Sundays, certain popular amusements would be legally allowed after church services, arose *not* only on account of the resulting disturbance of the Sabbath day of rest. Rather, the more important source of this opposition was the fully premeditated disruption the decree implied of the ordered and organized life practiced by the Puritan saints. Moreover, the king's threat to punish severely every attack on the legality of these sporting activities had a single clear purpose: to banish this Puritan movement that, owing to its *anti-authoritarian ascetic* features, posed a danger to the state. Monarchical-feudal society protected the "pleasure seekers" against the crystallizing middle-class morality and the ascetic *conventicles* hostile to authority, just as today capitalist society seeks to protect "those willing to work" against the class-specific morality of workers and the trade unions hostile to authority.

In opposition to the feudal-monarchical society, the Puritans held firm to their most central feature in this struggle over the *Book of Sports*, namely, the principle of leading an organized life anchored in asceticism.

Actually, Puritanism's aversion to sports was not a fundamental one, even for the Quakers. However, sports must serve a rational end; they must promote the relaxation indispensable for further physical achievement. Hence, sports became suspect whenever they constituted a means for the purely spontaneous expression of unrestrained impulses. They were obviously absolutely reprehensible to the extent that they became means toward pure enjoyment or awakened competitive ambition, raw instincts, or the irrational desire to gamble. Quite simply, the enjoyment of life as if it were only *physical drives*, which pulls one equally away from work in a calling and from piety, was the enemy of rational asceticism as such. This enmity remained, regardless of whether the enjoyment of life presented itself in the form of monarchical-feudal society's sports or in the common man's visits to the dance floor or the tavern.

Correspondingly, Puritanism's position toward those aspects of culture devoid of any direct relevance to religious matters was also one of suspicion and strong hostility. That is not to say that a sombre, narrow-minded scorn for culture was contained in Puritan ideals. Precisely the opposite holds, at least for the sciences (*Wissenschaften*) (with the exception of Scholasticism, which was despised). Moreover, the great representatives of Puritanism were deeply submerged in the humanism of the Renaissance, the sermons in the Presbyterian wing drip with references to classical antiquity, and even the radicals (although they took offense at it) did not reject this humanist learning in theological polemics. Perhaps no country was ever so overpopulated with "graduates" as New England in the first generation of its existence. Even the satires of opponents, such as *Hudibras* [1663–78] by [Samuel] Butler [1612–80], turn quickly to the armchair scholarship and sophomoric dialectics of the Puritans. Their learning *in part* goes together with the high religious esteem for knowledge that followed from the Puritans' rejection of the Catholic *fides implicita* ["confusing faith," as the Puritans perceived it].

Matters are distinctly different as soon as one moves into the arena of nonscientific literature and to the realm of art which appeals to the senses. Asceticism now blankets like a frost the life of merry olde England. Its influence was apparent not only on secular festivals. The angry hatred of the Puritans persecuted all that smacked of "superstition" and all residuals of the dispensation of grace through magic or sacraments, including Christmas festivities, the may pole celebration, and all unrestricted use of art by the church. The survival in Holland of a public space within which the development of a masterful, often coarse and earthy, realistic art could occur demonstrates in the end that the authoritarian regimentation of morality by the Puritans was not able to exercise a complete domination. The influence of court society and the landlord stratum, as well as members of the lower middle class who had become wealthy and sought joy in life, all contested in Holland the impact of Puritanism. This resistance took place after the short domination of the Calvinist theocracy had dissolved into a staid state church. As a consequence of this development, Calvinism suffered a distinct loss in ascetic energy and thus its capacity to attract believers perceptibly declined.

The theater was reprehensible to the Puritans. As in literature and art, radical views could not survive once eroticism and nudity had been strictly banned from the realm of the possible. The notions of "idle talk," "superfluities," and "vain ostentation," all of which designated to the Puritans irrational, aimless, and thus not ascetic, behavior (and surely not conduct serving God's glory but only human goals), surfaced quickly. Hence, dispassionate instrumentalism was given a decisive upper hand over and against every application of artistic tendencies. This purposiveness was especially important wherever the direct decoration of the person was involved, as for example in respect to dress. The foundation in ideas for that powerful tendency to render styles of life uniform, which today supports the capitalist interest in the "standardization" of production, derived from the Puritans' rejection of all "glorification of human wants and desires."

Certainly, in the midst of these considerations, we should not forget that Puritanism contained within itself a world of contradictions. It must be recognized that the instinctive awareness among Puritan leaders of the eternal greatness of art certainly transcended the level of art appreciation found in the milieu of the [feudalism-oriented] "cavaliers." Furthermore, and even though his "conduct" would scarcely have found grace in the eyes of the Puritan God, a unique genius such as Rembrandt was, in the direction of his creativity, fundamentally influenced by his sectarian milieu. These acknowledgments, however, fail to alter the larger picture: the powerful turn of the personality in an inward-looking direction (which the further development of the Puritan milieu could cultivate and, in fact, co-determined) influenced literature for the most part. Even in this realm, however, the impact of ascetic Protestantism would be felt only in later generations.

We cannot here investigate further the influences of Puritanism in all these ways. Nevertheless, we should note that *one* characteristic barrier always opposed ascribing legitimacy to the joy experienced from aspects of culture serving pure aesthetic pleasures or to the pure enjoyment of sports: *this pleasure should not cost anything.* Persons are only administrators of the cultural performances that the grace of God has offered. Hence, every dime expended for them must be justified, just as in the example of the servant in the Bible. It remains doubtful at least whether any part of this money should be spent for a purpose that serves one's own pleasure rather than the glory of God.

Who among us, whose eyes are open, has not seen manifestations of this outlook even at the present time?[5] The idea of a person's *duty* to maintain possessions entrusted to him, to which he subordinates himself as a dutiful steward or even as a "machine for producing wealth," lies upon his life with chilling seriousness. And as one's possessions become more valuable, the more burdensome becomes the feeling of responsibility to maintain them intact for God's glory and to increase their value through restless work – *if* the ascetic temper meets the challenge. The roots of this style of life also extend back to the Middle Ages (at least particular roots), as is true of so many components of the modern capitalist spirit. This spirit, however, first found its consistent ethical foundation in the ethic of ascetic Protestantism. Its significance for the development of [modern] capitalism is obvious.

Let us summarize the above. On the one hand, this-worldly Protestant asceticism fought with fury against the spontaneous *enjoyment* of possessions and constricted *consumption*, especially of luxury goods. On the other hand, it had the psychological effect of *freeing* the *acquisition of goods* from the constraints of the traditional economic ethic. In the process, ascetic Protestantism shattered the bonds restricting all striving for gain – not only by legalizing profit but also by perceiving it as desired by God (in the manner portrayed here). The struggle against the desires of the flesh and the attachment to external goods was *not*, as the Puritans explicitly attest (and also the great Quaker apologist, Barclay), a struggle against rational *acquisition*; rather, it challenged the irrational use of possessions. That which remained so familiar to feudal sensibilities – a high regard for the *external* display of luxury consumption – was condemned by the Puritans as a deification of human wants and desires. According to them, God wanted a rational and utilitarian use of wealth on behalf of the basic needs of the person and the community.

Hence, this-worldly asceticism did *not* wish to impose *self-castigation* upon the wealthy. Instead, it wanted that wealth to be used for necessary, *practical*, and *useful* endeavors. The notion of "comfort," typically for the Puritans, encompasses the realm of the ethically permissible use of goods. Thus, it is naturally not by chance that one observes the development of the style of life attached to this notion, earliest and most clearly, precisely in those most consistent representatives of the Puritan life outlook: the Quakers. In opposition to the glitter and pretense of feudalism's pomp and display, which rests upon an unstable economic foundation and prefers a tattered elegance to low-key simplicity, the Puritans placed the ideal of the clean and solid comfort of the middle-class "home."

In terms of capitalism's *production* of wealth, asceticism struggled against greed. It did so in order to confront both the danger it presented to social order and its *impulsive* character. The Puritans condemned all "covetousness" and "mammonism," for both implied the striving for wealth – becoming rich – as an end in itself, and wealth as such constituted a temptation.

The nature of asceticism again becomes clear at this point. Its methodical-rational organization of life was the power "that perpetually wanted good and perpetually created evil,"[6] namely, evil in the manner conceived by asceticism: wealth and its temptations. For asceticism (together with the Old Testament and completely parallel to the ethical valuation of "good works") defined the pursuit of riches, if viewed as an *end* in itself, as the peak of reprehensibility. At the same time, it also viewed the acquisition of wealth, when it was the *fruit* of work in a vocational calling, as God's blessing. Even more important for this investigation, the religious value set on restless, continuous, and systematic work in a vocational calling was defined as absolutely the highest of all ascetic means for believers to testify to their elect status, as well as simultaneously the most certain and most visible means of doing so. Indeed, the Puritan's sincerity of belief must have been the most powerful lever conceivable working to expand the life outlook that we are here designating as the spirit of capitalism.[7]

Moreover, if we now combine the strictures against consumption with this unchaining of the striving for wealth, a certain external result [that is, one with an impact outside the realm of religion] now becomes visible: *the formation of capital* through *asceticism's compulsive saving*.[8] The restrictions that opposed the consumption of wealth indeed had their productive use, for profit and gain became used as *investment* capital.

Of course, the strength of this effect cannot be determined exactly in quantitative terms. The connection became so apparent in New England, however, that it did not escape early on the eye of a historian as distinguished as John Doyle. But it was also apparent in Holland, where a strict Calvinism ruled for only seven years. The greater simplicity of life that dominated the Dutch regions of ascetic Protestantism led, among the enormously wealthy, to an excessive desire to accumulate capital. Furthermore, it is evident that the tendency for middle-class fortunes to be used for the acquisition of noble status (which has existed in all epochs and countries, and even today quite significantly in Germany) must have been inhibited to a measurable extent by the hostility of Puritanism to all feudal forms of life. English writers on the mercantilism of the seventeenth century traced the superiority of Dutch over English capitalism back to the English practice (as in Germany) of regularly investing newly acquired fortunes in land. On this basis (for the purchase of land is not the only issue), newly wealthy persons sought to make the transition to feudal habits of life and to noble status. The result was clear: such land could not be used for capitalist investment.

An esteem for *agriculture* was even present among the Puritans. Indeed, it constituted a particularly important arena for making a living (for example, in the case of Baxter) and was highly conducive to piety. Yet the Puritan engagement in agriculture diverged from feudalism: it involved productive farming rather than merely owning land as a landlord. In the eighteenth century, it was oriented more toward "rational" commercial farming than toward the acquisition of a country manor and entry into the nobility. Since the seventeenth century, the division between the "squirearchy," which were the social carriers of "merry olde England," and the Puritan circles, whose societal power varied across a broad spectrum, cut through English society. Both streams – on the one hand a spontaneous and naive taking pleasure in life and on the other a strictly regulated, reserved self-control and ethical restraint – stand even today alongside each other in any portrait of the English "national character." A similarly sharp polarity runs through the earliest history of North American colonization between the "adventurers," who wanted to build plantations with the labor of indentured servants and to live like feudal lords, and the middle-class frame of mind of the Puritans.

As far as its power extended, the Puritan life outlook promoted under all circumstances the tendency toward a middle-class, economically *rational* organization of life. This outlook was, of course, far more important than the mere facilitating of the formation of capital. Indeed, it was the most substantial and, above all, only consistent social carrier of this middle-class mode of organizing life. Just this rational organization of life stands at the source of modern "economic man" (*Wirtschaftsmenschen*).

Of course, these Puritan ideals of life failed to meet the challenge whenever the test – the "temptations" of wealth (which were well known even to the Puritans themselves) – became too great. We find the most sincere followers of the Puritan spirit very frequently among those in the middle class who operated small businesses, among farmers and the *beati possidentes* [those in possession of salvation] – all of whom must be understood as having been at the beginning of an *upwardly mobile* journey. Yet we find that many in these groups were prepared quite frequently to betray the old ideals. Such betrayal even occurred among the Quakers. The predecessor of this-worldly asceticism, the monastic asceticism of the Middle Ages, repeatedly fell victim to this same fate. Whenever the rational organization of the economy had fully developed its productive powers in the cloister milieu, which was characterized by a strict regulation of life as a whole and limited consumption, then the accumulated wealth was either used to acquire land and noble status (as occurred in the era before the Reformation) or it threatened the dissolution of monastic discipline. One of the numerous "reform movements" in monasticism had to intervene if this occurred. In a certain sense, the entire history of the religious orders reveals a constantly renewed struggle with the problem of the secularizing effects of wealth.

On a larger scale, the same is true for Puritanism's this-worldly asceticism. The powerful "revival" of Methodism, which preceded the flowering of English industrialism near the end of the eighteenth century, can be appropriately compared with the "reform movements" in the monastic orders. A passage from John Wesley himself can be noted now, for it is well suited to stand as a motto for all that has been stated here. It indicates how the main figures in the ascetic movements were themselves completely aware of the apparently so paradoxical relationship presented here and understood these connections fully.

> I fear, wherever riches have increased, the essence of religion has decreased in the same proportion. Therefore I do not see how it is possible, in the nature of things, for any revival of true religion to continue long. For religion must necessarily produce both industry and frugality, and these cannot but produce riches. But as riches increase, so will pride, anger, and love of the world in all its branches. How then is it possible that Methodism, that is, a religion of the heart, though it flourishes now as a green bay tree, should continue in this state? For the Methodists in every place grow diligent and frugal; consequently they increase their possession of material goods. Hence they proportionately increase in pride, in anger, in the desire of the flesh, the desire of the eyes, and the pride of life. So, although the form of religion remains, the spirit is swiftly vanishing away. Is there no way to prevent this continual decay of pure religion? We ought not to prevent people from being diligent and frugal; *we must exhort all Christians to gain all they can, and to save all they can; that is, in effect, to grow rich.* [Weber's emphasis] [1920]

(There follows the admonition that those who have "acquired all they can and saved all they can" should also "give all they can" – in order to grow in grace and to assemble a fortune in heaven.) In this passage from Wesley one sees the connection, in all its details, illuminated in the analysis above. [1920]

Exactly as Wesley noted here, the significance for economic development of the powerful early religious movements was to be found mainly in the ascetic effects of their *socialization*. To him, their full *economic* impact developed, as a rule, only after the peak of their *pure* religious enthusiasm. As the paroxysms of the search for God's kingdom gradually dissolved into the dispassionate virtues of the vocational calling and the religious roots of the movement slowly withered, a utilitarian orientation to the world took hold. In the popular imagination, if we follow [the Irish scholar of English and French literature Edward] Dowden [1843–1913], "Robinson Crusoe" – the *isolated economic man* (who is engaged in missionary activities in his spare time) – now took the place of Bunyan's "pilgrims" scurrying through the "amusement park of vanity" on their solitary spiritual quest for God's kingdom. If then, further, the basic principle "to make the best of *both* worlds" came to prevail, then, finally (as Dowden similarly already observed) the good conscience had also to be included among the series of factors comprising the comfortable, middle-class life (as is so beautifully expressed in the German adage about the "soft pillow"). That which the religiously lively epoch of the seventeenth century bequeathed to its utilitarian heirs was above all a startlingly good conscience (we can say without hesitation, *pharisaically* good) as concerns the acquisition of money. Elsewhere, such gain and acquisition occurred alone on the basis of legal forms. Now, with Puritanism, every residual of the medieval proverb *deo placere vix potest* has disappeared.

A specifically *middle-class vocational ethos* (*Berufsethos*) arose. Now the middle-class employer became conscious of himself as standing in the full grace of God and as visibly blessed by Him. If he stayed within the bounds of formal correctness, if his moral conduct remained blameless, and if the use he made of his wealth was not offensive, this person was now allowed to follow his interest in economic gain, and indeed *should* do so. Moreover, the power of religious asceticism made available to the businessperson dispassionate and conscientious workers. Unusually capable of working, these employees attached themselves to their work, for they understood it as bestowing a purpose on life that was desired by God.

In addition, religious asceticism gave to the employer the soothing assurance that the unequal distribution of the world's material goods resulted from the special design of God's providence. In making such distinctions as well as in deciding who should be among the chosen few, God pursued mysterious aims unknown to terrestrial mortals. Calvin had argued early on (in a passage frequently cited) that the "people," the overwhelming majority of skilled and unskilled workers, would continue to obey God only if kept poor. The Dutch (Peter de la Court and others) "secularized" this statement; to them, most persons *worked* only if driven to do so by necessity. In turn, this formulation of a key idea regarding the functioning of the capitalist economy then merged into the plethora of theories on the "productivity" of low wages. Here again, and in full conformity with the developmental pattern we have repeatedly observed, as the religious roots of an idea died out a utilitarian tone then surreptitiously shoved itself under the idea and carried it further.

Now let us turn away from the Puritan employer and briefly toward the other side, namely, the perspective of the worker. Zinzendorf's branch of Pietism, for example, glorified workers who were loyal to their callings, lived in accord with the ideals of the apostles, and never strove for gain – hence, workers endowed with the charisma of Christ's disciples. Similar views were widespread, in an even more radical form, among the baptizing congregations in their early stages. Of course, the entire corpus of literature on asceticism, which is drawn from almost *all* religions [East and West], is permeated with the point of view that loyal work is highly pleasing to God, even if performed for low wages by people at a great disadvantage in life and without other opportunities. *Here* Protestant asceticism added nothing new as such. It dramatically deepened, however, this point of view. In addition, it created the norm on which its impact *exclusively depended*: the psychological *motivation* that arose out of the conception of work as a *calling* and as the means best suited (and in the end often as the *sole* means) for the devout to become certain of their state of salvation. Furthermore, on the other hard, in interpreting the employer's acquisition of money also as a "calling," Protestant asceticism legalized the exploitation of this particular willingness to work.[9]

It is obvious how powerfully the *exclusive* striving for the kingdom of God – through fulfillment of the duty to work in a vocational calling and through strict asceticism, which church discipline naturally imposed in particular upon the propertyless classes – must have promoted the "productivity" of work in the capitalist sense of the word. For the modern worker, the view of work as a "vocational calling" became just as characteristic as the view of gain as a "vocational calling" became for the modern employer. New at the time, this situation was reflected in the keen observations on Dutch economic power of the seventeenth century by the insightful Englishman Sir William Petty . . . He traced its growth back to the especially numerous "Dissenters" (Calvinists and Baptists) in Holland, who viewed *"work and the industrious pursuit of a trade as their duty to God."*

The "organic" societal organization, in the form of the fiscal monopoly it assumed in the Anglicanism under the Stuarts [1603–1714] and especially in [Archbishop William] Laud's [1573–1645][10] conceptions, involved specific features. First, a coalition of state and church with the "business monopolists" arose. Second, this alliance became anchored in Christian social ethics. The Puritans stood against this coalition. They passionately opposed *this* type of economy, one in which the state offered privileges to merchants, cottage industries, and colonial capitalism. Instead, Puritans upheld a type of capitalism in which a person's competence and initiative-taking capacity provided the individualistic *motivation* for rational-legal acquisition. In England, where the industrial monopolies privileged by the state as a whole soon disappeared, Puritanism decisively participated in the creation of newly emerging industries. It did so in spite of and against the state's authoritarian powers. [1920]

The Puritans [William] Prynne [1600–1669] and [Matthew] Parker [1504–74][11] rejected every common undertaking with "courtiers and operators" in the mold of large-scale capitalists, for they perceived such people as members of an ethically suspect class. Moreover, the Puritans did so on the basis of pride in their own superior middle-class business ethics (*Geschäftsmoral*). In turn, precisely this ethos constituted the true reason for the persecution of Puritans by large-scale capitalists. Even as late as [the eighteenth-century the novelist Daniel] Defoe [1660–1731] suggested a struggle against Puritans. He sought to win this conflict by arguing in favor of boycotts against all businesses that changed banks and the cancellation of bank and stock accounts. [1920]

The contrast between the two types of capitalist conduct paralleled to a very great extent the religious contrasts. Even in the eighteenth century the opponents of the Puritans repeatedly satirized them as carriers of a "spirit of shopkeepers" and persecuted them as the ruin of old English ideals. The contrast between Puritan and Jewish economic ethics is also anchored *here* and even contemporaries (Prynne) knew that the former, and not the latter, was the middle-class economic ethic. [1920]

One of the constitutive components of the modern capitalist spirit and, moreover, generally of modern civilization, was the rational organization of life on the basis of the *idea of the calling*. It was born out of the spirit of *Christian asceticism*. Our analysis should have demonstrated this point. If we now read again the passages from Benjamin Franklin cited at the beginning of this essay, we will see that the essential elements of the frame of mind he described as the "spirit of capitalism" are just those that we have conveyed above as the content of Puritan vocational asceticism.[12] In Franklin, however, this "spirit" exists without the religious foundation, which had already died out.

The idea that modern work in a vocational calling supposedly carries with it an *ascetic* imprint is, of course, also not new. The limitation of persons to specialized work, which necessitates their renunciation of the Faustian multi-dimensionality of the human species, is in our world today the precondition for doing anything of value at all. This is a lesson that already *Goethe*, at the peak of his wisdom in his *Wilhelm Meister's Years of Travel* [1829] and in his depiction of the final stage of life through his [most famous character] Faust [1808], wished to teach us. He instructs us that this basic component of asceticism in the middle-class style of life – if it wishes to be a style at all – involves today an inescapable interaction in which the conduct of "specialized activity," on the one hand, and "renunciation," on the other, mutually condition each other. For Goethe this acknowledgment implied a farewell to an era of full and beautiful humanity – and a renunciation of it. For such an era will repeat itself, in the course of our civilizational development, with as little likelihood as a reappearance of the epoch in which Athens bloomed.

The Puritan *wanted* to be a person with a vocational calling; today we *are forced* to be. For to the extent that asceticism moved out of the monastic cell, was transferred to the life of work in a vocational calling, and then commenced to rule over this-worldly morality, it helped to construct the powerful cosmos of the modern economic order. Tied to the technical and economic conditions at the foundation of mechanical and machine production, this cosmos today determines the style of life of all individuals born into it – *not* only those directly engaged in earning a living. This pulsating mechanism does so with overwhelming force. Perhaps it will continue to do so until the last ton of fossil fuel has burnt to ashes. According to Baxter, the concern for material goods should lie upon the shoulders of his saints like "a lightweight coat that could be thrown off at any time." Yet fate allowed a steel-hard casing (*stahlhartes Gehäuse*) to be forged from this coat. To the extent that asceticism attempted to transform and influence the world, the world's material goods acquired an increasing and, in the end, inescapable power over people – as never before in history.

Today the spirit of asceticism has fled from this casing, whether with finality who knows? Victorious capitalism, in any case, ever since it came to rest on a mechanical foundation, no longer needs asceticism as a supporting pillar. Even the optimistic temperament of asceticism's joyful heir, the Enlightenment, appears finally to be fading. And the idea of an "obligation to search for and then accept a vocational calling" now wanders around in our lives as the ghost of beliefs no longer anchored in the substance of religion. Persons today usually abandon any attempt to make sense of the notion of a vocational calling altogether wherever the "conduct of a vocation" cannot be explicitly connected to the highest cultural values of a spiritual nature or, conversely, wherever persons are not forced to experience it subjectively simply as economic coercion. The pursuit of gain, in the region where it has become most completely unchained and stripped of its religious-ethical meaning, the United States, tends to be associated with purely competitive passions. Not infrequently, these passions directly imprint this pursuit with the character of a sporting contest.[13]

No one any longer knows who will live in this steel-hard casing and whether entirely new prophets or a mighty rebirth of ancient ideas and ideals will stand at the end of this prodigious development. *Or,* however, if neither, whether a mechanized ossification, embellished with a sort of rigidly compelled sense of self-importance, will arise. Then, indeed, if ossification appears, the saying might be true for the "last humans"[14] in this long civilizational development:

> narrow specialists without mind, pleasure-seekers without heart; in its conceit, this nothingness imagines it has climbed to a level of humanity never before attained.

Here, however, we have fallen into the realm of value-judgments and judgments rooted in faith, with which this purely historical analysis should not be burdened. The further *task* is a different one: to chart the significance of ascetic rationalism.[15] The above sketch has only hinted at its importance.

Its significance for the content of a community-building, ethical *social policy* must now be charted, that is, for the type of organization and the functions of social communities, ranging from the conventicle to the state. Having done that, we must analyze the relationship of ascetic rationalism to the ideals and cultural influences of humanistic rationalism. Further, we must investigate the relationship of ascetic rationalism to the development of philosophical and scientific empiricism, to the unfolding of technology, and to the development of nonmaterial culture (*geistige Kulturgüter*) in general.[16] Finally, we need to pursue the historical course of ascetic rationalism, beginning with the first signs of this-worldly asceticism in the Middle Ages and moving all the way to its dissolution in pure utilitarianism. We should then need to trace this development in its *particular historical* manifestations and through the particular regions of the expansion of ascetic religious devotion. Only after the completion of such investigations can the *extent* of ascetic Protestantism's civilizational significance be demarcated in comparison to that of other elements of modern civilization that can be changed and shaped in response to the actions of persons.

This study has attempted, of course, merely to trace ascetic Protestantism's influence, and the particular *nature* of this influence, back to ascetic Protestantism's motives in regard to one, however important, point. The way in which Protestant asceticism was in turn influenced in its development and characteristic uniqueness by the entirety of societal-cultural conditions, and especially *economic* conditions, must also have its day. For sure, even with the best will, the modern person seems generally unable to imagine *how* large a significance those components of our consciousness rooted in religious beliefs have actually had upon culture, national character, and the organization of life. Nevertheless, it can not be, of course, the intention here to set a one-sided spiritualistic analysis of the causes of culture and history in place of an equally one-sided "materialistic" analysis. *Both* are *equally possible.*[17] Historical truth, however, is served equally little if either of these analyses claims to be the conclusion of an investigation rather than its preparatory stage.

## NOTES

1. Throughout this chapter, as well as earlier, Weber generally places this term in quotation marks in order to signify that national character must be understood as constructed from social forces (and religious forces in particular) rather than as a genetic predisposition [sk].

2. On St. Bartholomew's Day (August 24, 1572), which followed the marriage of the Protestant Henry of Navarre (later Henry IV) to a Catholic princess, thousands of French Protestants (Huguenots) were persecuted and murdered [sk].

3. Clearly, this turn of the religious ethic of course cannot be seen as a reflection of the actual economic conditions. Vocational specialization was far further developed in Italy than in England in the Middle Ages. [1920]

4. *This* is what is pivotal. To this statement should be added, once again, the general comment: whatever theology-oriented ethical theory developed conceptually is naturally for us not the important matter. Rather, central here is the question of what morality was *valid* in the *practical* life of believers.

5. In addition to *many* other examples, I remember one in particular. A manufacturer, who had been unusually successful in business and had become very wealthy in his later years, suffered from a stubborn digestive disorder. His physician advised him to enjoy daily a few oysters – yet he complied only after great resistance. That here the issue involved a residual of an "ascetic" disposition (and not simply something related to "stinginess") suspicious of all personal *enjoyment* of wealth becomes apparent *in the end* when one notes that this same manufacturer had made very significant philanthropic contributions throughout his lifetime and had always shown an "open hand" to those in need.

6. Weber is here playing on the words of Goethe's Mephistopheles, who characterizes himself as "that power which always intends evil, and always creates good" (see *Faust*, Act 1, lines 1336–37) [sk].

7. ... For those whose conscience remains troubled whenever an economic (or "materialistic" as one, unfortunately, says even today) interpretation is omitted from discussions on causality, let it be noted here that I find the influence of economic development on the destiny of the formation of religious ideas very significant. I will later seek to demonstrate how, in our cases, mutually interacting adaptive processes and relationships produced both economic development on the one hand and religious ideas on the other. [See the Economic Ethic of the World Religions series.] Nonetheless, by no means can the content of religious ideas be *deduced* from "economic" forces. These ideas are, and nothing can change this, actually, *for their part*, the most powerful elements shaping "national character'; they carry purely within themselves an autonomous momentum, lawful capacity (*Eigengesetzlichkeit*), and coercive power. Moreover, the *most important* differences – those between Lutheranism and Calvinism – are predominantly, to the extent that nonreligious forces play a part, conditioned by *political* forces.

8. Eduard Bernstein is thinking of this compulsive saving when he says: "Asceticism is a middle-class virtue." His discussions *are the first* to have suggested these important connections. However, the association is a far more comprehensive one than he suspects. Decisive was not merely capital accumulation; rather, central was the ascetic rationalization of the entire vocational life. . . .

9. And one more point: a notion that one so often works with today may well be questioned, namely, the assumption that the medieval craftsman's "enjoyment" of "that which he produced himself" was quite strong. One must

ask to what extent this enjoyment played a substantial role as a psychological motivating force. Undoubtedly, something important is touched upon here. At any rate, [with the arrival of Puritanism] asceticism *stripped away* from work all this-worldly appeal – which today has been destroyed by capitalism for eternity – and oriented work toward the next world. Work in a vocational calling *as such* was desired by God. In other words, the impersonal character of work today, which offers little enjoyment and is meaningless when considered from the point of view of each person, was at that time still transfigured and glorified by religion because desired by God. In the period of its origin capitalism required workers who stood available, for the sake of the *conscience*, to be economically exploited. Capitalism today sits in the saddle and is capable, without any other-worldly reward, of coercing a willingness to work. [The last sentence was added in 1920.]

10. Laud was a central figure in the seventeenth-century Anglican Church. He used his power effectively to suppress the Puritans [sk].

11. A controversial Puritan, Prynne's writings, especially on the theater, brought him into conflict with the Anglican Church and the English monarchy. He attacked the *Book of Sports*. Nevertheless, he later defended the monarchy, criticized Cromwell, and advocated a subjection of the clergy to the Crown. A moderate reformer, Parker became an archbishop in the Anglican Church and the subject of considerable criticism by the Puritans [sk].

12. That even the components here (which have not yet been traced back to their religious roots) – namely, the maxim honesty is the best policy (Franklin's discussion of *credit*) – are also of Puritan origins is a theme that belongs in a somewhat different context (see the "Protestant Sects" essay below). Only the following observation of J. S. Rowntree (*Quakerism, Past and Present* [London: Smith, Elder and Co., 1859], pp. 95–96), to which Eduard Bernstein called my attention, needs to be repeated:

> Is it merely a *coincidence*, or is it a *consequence*, that the lofty profession of spirituality made by the Friends has gone hand in hand with shrewdness and tact in the transaction of mundane affairs? Real piety favors the success of a trader by insuring his integrity and fostering habits of prudence and forethought. [These are] important items in obtaining that standing and credit in the commercial world which are requisites for the steady accumulation of wealth (see the "Protestant Sects" essay).

13. "Couldn't the old man be satisfied with his $75,000 a year and retire? No! The frontage of the store must be widened to 400 feet. Why? That beats everything, he says. Evenings, when his wife and daughter read together, he longs for bed. Sundays, in order to know when the day will be over, he checks his watch every five minutes. What a miserable existence!" In this manner the son-in-low (who had emigrated from Germany) of this prosperous dry-goods-man from a city on the Ohio River offered his judgment. Such a judgment would surely appear to the "old man" as completely incomprehensible. It could be easily dismissed as a symptom of the lack of energy of the Germans.

14. This phrase (*letzte Menschen*) is from Friedrich Nietzsche. It could as well be translated as "last people." It is normally rendered as "last men." The "last humans," to Nietzsche, are repulsive figures without emotion. Through their "little pleasures" they render everything small – yet they claim to have "invented happiness." See also below, pp. 255–7 [sk].

15. This term is a synonym for "ascetic Protestantism" and "spirit of asceticism" [sk].

16. This phrase (*geistige Kulturgüter*) refers to the entire spectrum of "products of the mind," ranging from mathematical ideas and philosophical theories to interpretations of art and history. In Weber's time, they were more frequently referred to as "cultural ideas" (*Kulturideen*) or, simply, "ideas" (*Ideen*) [sk].

17. The sketch above has intentionally taken up only the relationships in which an influence of religious ideas on "material" life is actually beyond doubt. It would have been a simple matter to move beyond this theme to a conventional "construction," according to which *all* that is "characteristic" of modern civilization is logically *deduced* out of Protestant rationalism. However, this sort of construction is better left to that type of dilettante who believes in the "unity" (*Einheitlichkeit*) of the "social psyche" and its reducibility to *one* formula. It should only further be noted that naturally the period of capitalist development *before* the development we have considered was *comprehensively co*-determined by Christian influences, both inhibiting and promoting.

# On the Relationship Between the Economy and the Development of Religions

From "Business Report and Discussion Contributions, German Sociological Association Convention," (1910) in *Gesammelte Aufsätze zur Soziologie und Sozialpolitik* [*Collected Essays on Sociology and Social Policy*], ed. Marianne Weber, trans. Stephen Kalberg (Tübingen: Mohr Verlag, 1924), pp. 464–5.

[It is uncontestably the case] . . . that the Reformation was first set in motion in regions economically immeasurably less developed than Italy, in particular in Florence and other Italian cities. . . . [One should not consider] religious development as a reflex of something else, namely, of economic conditions. This is not at all the case, in my opinion. One must remember the following if clarity is to be acquired regarding how economic and religious forces relate to one another.

In Scotland, as well as in France, the aristocracy led the Calvinist-Huguenot revolts (in Scotland entirely, in France prominently). And this was the case everywhere. The division into Protestantism and

Catholicism occurred, if viewed in reference to status groups and their hierarchical ordering in the sixteenth century, upward and downward; it included persons from the highest down to the lowest strata. However, changes took place in the course of the Reformation's further unfolding. It was surely not by chance – and economic forces here obviously played a significant role – that the Scottish aristocracy returned to the lap of the Episcopal Church and the Scottish entrepreneurial middle class flowed into the Scottish Free Church. Likewise, it was not an accident that the French aristocracy more and more abandoned the Huguenot flag and that the Huguenots, whatever remained of them in France, increasingly became middle class.

Yet even this transformation cannot be understood as one in which the middle class, for economic reasons, developed out of its own internal dynamics a suitably entrepreneurial religiosity. The reverse! The particular imprint of Scotland's middle class was a product, as described by John Keats, for example, of the men of the church particular to Scotland. And as concerns France, Voltaire, for example, was well aware of the correct line of causality. In short, it would be entirely incorrect – and it is only this point that I oppose – if one wanted to offer a one-sided economic interpretation. This would remain the case even should it be argued that the economy constitutes the main cause, or even that all else must be viewed as only a reflex of economic or similar forces.

# On the Work Ethic of Union Members and Pietists

From "On the Psychological Physics of Industrial Work," (1908–9) in *Studienausgabe der Max Weber – Gesamtausgabe Band I/11: Zur Psychophysik der industriellen Arbeit – Schriften und Reden, 1908–12*, ed. Wolfgang Schluchter, trans. Stephen Kalberg (Tübingen: Mohr Verlag, 1998), pp. 109–11.

Because these considerations have dealt briefly with the question of the relation between the general political-social habitus of the workers – let us say that which can be likened to a *"Weltanschauung"* – and their achievement in the workplace, it may be permitted at this point to ruminate on the question of the connection between this habitus and the profit that can be made from workers. Entirely a-ideological employers lacking vested interests have attempted to explain the work performance of union members adhering to Social Democracy. With great frequency and in highly varying industries, the *capacity* of this group of workers to achieve normally stands high above all other workers. . . . Record achievements [in the factory studied here] have been posted by the *entire* male work force, which has been described by the firm's higher administration as comprised of particularly "disciplined union members." With only one exception, the best workers in the firm are found in this group, as far as I can assess. . . . The accomplishments of union members stand at the top and high above the average worker.

Female workers present a different picture. Those who originate from Pietist circles in particular stand out. It is surely completely impossible that chance alone accounts for the fact that the two women who have advanced in both sections of seam sewing (simple and complex) to the level of "master" . . . belong to this religious group. Moreover, the two weavers of handkerchiefs, about whom the same can be said, performed [at levels high above] the average worker as measured by piecework daily results. . . . Finally, among the . . . hard-to-monitor polishing workers, Pietists were similarly prominent.

The consequences of "Protestant asceticism" – in other words, the internal relationship it created to work in a vocation "desired by God" – are here clearly expressed, as is "Pietism's" prohibition upon dancing and similar pleasures. And just in this manner the old component of this religious temper, which was one on the whole particularly "willing to work" and also "individualistic" in the religious sense of the word, while simultaneously patriarchal, became manifest in the antagonism of all these devout circles to all things related to unions. Workers socialized into such outlooks and habits are naturally extremely useful for the employer. Indeed, the common occurrence now seems extremely regrettable from the perspective of his interests – namely, the thorough dying out of *this* power of religiosity among male workers.

This transformation remains in place even though this study conveyed clearly that an unusually harsh sense of justice – although one that found expression in a thoroughly "individual" manner – and a stubborn advocacy of demands were notable precisely among the most competent "Pietistic" female workers. One would have to investigate very carefully the extent to which such a posture can still be found in a general way today. That it exists as a residue of the past appears *to me* very credible. If so, it belongs in that larger context which I have tried to analyze in other writings [see *The Protestant Ethic and the Spirit of Capitalism*]; that is, this posture was characteristic of forces that, to a certain degree at any rate, were effective in the early epochs of industrial capitalism.

It is most likely the case that socialization into a particular "*Weltansch-auung*" plays a role, to a strong extent, in the development among these "Pietistic" circles of workplace achievement. This must be said even though this factor is, of course, not *alone* decisive. On the other hand, the same cannot be said for the analogous case – the male work force:

the socialization into a certain *"Weltanschauung"* does *not* account for the high work performance (if it to some extent generally exists) of union members adhering to Social Democracy. It is quite plausible and natural for specific bright and shrewd workers, aware of their lucrative market value as "means of production," to become union members – and under modern conditions for the majority of these talented workers to become Social Democrats. Nonetheless, detailed analysis would be necessary to ascertain whether either early socialization into Socialism or a later introduction to its ideas – and Socialism *wishes* to be a surrogate for religion, even though on the basis of a polar opposite frame of mind – might be capable of awakening latent qualities translatable into increased achievement in the workplace.

# chapter 3

# Continuous Ethical Discipline

## The Protestant Sects and
## the Spirit of Capitalism

From "The Protestant Sects and the Spirit of Capitalism," in *The Protestant Ethic and the Spirit of Capitalism*, 3rd edn, trans. H. H. Gerth and C. Wright Mills (Los Angeles: Roxbury Publishing, 2002), pp. 127–30.

. . . Every old travel book reveals that formerly church-mindedness in America went unquestioned, as compared with recent decades, and was even far stronger. Here we are especially interested in one aspect of this situation. . . . If one looked more closely at the matter in the United States, one could easily see that the question of religious affiliation was almost always posed in social life and in business life which depended on permanent and credit relations. However, as mentioned above, the American authorities never posed the question. Why?

First, a few personal observations [from 1904] may serve as illustrations. On a long railroad journey through what was then Indian territory, the author, sitting next to a traveling salesman of "undertaker's hardware" (iron letters for tombstones), casually mentioned the still impressively strong church-mindedness. Thereupon the salesman remarked, "Sir, for my part everybody may believe or not believe as he pleases; but if I saw a farmer or a businessman not belonging to any church at all, I wouldn't trust him with fifty cents. Why pay me, if he doesn't believe in anything?" Now that was a somewhat vague motivation.

The matter became somewhat clearer from the story of a German-born nose-and-throat specialist, who had established himself in a large city on the Ohio River and who told me of the visit of his first patient. Upon the doctor's request, he lay down upon the couch to be examined with the [aid of a] nose reflector. The patient sat up once and remarked with dignity and emphasis, "Sir, I am a member of the ____ Baptist Church in

____ Street." Puzzled about what meaning this circumstance might have for the disease of the nose and its treatment, the doctor discreetly inquired about the matter from an American colleague. The colleague smilingly informed him that the patient's statement of his church membership was merely to say: "Don't worry about the fees." But why should it mean precisely that? Perhaps this will become still clearer from a third happening.

On a beautiful clear Sunday afternoon early in October I attended a baptism ceremony of a Baptist congregation. I was in the company of some relatives who were farmers in the backwoods some miles out of M. [a county seat] in North Carolina. The baptism was to take place in a pool fed by a brook which descended from the Blue Ridge Mountains, visible in the distance. It was cold and it had been freezing during the night. Masses of farmers' families were standing all around the slopes of the hills; they had come, some from great distances, some from the neighborhood, in their light two-wheeled buggies.

The preacher in a black suit stood waist deep in the pond. After preparations of various sorts, about ten persons of both sexes in their Sunday-best stepped into the pond, one after another. They avowed their faith and then were immersed completely – the women in the preacher's arms. They came up, shaking and shivering in their wet clothes, stepped out of the pond, and everybody "congratulated" them. They were quickly wrapped in thick blankets and then they drove home. One of my relatives commented that "faith" provides unfailing protection against sneezes. Another relative stood beside me, and being unchurchly in accordance with German traditions, he looked on, spitting disdainfully over his shoulder. He spoke to one of those baptized, "Hello, Bill, wasn't the water pretty cool?" and received the very earnest reply, "Jeff, I thought of some pretty hot place (Hell!), and so I didn't mind the cool water." During the immersion of one of the young men, my relative was startled.

"Look at him," he said. "I told you so!"

When I asked him after the ceremony, "Why did you anticipate the baptism of that man?" he answered, "Because he wants to open a bank in M."

"Are there so many Baptists around that he can make a living?"

"Not at all, but once being baptized he will get the patronage of the whole region and he will outcompete everybody."

Further questions of "why" and "by what means" led to the following conclusion: Admission to the local Baptist congregation follows only upon the most careful "probation" and after closest inquiries into conduct going back to early childhood (Disorderly conduct? Frequenting taverns? Dance? Theatre? Card Playing? Untimely meeting of liability? Other Frivolities?) The congregation still adhered strictly to the religious tradition.

Admission to the congregation is recognized as an absolute guarantee of the moral qualities of a gentleman, especially of those qualities required in business matters. Baptism secures to the individual the deposits of the whole region and unlimited credit without any competition. He is a "made man." Further observation confirmed that these, or at least very similar phenomena, recur in the most varied regions. In general, *only* those men had success in business who belonged to Methodist or Baptist or other *sects* or sectlike conventicles. When a sect member moved to a different place, or if he was a traveling salesman, he carried the certificate of his congregation with him; and thereby he found not only easy contact with sect members but, above all, he found credit everywhere. If he got into economic straits through no fault of his own, the sect arranged his affairs, gave guarantees to the creditors, and helped him in every way, often according to the Biblical principle, *mutuum date nihil inde sperantes* [Lend, expecting nothing in return] (Luke 6:35).

The expectation of the creditors that his sect, for the sake of their prestige, would not allow creditors to suffer losses on behalf of a sect member was not, however, decisive for his opportunities. What was decisive was the fact that a fairly reputable sect would only accept for membership one whose "conduct" made him appear to be morally qualified beyond doubt.

It is crucial that sect membership meant a certificate of moral qualification and especially of business morals for the individual. This stands in contrast to membership in a "church" into which one is "born" and which lets grace shine over the righteous and the unrighteous alike. Indeed, a church is a corporation which organizes grace and administers religious gifts of grace, like an endowed foundation. Affiliation with the church is, in principle, obligatory and hence proves nothing with regard to the member's qualities. A sect, however, is a voluntary association of only those who, according to the principle, are religiously and morally qualified. . . .

From "The Protestant Sects and the Spirit of Capitalism," in *The Protestant Ethic and the Spirit of Capitalism*, 3rd edn, trans. H. H. Gerth and C. Wright Mills (Los Angeles: Roxbury Publishing, 2002), pp. 132–4.

Today the kind of denomination [to which one belongs] is rather irrelevant. It does not matter whether one be Freemason,[1] Christian Scientist, Adventist, Quaker, or what not. What is decisive is that one be admitted to membership by "ballot," after an *examination* and an ethical *probation* in the sense of the virtues which are at a premium for the inner-worldly asceticism of Protestantism and hence, for the ancient puritan tradition. Then, the same effect could be observed.

Closer scrutiny revealed the steady progress of the characteristic process of "secularization," to which in modern times all phenomena that originated in religious conceptions succumb. Not only religious associations, hence sects, have this effect on American life. Sects exercised this influence, rather, in a steadily decreasing proportion. If one paid some attention it was striking to observe (even fifteen years ago) that surprisingly many men among the American middle classes (always outside of the quite modern metropolitan areas and the immigration centers) were wearing a little badge (of varying color) in the buttonhole, which reminded one very closely of the rosette of the French Legion of Honor.

When asked what it meant, people regularly mentioned an association with a sometimes adventurous and fantastic name. And it became obvious that its significance and purpose consisted in the following: Almost always the association functioned as a burial insurance, besides offering greatly varied services. But often, and especially in those areas least touched by modern disintegration, the association offered the member the (ethical) claim for brotherly help on the part of every brother who had the means. If he faced an economic emergency for which he himself was not to be blamed, he could make this claim. And in several instances that came to my notice at the time, this claim again followed the very principle, *mutuum date nihil inde sperantes*, or at least a very low rate of interest prevailed. Apparently, such claims were willingly recognized by the members of the brotherhood. Furthermore – and this is the main point in this instance – membership was again acquired through balloting after investigation and a determination of moral worth. And hence the badge in the buttonhole meant, "I am a gentleman patented after investigation and probation and guaranteed by my membership." Again, this meant in business life above all, tested *credit worthiness*. One could observe that business opportunities were often decisively influenced by such legitimation.

All these phenomena, which seemed to be rather rapidly disintegrating – at least the religious organizations – were essentially confined to the middle classes. Some cultured Americans often dismissed these facts briefly and with a certain angry disdain as "humbug" or backwardness, or they even denied them; many of them actually did not know anything about them, as was affirmed to me by William James. Yet these survivals were still alive in many different fields, and sometimes in forms which appeared to be grotesque.

These associations were especially the typical vehicles of social ascent into the circle of the entrepreneurial middle class. They served to diffuse and to maintain the bourgeois capitalist business ethos among the broad strata of the middle classes (the farmers included).

As is well known, not a few (one may well say the majority of the older generation) of the American "promoters," "captains of industry," of the multi-millionaires and trust magnates belonged formally to sects, especially to the Baptists. However, in the nature of the case, these persons were often affiliated for merely conventional reasons, as in Germany, and only in order to legitimate themselves in personal and social life – not in order to legitimate themselves as businessmen; during the age of the Puritans, such "economic supermen" did not require such a crutch, and their "religiosity" was, of course, often of a more than dubious sincerity. The middle classes, above all the strata ascending with and out of the middle classes, were the bearers of that specific religious orientation which one must, indeed, beware viewing among them as only opportunistically determined.

Yet one must never overlook that without the universal diffusion of these qualities and principles of a methodical way of life, qualities which were maintained through these religious communities, capitalism today, even in America, would not be what it is. In the history of any economic area on earth there is no epoch, [except] those quite rigid in feudalism or patrimonialism, in which capitalist figures of the kind of Pierpont Morgan, Rockefeller, Jay Gould, et al. were absent. Only the technical *means* which they used for the acquisition of wealth have changed (of course!). *They* stood and they stand "beyond good and evil." But, however high one may otherwise evaluate their importance for economic transformation, they have never been decisive in determining what economic mentality was to dominate a given epoch and a given area. Above all, they were not the creators and they were not to become the bearers of the specifically Occidental middle class mentality. . . .

From "The Protestant Sects and the Spirit of Capitalism," in *The Protestant Ethic and the Spirit of Capitalism*, 3rd edn, trans. H. H. Gerth and C. Wright Mills (Los Angeles: Roxbury Publishing, 2002), pp. 137–8.

The tremendous social significance of admission to full enjoyment of the rights of the sectarian congregation, especially the privilege of being admitted to the *Lord's Supper*, worked among the sects in the direction of breeding that ascetist professional ethic which was adequate to modern capitalism during the period of its origin. It can be demonstrated that everywhere, including Europe, the religiosity of the ascetist sects has for several centuries worked in the same way as has been illustrated by the personal experiences mentioned above for [the case of] America.

When focusing on the religious background of these Protestant sects, we find in their literary documents, especially among those of the Quakers and Baptists up to and throughout the seventeenth century, again and again jubilation over the fact that the sinful "children of the world" distrust one another in business but that they have confidence in the religiously determined righteousness of the pious.

Hence, they give credit and deposit their money only with the pious, and they make purchases in their stores because there, and there alone, they are given honest and *fixed prices*. As is known, the Baptists have always claimed to have first raised this price policy to a principle. In addition to the Baptists, the Quakers raise the claim, as the following quotation shows, to which Mr. Eduard Bernstein drew my attention at the time:

But it was not only in matters which related to the law of the land where the primitive members held their words and engagements sacred. This trait was remarked to be true of them in their concerns of trade. On their first appearance as a society, they suffered as tradesmen because others, displeased with the peculiarity of their manners, withdrew their custom from their shops. But in a little time the great outcry against them was that they got the trade of the country into their hands. This outcry arose in part from a strict exemption of all commercial agreements between them and others and *because they never asked two prices for the commodities they sold.*

The view that the gods bless with riches the man who pleases them, through sacrifice or through his kind of conduct, was indeed diffused all over the world. However, the Protestant sects consciously brought this idea into connection with this kind of religious conduct, according to the principle of early capitalism: "Honesty is the best policy." This connection is found, although not quite exclusively, among these Protestant sects, but with characteristic continuity and consistency it is found *only* among them.

The whole typically bourgeois ethic was from the beginning common to all asceticist sects and conventicles and it is identical with the ethic practiced by the sects in America up to the very present. The Methodists, for example, held to be forbidden:

(1)   To make words when buying and selling ("haggling").
(2)   To trade with commodities before the custom tariff has been paid on them.
(3)   To charge rates of interest higher than the law of the country permits.
(4)   "To gather treasures on earth" (meaning the transformation of investment capital into "funded wealth").
(5)   To borrow without being sure of one's ability to pay back the debt.
(6)   Luxuries of all sorts.

But it is not only this ethic, already discussed in detail, which goes back to the early beginnings of asceticist sects. Above all, the social premiums, the means of discipline, and, in general, the whole organizational basis of Protestant sectarianism with all its ramifications reach back to those beginnings. The survivals in contemporary America are the derivatives of a religious regulation of life which once worked with penetrating efficiency. . . .

From "The Protestant Sects and the Spirit of Capitalism," in *The Protestant Ethic and the Spirit of Capitalism*, 3rd edn, trans. H. H. Gerth and C. Wright Mills, slightly revised by Stephen Kalberg (Los Angeles: Roxbury Publishing, 2002), pp. 144–7.

. . . During the Middle Ages it was also possible to proceed through the disciplinary powers of the church against a bishop who would not pay his debts, and, as Aloys Schulte has beautifully shown, this possibility gave the bishop a credit rating over and above a secular prince. Likewise, the fact that a Prussian Lieutenant was subject to discharge if he was incapable of paying off debts provided a higher credit rating for him. And the same held for the German fraternity student. Oral confession and the disciplinary power of the church during the Middle Ages also provided the means to enforce church discipline effectively. Finally, to secure a legal claim, the opportunity provided by the oath was exploited to secure excommunication of the debtor.

In all these cases, however, the forms of behavior that were favored or tabooed through such conditions and means differed totally from those which Protestant asceticism bred or suppressed. With the lieutenant, for instance, or the fraternity student, and probably with the bishop as well, the enhanced credit rating certainly did not rest upon the breeding of personal qualities suitable for business; and following up this remark directly: even though the effects in all three cases were intended to have the same direction, they were worked out in quite different ways. The medieval, like the Lutheran church discipline, first, was vested in the hands of the ministerial officeholder; secondly, this discipline worked – as far as it was effective at all – through authoritarian means; and, thirdly, it punished and placed premiums upon concrete individual acts.

The church discipline of the Puritans and of the sects was vested, first, at least in part and often wholly, in the hands of laymen. Secondly, it worked through the necessity of one's having to hold one's own; and, thirdly, it bred or, if one wishes, selected qualities. The last point is the most important one.

The member of the sect (or conventicle) had to have qualities of a certain kind in order to enter the community circle. Being endowed with these qualities was important for the development of rational modern capitalism. In order to hold his own in this circle the member had to *testify* repeatedly that he was endowed with these qualities. They were constantly and continuously bred in him. For, like his bliss in the beyond, his whole social existence in the here and now depended upon his "testifying" to his belief. The Catholic confession of sins was, to repeat, by comparison a means of *relieving* the person from the tremendous internal pressure under which the sect member in his conduct was constantly held. . . .

According to all experience there is no stronger means of breeding traits than through the necessity of holding one's own in the circle of one's associates. The continuous and unobtrusive ethical discipline of the sects was, therefore, related to authoritarian church discipline as rational breeding and selection are related to ordering and forbidding.

In this as in almost every other respect, the Puritan sects are the most specific bearers of the inner-worldly form of asceticism. Moreover, they are the most consistent and, in a certain sense, the only consistent

antithesis to the universalist Catholic Church – a compulsory organization for the administration of grace. The Puritan sects put the most
powerful individual interest of social self-esteem in the service of this
breeding of traits. Hence *individual* motives and personal self-interests were
also placed in the service of maintaining and propagating the "middle
class" Puritan ethic, with all its ramifications. This is absolutely decisive
for its penetrating and for its powerful effect.

To repeat, it is not the ethical *doctrine* of a religion, but that form of
ethical conduct upon which *psychological rewards* are placed that matters.[2]
Such rewards operate through the form and the condition of the respective goods of salvation. And such conduct constitutes "one's" specific "ethos"
in the sociological sense of the word. For Puritanism, that conduct was a
certain methodical, rational way of life which – given certain conditions
– paved the way for the "spirit" of modern capitalism. The rewards were
placed upon "testifying" before God in the sense of attaining salvation –
which is found in *all* Puritan denominations – and "testifying" before men
in the sense of socially holding one's own within the Puritan sects. Both
aspects were mutually supplementary and operated in the same direction: they helped to deliver the "spirit" of modern capitalism, its specific
*ethos:* the ethos of the modern *bourgeois middle classes.*

The ascetic conventicles and sects formed one of the most important
historical foundations of modern "individualism." Their radical break away
from patriarchal and authoritarian bondage, as well as their way of
interpreting the statement that one owes more obedience to God than to
man, were especially important.

Finally, in order to understand the nature of these ethical effects, a
comparative remark is required. In the *guilds* of the Middle Ages there
was frequently a control of the general ethical standard of the members
similar to that exercised by the discipline of the ascetic Protestant sects.
But the unavoidable difference in the effects of guild and of sect upon
the economic conduct of the individual is obvious.

The guild united members of the same occupation; hence it united
*competitors*. It did so in order to limit competition as well as the rational
striving for profit which operated through competition. The guild trained
for "civic" virtues and, in a certain sense, was the bearer of middle class
"rationalism" (a point which will not be discussed here in detail). The guild
accomplished this through a "subsistence policy" and through traditionalism. In so far as guild regulation of the economy gained effectiveness,
its practical results are well known.

The sects, on the other hand, united men through the selection and the
breeding of ethically qualified *fellow believers*. Their membership was not
based upon apprenticeship or upon the family relations of technically
qualified members of an occupation. The sect controlled and regulated
the members' conduct *exclusively* in the sense of formal *righteousness*

and methodical asceticism. It was devoid of the purpose of a material subsistence policy which handicapped an expansion of the rational striving for profit. The capitalist success of a guild member undermined the spirit of the guild – as happened in England and France – and hence capitalist success was shunned. But the capitalist success of a sect brother, if legally attained, testified of his worth and of his state of grace, and it raised the prestige and the propaganda chances of the sect. Such success was therefore welcome, as the several statements quoted above show. The organization of free labor in guilds, in their Occidental medieval form, has certainly – very much against their intention – not only been a handicap but also a precondition for the capitalist organization of labor which was, perhaps, indispensable.[3] But the guild, of course, could not give birth to the modern middle class capitalist *ethos*. Only the methodical way of life of the ascetic sects could legitimate and put a halo around the economic "individualist" impulses of the modern capitalist ethos.

## NOTES

1.  An assistant of Semitic languages in an eastern university told me that he regretted not having become "master of the chair," for then he would go back into business. When asked what good that would do the answer was: As a traveling salesman or seller he could present himself in a role famous for respectability. He could beat any competition and would be worth his weight in gold.
2.  Again we should like to stress emphatically this absolutely decisive point of the first of these two essays (*The Protestant Ethic and the Spirit of Capitalism*). It has been the fundamental mistake of my critics not to have taken notice of this very fact. . . .
3.  Here, in passing, we cannot analyze this rather involved causal relationship.

# part 3

# The Economy, the Workplace, and the Specialized Nature of Work in the Modern Epoch

## Introduction

Open, or "free," markets, Weber is convinced (Chapter 4), did not appear simply as a consequence of a "'goal-oriented' rational calculation with the technically most adequate available means." To him, conducive substantive rationalities had to be in place before "correct calculation" and the free market's formal rationality could develop. These terms are defined in this Part's opening selections, as is the distinction between "planned" and "open" markets. Major features of the modern bureaucratized workplace are then outlined: the separation of the worker from the means of production, the prominence attributed to examinations and certificates, and the centrality of discipline. Whether in educational institutions, the world of science, or on the factory floor, the specialization of work constitutes a common thread, according to Weber.

Although the spirit of capitalism must be noted as a central substantive condition along the winding path toward widespread free markets, Weber insists that complex patterns of social action also came into play. These are addressed in the first selections. They further illustrate his general position on economic development: the causal forces behind it – *constellations* of cultural, political, economic, status, legal, urban, and familial forces – must be acknowledged. To him, "the formal rationality of money calculation is dependent on certain quite specific substantive conditions" (1968a, p. 107). How did it occur that, in certain eras and certain regions, traditional action and traditional economic ethics, which had existed unchanged from time immemorial, were altered and indeed destroyed? Modernity, and in particular its "calculating attitude," rest upon a wide-ranging constellation of "value postulates."

Weber argues this general point also by comparing the market economy to the planned economy. Economic action in the latter is oriented "heteronomously"; that is, to a set of non-market rules or ideals. When held to comprehensively, such altruistic ideals inevitably lead to a "reduction in formal, calculating rationality" and to lower standards of living in the end. In an ideal-typical formulation, he then succinctly charts out "the conditions of maximum formal rationality of capital accounting."

In "Socialism"[1] (Chapter 5) Weber contends that the "separation of the worker from the tools of his trade" should not be seen, following Marx, as unique to the situation of the working class in privately owned industries. Rather, ownership today remains *in organizations* rather than in a class. State ownership will not alter this concentration of "the tools" (machines, laboratories, etc.) in, for example, factories, corporations, universities, and hospitals, Weber is convinced. Moreover, to him non-random forces stood behind this development toward the organization of economic activity in large-scale firms and factories. It occurred, on the one hand, as a consequence of the technologically more complex character of the tools and, on the other, as a result of the greater efficiency that follows wherever complex tasks are coordinated.

A further central feature of the modern economy is emphasized by Weber in a number of texts, namely, the specialization of tasks. The modern economy requires specialists; it "cannot be run in any other way." Yet this precondition also leads in the direction of large-scale organizations, for the discrete tasks carried out by specialists must be ordered and coordinated. The administrators, managers, clerks, and officials who do so acquire a central place in the modern economy – regardless of whether the bourgeoisie or the state owns the means of production. A "dictatorship of the official, not of the worker [is] on the advance," and industrialism's large-scale organization of production will alter "the spiritual face of mankind almost to the point of unrecognizability."

Attentive always to background cultural forces, Weber addresses also the manner in which discipline – "the consistently rationalized, methodically prepared and exact execution of the received order" – constitutes a central cornerstone underpinning bureaucratization. The impersonal and "unfailingly neutral" character of discipline "places [it] at the disposal of every power that claims its service" – and hence it stands in the most strict opposition to all personal devotion to charismatic figures. The feudal knight's strong orientation to a code of personal honor also contrasts clearly to the rational calculation and "orientation toward a purpose [and] a common cause" typical of discipline.

The suitability of discipline, which "puts the drill for the sake of habitual routinized skill" at the forefront, for the factory workplace is evident.

Indeed, Weber identifies the rigorous discipline practiced in the military as the "ideal model for the modern capitalist factory." When disciplined, the "optimal profitability" of workers can be calculated, for the "psychophysical apparatus of man is [in the factory] completely adjusted to the ... machines."[2] As rationalization occurs, especially in the factory and the administration of the state, discipline expands inexorably.

The subsequent readings in this Part explore the ramifications of these significant transformations of the workplace. The replacement of "the cultivated man" by "the specialist" is first examined (Chapter 6). Weber renders these ideal types in stark terms. He characterizes their struggle, and its ultimate outcome, as arising out of bureaucratization and the increasing importance of specialized knowledge in the modern epoch. The unequivocal expansion of certificates and examinations in higher education institutions is a manifestation of this importance. Whereas in earlier epochs "proof of ancestry" opened doors and established privileges, today "full bureaucratization" brings the examination irresistibly to the fore as the "universal instrument" leading the way to the "patent of education."

Scientific research, Weber emphasizes in his classical essay, "Science as a Vocation," (SV) is also undergoing massive specialization. This transformation is both inevitable and appropriate, he contends. The "definitive and good accomplishment" requires narrow training in demarcated sub-areas and an orientation to theoretical and empirical problems posed within them. Although scientific work is consequently quite tedious, the scientist must have an enthusiasm for and commitment to his or her endeavor. A true "calling" for science is possessed only by scholars, even as they pursue their specialized research tasks and extremely narrow conjectures, who are awakened by a "strange intoxication"; "without this you have *no* calling for science." Moreover, however specialized and bureaucratized, science exists in the end, Weber is convinced, only on the basis of new ideas and inspiration. Scientists must have ideas, yet they occur "when they please" and "cannot be forced." How do they arise at all in highly bureaucratized and specialized settings?, he wonders.

Weber sees these features – the separation of the worker from the means of production, the specialist character of scientific research and labor in general, and the centrality of examinations, certificates, and discipline – as indigenous to the modern economy and workplace. Nonetheless, he typically is convinced that even seemingly universal and standard features of modern capitalism must be acknowledged as varying in weight and scope in the various modern economies depending on arrays of background historical factors. The final reading in this Part forcefully affirms this notion central throughout Weber's sociology (Chapter 7).

He undertook to compare German and American capitalism by reference to underlying economic and political constellations in a lecture given in St Louis in 1904 at the World's Fair.[3] These "new" and "old" civilizations varied distinctly along many axes, and these differences shaped the particular contours of modern capitalism in each country dramatically. Weber's lecture stresses that any attempt to transpose understandings of American capitalism onto Germany, or vice versa, would only lead, owing to significant underlying historical divergence, to "entirely wrong conclusions." What differences did he have in mind?

His discussion focuses on the many forces in Germany that stand opposed to "money-making and its representatives." Written at the same time as *The Protestant Ethic and the Spirit of Capitalism*, this lecture emphasizes the "much more complicated social organization" in Germany where, over many centuries, a large stratum of state officials became powerful, together with a conservative, anti-capitalist Church and an "aristocracy" which dominated educational institutions. All opposed "the power of money-makers" and, in a "settled" Germany "less adventurous" than the United States, circumscribed dramatically any free space for the pursuit of profit. Americans find these developments "difficult to understand," he concedes. Capitalism in Europe assumes an "authoritarian stamp," Weber contends, in contrast to the "citizens' equality of rights" widespread in America.

The entrepreneurial economic culture called forth by the spirit of capitalism could more easily expand in the United States, Weber holds, which remained unburdened by any of these old civilization formations. Cognizance must be taken of the different *milieu*, he contends here and throughout his comparative-historical studies. When moving toward modern capitalism, countries do not stand on a level playing field, as little as they do when moving toward modern democracy. Nor are the different historical contexts shattered and banished by the wheels of modern capitalism to the same extent or in the same manner.

## NOTES

1. This text is from a lecture Weber gave in 1918 at a convention of Austrian army officers. Hence, its more informal tone.
2. This theme is treated in depth by Weber (see 1995).
3. Weber was invited to this "Universal Exposition" by his former colleague at Freiburg University, Hugo Münsterberg, then teaching in the Psychology Department at Harvard University. Owing to his illness, this was Weber's first lecture in more than six years.

# chapter 4

# Market and Planned Economies

## MODERN CAPITALISM'S SUBSTANTIVE CONDITIONS

## Formal and Substantive Rationality of Economic Action

From *Economy and Society: An Outline of Interpretive Sociology*, eds Guenther Roth and Claus Wittich, trans. Talcott Parsons, revised by Guenther Roth and Claus Wittich, and Stephen Kalberg (Berkeley, CA: University of California Press, 1978), pp. 85–6.

The term "formal rationality of economic action" will be used to designate the extent of *calculation* which is technically possible and which is actually applied. "Substantive rationality," on the other hand, is the degree to which the provisioning of given groups of persons (no matter how delimited) with goods is shaped by economically-oriented social action under specific (past, present, or potential) *value postulates (wertende Postulate)*, regardless of the nature of these ends. These may be of a great variety. . . .

1.  A system of economic activity will be called "formally" rational according to the degree to which the provision for needs, which is essential to every rational economy, is capable of being expressed in numerical, calculable terms, and is so expressed. In the first instance, it is quite independent of the technical form these calculations take, particularly whether estimates are expressed in money or in kind. The concept is thus unambiguous, at least in the sense that expression in money terms yield the highest degree of formal calculability. Naturally, even this is true only relatively, so long as other things are equal.

2. The concept "substantive rationality," on the other hand, is full of ambiguities. It conveys only one element common to all "substantive" analyses: namely, that they do not restrict themselves to note the purely formal and (relatively) unambiguous fact that action is based on "goal-oriented" rational calculation with the technically most adequate available methods, but apply ethical, political, utilitarian, hedonistic, feudal (*ständisch*), egalitarian, or whatever *demands*, and measure the results of the economic action, however formally "rational" in the sense of correct calculation they may be, against these scales of "value rationality" or "*substantive* goal rationality."

There is an infinite number of possible value scales for this type of rationality, of which the socialist and communist standards constitute only one group. The latter, although by no means unambiguous in themselves, always involve elements of social justice and equality. Others are criteria of status distinctions, or of the capacity for power, especially of the war capacity, of a political unit; all these and many others are of potential "substantive" significance. These points of view are, however, significant only as bases from which to judge the *outcome* of economic action. In addition and quite independently, it is possible to judge from an ethical, ascetic, or esthetic point of view the *spirit* of economic activity (*Wirtschaftsgesinnung*) as well as the *instruments* of economic activity. All of these approaches may consider the "purely formal" rationality of calculation in monetary terms as of quite secondary importance or even as fundamentally inimical to their respective ultimate ends, even before anything has been said about the consequences of the specifically modern calculating attitude. There is no question in this discussion of attempting value judgments in this field, but only of determining and delimiting what is to be called "formal."

# Market Economies and Planned Economies

From *Economy and Society: An Outline of Interpretive Sociology*, eds Guenther Roth and Claus Wittich, trans. Talcott Parsons, revised by Guenther Roth and Claus Wittich, and slightly revised by Stephen Kalberg (Berkeley, CA: University of California Press, 1978), pp. 109–11.

Want satisfaction will be said to take place through a "market economy" so far as it results from action oriented to advantages in exchange on the basis of self-interest and where co-operation takes place only through the exchange process. It results, on the other hand, from a "planned economy" so far as economic action is oriented systematically to an established substantive order, whether agreed or imposed, which is valid within an organization.

Want satisfaction through a market economy normally, and in proportion to the degree of rationality, presupposes money calculation. Where capital accounting is used it presupposes the economic separation of the budgetary unit (household) and the enterprise. Want satisfaction by means of a planned economy is dependent, in ways which vary in kind and degree according to its extensiveness, on calculation in kind as the ultimate basis of the *substantive* orientation of economic action. Formally, however, the action of the producing individual is oriented to the instructions of an administrative staff, the existence of which is indispensable.

In a market economy the individual units are autocephalous and their action is autonomously oriented. In the administration of budgetary units (households), the basis of orientation is the marginal utility of money holdings and of anticipated money income; in the case of intermittent entrepreneurship (*Gelegenheitserwerben*), the probabilities of market gain, and in the case of profit-making enterprises, capital accounting is the basis of orientation. In a planned economy, all economic action, so far as "planning" is really carried through, is oriented heteronomously and in a strictly "budgetary" manner, to rules which enjoin certain modes of action and forbid others, and which establish a system of rewards and punishments. When, in a planned economy, the prospect of additional individual income is used as a means of stimulating self-interest, the type and direction of the action thus rewarded is substantively heteronomously determined.

It is possible for the same thing to be true of a market economy, though in a formally voluntary way. This is true wherever the unequal distribution of wealth, and particularly of capital goods, forces the non-owning group to comply with the authority of others in order to obtain any return at all for the utilities they can offer on the market – either with the authority of a wealthy householder, or with the decisions, oriented to capital accounting, of the owners of capital or of their agents. In a purely capitalistic organization of production, this is the fate of the entire working class.

The following are decisive as elements of the motivation of economic activity under the conditions of a market economy: (1) For those without substantial property: (a) the fact that they run the risk of going entirely without provisions, both for themselves and for those personal dependents, such as children, wives, sometimes parents, whom the individual typically maintains on his own account; (b) that, in varying degrees subjectively they value economically productive work as a mode of life. (2) For those who enjoy a privileged position by virtue of wealth or the education which is usually in turn dependent on wealth: (a) opportunities for large income from profitable undertakings; (b) ambition; (c) the valuation as a "calling" of types of work enjoying high prestige, such as intellectual work, artistic performance, and work involving high technical competence. (3) For those sharing in the fortunes of profit-making enterprises: (a) the risk to the individual's own capital, and his own opportunities for profit, combined with (b) the valuation of rational acquisitive activity as a "calling." The latter may be significant as a proof of the individual's own achievement or as a symbol and a means of autonomous control over the individuals subject to his authority, or of control over economic advantages which are culturally or materially important to an indefinite plurality of persons – in a word, power.

A planned economy oriented to want satisfaction must, in proportion as it is radically carried through, weaken the incentive to labor so far as the risk of lack of support is involved. For it would, at least so far as there is a rational system of provision for wants, be impossible to allow a worker's dependents to suffer the full consequences of his lack of efficiency in production. Furthermore, autonomy in the direction of organized productive units would have to be greatly reduced or, in the extreme case, eliminated. Hence it would be impossible to retain capital risk and proof of merit by a formally autonomous achievement. The same would be true of autonomous power over other individuals and important features of their economic situation.

Along with opportunities for special material rewards, a planned economy may have command over certain ideal motives of what is in the broadest sense an altruistic type, which can be used to stimulate a level of achievement in economic production comparable to that which autonomous orientation to opportunities for profit, by producing for the satisfaction of effective demand, has empirically been able to achieve in a market economy. Where a planned economy is radically carried out, it must further accept the inevitable reduction in formal, calculatory rationality which would result from the elimination of money and capital accounting.

Substantive and formal (in the sense of exact *calculation*) rationality are, it should be stated again, after all largely distinct problems. This fundamental and, in the last analysis, unavoidable element of irrationality in economic systems is one of the important sources of all "social" problems, and above all, of the problems of socialism.

# The Conditions of Maximum Formal Rationality of Capital Accounting

From *Economy and Society: An Outline of Interpretive Sociology,* eds Guenther Roth and Claus Wittich, trans. Talcott Parsons, revised by Guenther Roth and Claus Wittich (Berkeley, CA: University of California Press, 1978), pp. 161–2.

The following are the principal conditions necessary for obtaining a maximum of formal rationality of capital accounting in production enterprises: (1) complete appropriation of all material means of production by owners and the complete absence of all formal appropriation of opportunities for profit in the market; that is, market freedom; (2) complete autonomy in the selection of management by the owners, thus complete absence of formal appropriation of rights to managerial functions; (3) complete absence of appropriation of jobs and of opportunities for earning by workers and, conversely, the absence of appropriation of workers by owners. This implies free labor, freedom of the labor market, and freedom in the selection of workers; (4) complete absence of substantive regulation of consumption, production, and prices, or of other forms of regulation which limit freedom of contract or specify conditions of exchange. This may be called substantive freedom of contract; (5) complete calculability of the technical conditions of the production process; that is, a mechanically rational technology; (6) complete calculability of the functioning of public administration and the legal order and a reliable purely formal guarantee of all contracts by the political authority. This is a formally rational administration and law; (7) the most complete separation possible of the enterprise and its conditions of success and failure from the household or private budgetary unit and its property interests. It is particularly important that the capital at the disposal of the enterprise should be clearly distinguished from the private wealth of the owners, and should not be subject to division or dispersion through inheritance. For large-scale enterprises, this condition tends to approach an optimum from a formal point of view: in the fields of transport, manufacture, and mining, if they are organized in corporate form with freely transferrable shares and limited liability, and in the field of agriculture, if there are relatively long-term leases for large-scale production units; (8) a monetary system with the highest possible degree of formal rationality.

# chapter 5

# The Separation of the Worker from the Means of Production, the Spread of Officialdom, and Organizational Discipline in the Factory

From "Socialism," in *Max Weber*, ed. J. E. T. Eldridge, trans. D. Hÿtch (London: Nelson, 1972), pp. 197–9.

In large states everywhere modern democracy is becoming a bureau-cratised democracy. And it must be so; for it is replacing the aristocratic or other titular officials by a paid civil service. It is the same everywhere, it is the same within the parties too. This is inevitable, and is the first fact which socialism has to reckon with: the necessity for years of specialist training, for increasingly extensive specialisation and for administration by a specialist civil service trained in this manner. The modern economy cannot be run in any other way.

However, this inescapable universal bureaucratisation is, in particular, that which is concealed behind one of the most frequently quoted socialist slogans – the slogan of the "separation of the worker from the tools of his trade." What does that mean? The worker is, so we are told "separated" from the material resources with which he produces, and on this separation rests the wage slavery in which he finds himself. In this they have in mind the fact that in the Middle Ages the worker was the owner of the technical tools with which he produced, while the modern worker, of course, neither does nor can own his tools whether the mine or factory in question is run by an employer or the state. They have in mind, further, that the artisan himself bought the raw materials which he processed, while that is not the case, and cannot be, with the paid worker of today; and that accordingly the product was in the Middle Ages, and is still, in places where crafts survive, at the disposal of the individual craftsman, who can sell it on the market and turn it to his own profit; while in a large concern it is at the disposal not of the worker but of the owner of these tools of the trade, who again may be the state or a private employer. That is true, but the fact is by no means peculiar to the process of economic production. We encounter the same thing, for example, within the university. The old-time lecturer and university professor worked with the books and the technical resources which they procured or made for themselves; chemists, for instance, produced the things which were required by scientific industry. The mass of today's manpower within the modern university set-up, particularly the assistants in the big faculties, are on the contrary in precisely the same situation as any worker in this respect. They can be given notice at any time. Their rights in the domain of the faculty are no different from those of the worker in the domain of the factory. They must conduct themselves, just like the latter, in accordance with the regulations in force. They have no ownership of the materials or apparatus, machines, etc. which are used in a chemical, physical or biological faculty or a clinic; these are rather the property of the state but are managed by the director of the department who levies charges for the purpose, while the assistant receives an income which does not fundamentally differ in amount from that of a trained worker. . . .

Everywhere we find the same thing: the tools within the factory, the state administration, the army and the university faculties are concentrated by means of a bureaucratically constructed human machine in the hands of him who controls this machine. This is due partly to purely technical considerations, to the nature of modern tools – machines, guns, etc. – but partly simply to the greater efficiency of this kind of co-operation: to the development of "discipline," army, office, shop-floor and factory discipline. In any event it is a serious mistake to think that this separation of the worker from the tools of his trade is something peculiar to industry and, moreover, to *private* industry. The basic state of affairs is unaltered when the person of the head of this machine changes, when, say, a state president or minister controls it instead of a private industralist. The "separation" from the means continues in any case. As long as there are mines, furnaces, railways, factories and machines, they will never be the property of an individual or of several individual workers in the sense in which the materials of a medieval craft were the property of one guild-master or of a local trade association or guild. That is out of the question because of the nature of present-day technology. . . .

From "Socialism," in *Max Weber*, ed. J. E. T. Eldridge, trans. D. Hÿtch (London: Nelson, 1972), pp. 200–2.

What characterises our current situation is this, that private economy, bound up with private bureaucratic organisation and hence with the separation of the worker from the tools of his trade, dominates the sphere of *industrial* production which has never before in history borne these two characteristics together on such a scale; and this process coincides with the establishment of mechanical production within the factory, thus with a local accumulation of labour on the same premises, enslavement to the machine and common working discipline within the machine-shop or pit. It is the discipline which lends the contemporary mode of "separation" of worker from materials its particular stamp. . . .

This subjection to working discipline is so extraordinarily marked for the industrial worker because, in contrast to, say, a slave plantation or a socage-farm, modern industry functions on the basis of an extraordinarily keen process of *selection*. A modern factory proprietor does not employ just any worker, just because he might work for a low wage. Rather he puts the man at the machine on piece-wages and says: "All right, now work, I shall see how much you earn"; and if the man does not prove himself capable of earning a certain minimum wage he is told: "We are sorry, you are not suited to this occupation, we cannot use you." He is dismissed because the machine is not working to capacity unless the man in front of it knows how to utilise it fully. Everywhere it is the same, or similar. Every modern concern, in contrast to those of antiquity which employed slave labour, where the lord was bound to the slaves he owned – if one of them died, it was a capital loss for him – rests on the principle of selection, and this selection on the other hand is intensified to the extreme by competition between employers, which constrains the individual employer to certain maximum wages: the inherent necessity of the worker's earnings corresponds to the inherent necessity of the discipline.

If the worker goes to the employer today and says: "We cannot live on these wages and you could pay us more," in nine out of ten cases – I mean in peacetime and in those branches where there is really fierce competition – the employer is in a position to show the workers from his books that it is impossible; my competitor pays such and such wages; if I pay you even only so much more, all the profit I could pay to the shareholders disappears from my books, I could not carry on the business, for I would get no credit from the bank. Thereby he is very often just stating the naked truth. There is the additional point that under the pressure of competition profitability depends on as much human labour as possible being eliminated by labour-saving machines, and especially the highest-paid variety who cost the business most. Hence skilled workers must be replaced by unskilled workers or workers trained directly at the machine. This process is inevitable and is continually occurring.

Socialism terms all this the "domination of men by matter," which means the domination of the end (supply meeting demand) by the means. It recognises that, while in the past there were individuals who could be held responsible for the fate of the client, bondsman or slave, this is impossible today. Therefore it attacks not individuals but the organisation of production as such. Any educated socialist will absolutely decline to hold an individual employer responsible for the worker's destined fate, but he will say it is inherent in the system, in the plight into which all parties, employer and employed, find themselves driven. . . .

From "Socialism," in *Max Weber*, ed. J. E. T. Eldridge, trans. D. Hÿtch (London: Nelson, 1972), pp. 203–4.

[Under socialism] the workers would very soon find out that the lot of a miner is not affected in the slightest by whether the pit is privately or state-owned. The life of a worker in the coal-mines of the Saar is just the same as in a private mining company: if the pit is badly run, i.e. is not very profitable, then things are bad for the men too. The difference, however, is that to strike against the state is impossible, hence that under this kind of state socialism the dependence of the worker is quite substantially increased. That is one of the reasons why social democracy generally rejects this nationalisation of the economy, this form of socialism. It is a consortium of syndicates. The decisive factor is, as before, profit; the question of what is earned by the individual industrialists who have joined forces in the syndicate and of whom one is now the treasurer continues to determine the lines along which the economy is run. And the distressing thing would be that, while at present the political and private industrial administrations (of syndicates, banks, and giant concerns) stand side by side as separate bodies, and therefore industrial power can still be curbed by political power, the two administrations would then be one body with common interest and could no longer be checked. . . .

From "Socialism," in *Max Weber*, ed. J. E. T. Eldridge, trans. D. Hÿtch (London: Nelson, 1972), p. 209.

. . . Above all, however, [socialism] means on the one hand the spread of officialdom, of specialist, commercially or technically trained clerks, but on the other, the propagation of men of *private means*, i.e. a class who just draw dividends and interest, without doing mental work for it, as the employer does, but who, with all their financial interests, are committed to the capitalist system. Public and trust concerns, however, are strongly and quite exclusively dominated by the *official*, not the worker, who has more difficulty in achieving anything by strike action here than against private employers. It is the dictatorship of the official, not that of the worker, which, for the present at any rate, is on the advance.

From "A Research Strategy for the Study of Occupational Careers and Mobility Patterns," in *Max Weber*, ed. J. E. T. Eldridge, trans. D. Hÿtch slightly revised by Stephen Kalberg (London: Nelson, 1972), pp. 154–5.

Only all these investigations combined could furnish a picture of the *cultural significance* of the process of development being undergone by major industry before our eyes. The cultural problems which it ultimately brings are of enormous extent. In a memorandum for the subcommittee A. Weber stressed – in agreement with the view of many of us – that the structure of that peculiar "system" which has been thrust upon the population by the organisation of large-scale industrial production transcends even the scope of the question of "capitalist" or "socialist" organisation of production in its significance for their fate, because the existence of this "equipment" *as such is independent* of this alternative. Indeed, the modern workshop with its official hierarchy, its discipline, its chaining of worker to machine, its agglommeration and yet at the same time (compared, say, with the spinning-rooms of the past) its isolation of workers',[1] its huge calculating machinery, stretching right down to the simplest manipulation of the worker, *is* – conceptually – independent of it. It has far-reaching specific effects, entirely peculiar to itself, on men and their "style of living."

Certainly, however – and here, again, would lie the limitation of that point of view – the substitution of *any* form of common economic "solidarity" for today's selection on the principle of private economic viability, chaining as it does the whole existence of those confined within the factory, whether directing or obeying, to the outcome of the employer's *private* cost and profit calculations, would radically change the spirit found today in this great edifice, and no one can even surmise with what consequences. These prospects do not enter into consideration for the present survey; it may content itself, for its vindication, with the fact that the "system" as it is today, with the effects it has . . ., has changed, and will go on changing, the spiritual face of mankind almost to the point of unrecognisability.

NOTE

1.  The question of how far conversation is or is not possible at work, and why, the question of what qualities (professional and otherwise) achieve respect among fellow-workers, the direction of *ethical* value-judgments among the workers – all these and similar questions need to be studied in the way in which they are determined by the workshop "community" (which, basically, is not a community) and by the predominance (to be examined in terms of its degree) of purely *pecuniary* involvement with work.

# Organizational Discipline in the Factory

From *Economy and Society: An Outline of Interpretive Sociology*, eds Guenther Roth and Claus Wittich, trans. by H. H. Gerth and C. Wright Mills, revised by Guenther Roth and Claus Wittich, and Stephen Kalberg (Berkeley, CA: University of California Press, 1978), pp. 1149–50.

[R]*ational discipline* . . . eradicates not only personal charisma but also stratification by status groups, or at least transforms them in a rationalizing direction.

The content of discipline is nothing but the consistently rationalized, methodically prepared and exact execution of the received order, in which all personal criticism is unconditionally suspended and the actor is unswervingly and exclusively set for carrying out the command. In addition, this conduct under orders is uniform. The effects of this uniformity derive from its quality as social action within a mass structure. Those who obey are not necessarily a simultaneously obedient or an especially large mass, nor are they necessarily united in a specific locality. What is decisive for discipline is that the obedience of a plurality of men is rationally uniform. . . .

Discipline in general, like its most rational offspring, bureaucracy, is impersonal. Unfailingly neutral, it places itself at the disposal of every power that claims its service and knows how to promote it. This does not prevent it from being intrinsically alien to charisma as well as status honor, especially of a feudal sort. The berserk with manic seizures of frenzy and the feudal knight who measures swords with an equal adversary in order to gain personal honor are equally alien to discipline, the former because of the irrationality of his action, the latter because his attitude lacks matter-of-factness. Discipline puts the drill for the sake of habitual routinized skill in place of heroic ecstasy, loyalty, spirited enthusiasm for a leader and personal devotion to him, the cult of honor, or the cultivation of personal fitness as an art. Insofar as discipline appeals to firm ethical motives, it presupposes a sense of duty and conscience – "men of conscience" versus "men of honor" in Cromwell's terms. . . .

The sociologically decisive points, however, are, first, that everything is rationally calculated, especially those seemingly imponderable and irrational emotional factors – in principle, at least, calculable in the same manner as the yields of coal and iron deposits. Secondly, devotion is normally impersonal, oriented toward a purpose, a common cause, a rationally intended goal, not a person as such, however personally tinged devotion may be in the case of a fascinating leader. . . .

From *Economy and Society: An Outline of Interpretive Sociology*, eds Guenther Roth and Claus Wittich, trans. by H. H. Gerth and C. Wright Mills, revised by Guenther Roth and Claus Wittich (Berkeley, CA: University of California Press, 1978), p. 1156.

No special proof is necessary to show that military discipline is the ideal model for the modern capitalist factory, as it was for the ancient plantation. However, organizational discipline in the factory has a completely rational basis. With the help of suitable methods of measurement, the optimum profitability of the individual worker is calculated like that of any material means of production. On this basis, the American system of "scientific management" triumphantly proceeds with its rational conditioning and training of work performances, thus drawing the ultimate conclusions from the mechanization and discipline of the plant. The psycho-physical apparatus of man is completely adjusted to the demands of the outer world, the tools, the machines – in short, it is functionalized, and the individual is shorn of his natural rhythm as determined by his organism; in line with the demands of the work procedure, he is attuned to a new rhythm through the functional specialization of muscles and through the creation of an optimal economy of physical effort. This whole process of rationalization, in the factory as elsewhere, and especially in the bureaucratic state machine, parallels the centralization of the material implements of organization in the hands of the ruler. Thus, discipline inexorably takes over ever larger areas as the satisfaction of political and economic needs is increasingly rationalized. This universal phenomenon more and more restricts the importance of charisma and of individually differentiated conduct.

# chapter 6

# The "Specialist" and the "Cultivated Man"

## CERTIFICATES AND THE ORIGIN OF IDEAS IN SCIENCE

From *Economy and Society: An Outline of Interpretive Sociology*, eds Guenther Roth and Claus Wittich, trans. by H.H. Gerth and C. Wright Mills, revised by Guenther Roth and Claus Wittich (Berkeley, CA: University of California Press, 1978), pp. 998–1002.

... [T]he bureaucratization of all domination very strongly furthers the development of "rational matter-of-factness" and the personality type of the professional expert. This has far-reaching ramifications, but only one important element of the process can be briefly indicated here: its effect upon the nature of education and personal culture (*Erziehung und Bildung*).

Educational institutions on the European continent, especially the institutions of higher learning – the universities, as well as technical academics, business colleges, gymnasia, and other secondary schools –, are dominated and influenced by the need for the kind of "education" which is bred by the system of specialized examinations or tests of expertise (*Fachprüfungswesen*) increasingly indispensable for modern bureaucracies.

The "examination for expertise" in the modern sense was and is found also outside the strictly bureaucratic structures: today, for instance, in the so-called "free" professions of medicine and law, and in the guild-organized trades. . . .

Only the modern development of full bureaucratization brings the system of rational examinations for expertise irresistibly to the fore. The American Civil-Service Reform movement gradually imports expert training and specialized examinations into the United States; the examination system also advances into all other countries from its main (European) breeding ground, Germany. The increasing bureaucratization of administration enhances the importance of the specialized examination in England. In China, the attempt to replace the old semi-patrimonial bureaucracy by a modern bureaucracy brought the expert examination; it took the place of the former and quite differently structured system of examinations. The bureaucratization of capitalism, with its demand for expertly trained technicians, clerks, etc., carries such examinations all over the world.

This development is, above all, greatly furthered by the social prestige of the "patent of education" acquired through such specialized examinations, the more so since this prestige can again be turned to economic advantage. The role played in former days by the "proof of ancestry," as prerequisite for equality of birth, access to noble prebends and endowments and, wherever the nobility retained social power, for the qualification to state offices, is nowadays taken by the patent of education. The elaboration of the diplomas from universities, business and engineering colleges, and the universal clamor for the creation of further educational certificates in all fields serve the formation of a privileged stratum in bureaus and in offices. Such certificates support their holders' claims for connubium with the notables (in business offices, too, they raise hope for preferment with the boss's daughter), claims to be admitted into the circles that adhere to "codes of honor," claims for a "status-appropriate" salary instead of a wage according to performance, claims for assured advancement and old-age insurance, and, above all, claims to the monopolization of socially and economically advantageous positions. If we hear from all sides demands for the introduction of regulated curricula culminating in specialized examinations, the reason behind this is, of course, not a suddenly awakened "thirst for education," but rather the desire to limit the supply of candidates for these positions and to monopolize them for the holders of educational patents. For such monopolization, the "examination" is today the universal instrument – hence its irresistible advance. As the curriculum required for the acquisition of the patent of education requires considerable expenses and a long period of gestation, this striving implies a repression of talent (of the "charisma") in favor of property, for the intellectual costs of the educational patent are always low and decrease, rather than increase, with increasing volume. . . .

Social prestige based upon the advantage of schooling and education as such is by no means specific to bureaucracy. On the contrary. But educational prestige in other structures of domination rests upon substantially different foundations with respect to content. Expressed in slogans, the "cultivated man," rather than the "specialist," was the end sought by education and the basis of social esteem in the feudal, theocratic, and patrimonial structures of domination, in the English administration by notables, in the old Chinese patrimonial bureaucracy, as well as under the rule of demagogues in the Greek states during the so-called Democracy.

The term "cultivated man" is used here in a completely value-neutral sense; it is understood to mean solely that a quality of life conduct which *was held to be* "cultivated" was the goal of education, rather than a specialized training in some expertise. Such education may have been aimed at a knightly or at an ascetic type, at a literary type (as in China) or at a gymnastic-humanist type (as in Hellas), or at a conventional "gentleman" type of the Anglo-Saxon variety. A personality "cultivated" in this sense formed the educational ideal stamped by the structure of domination and the conditions of membership in the ruling stratum of the society in question. The qualification of this ruling stratum rested upon the possession of a "plus" of such *cultural quality* (in the quite variable and value-neutral sense of the term as used here), rather than upon a "plus" of expert knowledge. Military, theological and legal expertise was, of course, intensely cultivated at the same time. But the point of gravity in the Hellenic, in the medieval, as well as in the Chinese educational curriculum was formed by elements entirely different from those which were "useful" in a technical sense.

Behind all the present discussions about the basic questions of the educational system there lurks decisively the struggle of the "specialist" type of man against the older type of the "cultivated man," a struggle conditioned by the irresistibly expanding bureaucratization of all public and private relations of authority and by the ever-increasing importance of experts and specialized knowledge. This struggle affects the most intimate aspects of personal culture. . . .

From "Science as a Vocation," in *From Max Weber: Essays in Sociology*, eds and trans. Hans H. Gerth and C. Wright Mills (New York: Oxford University Press, 1946), pp. 134–6.

. . . I believe that actually you wish to hear of something else, namely, of the *inward* calling for science. In our time, the internal situation, in contrast to the organization of science as a vocation, is first of all conditioned by the facts that science has entered a phase of specialization previously unknown and that this will forever remain the case. Not only externally, but inwardly, matters stand at a point where the individual can acquire the sure consciousness of achieving something truly perfect in the field of science only in case he is a strict specialist.

All work that overlaps neighboring fields, such as we occasionally undertake and which the sociologists must necessarily undertake again and again, is burdened with the resigned realization that at best one provides the specialist with useful questions upon which he would not so easily hit from his own specialized point of view. One's own work must inevitably remain highly imperfect. Only by strict specialization can the scientific worker become fully conscious, for once and perhaps never again in his lifetime, that he has achieved something that will endure. A really definitive and good accomplishment is today always a specialized accomplishment. And whoever lacks the capacity to put on blinders, so to speak, and to come up to the idea that the fate of his soul depends upon whether or not he makes the correct conjecture at this passage of this manuscript may as well stay away from science. He will never have what one may call the "personal experience" of science. Without this strange intoxication, ridiculed by every outsider; without this passion, this "thousands of years must pass before you enter into life and thousands more wait in silence" – according to whether or not you succeed in making this conjecture; without this, you have *no* calling for science and you should do something else. For nothing is worthy of man as man unless he can pursue it with passionate devotion.

Yet it is a fact that no amount of such enthusiasm, however sincere and profound it may be, can compel a problem to yield scientific results. Certainly enthusiasm is a prerequisite of the "inspiration" which is decisive. Nowadays in circles of youth there is a widespread notion that science has become a problem in calculation, fabricated in laboratories or statistical filing systems just as "in a factory," a calculation involving only the cool intellect and not one's "heart and soul." First of all one must say that such comments lack all clarity about what goes on in a factory or in a laboratory. In both some idea has to occur to someone's mind, and it has to be a correct idea, if one is to accomplish anything worthwhile. And such intuition cannot be forced. It has nothing to do with any cold calculation. Certainly calculation is also an indispensable prerequisite. No sociologist, for instance, should think himself too good, even in his old age, to make tens of thousands of quite trivial computations in his head and perhaps for months at a time. One cannot with impunity try to transfer this task entirely to mechanical assistants if one wishes to figure something, even though the final result is often small indeed. But if no "idea" occurs to his mind about the direction of his computations and, during his computations, about the bearing of the emergent single results, then even this small result will not be yielded.

Normally such an "idea" is prepared only on the soil of very hard work, but certainly this is not always the case. Scientifically, a dilettante's idea may have the very same or even a greater bearing for science than that of a specialist. Many of our very best hypotheses and insights are due precisely to dilettantes. The dilettante differs from the expert, as Helmholtz has said of Robert Mayer, only in that he lacks a firm and reliable work procedure. Consequently he is usually not in the position to control, to estimate, or to exploit the idea in its bearings. The idea is not a substitute for work; and work, in turn, cannot substitute for or compel an idea, just as little as enthusiasm can. Both, enthusiasm and work, and above all both of them *jointly*, can entice the idea.

Ideas occur to us when they please, not when it pleases us. The best ideas do indeed occur to one's mind in the way in which Ihering describes it: when smoking a cigar on the sofa; or as Helmholtz states of himself with scientific exactitude: when taking a walk on a slowly ascending street; or in a similar way. In any case, ideas come when we do not expect them, and not when we are brooding and searching at our desks. Yet ideas would certainly not come to mind had we not brooded at our desks and searched for answers with passionate devotion.

However this may be, the scientific worker has to take into his bargain the risk that enters into all scientific work: Does an "idea" occur or does it not? He may be an excellent worker and yet never have had any valuable idea of his own. It is a grave error to believe that this is so only in science, and that things for instance in a business office are different from a laboratory. A merchant or a big industrialist without "business imagination," that is, without ideas or ideal intuitions, will for all his life remain a man who would better have remained a clerk or a technical official. He will never be truly creative in organization. Inspiration in the field of science by no means plays any greater role, as academic conceit fancies, than it does in the field of mastering problems of practical life by a modern entrepreneur. On the other hand, and this also is often misconstrued, inspiration plays no less a role in science than it does in the realm of art. It is a childish notion to think that a mathematician attains any scientifically valuable results by sitting at his desk with a ruler, calculating machines or other mechanical means. The mathematical imagination of a Weierstrass is naturally quite differently oriented in meaning and result than is the imagination of an artist, and differs basically in quality. But the psychological processes do not differ. Both are frenzy (in the sense of Plato's "mania") and "inspiration."

# chapter 7

# Old and New Civilizations

## CONTRASTING RURAL SOCIAL STRUCTURES IN GERMANY AND THE UNITED STATES

From "Capitalism and Rural Society in Germany," in *From Max Weber: Essays in Sociology*, eds and trans. Hans H. Gerth and C. Wright Mills (New York: Oxford University Press, 1946), pp. 364–5.

... The power of tradition inevitably predominates in agriculture; it creates and maintains types of rural population on the European Continent which do not exist in a new country, such as the United States; to these types belongs, first of all, the European peasant.

The European peasant is totally different from the farmer of England or of America. The English farmer today is sometimes quite a remarkable entrepreneur and producer for the market; almost always he has rented his estate. The American farmer is an agriculturist who has usually acquired, by purchase or by being the first settler, the land as his own property; but sometimes he rents it. In America the farmer produces for the market. The market is older than the producer in America. The European peasant of the old type was a man who, in most instances, inherited the land and who produced primarily for his own wants. In Europe the market is younger than the producer....

From "Capitalism and Rural Society in Germany," in *From Max Weber: Essays in Sociology*, eds and trans. Hans H. Gerth and C. Wright Mills (New York: Oxford University Press, 1946), pp. 369–72.

... Even in America, with its democratic traditions handed down by Puritanism as an everlasting heirloom, the [Civil War] victory over the planters' aristocracy was difficult and was gained with great political and social sacrifices. But in countries with old civilizations, matters are much more complicated. For there the struggle between the power of historical notions and the pressure of capitalist interests summon certain social forces to battle as adversaries of bourgeois capitalism. In the United States such forces were partly unknown, or stood partly on the side of the North. A few remarks concerning this may be made here.

In the countries of old civilization and limited possibilities for economic expansion, money-making and its representatives necessarily play a considerably smaller social role than in a country that is still new. The importance of the stratum of state officials is and must be much greater in Europe than in the United States. The much more complicated social organization makes a host of specially trained officials, employed for life, indispensable in Europe. In the United States only a much smaller number of them will exist, even after the movement of civil-service reform shall have attained all its aims. The jurist and administrative official in Germany, in spite of his shorter and more intensive education in preparation for the university, is about thirty-five years old when his time of preparation and his unsalaried activity is completed and he obtains a salaried office. Therefore, he can come only from wealthy circles; he is trained to unsalaried or low-salaried service and can find his reward for service only in the high social standing of his vocation. A character is thus stamped on him which is far from the interests of money-makers and which places him on the side of the adversaries of their dominion. . . .

The church belongs to the conservative forces in European countries; first, the Roman Catholic Church, which, in Europe, even on account of the multitude of its followers, is a power of quite different importance and character than it possesses in Anglo-Saxon countries; but also the Lutheran Church. Both of these churches support the peasant, with his conservative way of life, against the dominion of urban rationalist culture. The rural co-operative movement stands, to a great extent, under the guidance of clergymen, who are the only ones capable of leadership in the rural districts. Ecclesiastic, political, and economic points of view are here intermingled. In Belgium, the rural co-operatives are a means of the clerical party in their conflict against the socialists; the latter are supported by the consumers' unions and trade unions. In Italy, almost nobody finds credit with certain co-operatives unless he presents his confessional certificate. Likewise, a landed aristocracy finds strong backing in the church, although the Catholic Church is, in social regards, more democratic nowadays than formerly. The church is pleased with patriarchal labor relations because contrary to the purely commercial relations which capitalism creates, they are of a personal human character. The church holds the sentiment that the relation between a lord and a serf, rather than the bare commercial conditions created by the labor market, can be developed and penetrated ethically. Deep, historically conditioned contrasts, which have always separated Catholicism and Lutheranism from Calvinism, strengthen this anti-capitalistic attitude of the European churches.

Finally, in an old civilized country, the "aristocracy of education," as it likes to be called, is a definite stratum of the population without personal interests in economics; hence it views the triumphal procession of capitalism more skeptically and criticizes more sharply than can naturally and justly be the case in a country such as the United States.

As soon as intellectual and esthetic education has become a profession, its representatives are bound by an inner affinity to all the carriers of ancient social culture, because for them, as for their prototypes, their profession cannot and must not be a source of heedless gain. They look distrustfully upon the abolition of traditional conditions of the community and upon the annihilation of all the innumerable ethical and esthetic values which cling to these traditions. They doubt if the dominion of capital would give better, more lasting guaranties to personal liberty and to the development of intellectual, esthetic, and social culture which they represent than the aristocracy of the past has given. They want to be ruled only by persons whose social culture they consider equivalent to their own; therefore, they prefer the rule of the economically independent aristocracy to the rule of the professional politician. Thus, it happens nowadays in the civilized countries – a peculiar and, in more than one respect, a serious fact – that the representatives of the highest interests of culture turn their eyes back, and, with deep antipathy standing opposed to the inevitable development of capitalism, refuse to co-operate in rearing the structure of the future. Moreover, the disciplined masses of workingmen created by capitalism are naturally inclined to unite in a class party, if new districts for settlement are no longer available, and if the workingman is conscious of being forced to remain inevitably a proletarian as long as he lives, which is bound to come about sooner or later also in [the United States], or has already come about. The progress of capitalism is not hemmed in by this; the workingman's chances to gain political power are insignificant. Yet they weaken the political power of the bourgeoisie and strengthen the power of the bourgeois' aristocratic adversaries. The downfall of German bourgeois liberalism is based upon the joint effectiveness of these motives.

Thus, in [European] countries, where a rural community, aristocratically differentiated, exists, a complex of social and political problems arises. An American finds it difficult to understand the importance of agrarian questions on the European continent, especially in Germany, even in German politics. He will arrive at entirely wrong conclusions if he does not keep before his eyes these great complexes. A peculiar combination of motives is effective in these old countries and explains the deviation of European from American conditions. Besides the necessity for strong military preparedness, there are essentially two factors: *First*, something which never existed in the greater part of America, which may be designated as "backwardness," that is, the influence of a gradually disappearing older form of rural society.

The second set of circumstances which have not yet become effective in America, but to which this country – so elated by every million of increased population and by every rise of the valuation of the land – will unavoidably be exposed exactly as Europe has been, is the density of population, the high value of the land, the stronger differentiation of occupations, and the peculiar conditions resulting therefrom.

Under all these conditions, the rural community of old civilized countries faces capitalism which is joined with the influence of great political and social powers only known to old countries. Even today under these circumstances, capitalism produces effects in Europe which can be produced in America only in the future. In consequence of all those influences, European capitalism, at least on the Continent, has a peculiar authoritarian stamp, which contrasts with the citizen's equality of rights and which is usually distinctly felt by Americans. . . .

From "Capitalism and Rural Society in Germany," in *From Max Weber: Essays in Sociology*, eds and trans. Hans H. Gerth and C. Wright Mills (New York: Oxford University Press, 1946), p. 383.

. . . For while it is correct to say that the burden of historical tradition does not overwhelm the United States, and that the problems originating from the power of tradition do not exist here, yet the effects of the power of capitalism are the stronger, and will, sooner or later, further the development of land monopolies. When the land has become costly enough to secure a certain rent; when the accumulation of large fortunes has reached a still higher point than today; when, at the same time, the possibility of gaining proportionate profits by constant, new investments in trade and industry has been diminished so that the "captains of industry," as has occurred everywhere in the world, begin to strive for hereditary preservation of their possessions instead of new investments bringing both profit and risk – then, indeed, the desire of the capitalist families to form a "nobility" will arise, probably not in form though in fact. The representatives of capitalism will not content themselves any longer with such harmless play as pedigree studies and the numerous pranks of social exclusiveness which are so startling to the foreigner. Only when capital has arrived at this course and begins to monopolize the land to a great extent, will a great rural social question arise in the United States, a question which cannot be cut with the sword, as was the slave question. . . .

From "Capitalism and Rural Society in Germany," in *From Max Weber: Essays in Sociology*, eds and trans. Hans H. Gerth and C. Wright Mills (New York: Oxford University Press, 1946), p. 385.

The United States . . . has no old aristocracy; hence the tensions caused by the contrast between authoritarian tradition and the purely commercial character of modern economic conditions do not exist. Rightly it celebrates the purchase of this immense territory, in whose center we are here [St Louis], as the real historical seal imprinted upon its democratic institutions; without this acquisition, with powerful and warlike neighbors at its side, it would be forced to wear the coat of mail like ourselves, who constantly keep in the drawer of our desks the march order in case of war. But on the other hand, the greater part of the problems for whose solution we are now working will approach America within only a few generations. The way in which they will be solved will determine the character of the future culture of this continent. It was perhaps never before in history made so easy for any nation to become a great civilized power as for the American people. Yet, according to human calculation, it is also the last time, as long as the history of mankind shall last, that such conditions for a free and great development will be given; the areas of free soil are now vanishing everywhere in the world.

# part 4

# Stratification and Inequality

## Introduction

Max Weber's essay, "Class, Status, Party," is universally viewed as offering a strong criticism of Marx's explanation for inequality (Chapter 8). It introduced ideal types into sociology – status and status groups (*Stand*) – that became widely influential. To this day they are used as pivotal concepts for the analysis of a wide variety of social phenomena. Weber's wide-ranging analytic treatment of inequality in groups can briefly be summarized.

Following Marx, Weber is convinced that ownership centrally influences one's class situation and the "distribution of power in groups" generally. What is basic is property and lack of property; once defined, "naked economic power" and "naked possession," or lack thereof, chart out a person's "specific life chances." Although private property constitutes the single foundation for social stratification for Marx, Weber contends that power is distributed pluralistically: ownership is important, he recognizes, but so are status and "parties."

One's "status situation" involves a "social estimation of honor." Here claims to social esteem, and acknowledgment of it, orient social action. Ways of conducting life, which rest upon discrete socialization processes and hereditary and occupational prestige, come to the fore (1968a, pp. 305–6; see also 1946e, p. 300).

A status group appears when persons share a lifestyle, consumption patterns, common conventions, specific notions of honor and, conceivably, economic and particular status monopolies. Stratification by status always implies the monopolization by some groups of "ideal and material goods or opportunities," as well as, to the same extent, social distance and exclusiveness. Status differences become apparent whenever social interaction is restricted or lacking. Distinguished families throughout the world permit courtship of their daughters only by status peers and stigmatize the parvenu, and members of "old families," such as the descendants of the Pilgrim Fathers, Pocahontas, and the First Families of Virginia, have frequently cultivated a variety of techniques of exclusiveness. The marketplace, on the contrary, rather than cultivating personal distinctions in respect to social honor, levels persons down to their monetary relationship to the market.

These ideal types – classes and status groups – differ in a further significant manner, according to Weber: their capacity to call forth social action varies. Here his critique of Marx is also evident. Weber is convinced that a shared situation in terms of property ownership (or lack thereof) does not itself call forth the orientation of persons to each other and common social action, as Marx believed. Only "mass behavior" – Weber's term for a type of action similar to imitative and reactive action that lacks, unlike *social* action, a meaningful orientation to others (see above, pp. 8–13) – may result when workers are discontened. A transformation of complaints into collective activity may *not* take place as a consequence of similar life chances grounded in property; "grumbling" alone may occur among those without property. Whether social action crystallizes, and whether associations promoting concerted activities and "class action" arise, depend on a series of further forces, Weber insists, such as "general cultural conditions," the degree of contrasts – and their recognizability – across classes, and "the transparency of the connections between the causes and the consequences of the 'class situation' " (p. 154).

Status situations call forth social action with far greater likelihood, he argues. Indeed, unlike classes, status groups, owing to the evaluation they imply of one's own situation relative to that of others as well as a subjective awareness of common conventions, values, and styles of life, "are normally groups," albeit at times amorphous. At other times status groups become firm and even closed in defense of "ideal and material interests." They have, Weber is convinced, throughout history stood against "the market principle" and hindered its development.

Viewed through a broad comparative-historical lens, the dominant mode of stratification varies, Weber argues against Marx's universal postulate, across civilizations and epochs. A "stratification by status" permeated the societies of Antiquity and the Middle Ages in particular, he recalls, effectively restricting free market competition, as well as class conflict and the unmediated orientation to material interests. Guilds, for example, now and then in the Middle Ages struggled more fervently over questions of precedence in festival processions than over economic issues (see 1958, pp. 34, 125). In the modern West, on the other hand, class situation has become more central (see 1946e, p. 301). After all, the origin of status groups is "normally co-determined by economic forces" when high status assumes an ostentatious lifestyle. Attending once again to a background milieu, Weber notes that stratification by status is more likely whenever relationships of production and distribution are stable, and naked class situation becomes prominent in eras of great technological and economic change. When the tempo of the transformations recedes, a reinvigoration of status structures occurs and social honor becomes more salient.

The ideal types "class" and "status" also render succinctly Weber's position in regard to the course of history: it can never be depicted accurately as an evolutionary line of linear progress. As captured by ideal types, groups "close" – and indeed may become quite rigid as ideal and material interests collapse to sustain them. Technological innovations, population changes, charismatic figures, and even the material interests of a powerful bourgeoisie may be unable to alter these groupings. Moreover, "class" and "status" demonstrate vividly how groups – how they originate and how they interact in fluctuating relationships of antagonism and affinity – stand at the center of Weber's sociology. This level of analysis calls into question directly the use in sociology of global and non-empirical concepts – "class conflict" and "society," for example – as heuristic tools, as well as all attempts to proclaim, as empirically accurate, overarching historical trends.

Weber's refusal to formulate such generalities is apparent throughout "Class, Status, Party," though in particular in respect to three themes. First, he charts out on several occasions the ways in which laws, and even legal monopolies over official positions, may develop from the conventions indigenous to a status group – or may not, depending upon the influence of the status group and the social context of facilitating and opposing forces. Cases must be examined on an individual basis. Second, in respect to the origins of status groups, questions must be asked regarding whether they arose from ethnic groups, class situation, or political associations, for example. Clear general conclusions cannot be drawn. Third, in certain cases status groups may develop into castes, Weber sees, or much firmer groupings rooted in and sustained by religious rituals. Whether this occurs, as in India, depends also upon arrays of historical developments rather than general evolutionary patterns.

Nonetheless, in this essay several generalizations *are* formulated – that is, as ideal types. Rather than sweeping and wide-ranging, they remain distinctly rooted in the milieu within which each status group is embedded. For example, the dignity of people in "negatively privileged status groups" arises, Weber contends, from a vision of their future situation, whereas the dignity of "positively privileged status groups" arises out of a sense of their "being" and social honor in the present; status groups high in prestige abhor physical labor; and the stigmatization of the parvenu is greater where the status order is firm.

Finally, Weber emphasizes in "Class, Status, Party" that the distribution of power in groups is influenced not only by the economic order (classes) and the social order (status groups), but also by "parties." Parties are organized groups oriented toward the acquisition of power and the attempt systematically to reach this goal. People are brought together within groupings operating under a set of statutes or laws – "they are associated" – in pursuit of this aim.

Two short essays on German society in Weber's time round out this Part. Both vividly capture how, for him, inequality can be conceptualized by class and status. In "National Character and the Junkers" (Chapter 9) Weber depicts Germany as a nation without a viable aristocracy. Moreover, the conventions of its most prestigious stratum, the Junkers in Prussia, "are not suited to mold and unify the nation"; they also cannot be "democratized." The importance of status groups for a nation's political culture as a whole is then delineated, not least through a number of contrasts with England and Spain. Weber also draws attention to the dominant mode of upward mobility in Germany. Finally, he notes that "political democratization" (the right to vote and to elect parliaments, etc.) must be kept analytically separate from "social democratization" (social egalitarianism). He sees "new aristocracies" as arising in a heretofore quite egalitarian society, namely, the United States.

The final selection, from *Zur Politik im Weltkrieg* (Chapter 10), further illustrates Weber's thinking on inequality. Because it is taken from his political writings, in places it uses a more forceful language than is found in his sociology texts. Writing during World War I, he proposes the adoption of universal suffrage for the election of a parliament in Germany. Only such a parliament will serve as a counterweight to growing social and economic inequality, he contends.

# chapter 8

# The Distribution of Power Within the Group

## CLASS, STATUS, PARTY

From *Economy and Society: An Outline of Interpretive Sociology*, eds Guenther Roth and Claus Wittich, trans. H. H. Gerth and C. Wright Mills, revised by Guenther Roth and Claus Wittich, and Stephen Kalberg. All subheadings by H. H. Gerth and C. Wright Mills (Berkeley, CA: University of California Press, 1978), pp. 926–39.

A. ECONOMICALLY DETERMINED POWER AND THE STATUS ORDER. The formation of every legal order directly influences the distribution of power, economic or otherwise, within its respective group. This is true of all legal orders and not only that of the state. In general, we understand by "power" the chance of a man or a number of men to realize their own will in a social action even against the resistance of others who are participating in the action.

"Economically conditioned" power is not, of course, identical with "power" as such. On the contrary, the emergence of economic power may be the consequence of power existing on other grounds. Man does not strive for power only in order to enrich himself economically. Power, including economic power, may be valued for its own sake. Very frequently the striving for power is also conditioned by the social honor it entails. Not all power, however, entails social honor: The typical American [Political] Boss, as well as the typical big speculator, deliberately relinquishes social honor. Quite generally, "mere economic" power, and especially "naked" money power, is by no means a recognized basis of social honor. Nor is power the only basis of social honor. Indeed, social honor, or prestige, may even be the basis of economic power, and very frequently has been. Power, as well as honor, may be guaranteed by the legal order, but, at least normally, it is not their primary source. The legal order is rather an additional factor that enhances the chance to hold power or honor; but it can not always secure them.

The way in which social honor is distributed in a large group between groups typically participating in its distribution we call the "social order." The social order and the economic order are related in a similar manner to the legal order. However, the economic order merely defines the way in which economic goods and services are distributed and used. Of course the status order is strongly influenced by it, and in turn reacts upon it.

Now "classes," "status groups," and "parties" are phenomena of the distribution of power within a large group.

B. DETERMINATION OF CLASS SITUATION BY MARKET SITUATION. In our terminology, "classes" are not groups; they merely represent possible, and frequent, bases for social action. We may speak of a "class" when (1) a number of people have in common a specific causal component of their life chances, insofar as (2) this component is represented exclusively by economic interests in the possession of goods and opportunities for income, and (3) is represented under the conditions of the commodity or labor markets. This is "class situation."

It is the most elemental economic fact that the way in which the disposition over material property is distributed among a plurality of people, meeting competitively in the market for the purpose of exchange, in itself creates specific life chances. The mode of distribution, in accord with the law of marginal utility, excludes the non-wealthy from competing for highly valued goods; it favors the owners and, in fact, gives to them a monopoly to acquire such goods. Other things being equal, the mode of distribution monopolizes the opportunities for profitable deals for all those who, provided with goods, do not necessarily have to exchange them. It increases, at least generally, their power in the price struggle with those who, being propertyless, have nothing to offer but their labor or the resulting products, and who are compelled to get rid of these products in order to subsist at all. The mode of distribution gives to the propertied a monopoly on the possibility of transferring property from the sphere of use as "wealth" to the sphere of "capital," that is, it gives them the entrepreneurial function and all chances to share directly or indirectly in returns on capital. All this holds true within the area in which pure market conditions prevail. "Property" and "lack of property" are, therefore, the basic categories of all class situations. It does not matter whether these two categories become effective in the struggles over prices or in competition generally.

Within these categories, however, class situations are further differentiated: on the one hand, according to the kind of property that is usable for returns; and, on the other hand, according to the kind of services that can be offered in the market. Ownership of dwellings; workshops; warehouses; stores; agriculturally usable land in large or small holdings – a quantitative difference with possibly qualitative consequences; ownership of mines; cattle; men (slaves); disposition over mobile instruments of production, or capital goods of all sor        ⁀        iects that can easily be exchanged for money; ⟨        of one's own labor or of others' labor differing according to their various distances from consumability; disposition over transferable monopolies of any kind – all these distinctions differentiate the class situations of the propertied just as does the "meaning" which they can give to the use of property, especially to property which has money equivalence. Accordingly, the propertied, for instance, may belong to the class of rentiers or to the class of entrepreneurs.

Those who have no property but who offer services are differentiated just as much according to their kinds of services as according to the way in which they make use of these services, in a continuous or discontinuous relation to a recipient. But common to the concept of class is always that the kind of chance in the *market* is the decisive moment which presents a shared condition for the individual's fate. "Class situation" is, in this sense, ultimately "market situation." The effect of naked possession *per se*, which among cattle breeders gives over the non-owning slave or serf into the power of the cattle owner, is only a fore-runner of real "class" formation. However, in the cattle loan and in the naked severity of the law of debts in such groups for the first time mere "possession" as such emerges as decisive for the fate of the individual; this is much in contrast to crop-raising groups, which are based on labor. The creditor-debtor relation becomes the basis of "class situations" first in the cities, where a "credit market," however primitive, with rates of interest increasing according to the extent of need and factual monopolization of lending in the hands of a plutocracy could develop. Therewith "class struggles" begin.

Those men whose fate is not determined by the chance of using goods or services for themselves on the market, e.g., slaves, are not, however, a class in the technical sense of the term. They are, rather, a status group.

C. SOCIAL ACTION FLOWING FROM CLASS INTEREST. According to this terminology, the factor that creates "class" is unambiguously economic interest, and indeed, only those interests involved in the existence of the market. Nevertheless, the concept of class-interest is an ambiguous one: even as an empirical concept it is ambiguous as soon as one understands by it something other than the factual direction of interests following with a certain probability from the class situation for a certain average of those people subjected to the class situation. The class situation and other circumstances remaining the same, the direction in which the individual worker, for instance, is likely to pursue his interests may vary widely, according to whether he is constitutionally qualified for the task at hand to a high, to an average, or to a low degree. In the same way, the direction of interests may vary according to whether or not social action of a larger or smaller portion of those commonly affected by the class situation, or even an association among them, e.g., a trade union, has grown out of the class situation, from which the individual may expect promising results for himself. The emergence of an association or even of *social* action from a common class situation is by no means a universal phenomenon.

The class situation may be restricted in its efforts to the generation of essentially *similar* reactions, that is to say, within our terminology, of "mass behavior." However, it may not even have this result. Furthermore, often merely amorphous social action emerges. For example, the "grumbling" of workers known in ancient Oriental ethics: The moral disapproval of the work-master's conduct, which in its practical significance was probably equivalent to an increasingly typical phenomenon of precisely the latest industrial development, namely, the slowdown of laborers by virtue of tacit agreement. The degree to which "social action" and possibly associations emerge from the "mass behavior" of the members of a class is linked to general cultural conditions, especially to those of an intellectual sort. It is also linked to the extent of the contrasts that have already evolved, and is especially linked to the *transparency* of the connections between the causes and the consequences of the "class situation." For however different life chances may be, this fact in itself, according to all experience, by no means gives birth to "class action" (social action by the members of a class). For that, the real conditions and the results of the class situation must be distinctly recognizable. For only then the contrast of life chances can be felt not as an absolutely given fact to be accepted, but as a resultant from either (1) the given distribution of property, or (2) the structure of the concrete economic order. It is only then that people may react against the class structure not only through acts of intermittent and irrational protest, but in the form of rational association. There have been "class situations" of the first category (1), of a specifically naked and transparent sort, in the urban centers of Antiquity and during the Middle Ages; especially then when great fortunes were accumulated by factually monopolized trading in local industrial products or in foodstuffs; furthermore, under certain conditions, in the rural economy of the most diverse periods, when agriculture was increasingly exploited in a profit-making manner. The most important historical example of the second category (2) is the class situation of the modern proletariat.

D. TYPES OF CLASS STRUGGLE. Thus every class may be the carrier of any one of the innumerable possible forms of class action, but this is not necessarily so. In any case, a class does not in itself constitute a group. To treat "class" conceptually as being equivalent to "group" leads to distortion. That men in the same class situation regularly react in mass actions to such tangible situations as economic ones in the direction of those interests that are most adequate to their average number is an important and after all simple fact for the understanding of historical events. However, this fact must not lead to that kind of pseudo-scientific operation with the concepts of "class" and "class interests" which is so frequent these days and which has found its most classic expression in the statement of a talented author to the effect that the individual may be in error concerning his interests but that the "class" is "infallible" about its interests.

If classes as such "are" not groups, nevertheless class situations emerge only on the basis of social action. However, social action that brings forth class situations is not basically action among members of the identical class; rather it is social action *between* members of different classes. Social actions that directly determine the class situation of the worker and the entrepreneur are: the labor market, the commodities market, and the capitalistic enterprise. But, in its turn, the existence of a capitalistic enterprise presupposes that a very specific kind of social action exists to protect the possession of goods *per se*, and especially the power of individuals to dispose, in principle freely, over the means of production: a certain kind of legal order. Each kind of class situation, and above all when it rests upon the power of property *per se*, will become most clearly efficacious when all other determinants of reciprocal relations are, as far as possible, eliminated in their significance. It is in this way that the use of the power of property in the market obtains its most sovereign importance.

Now status groups hinder the consistent carrying through of the sheer market principle. In the present context they are of interest only from this one point of view. Before we briefly consider them, note that not much of a general nature can be said about the more specific kinds of antagonism between classes (in our meaning of the term). The great shift, which has been going on continuously in the past, and up to our times, may be summarized, although at a cost of some precision: the struggle in which class situations are effective has progressively shifted from consumption credit toward, first, competitive struggles in the commodity market and then toward wage disputes on the labor market. The "class struggles" of Antiquity – to the extent that they were genuine class struggles and not struggles between status groups – were initially carried on by peasants and perhaps also artisans threatened by debt bondage and struggling against urban creditors. . . .

E. STATUS HONOR. In contrast to classes, *Stände* (*status groups*) are normally groups. They are, however, often of an amorphous kind. In contrast to the purely economically determined "class situation," we wish to designate as *status situation* every typical component of the life of people that is determined by a specific, positive or negative, social estimation of *honor*. This honor may be connected with any quality shared by a plurality, and, of course, it can be knit to a class situation: class distinctions intertwine in the most varied ways with status distinctions. Property as such does not always lead to status recognition, but in the long run it does, and with extraordinary regularity. In the subsistence economy of neighborhood associations, it is often simply the richest who is the "chieftain." However, this often is only an honorific preference. In the so-called pure modern "democracy," that is, one devoid of any expressly ordered status privileges for individuals, it may be, for example, that only the families coming under approximately the same tax class dance with one another. This illustration is reported of certain smaller Swiss cities. But status honor must not necessarily be linked with a "class situation." On the contrary, it normally stands in sharp opposition to the pretensions of sheer property.

Both propertied and propertyless people can belong to the same status group, and frequently they do with very tangible consequences. This "equality" of social esteem may, however, in the long run become quite precarious. The equality of status among American gentlemen, for instance, is expressed by the fact that outside the subordination determined by the different functions of business, it would be considered strictly repugnant – wherever the old tradition still prevails – if even the richest boss, while playing billiards or cards in his club would not treat his clerk as in every sense fully his equal in birthright, but would bestow upon him the condescending status-conscious "benevolence" which the German boss can never banish from his demeanor. This is one of the most important reasons why in America the German clubs have never been able to attain the attraction that the American clubs have.

In content, status honor is normally expressed by the fact that above all else a specific *style of life* is expected from all those who wish to belong to the circle. Linked with this expectation are restrictions on social intercourse (that is, socializing which is not subservient to economic or any other purposes). These restrictions may confine normal marriages to within the status circle and may lead to complete endogamous closure. Whenever this is not a merely isolated and socially irrelevant imitation of another style of life, but consensual action of this closing character, the status development is under way.

In its characteristic form, stratification by status groups on the basis of conventional styles of life is developing at the present time in the United States out of its long-standing democracy. For example, only the resident of a certain street ("the Street") is considered as belonging to "society" and as an appropriate social partner, and is visited and invited. Above all, this stratification develops in such a way as to make for strict submission to the fashion that is dominant at a given time in "society." This submission to fashion also exists among men in America to a degree unknown in Germany; it appears as an indication of the fact that a given man puts forward a *claim* to qualify as a gentleman. This submission decides, at least *prima facie*, that he will be treated as such. And this recognition becomes just as important for his employment chances in swank establishments, and above all, for social acceptance and marriage with "esteemed" families, as the qualification for dueling among Germans.

As for the rest, status honor is usurped by certain families resident for a long time, and, of course, correspondingly wealthy (e.g. F.F.V., the First Families of Virginia), or by the actual or alleged descendants of the "Indian Princess" Pocahontas, of the Pilgrim fathers, or of the Knicker-bockers, the members of almost inaccessible sects and all sorts of circles setting themselves apart by means of any other characteristics and badges. In this case stratification is purely conventional and rests largely on usurpation (as does normally almost all status honor in its beginning). But the road to legal privilege, positive or negative, is easily traveled as soon as a certain stratification of the social order has in fact been "lived in" and has achieved stability as a consequence of a stable distribution of economic power.

F. ETHNIC SEGREGATION AND CASTE. Where the consequences have been realized to their full extent, the status group evolves into a closed caste. Status distinctions are then guaranteed not merely by conventions and laws, but also by religious rituals. This occurs in such a way that every physical contact with a member of any caste that is considered to be lower by the members of a higher caste is considered as making for a ritualistic impurity and a stigma which must be expiated by a religious act. In addition, individual castes develop in part quite distinct cults and gods.

In general, however, the status structure reaches such extreme consequences only where there are underlying differences which are held to be "ethnic." The caste is, indeed, the normal form in which ethnic groups that believe in blood relationship and exclude exogamous marriage and social intercourse are "associated" with one another. Such a caste situation is part of the phenomenon of pariah peoples and is found all over the world. These people form social groups, acquire specific occupational traditions of handicrafts or of other arts, and cultivate a belief in their ethnic commonality. They live in a diaspora strictly segregated from all personal socializing, except that of an unavoidable sort, and their situation is legally precarious. Yet, by virtue of their economic indispensability, they are tolerated, indeed frequently privileged, and they live interspersed in political groups. The Jews are the most impressive historical example.

A status segregation grown into a "caste" differs in its structure from a mere "ethnic" segregation: the caste structure transforms the horizontal and unconnected coexistences of ethnically segregated groups into a vertical social hierarchy of super- and subordination. Correctly formulated: a comprehensive association integrates the ethnically divided groups into social action that is specifically political. They differ precisely in this way: ethnic co-existence, based on mutual repulsion and disdain, allows each ethnic group to consider its own honor as the highest one; the caste structure brings about a social subordination and an acknowledgement of "more honor" in favor of the privileged caste and status groups. This is due to the fact that in the caste structure ethnic distinctions as such have become "functional" distinctions within the political association (warriors, priests, artisans that are politically important for war and for building, and so on). But even pariah peoples who are most despised (for example, the Jews) are usually apt to continue cultivating the belief in their own specific "honor," a belief that is equally unique to ethnic and to status groups.

However, with the negatively privileged status groups the sense of dignity – namely, the subjective influence of social honor and expectations regarding social conventions that the positively privileged status group raises for the deportment of its members – takes a different turn. The sense of dignity that characterizes positively privileged status groups is naturally related to their "being" which does not transcend itself, that is, it is related to their "beauty and competence" (καλοκἀγαθία). Their kingdom is "of this world." They live for the present and by exploiting their great past. The sense of dignity of the negatively privileged strata naturally refers to a future lying beyond the present, whether it is of this life or of another. In other words, it must be nurtured by the belief in a providential mission and by a belief in a specific honor before God, The chosen people's dignity is nurtured by a belief either that in the beyond "the last will be the first," or that in this life a Messiah will appear to bring forth into the light of the world which has cast them out the hidden honor of the pariah people. This simple state of affairs, and not the resentment which is so strongly emphasized in Nietzsche's much-admired construction in the *Genealogy of Morals*, is the source of the religiosity cultivated by pariah status groups; moreover, resentment applies only to a limited extent; for one of Nietzsche's main examples, Buddhism, it is not at all applicable.

For the rest, the development of status groups from ethnic segregations is by no means the normal occurrence. On the contrary. Since objective "racial differences" are by no means behind every subjective sentiment of an "ethnic" community, the question of an ultimately racial foundation of status stratification is rightly a question of the concrete individual case. Very frequently a status group is instrumental in the production of a thoroughbred anthropological type. Certainly status is to a high degree effective in producing groups, for it selects personally qualified individuals (e.g. the knighthood selects those who are fit for warfare, physically and psychically). But such selection is far from being the only, or the predominant, way in which status groups are formed; political membership or class situation has at all times been at least as frequently decisive. And today the class situation is by far the predominant factor. After all, the possibility of a style of life expected for members of a status group is normally co-determined economically.

G. STATUS PRIVILEGES. For all practical purposes, stratification by status goes hand in hand with a monopolization of ideal and material goods or opportunities in a manner we have come to know as typical. Besides the specific status honor, which always rests upon distance and exclusiveness, honorific preferences may consist of the privilege of wearing special costumes, of eating special dishes taboo to others, of carrying arms (which is most obvious in its consequences), and the right to be a dilettante in artistic expression (playing of certain musical instruments, for example). However, monopolies of material goods and opportunities provide the most effective motives for the exclusiveness of a status group; although in themselves rarely sufficient, almost always they come into play to some extent. Within a status circle there is the question of intermarriage: the interest of the families in the monopolization of potential bridegrooms is at least of equal importance and is parallel to the interest in the monopolization of daughters. The daughters of the members must be provided for.

With an increased closure of the status group, the conventional preferential opportunities for special employment grow into a legal monopoly of special offices for the members. Certain goods become objects for monopolization by status groups, typically, entailed estates, and frequently also the possession of serfs or bondsmen and, finally, special trades. This monopolization occurs positively when the status group is *exclusively* entitled to own and to manage them; and negatively when, in order to maintain its specific way of life, the status group must *not* own and manage them. For the decisive role of a "style of life" in status "honor" means that status groups are the specific bearers of all "conventions".

In whatever way it may be manifest, all "stylization" of life either originates in status groups or is at least conserved by them. Even if the principles of status conventions differ greatly, they reveal certain typical traits, especially among the most privileged strata. Quite generally, among privileged status groups there is a status disqualification that operates against the performance of common physical labor. This disqualification is now "setting in" in America against the old tradition of esteem for labor. Very frequently every rational economic pursuit, and especially entrepreneurial activity, is looked upon as a disqualification of status. Artistic and literary activity is also considered degrading work as soon as it is exploited for income, or at least when it is connected with hard physical exertion. An example is the sculptor working like a mason in his dusty smock as over against the painter in his salon-like studio and those forms of musical practice that are acceptable to the status group.

H. ECONOMIC CONDITIONS AND EFFECTS OF STATUS STRATIFICATION. The frequent disqualification of the "gainfully employed" as such is a direct result of the principle of status stratification, and of course, of this principle's opposition to a distribution of power regulated exclusively through the market. These two factors operate along with various individual ones, which will be touched upon below.

We have seen above that the market and its processes know no "regard to the person": "matter-of-fact" interests dominate it. It knows nothing of honor. The status order means precisely the reverse: stratification in terms of honor and styles of life specific to status groups as such. The status order would be threatened at its very root if mere economic acquisition and naked economic power still bearing the stigma of its extra-status origin could bestow upon anyone who has won them the same or even greater "honor" as the vested interests claim for themselves. After all, given equality of status honor, property *per se* represents an addition even if it is not overtly acknowledged to be such.

Therefore all groups having interests in the status order react with special sharpness precisely against the pretensions of purely economic acquisition. In most cases they react the more vigorously the more they feel themselves threatened. Calderon's respectful treatment of the peasant, for instance, as opposed to Shakespeare's simultaneous ostensible disdain of the *canaille* [mob] illustrates the different way in which a firmly established status order reacts as compared with a status order that has become economically precarious. This is an example of a state of affairs that recurs everywhere. Precisely because of the rigorous reactions against the claims of property *per se*, the "parvenu" is never accepted, personally and without reservation, by the privileged status groups, no matter how completely his style of life has been adjusted to theirs. They will only accept his descendants who have been educated in the conventions of their status group and who have never besmirched its honor by their own economic labor.

As to the general *effect* of stratification through status only one consequence can be stated, but it is a very important one: the hindrance of the free development of the market. This occurs first for those goods that status groups directly withhold from free exchange by monopolization, which may be effected either through laws or conventions. For example, in many Hellenic cities during the "status era" and also originally in Rome, the inherited estate (as shown by the old formula for placing spendthrifts under a guardian) was monopolized, as were the estates of knights, peasants, priests, and especially the clientele of the craft and merchant guilds. The market is restricted, and the power of naked property *per se*, which gives its stamp to "class formation," is pushed into the background. The results of this process can he most varied. Of course, they do not necessarily weaken the contrasts in the economic situation. Frequently they strengthen these contrasts, and in any case, where stratification by status permeates a group as strongly as was the case in all political groups of Antiquity and of the Middle Ages, one can never speak of a genuinely free market competition as we understand it today.

There are wider effects than this direct exclusion of special goods from the market. From the conflict between the status order and the purely economic order mentioned above, it follows that in most instances the notion of honor peculiar to status absolutely abhors that which is essential to the market: hard bargaining. Honor abhors hard bargaining among peers and occasionally it taboos it for the members of a status group in general. Therefore, everywhere some status groups, and usually the most influential, consider almost any kind of overt participation in economic acquisition as absolutely stigmatizing.

With some over-simplification, one might thus say that classes are stratified according to their relations to the production and acquisition of goods; whereas status groups are stratified according to the principles of their *consumption* of goods as represented by special "styles of life." An "occupational status group," too, is a status group proper. For normally it successfully claims social honor only on the basis of the special style of life conditioned by the occupation.

The differences between classes and status groups frequently overlap. It is precisely those status groups most strictly segregated in terms of honor (viz. the Indian castes) that today show, although within very rigid limits, a relatively high degree of indifference to "acquisition." However, the Brahmins seek to acquire goods in the most diverse ways.

As to the general economic conditions making for the predominance of stratification by status, only the following can be said. When the bases of the acquisition and distribution of goods are relatively stable, stratification by status is favored. Every technological repercussion and economic transformation threatens stratification by status and pushes the class situation into the foreground. Epochs and countries in which the naked class situation is of predominant significance are regularly the periods of technical and economic transformations. And every slowing down of the change in economic stratification leads, in due course, to the growth of status structures and makes for a resuscitation of the important role of social honor.

I. PARTIES. Whereas the genuine place of classes is within the economic order, the place of status groups is within the social order, that is, within the sphere of the distribution of honor. From within these spheres, classes and status groups influence one another and the legal order and are in turn influenced by it. "*Parties*" reside in the sphere of "power." Their action is oriented toward the acquisition of social "power," that is to say, toward influencing social action no matter what its content may be. In principle, parties may exist in a social club as well as in a state. As over against the actions of classes and status groups, for which this is not necessarily the case, party-oriented social action always involves association – for it is always directed toward a goal which is striven for in a planned manner. This goal may be "impersonal" (the party may aim at realizing a program for ideal or material purposes), or the goal may be "personal" (sinecures, power, and from these, honor for the leader and the followers of the party). Usually the party aims at all such goals simultaneously. Parties are, therefore, only possible within groups that have an associational character, that is, some rational order and a staff of persons available who are ready to enforce it. For parties aim precisely at influencing this staff, and if possible, to recruit from it party members.

In any individual case, parties may represent interests determined through class situation or status situation, and they may recruit their following respectively from one or the other. But they need he neither purely class nor purely status parties; in fact, they are more likely to be mixed types, and sometimes they are neither. They may represent ephemeral or enduring formations. Their means of attaining power may be quite varied, ranging from naked violence of any sort to canvassing for votes with coarse or subtle means: money, social influence, the force of speech, suggestion, clumsy hoax, and so on to the rougher or more artful tactics of obstruction in parliamentary bodies.

The sociological structure of parties differs in a basic way according to the kind of social action which they struggle to influence; that means, they differ according to whether or not the group is stratified by status or by classes. Above all else, they vary according to the structure of authority within groups. For their leaders normally deal with its conquest. In our general terminology, parties are not only products of modern forms of authority. We shall also designate as parties the ancient and medieval ones, despite the fact that their structure differs basically from modern parties. Since a party always struggles for political control (*Herrschaft*), its organization too is frequently strictly "oriented to authority." Because of these variations between the forms of authority, it is impossible to say anything about the structure of parties without discussing them first. [See *E&S*, pp. 941–1211]. . . .

Before we do this, we should add one more general observation about classes, status groups and parties: The fact that they presuppose an association that overarches them, and in particular politically-oriented social action, does not mean that they are confined to it. On the contrary, at all times it has been the order of the day that such association (even when it aims at the use of military force in common) reaches beyond the state boundaries [see on parties also *E&S*, pp. 285–8]. . . .

# chapter 9

# Germany as a Nation
# of Commoners

From "National Character and the Junkers," in *From Max Weber: Essays in Sociology*,
eds and trans. Hans H. Gerth and C. Wright Mills, slightly revised by Stephen Kalberg
(New York: Oxford University Press, 1946 [1917]), pp. 386–8.

... The Junkers of the east are frequently (and often unjustly) vilified;
they are just as frequently (and as often unjustly) idolized. Anyone
who knows them personally will certainly enjoy their company at the
hunt, over a good glass, or at cards; and in their hospitable homes, everything is genuine. But everything becomes spurious when one stylizes
this essentially "bourgeois" stratum of entrepreneurs into an "aristocracy."

Economically, the Junkers are entirely dependent upon working as
agricultural entrepreneurs; they are engaged in the struggle of economic interests. Their social and economic struggle is just as ruthless as
that of any manufacturer. Ten minutes in their circle shows one that they
are plebeians. Their very virtues are of a thoroughly robust and plebeian
nature. Minister von Miquel once stated (privately!) that "Nowadays
an East German feudal estate cannot support an aristocratic household,"
and he was quite correct. If one tries to mold such a stratum into an
aristocracy, replete with feudal gestures and pretensions, a stratum now
dependent upon routine managerial work of a capitalistic nature, the
only result which can be irrevocably attained is the *physiognomy of a
parvenu*. Those traits of our political and general conduct in the world which
bear this stamp are determined, though not exclusively, by the fact that
we have fed aristocratic pretensions to strata which simply lack the
qualifications.

The Junkers are only one instance of this point. Among us the absence
of men of cosmopolitan education is, of course, not only due to the physiognomy of the Junkers; it is also a result of the pervasive, "middle class"
character of all those strata which have been the specific bearers of the
Prussian polity during the time of its poverized but glorious ascendancy.
The old officers' families, in their highly honorific way, cultivate in their
often extremely modest economic conditions the tradition of the old

Prussian army. The civil-servant families are of the same hue. It does not matter whether or not these families are of noble birth; economically, socially, and according to their horizon, they constitute a bourgeois middle-class group. In general, the social forms of the German officer corps are absolutely appropriate to the nature of the stratum, and in their decisive features they definitely resemble those of the officer corps of the democracies (of France and also of Italy). But these traits immediately become a caricature when non-military circles consider them as a model for their conduct. This holds, above all, when they are blended with social forms derived from the "pennalism" of the schools for bureaucracy. Yet, such is the case with us.

It is well known that the student fraternities constitute the typical social education of aspirants for non-military offices, sinecures, and the liberal professions of high social standing. The "academic freedom" of dueling, drinking, and class cutting stems from a time when other kinds of freedom did not exist in Germany and when only the stratum of literati and candidates for office was privileged in such liberties. The inroad, however, which these conventions have made upon the bearing of the "academically certified man" of Germany cannot be eliminated even today. This type of man has always been important among us, and becomes increasingly so. Even if the mortgages on fraternity houses and the necessity for the alumni to bear their interest did not take care of the economic immortality of the student fraternities, this type would hardly disappear. On the contrary, the fraternity system is steadily expanding [1917]; for the social connections of the fraternities nowadays constitute a specific way of selecting officials. And the officers' commission with its prerequisite qualification for dueling, visibly guaranteed through the colored fraternity ribbon, gives access to "society."

To be sure, the drinking compulsions and dueling techniques of the fraternities are increasingly adjusted to the needs of the weaker constitutions of aspirants to the fraternity ribbon, who for the sake of connections become more and more numerous. Allegedly, there are even teetotalers in some of these dueling corps. The intellectual inbreeding of the fraternities, which has continuously increased during recent decades, is a decisive factor. Fraternities have reading rooms of their own and special fraternity papers, which the alumni provide exclusively with well-meant "patriotic" politics of an unspeakably petty-bourgeois character. Social intercourse with classmates of a different social or intellectual background is shunned or at least made very difficult. With all this, fraternity connections are constantly expanding. A sales clerk who aspires to qualify for an officer's commission as a prerequisite of marriage into "society" (particularly with the boss's daughter) will enroll in one of the business colleges which are frequented largely because of their fraternity life. . . .

From "National Character and the Junkers," in *From Max Weber: Essays in Sociology*, eds and trans. Hans H. Gerth and C. Wright Mills, slightly revised by Stephen Kalberg (New York: Oxford University Press, 1946), pp. 390–3.

. . . It is equally important that there is no social form of German gentility. For despite the occasional boasting of our literati, it is completely untrue that individualism exists in Germany in the sense of freedom from conventions, in contrast to the conventions of the Anglo-Saxon gentleman or of the Latin salon type of man. Nowhere are there more rigid and compelling conventions than those of the German "fraternity man." These conventions directly and indirectly control just as large a part of the progeny of our leading strata as do the conventions of any other country. Wherever the forms of the officer corps do not hold, these fraternity conventions constitute "the German form"; for the effects of the dueling corps conventions largely determine the forms and conventions of the dominant strata of Germany: of the bureaucracy and of all those who wish to be accepted in "society," where bureaucracy sets the tone. And these forms are certainly not genteel.

From a political point of view, it is still more important that, in contrast to the conventions of Latin and Anglo-Saxon countries, these German forms are simply not suited to serve as a model for the whole nation down to the lowest strata. They are not suited to mold and unify the nation in its gesture as a *Herrenvolk*, self-assured in its overt conduct in the way in which Latin and Anglo-Saxon conventions have succeeded.

It is a grave error to believe that "race" is the decisive factor in the striking lack of grace and dignity in the overt bearing of the German. The German-Austrian's demeanor is formed by a genuine aristocracy. He does not lack these qualities, in spite of identical race, whatever else his weaknesses may be.

The forms that control the Latin type of personality, down to the lowest strata, are determined by imitation of the cavalier as evolved since the sixteenth century.

The Anglo-Saxon conventions also mold personalities down into the lower strata. They stem from the social habits of the gentry stratum, which has set the tone in England since the seventeenth century. The gentry emerged during the later Middle Ages from a peculiar blend of rural and urban notables, namely "gentlemen," who became the bearers of "self-government."

In all these cases it has been of consequence that the decisive features of the relevant conventions and gestures could be easily and universally imitated and hence could be democratized. But the conventions of the academically examined candidates for office in Germany, of those strata which they influence, and, above all, the habits for which the dueling corps conditions its men – these were and are obviously not suited for imitation by any circles outside of the examined and certified strata. In particular, they cannot be imitated by the broad masses of the people; they cannot be democratized, although, or rather precisely because, in essence these conventions are by no means cosmopolitan or otherwise aristocratic. They are thoroughly plebeian in nature.

The neo-Latin code of honor, as well as the quite different Anglo-Saxon code, has been suitable for far-reaching democratization. The specifically German concept of qualification for dueling, however, is not suited for being democratized, as one can easily see. This concept is of great political bearing, but the politically and socially important point is not – as is frequently held – that a so-called "code of honor" in the narrower sense exists in the officer corps. It is absolutely in place there. The fact that a Prussian *Landrat* [county executive] must qualify himself for dueling, in the sense of the pennalist duel corps, in order to maintain himself in his post – that is what is politically relevant. This also holds for any other administrative official who is easily removable. It is in contrast, for instance, to the *Amtsrichter* [judge of a lower court], who, by virtue of the law, is "independent," and who because of this independence is socially déclassé as compared to the *Landrat*. As with all other conventions and forms supported by the structure of bureaucracy and decisively fashioned by the idea of German student honor, from a formal point of view the concept of dueling qualification constitutes a caste convention because of its peculiar nature. None of these forms can be democratized. In substance, however, they are not of an aristocratic but of an absolutely plebeian character, because they lack all esthetic dignity and all genteel cultivation. It is this inner contradiction that invites ridicule and has such unfavorable political effects.

Germany is a nation of plebeians. Or, if it sounds more agreeable, it is a nation of commoners. Only on this basis could a specifically "German form" grow.

Socially, democratization brought about or promoted by the new political order – and that is what should be discussed here – would not destroy the value of aristocratic forms, since there are no such forms. Nor could it deprive such values of their exclusiveness and then propagate them throughout the nation, as was done with the forms of the Latin and Anglo-Saxon aristocracies. The form values of the degree-hunter qualifying for duels are not sufficiently cosmopolitan to support personal poise even in their own stratum. As every test shows, these forms do not always suffice even to hide the actual insecurity before a foreigner who is educated as a man of the world. The endeavor to hide such insecurity often takes the form of "pertness," which, in the main, stems from awkwardness and appears as poor breeding.

We shall not discuss whether political "democratization" would actually result in social democratization. Unlimited political "democracy" in America, for instance, does not prevent the growth of a raw plutocracy or even an "aristocratic" prestige group, which is slowly emerging. The growth of this "aristocracy" is culturally and historically as important as that of plutocracy, even though it usually goes unnoticed.

The development of a truly cultured "German form," which is at the same time suitable for the character of the socially dominant stratum of commoners, lies in the future. The incipient development of such civil conventions in the Hanseatic cities has not been continued under the impact of political and economic changes sine 1870. And the present war [World War I] has blessed us with a great many parvenus, whose sons will ardently acquire the usual duel corps conventions at the universities. These conventions do not raise any demands for a cultured tradition; they serve as a convenient way of taming men for qualifying as an applicant for officer commissions. Hence, for the time being there is no hope for a change. In any case, this much holds: if "democratization" should result in eliminating the social prestige of the academically certified man – which is by no means certain and which cannot be discussed here – then no politically valuable social forms would be abolished in Germany. Since they do not exist, they cannot be eliminated. Democracy could perhaps then free the road for the development of valuable forms suitable to our civic, social, and economic structure, which therefore would be "genuine" and cultured values.

One cannot invent such values, just as one cannot invent a style. Only this much (in an essentially negative and formal way) can be said, and it holds for all values of this nature: such forms can never be developed on any other basis than upon an attitude of personal distance and reserve. In Germany this prerequisite of all personal dignity has frequently been lacking among both high and low. The latest literati, with their urge to brag about and to print their personal "experiences" – erotical, religious, or what not – are the enemies of all dignity, no matter of what sort. "Distance," however, can by no means be gained exclusively through a lofty and "aristocratic" contrasting of one's self from the "far too many," as is maintained by the various and misconceived "prophecies" which go back to Nietzsche. On the contrary, when today it is in need of this inner support, distance is always spurious. Perhaps the necessity of maintaining one's inner dignity in the midst of a democratic world can serve as a test of the genuineness of dignity.

# chapter 10

# The Counterbalancing of Economic and Social Inequality by Universal Suffrage[1]

From "Suffrage and Democracy in Germany." (1917) in *Studienausgabe der Max Weber – Gesamtausgabe Band 1/15: Zur Politik im Weltkrieg–Schriften und Reden 1914–1918*, ed. Wolfgang Mommsen, trans. Stephen Kalberg (Tübingen: Mohr Verlag, 1988), pp. 170–2.

Equality in respect to the right to vote means first of all simply nothing other than that, as concerns this aspect of social life, the individual is *not* considered – as is otherwise the case – according to his distinct position in the occupational and family domains, on the one hand and, on the other, in terms of the particular features of his material or social situation. Rather, only the person *as a citizen* is considered. The unity of the nation-state, which replaces the divisiveness that reigns across the private spheres of life, here becomes evident.

The equality of citizens in nation-states has of course nothing whatsoever to do with a theory of some kind of natural "equality" among human beings. On the contrary, citizen equality can be viewed basically as a certain counterweight against social *inequalities* – and these were *not at all* grounded in natural distinctions. Rather, standing in the sharpest contrast to any natural qualities, social inequalities were created from societal conditions, above all from forces related to the wallet. As long as the society of today continues to exist – even if only in some related form, and it possesses a very stubborn quality – inequalities in the external conditions of life will also endure, above all in regard to *property*. Moreover, although social relationships of dependence, which are rooted in inequalities in regard to property ownership, may become less harsh, they can never be entirely eliminated. And those who have acquired privileges in this manner will never even come close to losing their influence, which extends far beyond their numbers, on national policy.

Similarly, the nature of the organization of the modern state and economy continuously bestows a privileged position upon *specialized education* and, in the process, of *Bildung*, or the acquisition of humanities-based knowledge (which, although not identical to specialized training is promoted by it, also through purely technical modes of education). Its possession constitutes the strongest element that makes for status distinctions in modern society. Just for this reason it makes sense to have a law on suffrage for the election of parliamentarians that opposes this inequality with significant force; namely, a counterbalance – rooted in superior numbers – to the privileged strata is established as a consequence of this law's endowment of the masses with electoral equality. This universal suffrage law will create a parliament that functions, at least in respect to the election, as a *monitoring* body and as a locus for the *selection of leaders*.

Moreover, an openly elected parliament becomes even more indispensable if we turn to the economy. Let us assume that, as a consequence of [World War I], a *permanent* and wide-ranging "organization" of the economy into interest groupings will unfold *in which state officials participate*; that is, a bureaucratically "supervised" or "co-administered" economy will come into being. On behalf of its regulation (or, better said, certain important branches of it), firm and lasting relationships would then develop between the state's offices and rigid occupational cooperatives. Have even any single one of our chattering intellectuals, who have all been childishly so enthusiastic about the prospect of this development, actually considered what would *politically* come out of this situation if simultaneously a further development fails to occur – namely, a tremendous increase in the power of a parliament *not* organized along occupational lines? These literati are under the illusion that "the state" will be the wise regulator of the economy. *The reverse!* The bankers and capitalist entrepreneurs, whom the intellectuals hate so much, would then become *the unlimited and uncontrolled masters of the state!*

For if the economy is "organized" into a machinery of large and small capitalist *cartels* of every type and the very formation of its own will (*Willensbildung*) is placed into the hand of just *these* "cooperative" organizations, *who on earth then is "the state?"* Even the participation of the state in the coal syndicate and in mining generally means, practically, that the Treasury Department is *not* interested in the best possible provision of the nation with inexpensive coal, but in *high rents* from its mines. Moreover, this participation means that private and public mining companies and bureaucracies are *identical* in respect to this interest, and that they both stand opposed to the interests of workers as well as consumers of coal.

Every further advance of *state*-directed cartellization obviously means nothing other than a further propagation of this situation. It should not be considered here whether this development might be unavoidable. Yet one could note that it is immeasurably naïve to believe, as do our ink-slinging ideologists, that *in this manner* the highly repugnant domination of interests in "profit" and the production of goods for "gain" will be eliminated or weakened in favor of a "natural economy" – a "communal economy" in which an interest exists in the best possible (that is, the most inexpensive) provisioning of *people* desiring and consuming commodities. What groundless nonsense! This would only mean that the interests of capitalist producers and industrialists, as represented by the cartels, *would exclusively and entirely dominate the state.*

This will occur *unless* this manner of organizing producer interests is confronted by a power strong enough to monitor these interests and to steer them according to the *needs* of the population. However, the *needs* of a person do *not* congeal in response to his or her position in the commodities *production* mechanism. The worker *needs* bread, an apartment, and clothes precisely in *the same* manner, regardless of the type of factory in which he works.

Thus, just when this mode of organizing the economy into cartels appears on the immediate horizon, it becomes absolutely necessary to establish *before* its functioning begins – that is, right now – a parliament elected on the basis of universal suffrage and endowed with completely sovereign power. Such a body would be capable, because it is *not* organized according to types of economic activity oriented to the production of goods but rather according to the principle by which the *needs* of the masses are represented, of standing in opposition to the cartellization of the economy. And parliament's power must be sovereign to a degree essentially greater than has heretofore existed, for the distribution of power until the present has *not* sufficed to shatter the power of industrial interests and the naturally-given domination of the Department of the Treasury in state-run firms. This must be viewed as a *negative* reason to institute universal suffrage.

There is, however, also a positive reason. Viewed from a purely "national politics" perspective, universal suffrage stands in a close relationship to that equality of certain *destinies* created by the modern state. All are "equal" before death; people are almost equal in regard to the indispensable necessities of physical life. Just these most ordinary and, on the other hand, most solemn and majestic necessities encompass also the equalities that the modern state offers to all its citizens in a truly permanent and unquestionable manner: merely, physical safety, a minimal standard of living that allows survival, and death upon the military field of battle. All inequalities common to us from the political laws of the past derived in the end from inequalities in respect to qualification for the *military*, and these were economically determined. This question of one's military qualification is absent in the bureaucratized state and army.

Standing in opposition to the universal leveling and inescapable domination that appears with bureaucracies, which first enabled the formulation of the modern concept "citizen," is the power mechanism of the ballot. It exists now simply as the *single* power mechanism *capable* of, in any way, giving into the hands of those subject to the bureaucracy a minimum of co-determination in the affairs of the community for which they are obliged to die.


## NOTE

1. This selection is from Weber's political writings and hence includes, at points, polemical formulations.

# part 5

# Authority in
# the Modern Epoch

## Introduction

Many social thinkers in Europe at the dawning of the twentieth century were overwhelmed by the intensity and scale of the social changes encompassing them. Urbanization, industrialization, and secularization were all proceeding at an uneasy tempo and in unknown directions. To many in Germany, these transformations overwhelmed and cast aside an earlier world still endowed with dignity. Although Weber cannot be counted among those who retreated from the modern era and sought a return to a world of the past putatively more stable and worthy, he viewed the new "cosmos" with great trepidation. All traditional forms of authority, whether based on religion, the patriarchy of the clan and tribe, feudalism, or monarchy ("patrimonialism"), were collapsing; they no longer commanded respect. His interest in the conditions under which people subjectively view commands as legitimate and obey them – authority (*Herrschaft*) – arose out of his concern.

While many foresaw an horrendous vacuum and even a reign of chaos, Weber argued that a qualitatively new type of authority had crystallized in the modern era. He called it "rational-legal," or "bureaucratic." So much of life in the rapidly changing world took place outside of the family and surely separate from the feudal manor and the rule of monarchs. The bureaucracy, manifest comprehensively alike in state offices, hospitals, the army, universities, legal institutions, and the workplace in general, cast its authority broadly across public life – hence, to Weber, creating patterns of social action and to the same extent circumscribing the free play of practical rationality. How does he define authority generally and, of direct importance in this volume, its modern manifestation: bureaucratic authority?[1]

Why, actually, do people obey authority? Rather than a "social fact," an expression of natural laws, or an inevitable culmination of historical evolutionary forces, authority implies for Weber nothing more than the empirical probability that a definable group of individuals (as a result of various motives) will orient their social action to giving directives or commands, that another definable group (as a result of various motives) will orient their social action to obedience, and that commands and directives are in fact, to a sociologically relevant degree, empirically carried out.[2] In his famous formulation, authority refers "to the likelihood that a demarcated command will find obedience among a specific circle of persons" (p. 179). It may be ascribed to diverse individuals, such as judges, civil servants, bankers, craftsmen, and tribal chiefs. All exercise authority wherever obedience is claimed and in fact called forth.

Weber's major concern focusses upon *legitimate* authority, or the relationship characterized by the attribution of a degree of legitimacy to the authority. For this reason, obedience, importantly, acquires a voluntary element. Whether anchored in unreflective habit or custom, an emotional attachment to the authorities or fear of them, values or ideals, or purely material interests and a calculation of advantage, a necessary minimum of compliance, unlike sheer *power*, always exists in the case of legitimate authority: "In general, it should be kept clearly in mind that the basis of every authority, and correspondingly of every kind of willingness to obey, is a *belief*, a belief by virtue of which persons exercising authority are lent prestige" (1968a, p. 263).

Weber goes to great pains to distinguish legitimate authority from power; indeed, his classic formulation of this distinction has been accepted throughout the social sciences for generations. He defines power as "the likelihood that one person in a social relationship will be able, even despite resistance, to carry out his own will" (p. 179), and sees power as ubiquitous – present even in social gatherings, lecture halls, and congregations, as well as the realm of politics. Because they are rooted in a belief, legitimate authority relationships to Weber are more enduring and stable than power relationships, which rest on force alone.

In essence, authorities seek to convince themselves of their *right* to exercise authority and attempt to implant the view, in demarcated groups of people, that this right is deserved. If they succeed, a willingness to obey arises, in the form of patterned social action, that secures their authority far more effectively than would sheer coercion. The character of the typical belief, or claim to legitimacy, provides Weber with the criteria he utilizes to classify the major types of authority into ideal-typical models. From the vantage point of his wide-ranging comparative-historical studies, he argues that all ruling powers, whether "profane or religious, political as well as unpolitical," can be understood as appealing to *rational-legal*,

The "pure" types of domination correspond to these three possible types of legitimation. The forms of domination occurring in historical reality constitute combinations, mixtures, adaptations, or modifications of these "pure" types.

Social action that is rationally associated within a form of domination locates its specific type in the "bureaucracy." "Patriarchalism" typically represents social action that is linked into traditional authority relationships. The "charismatic" form of domination does not rest upon either authority grounded in tradition or rationally enacted rules; rather, it is legitimated by a particular personality.

## NOTE

1. *Arbiter elegantiarum* – According to Tacitus (*Ann.* XVI 18). Gaius Petronius, who is probably identical with the satirist Petronius Arbiter, was called by Nero the "arbiter of elegance" to whose judgment he bowed in matters of taste. [Max Rheinstein]

# Domination and Legitimacy

From *Economy and Society: An Outline of Interpretive Sociology*, eds Guenther Roth and Claus Wittich, trans. Talcott Parsons, revised by Guenther Roth and Claus Wittich, and Stephen Kalberg (Berkeley, CA: University of California Press, 1978), pp. 212–13.

Domination was defined . . . as the probability that certain specific commands (or all commands) will be obeyed by a given group of persons. It thus does not include every mode of exercising "power" or "influence" over other persons. Domination ("authority") in this sense may be based on the most diverse motives of compliance: all the way from simple habituation to the most purely rational calculation of advantage. Hence every genuine form of domination implies a minimum of voluntary compliance, that is, an *interest* (based on ulterior motives or genuine acceptance) in obedience.

Not every case of domination makes use of economic means; still less does it always have economic objectives. However, normally the rule over a considerable number of persons requires a staff, that is, a *special* group which can normally be trusted to execute the general policy as well as the specific commands. The members of the administrative staff may be bound to obedience to their superior (or superiors) by custom, by affectual ties, by a purely material complex of interests, or by value-based motives. The type of these motives largely determines the type of domination. *Purely* material interests and calculations of advantages as the basis of solidarity between the chief and his administrative staff result, in this as in other connexions, in a relatively unstable situation. Normally other elements, affectual and value-rational, supplement such interests. In certain exceptional cases the former alone may be decisive. In everyday life these relationships, like others, are governed by custom and material calculation of advantage. But custom, interests, purely affectual or value-based motives of solidarity, do not form a sufficiently reliable basis for a given domination. In addition there is normally a further element, the belief in *legitimacy*.

Experience shows that in no instance does domination voluntarily limit itself to the appeal to material or affectual or ideal motives as a basis for its continuance. In addition every such system attempts to establish and to cultivate the belief in its legitimacy. But according to the kind of legitimacy which is claimed, the type of obedience, the kind of administrative staff developed to guarantee it, and the mode of exercising authority, will all differ fundamentally. Equally fundamental is the variation in effect. Hence, it is useful to classify the types of domination according to the kind of claim to legitimacy typically made by each. . . .

# The Three Pure Types of Domination

From *Economy and Society: An Outline of Interpretive Sociology*, eds Guenther Roth and Claus Wittich, trans. Talcott Parsons, revised by Guenther Roth and Claus Wittich, and Stephen Kalberg (Berkeley, CA: University of California Press, 1978), pp. 215–16.

There are three pure types of legitimate domination. The validity of the claims to legitimacy may be based on:

1. Rational grounds – resting on a belief in the legality of enacted orders [e.g., civil service rules] and the right of those elevated to authority under such orders to issue commands (legal authority).
2. Traditional grounds – resting on an established belief in the sanctity of immemorial traditions and the legitimacy of those exercising authority under them (traditional authority); or finally.
3. Charismatic grounds – resting on devotion to the exceptional sanctity, heroism or exemplary character of an individual person, and of the orders revealed or ordained by him (charismatic authority).

In the case of legal authority, obedience is owed to the legally established *impersonal order*. It extends to the persons exercising the authority of office under it by virtue of the formal legality of their commands and only within the scope of authority of the office. In the case of traditional authority, obedience is owed to the *person* of the chief who occupies the traditionally sanctioned position of authority and who is (within its sphere) bound by tradition. But here the obligation of obedience is a matter of personal loyalty within the area of accustomed obligations. In the case of charismatic authority, it is the charismatically qualified leader as such who is obeyed by virtue of personal trust in his revelation, his heroism or his exemplary qualities so far as they fall within the scope of the individual's belief in his charisma.[1]

## NOTE

1. The fact that none of these three ideal types . . . is usually to be found in historical cases in "pure" form, is naturally not a valid objection to attempting their conceptual formulation in the sharpest possible form. In this respect the present case is no different from many others. Later on . . . the transformation of pure charisma by the process of routinization will be discussed [see pp. 217–20] and thereby the relevance of the concept to the understanding of empirical systems of authority considerably increased. But even so it may be said of every historical phenomenon of authority that it is not likely to be "as an open book." Analysis in terms of sociological types has, after all, as compared with purely empirical historical investigation, certain advantages which should not be minimized. That is, it can in the particular case of a concrete form of authority determine what conforms to or approximates such types as "charisma," "hereditary charisma," "the charisma of office," "patriarchy," "bureaucracy," the authority of status groups, and in doing so it can work with relatively unambiguous concepts. But the idea that the whole of concrete historical reality can be exhausted in the conceptual scheme about to be developed is as far from the author's thoughts as anything could be. [This endnote appeared as an "excerpt" (printed in smaller case) in *E&S*.]

# chapter 12

# The Bureaucracy I

## EXTERNAL FORM, TECHNICAL SUPERIORITY, ETHOS, AND INEQUALITY

## External Form

From *Economy and Society: An Outline of Interpretive Sociology*, eds Guenther Roth and Claus Wittich, trans. H. H. Gerth and C. Wright Mills, revised by Guenther Roth and Claus Wittich (Berkeley, CA: University of California Press, 1978), pp. 956–8.

Modern officialdom functions in the following manner:

I. There is the principle of official *jurisdictional areas*, which are generally ordered by rules, that is, by laws or administrative regulations. This means:

(1)   The regular activities required for the purposes of the bureaucratically governed structure are assigned as official duties.

(2)   The authority to give the commands required for the discharge of these duties is distributed in a stable way and is strictly delimited by rules concerning the coercive means, physical, sacerdotal, or otherwise, which may be placed at the disposal of officials.

(3)   Methodical provision is made for the regular and continuous fulfillment of these duties and for the exercise of the corresponding rights; only persons who qualify under general rules are employed.

   In the sphere of the state these three elements constitute a bureaucratic *agency*; in the sphere of the private economy they constitute a bureaucratic *enterprise*. Bureaucracy, thus understood, is fully developed in political and ecclesiastical communities only in the modern state, and in the private economy only in the most advanced institutions of capitalism.

Permanent agencies, with fixed jurisdiction, are not the historical rule but rather the exception. This is even true of large political structures such as those of the ancient Orient, the Germanic and Mongolian empires of conquest, and of many feudal states. In all these cases, the ruler executes the most important measures through personal trustees, table-companions, or court-servants. Their commissions and powers are not precisely delimited and are temporarily called into being for each case.

II. The principles of *office hierarchy* and of channels of appeal (*Instanzenzug*) stipulate a clearly established system of super- and subordination in which there is a supervision of the lower offices by the higher ones. Such a system offers the governed the possibility of appealing, in a precisely regulated manner, the decision of a lower office to the corresponding superior authority. With the full development of the bureaucratic type, the office hierarchy is *monocratically* organized. The principle of hierarchical office authority is found in all bureaucratic structures: in state and ecclesiastical structures as well as in large party organizations and private enterprises. It does not matter for the character of bureaucracy whether its authority is called "private" or "public."

When the principle of jurisdictional "competency" is fully carried through, hierarchical subordination – at least in public office – does not mean that the "higher" authority is authorized simply to take over the business of the "lower." Indeed, the opposite is the rule; once an office has been set up, a new incumbent will always be appointed if a vacancy occurs.

III. The management of the modern office is based upon written documents (the "files"), which are preserved in their original or draft form, and upon a staff of subaltern officials and scribes of all sorts. The body of officials working in an agency along with the respective apparatus of material implements and the files makes up a *bureau* (in private enterprises often called the "counting house," *Kontor*).

In principle, the modern organization of the civil service separates the bureau from the private domicile of the official and, in general, segregates official activity from the sphere of private life. Public monies and equipment are divorced from the private property of the official. This condition is everywhere the product of a long development. Nowadays, it is found in public as well as in private enterprises; in the latter, the principle extends even to the entrepreneur at the top. In principle, the *Kontor* (office) is separated from the household, business from private correspondence, and business assets from private wealth. The more consistently the modern type of business management has been carried through, the more are these separations the case. The beginnings of this process are to be found as early as the Middle Ages.

It is the peculiarity of the modern entrepreneur that he conducts himself as the "first official" of his enterprise, in the very same way in which the ruler of a specifically modern bureaucratic state [Frederick II of Prussia] spoke of himself as "the first servant" of the state. The idea that the bureau activities of the state are intrinsically different in character from the management of private offices is a continental European notion and, by way of contrast, is totally foreign to the American way.

IV. Office management, at least all specialized office management – and such management is distinctly modern – usually presupposes thorough training in a field of specialization. This, too, holds increasingly for the modern executive and employee of a private enterprise, just as it does for the state officials.

V. When the office is fully developed, official activity demands the *full working capacity* of the official, irrespective of the fact that the length of his obligatory working hours in the bureau may be limited. In the normal case, this too is only the product of a long development, in the public as well as in the private office. Formerly the normal state of affairs was the reverse: Official business was discharged as a secondary activity.

VI. The management of the office follows *general rules*, which are more or less stable, more or less exhaustive, and which can be learned. Knowledge of these rules represents a special technical expertise which the officials possess. It involves jurisprudence, administrative or business management.

The reduction of modern office management to rules is deeply embedded in its very nature. The theory of modern public administration, for instance, assumes that the authority to order certain matters by decree – which has been legally granted to an agency – does not entitle the agency to regulate the matter by individual commands given for each case, but only to regulate the matter abstractly. This stands in extreme contrast to the regulation of all relationships through individual privileges and bestowals of favor, which, as we shall see, is absolutely dominant in patrimonialism, at least in so far as such relationships are not fixed by sacred tradition. . . .

From *Economy and Society: An Outline of Interpretive Sociology*, eds Guenther Roth and Claus Wittich, trans. H. H. Gerth and C. Wright Mills, revised by Guenther Roth and Claus Wittich, slightly revised by Stephen Kalberg (Berkeley, CA: University of California Press, 1978), pp. 960–1.

Typically, the bureaucratic official is appointed by a superior authority. An official elected by the governed is no longer a purely bureaucratic figure. Of course, a formal election may hide an appointment – in politics especially by party bosses. This does not depend upon legal statutes, but upon the way in which the party mechanism functions. Once firmly organized, the parties can turn a formally free election into the mere acclamation of a candidate designated by the party chief, or at least into a contest, conducted according to certain rules, for the election of one of two designated candidates.

In all circumstances, the designation of officials by means of an election modifies the rigidity of hierarchical subordination. In principle, an official who is elected has an autonomous position vis-à-vis his superiors, for he does not derive his position "from above" but "from below," or at least not from a superior authority of the official hierarchy but from powerful party men ("bosses"), who also determine his further career. The career of the elected official is not primarily dependent upon his chief in the administration. The official who is not elected, but appointed by a superior, normally functions, from a technical point of view, more accurately because it is more likely that purely functional points of consideration and qualities will determine his selection and career....

From *Economy and Society: An Outline of Interpretive Sociology*, eds Guenther Roth and Claus Wittich, trans. H. H. Gerth and C. Wright Mills, revised by Guenther Roth and Claus Wittich, slightly revised by Stephen Kalberg (Berkeley, CA: University of California Press, 1978), p. 963.

... The official as a rule receives a *monetary* compensation in the form of a *salary*, normally fixed, and the old age security provided by a pension. The salary is not measured like a wage in terms of work done, but according to "status," that is, according to the kind of function (the "rank") and, possibly, according to the length of service. The relatively great security of the official's income, as well as the rewards of social esteem, make the office a sought-after position, especially in countries which no longer provide opportunities for colonial profits. In such countries, this situation permits relatively low salaries for officials.

... The official is set for a "career" within the hierarchical order of the public service. He expects to move from the lower, less important and less well paid, to the higher positions. The average official naturally desires a mechanical fixing of the conditions of promotion: if not of the offices, at least of the salary levels. He wants these conditions fixed in terms of "seniority," or possibly according to grades achieved in a system of examinations. Here and there, such grades actually form a *character indelebilis* of the official and have lifelong effects on his career. To this is joined the striving to reinforce the right to office and to increase status group closure and economic security. All of this makes for a tendency to consider the offices as "prebends" of those qualified by educational certificates. The necessity of weighing general personal and intellectual qualifications without concern for the often subaltern character of such patents of specialized education, has brought it about that the highest political offices, especially the "ministerial" positions, are as a rule filled without reference to such certificates....

From "The Social Psychology of the World Religions," in *From Max Weber: Essays in Sociology*, eds and trans. Hans H. Gerth and C. Wright Mills (New York: Oxford University Press, 1946), p. 299.

With the triumph of *formalist* juristic rationalism, the legal type of domination appeared in the Occident at the side of the transmitted types of domination. Bureaucratic rule was not and is not the only variety of legal authority, but it is the purest. The modern state and municipal official, the modern Catholic priest and chaplain, the officials and employees of modern banks and of large capitalist enterprises represent, as we have already mentioned, the most important types of this structure of domination.

The following characteristic must be considered decisive for our terminology: in legal authority, submission does not rest upon the belief and devotion to charismatically gifted persons, like prophets and heroes, or upon sacred tradition, or upon piety toward a personal lord and master who is defined by an ordered tradition, or upon piety toward the possible incumbents of office fiefs and office prebends who are legitimized in their own right through privilege and conferment. Rather, submission under legal authority is based upon an *impersonal* bond to the generally defined and functional "duty of office." The official duty – like the corresponding right to exercise authority: the "jurisdictional competency" – is fixed by *rationally established* norms, by enactments, decrees, and regulations, in such a manner that the legitimacy of the authority becomes the legality of the general rule, which is purposely thought out, enacted, and announced with formal correctness.

# The Technical Superiority of Bureaucratic Organization over Administration by Notables

From *Economy and Society: An Outline of Interpretive Sociology*, eds Guenther Roth and Claus Wittich, trans. H. H. Gerth and C. Wright Mills, revised by Guenther Roth and Claus Wittich, slightly revised by Stephen Kalberg (Berkeley, CA: University of California Press, 1978), pp. 973–5.

The decisive reason for the advance of bureaucratic organization has always been its purely *technical* superiority over any other form of organization. The fully developed bureaucratic apparatus compares with other organizations exactly as does the machine with the non-mechanical modes of production. Precision, speed, unambiguity, knowledge of the files, continuity, discretion, unity, strict subordination, reduction of friction and of material and personal costs – these are raised to the optimum point in the strictly bureaucratic administration, and especially in its monocratic form. As compared with all collegiate, honorific, and avocational forms of administration, trained bureaucracy is superior on all these points. And as far as complicated tasks are concerned, paid bureaucratic work is not only more precise but, in the last analysis, it is often cheaper than even formally unremunerated honorific service.

Honorific arrangements make administrative work a subsidiary activity: an avocation and, for this reason alone, honorific service normally functions more slowly. Being less bound to schemata and more formless, it is less precise and less unified than bureaucratic administration, also because it is less dependent upon superiors. Because the establishment and exploitation of the apparatus of subordinate officials and clerical services are almost unavoidably less economical, honorific service is less continuous than bureaucratic and frequently quite expensive. This is especially the case if one thinks not only of the money costs to the public treasury – costs which bureaucratic administration, in comparison with administration by notables, usually increases – but also of the frequent economic losses of the governed caused by delays and lack of precision. Permanent administration by notables is normally feasible only where official business can be satisfactorily transacted as an avocation.

With the qualitative increase of tasks the administration has to face, administration by notables reaches its limits – today even in England. Work organized by collegiate bodies, on the other hand, causes friction and delay and requires compromises between colliding interests and views. The administration, therefore, runs less precisely and is more independent of superiors; hence, it is less unified and slower. All advances of the Prussian administrative organization, for example, have been and will in the future be advances of the bureaucratic, and especially of the monocratic, principle.

Today, it is primarily the capitalist market economy which demands that the official business of public administration be discharged precisely, unambiguously, continuously, and with as much speed as possible. Normally, the very large modern capitalist enterprises are themselves unequalled models of strict bureaucratic organization. Business management throughout rests on increasing precision, steadiness, and, above all, speed of operations. This, in turn, is determined by the peculiar nature of the modern means of communication, including, among other things, the news service of the press. The extraordinary increase in the speed by which public announcements, as well as economic and political facts, are transmitted exerts a steady and sharp pressure in the direction of speeding up the tempo of administrative reaction towards various situations. The optimum of such reaction time is normally attained only by a strictly bureaucratic organization. (The fact that the bureaucratic apparatus also can, and indeed does, create certain definite impediments for the discharge of business in a manner best adapted to the individuality of each case does not belong in the present context.)

Bureaucratization offers above all the optimum possibility for carrying through the principle of specializing administrative functions according to purely objective considerations. Individual performances are allocated to functionaries who have specialized training and who by constant practice increase their expertise. "Objective" discharge of business primarily means a discharge of business according to *calculable rules* and "without regard for persons."

"Without regard for persons," however, is also the watchword of the market and, in general, of all pursuits of naked economic interests. Consistent bureaucratic domination means the leveling of "status honor." Hence, if the principle of the free market is not at the same time restricted, it means the universal domination of the "class situation." That this consequence of bureaucratic domination has not set in everywhere proportional to the extent of bureaucratization is due to the differences between possible principles by which polities may supply their requirements. However, the second element mentioned, calculable rules, is the most important one for modern bureaucracy. The peculiarity of modern culture, and specifically of its technical and economic basis, demands this very "calculability" of results. When fully developed, bureaucracy also stands, in a specific sense, under the principle of *sine ira ac studio*. Bureaucracy develops the more perfectly, the more it is "dehumanized," the more completely it succeeds in eliminating from official business love, hatred, and all purely personal, irrational, and emotional elements which escape calculation. This is appraised as its special virtue by capitalism.

The more complicated and specialized modern culture becomes, the more its external supporting apparatus demands the personally detached and strictly objective *expert*, in lieu of the lord of older orders who was moved by personal sympathy and favor, by grace and gratitude. The bureaucracy offers the structure demanded by the external apparatus of modern culture in the most favorable combination. In particular, only bureaucracy has established the foundation for the administration of a rational law conceptually systematized on the basis of "statutes," such as the later Roman Empire first created with a high degree of technical perfection. During the Middle Ages, the reception of this [Roman] law coincided with the bureaucratization of legal administration: The advance of the rationally trained expert displaced the old trial procedure which was bound to tradition or to irrational presuppositions. . . .

From *Economy and Society: An Outline of Interpretive Sociology*, eds Guenther Roth and Claus Wittich, trans. H. H. Gerth and C. Wright Mills, revised by Guenther Roth and Claus Wittich, slightly revised by Stephen Kalberg (Berkeley, CA: University of California Press, 1978), pp. 979–80.

... The only decisive point for us is that in principle a system of rationally debatable "reasons" stands behind every act of bureaucratic administration, namely, either subsumption under norms, or a weighing of ends and means.

In this context, too, the position intrinsic to all "democratic" currents, in the sense of currents that would minimize "domination," is necessarily ambiguous. "Equality before the law" and the demand for legal guarantees against arbitrariness demand a formal and rational "objectivity" of administration, as opposed to the personal discretion flowing from the "grace" of the old patrimonial domination. If, however, an "ethos" – not to speak of other impulses – takes hold of the masses on some individual question, its postulates of *substantive* justice, oriented toward some concrete instance and person, will unavoidably collide with the formalism and the rule-bound and cool "matter-of-factness" of bureaucratic administration. Emotions must in that case reject what reason demands.

The propertyless masses especially are not served by the formal "equality before the law" and the "calculable" adjudication and administration demanded by bourgeois interests. Naturally, in their eyes justice and administration should serve to equalize their economic and social life-opportunities in the face of the propertied classes. Justice and administration can fulfill this function only if they assume a character that is "ethical" with respect to substantive content (*Kadi*-justice) and hence nonformal. Not only any sort of "popular justice" – which usually does not ask for rational reasons and "norms" – but also any intensive influence on the administration by so-called "public opinion" – that is, concerted action born of irrational "sentiments" and usually staged or directed by party bosses or the press – thwarts the rational course of justice just as strongly, and under certain circumstances far more so, as the "star chamber" proceedings (*Kabinettsjustiz*) of absolute rulers used to be able to do.

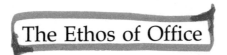

# The Ethos of Office

From *Economy and Society: An Outline of Interpretive Sociology*, eds Guenther Roth and Claus Wittich, trans. H. H. Gerth and C. Wright Mills, revised by Guenther Roth and Claus Wittich, slightly revised by Stephen Kalberg (Berkeley, CA: University of California Press, 1978), pp. 958–9.

That the office is a "vocation" (*Beruf*) finds expression, first, in the requirement of a prescribed course of training, which demands the entire working capacity for a long period of time, and in generally prescribed special examinations as prerequisites of employment. Furthermore, it finds expression in that the position of the official is in the nature of a "duty" (*Pflicht*). This determines the character of his relations in the following manner: Legally and actually, office holding is not considered ownership of a source of income, to be exploited for rents or emoluments in exchange for the rendering of certain services, as was normally the case during the Middle Ages and frequently up to the threshold of recent times, nor is office holding considered a common exchange of services, as in the case of free employment contracts. Rather, entrance into an office, including one in the private economy, is considered an acceptance of a specific duty of fealty to the purpose of the office (*Amtstreue*) in return for the grant of a secure existence. It is decisive for the modern loyalty to an office that, in the pure type, it does not establish a relationship to a *person*, like the vassal's or disciple's faith under feudal or patrimonial authority, but rather is devoted to *impersonal* and *functional* purposes. These purposes, of course, frequently gain an ideological halo from cultural values, such as state, church, community, party or enterprise, which appear as surrogates for a this-worldly or other-worldly personal ruler and which are embodied by a given group. . . .

From *Economy and Society: An Outline of Interpretive Sociology*, eds Guenther Roth and Claus Wittich, trans. H. H. Gerth and C. Wright Mills, revised by Guenther Roth and Claus Wittich, slightly revised by Stephen Kalberg (Berkeley, CA: University of California Press, 1978), pp. 1000–1.

. . . [B]ureaucracy strives everywhere for the creation of a "right to the office" by the establishment of regular disciplinary procedures and by the elimination of the completely arbitrary disposition of the superior over the subordinate official. The bureaucracy seeks to secure the official's position, his orderly advancement, and his provision for old age. . . .

. . . [B]ureaucracy, both in business offices and in public service, promotes the rise of a specific status group, just as did the quite different officeholders of the past. We have already pointed out that these status characteristics are usually also exploited for, and by their nature contribute to, the technical usefulness of bureaucracy in fulfilling its specific tasks. It is precisely against this unavoidable status character of bureaucracy that "democracy" reacts in its striving to put the election of officials for short terms in place of the appointment of officials and to substitute the recall of officials by referendum for a regulated disciplinary procedure. . . .

From *Economy and Society: An Outline of Interpretive Sociology*, eds Guenther Roth and Claus Wittich, trans. Claus Wittich, slightly revised by Stephen Kalberg (Berkeley, CA: University of California Press, 1978), pp. 1403–4.

. . . It can easily be seen that [the bureaucracy's] effectiveness has definite limitations in the public and governmental realm as well as in the private economy. The "directing mind," the *moving* spirit – that of the entrepreneur here and of the politician there – differs in substance from the civil-service frame of mind of the official. It is true that the entrepreneur, too, works in an office, just like the army leader, who is formally not different from other officers. If the president of a large enterprise is a salaried employee of a joint stock corporation, then he is *legally* an official like many others. In political life the same is true of the head of a political agency. The governing minister is *formally* a salaried official with pension rights. The fact that according to all constitutions he can be dismissed or resign at any time differentiates his position from that of most, but not all other officials. Far more striking is the fact that he, and he alone, does not need to prove formal specialized training. This indicates that the meaning of his position distinguishes him, after all, from other officials, as it does the entrepreneur and the corporation president in the private economy. Actually, it is more accurate to say that he is *supposed* to be something different. And so it is indeed. If a man in a leading position is an "official" in the spirit of his performance, no matter how qualified – a man, that is, who works dutifully and honorably according to rules and instruction –, then he is as useless at the helm of a private enterprise as of a government. . . .

The difference is rooted only in part in the kind of performance expected. Independent decision-making and imaginative organizational capabilities in matters of detail are usually also demanded of the bureaucrat, and very often expected even in larger matters. The idea that the bureaucrat is absorbed in subaltern routine and that only the "director" performs the interesting, intellectually demanding tasks is a preconceived notion of the literati. . . . The difference lies, rather, in the kind of *responsibility*, and this does indeed determine the different demands addressed to both kinds of positions. An official who receives a directive which he considers wrong can, and is supposed to, object to it. If his superior insists on its execution, it is his duty and even his honor to carry it out as if it corresponded to his innermost conviction, and to demonstrate in this fashion that his sense of duty stands above his personal preference. It does not matter whether the imperative mandate originates from an "agency," a "corporate body" or an "assembly." This is the ethos of *office*.

A political leader acting in this way would deserve contempt. He will often be compelled to make compromises, that means, to sacrifice the less important to the more important. If he does not succeed in demanding of his ruler, be he a monarch or the people: "You either give me now the authorization I want from you, or I will resign," he is a miserable *Kleber* [one who sticks to his post] – as Bismarck called this type – and not a leader. "To be above parties" – in truth, to remain outside the realm of the struggle for power – is the official's role, while this struggle for personal power, and the resulting personal responsibility, is the lifeblood of the politician as well as of the entrepreneur.

# Inequality

From *Economy and Society: An Outline of Interpretive Sociology*, eds Guenther Roth and Claus Wittich, trans. Talcott Parsons, revised by Guenther Roth and Claus Wittich (Berkeley, CA: University of California Press, 1978), p. 225.

Bureaucratic administration means fundamentally domination through knowledge. This is the feature of it which makes it specifically rational. This consists on the one hand in technical knowledge which, by itself, is sufficient to ensure it a position of extraordinary power. But in addition to this, bureaucratic organizations, or the holders of power who make use of them, have the tendency to increase their power still further by the knowledge growing out of experience in the service. For they acquire through the conduct of office a special knowledge of facts and have available a store of documentary material peculiar to themselves.

From *Economy and Society: An Outline of Interpretive Sociology*, eds Guenther Roth and Claus Wittich, trans. H. H. Gerth and C. Wright Mills, revised by Guenther Roth and Claus Wittich, slightly revised by Stephen Kalberg (Berkeley, CA: University of California Press, 1978), pp. 989–94.

It is clear that the bureaucratic organization of a social structure, and especially of a political one, can and regularly does have far-reaching economic consequences. But what sort of consequences? Of course, in any individual case it depends upon the distribution of economic and social power, and especially upon the sphere that is occupied by the emerging bureaucratic mechanism. The consequences of bureaucracy depend therefore upon the direction which the powers using the apparatus give to it. Very frequently a crypto-plutocratic distribution of power has been the result.

In England, but especially in the United States, party donors regularly stand behind the bureaucratic party organizations. They have financed these parties and have been able to influence them to a large extent. The breweries in England, and in Germany the so-called "heavy industry" and the Hansa League with their election funds, are well enough known in this respect. In political, and especially in state formations, too, bureaucratization and social leveling – with the associated breaking up of the opposing local and feudal privileges – have in modern times frequently benefitted the interests of capitalism or have been carried out in direct alliance with capitalist interests; witness the great historical alliance of the absolute princes with capitalist interests. In general, a legal leveling and destruction of firmly established local structures ruled by notables has usually tended to expand capitalism's sphere of movement. But, on the other hand, there is also an effect of bureaucratization that meets the petty-bourgeois interest in a safe traditional "living," or even a state-socialist effect that strangulates opportunities for private profit. This has undoubtedly been active in several cases of historically far-reaching importance, particularly during Antiquity; it is perhaps also to be expected in future developments in our world. . . .

. . . We must remember the fact which we have encountered several times and which we shall have to discuss repeatedly: that "democracy" as such is opposed to the "rule" of bureaucracy, in spite and perhaps because of its unavoidable yet unintended promotion of bureaucratization. Under certain conditions, democracy creates palpable breaks in the bureaucratic pattern and impediments to bureaucratic organization. Hence, one must in every individual historical case analyze in which of the special directions bureaucratization has there developed.

For this reason, it must also remain an open question whether the *power* of bureaucracy is increasing in the modern states in which it is spreading. The fact that bureaucratic organization is technically the most highly developed power instrument in the hands of its controller does not determine the weight that bureaucracy as such is capable of procuring for its own opinions in a particular social structure. The ever-increasing "indispensability" of the officialdom, swollen to the millions, is no more decisive on this point than is the economic indispensability of the proletarians for the strength of the social and political power position of that class (a view which some representatives of the proletarian movement hold).[1] If "indispensability" were decisive, the equally "indispensable" slaves ought to have held this position of power in any economy where slave labor prevailed and consequently freemen, as is the rule, shunned work as degrading. Whether the power of bureaucracy as such increases cannot be decided *a priori* from such reasons. The drawing in of economic interest groups or other non-official experts, or the drawing in of lay representatives, the establishment of local, inter-local, or central parliamentary or other representative bodies, or of occupational associations – these *seem* to run directly against the bureaucratic tendency. How far this appearance is the truth must be discussed in another chapter, rather than in the framework of this purely formal and typological (*kasuistisch*) discussion. In general, only the following can be said here:

The power position of a fully developed bureaucracy is always great, under normal conditions overtowering. The political "ruler" always finds himself, vis-à-vis the trained official, in the position of a dilettante facing the expert. This holds whether the "ruler," whom the bureaucracy serves, is the "people" equipped with the weapons of legislative initiative, referendum, and the right to remove officials; or a parliament elected on a more aristocratic or more democratic basis and equipped with the right or the *de facto* power to vote a lack of confidence; or an aristocratic collegiate body, legally or actually based on self-recruitment; or a popularly elected president or an "absolute" or "constitutional" hereditary monarch. . . .

Every bureaucracy seeks further to increase this superiority of the professional insider through the means of *keeping secret* its knowledge and intentions. Bureaucratic administration always tends to exclude the public, to hide its knowledge and action from criticism as well as it can. Prussian church authorities now threaten to use disciplinary measures against pastors who make reprimands or other admonitory measures in any way accessible to third parties, charging that in doing so they become "guilty" of facilitating a possible criticism of the church authorities. The treasury officials of the Persian Shah have made a secret science of their budgetary art and even use a secret script. The official statistics of Prussia, in general, make public only what cannot do any harm to the intentions of the power-wielding bureaucracy. This tendency toward secrecy is in certain administrative fields a consequence of their objective nature: namely, wherever power interests of the given structure of domination *toward the outside* are at stake, whether this be the case of economic competitors of a private enterprise or that of potentially hostile foreign polities in the public field.

If it is to be successful, the management of diplomacy can be publicly supervised only to a very limited extent. The military administration must insist on the concealment of its most important measures with the increasing significance of purely technical aspects. Political parties do not proceed differently, in spite of all the ostensible publicity of the party conventions and "Catholic Congresses" (*Katholikentage*).[2] With the increasing bureaucratization of party organizations, this secrecy will prevail even more. Foreign trade policy, in Germany for instance, brings about a concealment of production statistics. Every fighting posture of a social structure toward the outside tends in itself to have the effect of buttressing the position of the group in power.

However, the pure power interests of bureaucracy exert their effects far beyond these areas of functionally motivated secrecy. The concept of the "office secret" is the specific invention of bureaucracy, and few things it defends so fanatically as this attitude which, outside of the specific areas mentioned, cannot be justified with purely functional arguments. In facing a parliament, the bureaucracy fights, out of a sure power instinct, every one of that institution's attempts to gain through its own means (as, e.g., through the so-called "right of parliamentary investigation") expert knowledge from the interested parties. Bureaucracy naturally prefers a poorly informed, and hence powerless, parliament – at least insofar as this ignorance is compatible with the bureaucracy's own interests. . . .

Only the expert knowledge of private economic interest groups in the field of "business" is superior to the expert knowledge of the bureaucracy. This is so because the exact knowledge of facts in their field is of direct significance for economic survival. Errors in official statistics do not have direct economic consequences for the responsible official, but miscalculations in a capitalist enterprise are paid for by losses, perhaps by its existence. Moreover, the "secret," as a means of power, is more safely hidden in the books of an enterprise than it is in the files of public authorities. For this reason alone authorities are held within narrow boundaries when they seek to influence economic life in the capitalist epoch, and very frequently their measures take an unforeseen and unintended course or are made illusory by the superior expert knowledge of the interested groups. . . .

. . . [T]he ruler, who increasingly turns into a "dilettante," at the same time exploits expert knowledge and – what frequently remains unnoticed – seeks to fend off the threatening dominance of the experts. He keeps one expert in check by others, and by such cumbersome procedures seeks personally to gain a comprehensive picture as well as the certainty that nobody prompts him into arbitrary decisions.

NOTES

1. This is directed, among others, at Robert Michels, to whom Weber wrote in November 1906:

> Indispensability in the economic process means nothing, absolutely nothing for the power position and power chances of a class. At a time when no "citizen" worked, the slaves were ten times, nay a thousand times, as necessary as is the proletariat today. What does that matter? The medieval peasant, the Negro of the American South, they were all absolutely "indispensable.". . . The phrase contains a dangerous illusion.

... Political democratization is the only thing which can perhaps be achieved in the foreseeable future, and that would be no mean achievement. ... I cannot prevent you from believing in more, but I cannot force myself to do so.

Quoted in Wolfgang Mommsen, *Max Weber und die deutsche Politik. 1890–1920* (Tübingen: Mohr, 1959), 97 and 121 [Roth and Wittich].

2. *Katholikentag*: An annual conference established in 1858, under the direction of a central committee, to discuss ecclesiastical, political and social welfare issues and to represent German Catholicism before the public which was then largely Protestant. Discontinued during the Nazi period, the Congress has been meeting biannually since 1950 [Roth and Wittich].

# chapter 13

# The Bureaucracy II

## THE IMPACT UPON SOCIETY

## Leveling and "Passive" Democratization

*Economy and Society: An Outline of Interpretive Sociology*, eds Guenther Roth and Claus Wittich, trans. H. H. Gerth and C. Wright Mills, revised by Guenther Roth and Claus Wittich, slightly revised by Stephen Kalberg (Berkeley, CA: University of California Press, 1978), pp. 983–6.

Bureaucratic organization has usually become dominant on the basis of a – at least relative – leveling of economic and social differences. This leveling has been significant for administrative functions.

Bureaucracy inevitably accompanies modern *mass democracy*, in contrast to the democratic self-government of small homogeneous units. This results from its characteristic principle: the abstract regularity of the exercise of authority, which is a result of the demand for "equality before the law" in the personal and functional sense – hence, of the horror of "privilege," and the principled rejection of doing business "from case to case." Such regularity also follows from the social preconditions of its origin.

Every non-bureaucratic administration of a large social structure rests in some way upon the fact that an existing higher social, economic, or honorific ranking is brought into line with administrative functions and duties. This usually means that a direct or indirect economic or even "social" exploitation of position, which every sort of administrative activity bestows upon its bearers, is the compensation for the assumption of administrative functions. . . .

. . . Mass democracy which makes a clean sweep of the feudal, patrimonial, and – at least in intent – the plutocratic privileges in administration unavoidably has to put paid professional labor in place of the historically inherited "avocational" administration by notables. . . .

... The progress of bureaucratization within the state administration itself is a phenomenon paralleling the development of democracy, as is quite obvious in France, North America, and now in England. Of course, one must always remember that the term "democratization" can be misleading. The *demos* itself, in the sense of a shapeless mass, never "governs" larger associations, but rather is governed. What changes is only the way in which the executive leaders are selected and the measure of influence which the *demos*, or better, which social circles from its midst are able to exert upon the content and the direction of administrative activities by means of "public opinion." "Democratization," in the sense here intended, does not necessarily mean an increasingly active share of the subjects in government. This may be a result of democratization, but it is not necessarily the case.

We must expressly recall at this point that the political concept of democracy, deduced from the "equal rights" of the governed, includes these further postulates: (1) prevention of the development of a closed status group of officials in the interest of a universal accessibility of office, and (2) minimization of the authority of officialdom in the interest of expanding the sphere of influence of "public opinion" as far as practicable. Hence, wherever possible, political democracy strives to shorten the term of office through election and recall, and to be relieved from a limitation to candidates with special expert qualifications. Thereby democracy inevitably comes into conflict with the bureaucratic tendencies which have been produced by its very fight against the notables. The loose term "democratization" cannot be used here, in so far as it is understood to mean the minimization of the civil servants' power in favor of the greatest possible "direct" rule of the *demos*, which in practice means the respective party leaders of the *demos*. The decisive aspect here – indeed it is rather exclusively so – is the *leveling of the governed* in face of the governing and bureaucratically articulated group, which in its turn may occupy a quite autocratic position, both in fact and in form. ...

... In Russia, the destruction of the position of the old seigneurial nobility through the regulation of the *mestnichestvo* (rank order) system and the consequent permeation of the old nobility by an office nobility [under Peter the Great] were characteristic transitional phenomena in the development of bureaucracy. In China, the estimation of rank and the qualification for office according to the number of examinations passed have similar significance, although with an – at least in theory – even more pronounced rigour. In France the Revolution and, more decisively, Bonapartism have made the bureaucracy all-powerful. In the Catholic church, first the feudal and then all independent local intermediary powers were eliminated. This was begun by Gregory VII [1073–85] and continued through the Council of Trent [1592] and the Vatican Council

[1869–70], and it was completed by the edicts of Pius X [1903–14]. The transformation of these local powers into pure functionaries of the central authority was connected with the constant increase in the factual significance of the formally quite dependent *Kapläne* [auxiliary clergymen supervising lay organizations], a process which above all was based on the political party organization of Catholicism. Hence this process meant an advance of bureaucracy and at the same time of "passive" democratization, as it were, that is, the leveling of the ruled. In the same way, the substitution of the bureaucratic army for the self-equipped army of notables is everywhere a process of "passive" democratization, in the sense in which this applies to every establishment of an absolute military monarchy in the place of a feudal state or of a republic of notables. . . .

# The Expansion of Bureaucracy into All Fields

From *Economy and Society: An Outline of Interpretive Sociology*, eds Guenther Roth and Claus Wittich, trans. Talcott Parsons, revised by Guenther Roth and Claus Wittich, slightly revised by Stephen Kalberg (Berkeley, CA: University of California Press, 1978), pp. 223–4.

The development of modern forms of organization in *all* fields is nothing less than identical with the development and continual spread of bureaucratic administration. This is true of church and state, of armies, political parties, economic enterprises, interest groups, endowments, clubs, and many others. Its development is, to take the most striking case, at the root of the modern Western state. However many forms there may be which do not appear to fit this pattern, such as collegial representative bodies, parliamentary committees, soviets, honorary officers, lay judges, and what not, and however many people may complain about the "red tape," it would be sheer illusion to think for a moment that continuous administrative work can be carried out in any field except by means of officials working in offices. The whole pattern of everyday life is cut to fit this framework. If bureaucratic administration is, other things being equal, always the most [formal] rational type from a technical point of view, the needs of mass administration make it today completely indispensable. The choice is only that between bureaucratization or increasing dilettantism in the field of administration. . . .

When those subject to bureaucratic control seek to escape the influence of the existing bureaucratic apparatus, this is normally possible only by creating an organization of their own which is equally subject to bureaucratization. Similarly the existing bureaucratic apparatus is driven to continue functioning by the most powerful interests which are material and objective, but also ideal in character. Without it, a society like our own – with its separation of officials, employees, and workers from ownership of the means of administration, and its dependence on discipline and on technical training – could no longer function. The only exception would be those groups, such as the peasantry, who are still in possession of their own means of subsistence. Even in the case of revolution by force or of occupation by an enemy, the bureaucratic machinery will normally continue to function just as it has for the previous legal government.

From *Economy and Society: An Outline of Interpretive Sociology*, eds Guenther Roth and Claus Wittich, trans. H. H. Gerth and C. Wright Mills, revised by Guenther Roth and Claus Wittich, slightly revised by Stephen Kalberg (Berkeley, CA: University of California Press, 1978), pp. 980–4.

The bureaucratic structure goes hand in hand with the concentration of the material means of operation in the hands of upper level managers. This concentration occurs, for instance, in a well-known and typical fashion in the development of big capitalist enterprises, which find their essential characteristics in this process. A corresponding process occurs in public organizations [and in warfare]. . . .

. . . Only the bureaucratic army structure allows for the development of the professional standing armies which are necessary for the constant pacification of large territories as well as for warfare against distant enemies, especially enemies overseas. Further, military discipline and technical military training can normally be fully developed, at least to its modern high level, only in the bureaucratic army.

Historically, the bureaucratization of the army has everywhere occurred along with the shifting of army service from the shoulders of the propertied to those of the propertyless. Until this transfer occurs, military service is an honorific privilege of propertied men. . . .

. . . In this same way as with army organizations, the bureaucratization of administration in other spheres goes hand in hand with the concentration of resources. . . .

In the field of scientific research and instruction, the bureaucratization of the inevitable research institutes of the universities is also a function of the increasing demand for material means of operation. Liebig's laboratory at Giessen University was the first example of big enterprise in this field. Through the concentration of such means in the hands of the privileged head of the institute the mass of researchers and instructors are separated from their "means of production," in the same way as the workers are separated from theirs by the capitalist enterprises. . . .

... [I]n their own organizations the democratic mass parties have completely broken with traditional rule by notables based upon personal relationships and personal esteem. Such personal structures still persist among many old conservative as well as old liberal parties, but democratic mass parties are bureaucratically organized under the leadership of party officials, professional party and trade union secretaries, etc. In Germany, for instance, this has happened in the Social Democratic party and in the agrarian mass-movement; in England earliest in the caucus democracy of Gladstone and Chamberlain which spread from Birmingham in the 1870's. In the United States, both parties since Jackson's administration have developed bureaucratically. In France, however, attempts to organize disciplined political parties on the basis of an election system that would compel bureaucratic organization have repeatedly failed. The resistance of local circles of notables against the otherwise unavoidable bureaucratization of the parties, which would encompass the entire country and break their influence, could not be overcome. Every advance of simple election techniques based on numbers alone as, for instance, the system of proportional representation, means a strict and inter-local bureaucratic organization of the parties and therewith an increasing domination of party bureaucracy and discipline, as well as the elimination of the local circles of notables – at least this holds for large states. ...

From *Economy and Society: An Outline of Interpretive Sociology*, eds Guenther Roth and Claus Wittich, trans. H. H. Gerth and C. Wright Mills, revised by Guenther Roth and Claus Wittich, slightly revised by Stephen Kalberg (Berkeley, CA: University of California Press, 1978), p. 998.

Only with the bureaucratization of the state and of law in general can one see a definite possibility of a sharp conceptual separation of an "objective" legal order from the "subjective" rights of the individual which it guarantees, as well as that of the further distinction between "public" law, which regulates the relationships of the public agencies among each other and with the subjects, and "private" law which regulates the relationships of the governed individuals among themselves. These distinctions presuppose the conceptual separation of the "state," as an abstract bearer of sovereign prerogatives and the creator of legal norms, from all personal authority of individuals. These conceptual distinctions are necessarily remote from the nature of *pre*-bureaucratic, especially from patrimonial and feudal, structures of authority. They were first conceived and realized in urban communities; for as soon as their officeholders were appointed by periodic *elections*, the individual power-holder, even if he was in the highest position, was obviously no longer identical with the man who possessed authority "in his own right." Yet it was left to the complete depersonalization of administrative management by bureaucracy and the rational systematization of law to realize the separation of the public and the private sphere fully and in principle.

# On the Difficulty of Destroying Bureaucracy

From *Economy and Society: An Outline of Interpretive Sociology*, eds Guenther Roth and Claus Wittich, trans. H. H. Gerth and C. Wright Mills, revised by Guenther Roth and Claus Wittich, slightly revised by Stephen Kalberg (Berkeley, CA: University of California Press, 1978), pp. 987–9.

Once fully established, bureaucracy is among those social structures which are the hardest to destroy. Bureaucracy is *the* means of transforming social action into rationally organized action. Therefore, as an instrument of rationally organizing authority relations, bureaucracy was and is a power instrument of the first order for one who controls the bureaucratic apparatus. Under otherwise equal conditions, rationally organized and directed action (*Gesellschaftshandeln*) is superior to every kind of mass action (*Massenhandeln*) [see above, pp. 10–12] and also social action opposing it. Where administration has been completely bureaucratized, the resulting system of domination is practically indestructible.

The individual bureaucrat cannot squirm out of the apparatus into which he has been harnessed. In contrast to the "notable" performing administrative tasks as a honorific duty or as a subsidiary occupation (avocation), the professional bureaucrat is chained to his activity in his entire economic and ideological existence. In the great majority of cases he is only a small cog in a ceaselessly moving mechanism which prescribes to him an essentially fixed route of march. The official is entrusted with specialized tasks, and normally the mechanism cannot be put into motion or arrested by him, but only from the very top. The individual bureaucrat is, above all, forged to the common interest of all the functionaries in the perpetuation of the apparatus and the persistence of its rationally exercised domination.

The ruled, for their part, cannot dispense with or replace the bureaucratic apparatus once it exists, for it rests upon expert training, a functional specialization of work, and an attitude set on habitual virtuosity in the mastery of single yet methodically integrated functions. If the apparatus stops working, or if its work is interrupted by force, chaos results, which it is difficult to master by improvised replacements from among the governed. This holds for public administration as well as for private economic management. Increasingly the material fate of the masses depends upon the continuous and correct functioning of the ever more bureaucratic organizations of private capitalism, and the idea of eliminating them becomes more and more utopian.

Increasingly, all order in public and private organizations is dependent on the system of files and the discipline of officialdom, that means, its habit of painstaking obedience within its wonted sphere of action. The latter is the more decisive element, however important in practice the files are. The naive idea of Bakuninism of destroying the basis of "acquired rights" together with "domination" by destroying the public documents overlooks that the settled orientation of *man* for observing the accustomed rules and regulations will survive independently of the documents. Every reorganization of defeated or scattered army units, as well as every restoration of an administrative order destroyed by revolts, panics, or other catastrophes, is effected by an appeal to this conditioned orientation, bred both in the officials and in the subjects, of obedient adjustment to such [social and political] orders. If the appeal is successful it brings, as it were, the disturbed mechanism to "snap into gear" again.

The objective indispensability of the once-existing apparatus, in connection with its peculiarly "impersonal" character, means that the mechanism – in contrast to the feudal order based upon personal loyalty – is easily made to work for anybody who knows how to gain control over it. A rationally ordered officialdom continues to function smoothly after the enemy has occupied the territory; he merely needs to change the top officials. It continues to operate because it is to the vital interest of everyone concerned, including above all the enemy. After Bismarck had, during the long course of his years in power, brought his ministerial colleagues into unconditional bureaucratic dependence by eliminating all independent statesmen, he saw to his surprise that upon his resignation they continued to administer their offices unconcernedly and undismayedly, as if it had not been the ingenious lord and very creator of these tools who had left, but merely some individual figure in the bureaucratic machine which had been exchanged for some other figure. In spite of all the changes of masters in France since the time of the First Empire, the power apparatus remained essentially the same.

Such an apparatus makes "revolution," in the sense of the forceful creation of entirely new formations of authority, more and more impossible – technically, because of its control over the modern means of communication (telegraph etc.), and also because of its increasingly rationalized inner structure. The place of "revolutions" is under this process taken by *coups d'état*, as again France demonstrates in the classical manner since all successful transformations there have been of this nature.

From *Economy and Society: An Outline of Interpretive Sociology*, eds Guenther Roth and Claus Wittich, trans. Claus Wittich (Berkeley, CA: University of California Press, 1978), p. 1401.

Bureaucracy is distinguished from other historical agencies of the modern rational order of life in that it is far more persistent and "escape-proof." History shows that wherever bureaucracy gained the upper hand, as in China, Egypt and, to a lesser extent, in the later Roman empire and Byzantium, it did not disappear again unless in the course of the total collapse of the supporting culture. Yet these were still, relatively speaking, highly irrational forms of bureaucracy: "Patrimonial bureaucracies." In contrast to these older forms, modern bureaucracy has one characteristic which makes its "escape-proof" nature much more definite: rational specialization and training. . . . Wherever the modern specialized official comes to predominate, his power proves practically indestructible since the whole organization of even the most elementary want satisfaction has been tailored to his mode of operation.

# chapter 14

# Past and Present

## CHARISMATIC AUTHORITY AND ITS ROUTINIZATION

From "The Social Psychology of the World Religions," in *From Max Weber: Essays in Sociology*, eds and trans. H. H. Gerth and C. Wright Mills (New York: Oxford University Press, 1946), pp. 295–6.

... [T]he term "charisma" shall be understood to refer to an *extraordinary* quality of a person, regardless of whether this quality is actual, alleged, or presumed. "Charismatic authority," hence, shall refer to a rule over men, whether predominantly external or predominantly internal, to which the governed submit because of their belief in the extraordinary quality of the specific *person*. The magical sorcerer, the prophet, the leader of hunting and booty expeditions, the warrior chieftain, the so-called "Caesarist" ruler, and, under certain conditions, the personal head of a party are such types of rulers for their disciples, followings, enlisted troops, parties, et cetera. The legitimacy of their rule rests on the belief in and the devotion to the extraordinary, which is valued because it goes beyond the normal human qualities, and which was originally valued as supernatural. The legitimacy of charismatic rule thus rests upon the belief in magical powers, revelations and hero worship. The source of these beliefs is the "proving" of the charismatic quality through miracles, through victories and other successes, that is, through the welfare of the governed. Such beliefs and the claimed authority resting on them therefore disappear, or threaten to disappear, as soon as proof is lacking and as soon as the charismatically qualified person appears to be devoid of his magical power or forsaken by his god. Charismatic rule is not managed according to general norms, either traditional or rational, but, in principle, according to concrete revelations and inspirations, and in this sense, charismatic authority is "irrational."

From *Economy and Society: An Outline of Interpretive Sociology*, eds Guenther Roth and Claus Wittich, trans. Talcott Parsons, revised by Guenther Roth and Claus Wittich, slightly revised by Stephen Kalberg (Berkeley, CA: University of California Press, 1978), pp. 243–4.

An organized group subject to charismatic authority will be called a charismatic community (*Gemeinde*). It is based on an emotional form of communal relationship (*Vergemeinschaftung*). The administrative staff of a charismatic leader does not consist of "officials"; least of all are its members technically trained. It is not chosen on the basis of social privilege nor from the point of view of domestic or personal dependency. It is rather chosen in terms of the charismatic qualities of its members. The prophet has his disciples; the warlord his bodyguard; the leader, generally, his agents (*Vertrauensmänner*). There is no such thing as appointment or dismissal, no career, no promotion. There is only a call at the instance of the leader on the basis of the charismatic qualification of those he summons. There is no hierarchy; the leader merely intervenes in general or in individual cases when he considers the members of his staff lacking in charismatic qualification for a given task. There is no such thing as a bailiwick or definite sphere of competence, and no appropriation of official powers on the basis of social privileges. There may, however, be territorial or functional limits to charismatic powers and to the individual's mission. There is no such thing as a salary or a benefice.

Disciples or followers tend to live primarily in a communistic relationship with their leader on means which have been provided by voluntary gift. There are no established administrative organs. In their place are agents who have been provided with charismatic authority by their leader or who possess charisma of their own. There are no organized formal rules, or abstract legal principles, and hence no process of rational judicial decision oriented to them. But equally there is no legal wisdom oriented to judicial precedent. Formally concrete judgments are newly created from case to case and are originally regarded as divine judgments and revelations.

From a substantive point of view, every charismatic authority would have to subscribe to the proposition: "It is written . . . but I say unto you . . ." The genuine prophet, like the genuine military leader and every true leader in this sense, preaches, creates, or demands *new* obligations – most typically, by virtue of revelation, oracle, inspiration, or of his own will, which are recognized by the members of the religious, military, or party group because they come from such a source. Recognition is a duty. When such an authority comes into conflict with the competing authority of another who also claims charismatic sanction, the only recourse is to some kind of a contest, by magical means or an actual physical battle of the leaders. In principle, only one side can be right in such a conflict; the other must be guilty of a wrong which has to be expiated.

Since it is "extraordinary," charismatic authority is sharply opposed to rational, and particularly bureaucratic, authority, and to traditional authority, whether in its patriarchal, patrimonial, or estate variants, all of which are everyday forms of domination while the charismatic type is the direct antithesis of this. Bureaucratic authority is specifically rational in the sense of being bound to intellectually analysable rules, while charismatic authority is specifically irrational in the sense of being foreign to all rules. Traditional authority is bound to the precedents handed down from the past and to this extent is also oriented to rules. Within the sphere of its claims, charismatic authority repudiates the past, and is in this sense a specifically revolutionary force. It recognizes no appropriation of positions of power by virtue of the possession of property, either on the part of a chief or of socially privileged groups. The only basis of legitimacy for it is personal charisma so long as it is proved; that is, as long as it receives recognition and as long as the followers and disciples prove their usefulness charismatically.

From *Economy and Society: An Outline of Interpretive Sociology*, eds Guenther Roth and Claus Wittich, trans. Talcott Parsons, revised by Guenther Roth and Claus Wittich, slightly revised by Stephen Kalberg (Berkeley, CA: University of California Press, 1978), p. 246.

In its pure form charismatic authority has a character specifically foreign to everyday routine structures. The social relationships directly involved are strictly personal, based on the validity and practice of charismatic personal qualities. If this is not to remain a purely transitory phenomenon, but to take on the character of a permanent relationship – a "community" of disciples or followers or a party organization or any sort of political or hierocratic organization – it is necessary for the character of charismatic authority to become radically changed. Indeed, in its pure form charismatic authority may be said to exist only *in natu nascendi*. It cannot remain stable, but becomes either traditionalized or rationalized, or a combination of both.

The following are the principal motives underlying this transformation: (a) The ideal and also the material interests of the followers in the continuation and the continual reactivation of the community, (b) the still stronger ideal and also stronger material interests of the members of the administrative staff, the disciples, the party workers or others in continuing their relationship. Not only this, but they have an interest in continuing it in such a way that both from an ideal and a material point of view, their own position is put on a stable everyday basis. This means, above all, making it possible to participate in normal family relationships or at least to enjoy a secure social position in place of the kind of discipleship which is cut off from ordinary worldly connections, notably in the family and in economic relationships.

These interests generally become conspicuously evident with the disappearance of the personal charismatic leader and with the problem of succession. The way in which this problem is met – if it is met at all and the charismatic community continues to exist or now begins to emerge – is of crucial importance for the character of the subsequent social relationships.

From "The Social Psychology of the World Religions," in *From Max Weber: Essays in Sociology*, eds and trans. H. H. Gerth and C. Wright Mills (New York: Oxford University Press, 1946), p. 297.

Throughout early history, charismatic authority, which rests upon a belief in the sanctity or the value of the extraordinary, and traditionalist (patriarchical) domination, which rests upon a belief in the sanctity of everyday routines, divided the most important authoritative relations between them. The bearers of charisma, the oracles of prophets, or the edicts of charismatic war lords alone could integrate "new" laws into the circle of what was upheld by tradition. Just as revelation and the sword were the two extraordinary powers, so were they the two typical innovators. In typical fashion, however, both succumbed to routinization as soon as their work was done.

With the death of the prophet or the war lord the question of successorship arises. This question can be solved by *Kürung*, which was originally not an "election" but a selection in terms of charismatic qualification; or the question can be solved by the sacramental substantiation of charisma, the successor being designated by consecration, as is the case in hierocratic or apostolic succession; or the belief in the charismatic qualification of the charismatic leader's sib can lead to a belief in hereditary charisma, as represented by hereditary kingship and hereditary hierocracy. With these routinizations, *rules* in some form always come to govern. The prince or the hierocrat no longer rules by virtue of purely personal qualities, but by virtue of acquired or inherited qualities, or because he has been legitimized by an act of charismatic election. The process of routinization, and thus traditionalization, has set in.

Perhaps it is even more important that when the organization of authority becomes permanent, the staff supporting the charismatic ruler becomes routinized. The ruler's disciples, apostles, and followers became priests, feudal vassals and, above all, officials. The original charismatic community lived communistically off donations, alms, and the booty of war: they were thus specifically alienated from the economic order. The community was transformed into a stratum of aids to the ruler and depended upon him for maintenance through the usufruct of land, office fees, income in kind, salaries, and hence, through prebends.

# part 6

# The Nation, the Modern State, and Modern Law

## Introduction

This Part collects several of Weber's writings on the nation, the modern state, and modern law. The diverse ways in which they overlap and intersect in different contemporary societies is apparent from these selections.

To provide an empirically clear and persuasive definition of the nation, Weber holds (Chapter 15), constitutes a difficult task. Undoubtedly, a nation implies "*it is proper* to expect from certain groups a specific sentiment of solidarity in the face of other groups" – and hence, he argues, "[it] belongs in the sphere of values" (p. 225). On what basis, however, are these groups demarcated and what sort of social action should this solidarity call forth?

Through sets of empirical observations and examples, Weber rejects, as too imprecise, factors often thought to stand at the foundation of the sense of nationhood: a common language, religious creed, and the "common blood" of a specific ethnic group, although all may call forth sentiments of national solidarity to a significant degree under specific circumstances. Moreover, changes occur over time. A certain group might be viewed in one epoch as a "race" and in another as a nation; in one era workers may view themselves as citizens of a nation, in another as in solidarity with workers across many nations. The same may be said of intellectuals. A "homogeneous or historically constant attitude towards the idea [of the 'nation']" (p. 227) cannot be empirically demonstrated. And the actual meaning of "national sentiments" is fluid and varies in strength, for example, among Germans, French, and Spaniards; each group understands "solidarity toward the outside" in its own way.

Weber's search for an empirically grounded ideal type reveals nations to be extremely complex and "entirely ambiguous." Yet an *idea* – a providential "mission" – seems of overarching centrality if the indispensable solidarity sentiment is to appear, he argues; the group must become defined as one that cultivates and preserves a particular and irreplaceable "culture" mission. (For further discussion of this concept, see 1968a, pp. 395–8.) The state proves less ambiguous (Chapter 16).

Cited widely as the standard definition to this day, Weber sees the state as a type of organization – "a political organization . . . [that] successfully claims a *monopoly over the legitimate* physical coercion necessary for the implementation of its laws and decrees" (p. 230; see 1946c, p. 334). Hence, this ideal type renders the state, as opposed to the nation, purely in terms of its capacity to fulfill a task. The extent to which a "providential mission" or a "solidarity sentiment" arises and becomes connected to a particular state remains, to Weber, variable and a subject for case-by-case empirical investigation. Similarly, whether the state is more democratic or more authoritarian must be examined empirically.

He then notes how the state arose as a political organization and "legal order." Both religious and economic forces were particularly central. In particular, those people with an economic interest in the expansion of markets required the suppression of private violence and the creation of "rationally ordered guarantees" – and these came into existence only as the political organization expanded. With pacification disputes became increasingly the domain of judges. The state's laws and legal procedures will capture our attention in a moment. In order to define the state more precisely, two features emphasized by Weber must be noted.

He addresses, in "The Economic Foundations of Imperialism (pp. 230–8)," how power stands at the center of the "specific internal dynamic" of political organizations, how prestige may derive from this power and in turn feed its aggrandizement, and how "claims to prestige have always played into the origins of wars." As a consequence of an "unavoidable 'dynamic of power,'" the search for prestige by large political organizations calls forth other "bearers of prestige" and potentially quite dangerous competitive relationships across states. And groups with vested interests in the political organization may well cultivate the sentiment of prestige, which in turn enhances belief "in the actual existence of one's own might." Against Marx, Weber insists that economic interests alone cannot explain this dynamic.

This acknowledgment of both political and economic forces characterizes his subsequent discussion. Rather than originating out of trade alone, the *imperialism of states* arises from the intertwining of the state's "dynamic of power" with the market interests of capitalists. Weber here offers a very sober accounting of the many ways in which economic interests play a central role wherever states expand, and the manner in which the legal framework of states can be influenced, on behalf of imperialism, by the vested interests of powerful groupings. Far greater opportunities for profit, he argues, are offered by imperialist capitalism than the "'pacifist' tendency of expansion which aims merely at freedom of trade." The revival in Weber's time of imperialist capitalism was "not accidental" and a state-socialist or collective economy would "hardly change [this situation] fundamentally" (p. 226).

This selection also emphasizes throughout a further Weberian position fundamentally in opposition to Marx: the modern state – its laws, statutes, and legal procedures – possesses autonomy, despite the perpetual influence exercised upon it by arrays of groupings with economic interests.[1] We are now prepared to address Weber's characterization of "modern law" (Chapter 17).

Following the accustomed format in his writings, he examines at the outset the character of law in past epochs and then turns to its modern manifestations. Traditions or consensus across groups in earlier eras legitimized laws rather than states. Consensual groups (families and clans) or rational associations (guilds, for example) formulated the "particular" or "special law" of these "law communities." Membership in each derived from the "objective characteristics" of persons, such as place of birth, ethnicity, religious affiliation, occupation, etc. *Between* these communities law was created through agreements that prescribed atonement mechanisms; *among* group members conflicts were settled by patriarchs and by reference to tradition.

The membership of people in one all-encompassing "compulsory institution" and its formal "legal equality" – that is, the state, with its authority over all within its boundaries, even to use force – constituted a giant leap away from particularist law, one pushed by two great "rationalizing forces": the market economy's expansion was central, but also, *contra* Marx, "the bureaucratization of the activities of the organs of the consensual groups" (p. 240). Legal procedures that sought to establish guilt or innocence appeared as modern law crystallized, and judges, bound by oath to uphold these procedures and to interpret evidence impartially, came to the fore. Arbitrariness, "subjectivistic instability," and substantive justice retreated as notions of formal justice and formal rationality, rooted in abstract reasoning and codified law carried by political and economic groupings interested in stable and predictable legal procedures, became more widespread. Long-range planning in the marketplace could take place only within a legal framework that offered some degree of certainty.

In its most methodical form as manifest in the Continental Law tradition ("Pandectist Civil Law"), the formal rational law of the modern West renders decisions based upon "abstract legal propositions" and articulates a "gapless system" of codes capable of encompassing all social action with "legal logic." As well as other modern law, it also expands the rights held by individuals and offers them legal guarantees of freedoms (movement, conscience, contract, and property disposition) and "the autonomy to regulate . . . relations with others." The state provides the legal framework (constitutions, parliaments, etc.) and the implementing institutions (police, courts) for all these components of modern law. The final reading (Chapter 17) offers a brief, but penetrating, overview of many of this chapter's crucial themes.

## NOTE

1. This idea – that the state possesses an internal dynamic and autonomy, even an independent influence *vis-à-vis* the capitalist economy – became central in the "state-centered" school of American sociology that developed in the 1970s and 1980s (see Skocpol, 1979; Evans *et al.*, 1984) [sk].

# chapter 15

# *The Nation*

## A SENTIMENT OF SOLIDARITY AND THE "NATIONAL" IDEA

From *Economy and Society: An Outline of Interpretive Sociology*, eds Guenther Roth and Claus Wittich, trans. H. H. Gerth and C. Wright Mills, revised by Guenther Roth and Claus Wittich, slightly revised by Stephen Kalberg (Berkeley, CA: University of California Press, 1978), pp. 922–6.

If the concept of "nation" can in any way be defined unambiguously, it certainly cannot be stated in terms of empirical qualities common to those who count as members of the nation. In the sense of those using the term at a given time, the concept undoubtedly means, above all, that *it is proper* to expect from certain groups a specific sentiment of solidarity in the face of other groups. Thus, the concept belongs in the sphere of values. Yet, there is no agreement on how these groups should be delimited or about what concerted action should result from such solidarity.

In ordinary language, "nation" is, first of all, not identical with the "people of a state," that is, with the membership of a given polity. Numerous polities comprise groups who emphatically assert the independence of their "nation" in the face of other groups; or they comprise merely *parts* of a group whose members declare themselves to be one homogenous "nation" (Austria is an example for both). Furthermore, a "nation" is not identical with a community speaking the same language; that this by no means always suffices is indicated by the Serbs and Croats, the North Americans, the Irish, and the English. On the contrary, a common language does not seem to be absolutely necessary to a "nation." In official documents, besides "Swiss People" one also finds the phrase "Swiss Nation." And some language groups do not think of themselves as a separate "nation," for example, at least until recently, the White Russians. As a rule, however, the pretension to be considered a special "nation" is associated with a common language as a culture value of the masses; this is predominantly the case in the classic country of language conflicts, Austria, and equally so in Russia and in eastern Prussia. But this linkage of the common language and "nation" is of varying intensity; for instance, it is very low in the United States as well as in Canada.

"National" solidarity among men speaking the same language may be just as well rejected as accepted. Solidarity, instead, may be linked with differences in the other great culture value of the masses, namely, a religious creed, as is the case with the Serbs and Croats. National solidarity may be connected with differing social structure and mores and hence with "ethnic" elements, as is the case with the German Swiss and the Alsatians in the face of the Germans of the Reich, or with the Irish facing the British. Yet above all, national solidarity may be linked to memories of a common political destiny with other nations, among the Alsatians with the French since the Revolutionary War which represents their common heroic age, just as among the Baltic Barons with the Russians whose political destiny they helped to steer.

It goes without saying that "national" affiliation need not be based upon common blood. Indeed, especially radical "nationalists" are often of foreign descent. Furthermore, although a specific common anthropological type is not irrelevant to nationality, it is neither sufficient nor prerequisite to nation founding. Nevertheless, the idea of the "nation" is apt to include the notions of common descent and of an essential, though frequently indefinite, homogeneity. The "nation" has these notions in common with the sentiment of solidarity of ethnic communities, which is also nourished from various sources. . . . But the sentiment of ethnic solidarity does not by itself make a "nation." Undoubtedly, even the White Russians in the face of the Great Russians have always had a sentiment of ethnic solidarity, yet even at the present time they would hardly claim to qualify as a separate "nation." . . .

Whether the Jews may be called a "nation" is an old problem. Most of the time, the answer will be negative. At any rate, the answers of the Russian Jews, of the assimilating West-European and American Jews, and of the Zionists would vary in nature and extent. In particular, the question would be answered very differently by the peoples of their environment, for example, by the Russians on the one side and the Americans on the other – or at least by those Americans who at the present time still maintain American and Jewish nature to be essentially similar, as an American President[1] has asserted in an official document.

Those German-speaking Alsatians who refuse to belong to the German "nation" and who cultivate the memory of political union with France do not thereby consider themselves simply as members of the French "nation." The Negroes of the United States, at least at present, consider themselves members of the American "nation," but they will hardly ever be so considered by the Southern Whites.

Only fifteen years ago [approx. 1900], men knowing the Far East still denied that the Chinese qualified as a "nation"; they held them to be only a "race." Yet today, not only the Chinese political leaders but also the very same observers would judge differently. Thus it seems that a group of people under certain conditions may attain the quality of a nation through specific behavior, or they may claim this quality as an "attainment" – and within short spans of time at that.

There are, on the other hand, social groups that profess indifference to, and even directly relinquish, any evaluational adherence to a single nation. At the present time, certain leading strata of the class movement of the modern proletariat consider such indifference and relinquishment to be an accomplishment. Their argument meets with varying success, depending upon political and linguistic affiliations and also upon different strata of the proletariat; on the whole, their success is rather diminishing at the present time.

An unbroken scale of quite varied and highly changeable attitudes toward the idea of the "nation" is to be found among social strata within single groups to whom language usage ascribes the quality of "nations." The scale extends from emphatic affirmation to emphatic negation and finally complete indifference, as may be characteristic of the citizens of Luxembourg and of nationally "unawakened" peoples. Feudal strata, strata of officials, bourgeois strata of various occupational categories, strata of "intellectuals" do not have homogeneous or historically constant attitudes towards the idea.

The reasons for the belief that one represents a nation vary greatly, just as does the empirical conduct that actually results from affiliation or lack of it with a nation. The "national sentiments" of the German, the Englishman, the North American, the Spaniard, the Frenchman, or the Russian do not function in an identical manner – to take only the simplest illustration – in relation to the polity, with the geographical boundaries of which the "idea" of the nation may come into conflict. This antagonism may lead to quite different results. Certainly the Italians in the Austrian state would fight Italian troops only if coerced into doing so. Large portions of the German Austrians would today fight against Germany only with the greatest reluctance; they could not be relied upon. The German-Americans, however, even those valuing their [former] "nationality" most highly, would fight against Germany, not gladly, yet, given the occasion, unconditionally. The Poles in the German State would fight readily against a Russian Polish army but hardly against an autonomous Polish army. The Austrian Serbs would fight against Serbia with very mixed feelings and only in the hope of attaining common autonomy. The Russian Poles would fight more reliably against a German than against an Austrian army.

It is a well-known historical fact that within the same nation the intensity of solidarity felt toward the outside is changeable and varies greatly in strength. On the whole, this sentiment has grown even where internal conflicts of interest have not diminished. Only sixty years ago the [Prussian conservative] *Kreuzzeitung* [newspaper] still appealed for the intervention of the emperor of Russia in internal German affairs; today, in spite of increased class antagonism, this would be difficult to imagine.

In any case, the differences in national sentiment are both significant and fluid and, as is the case in all other fields, fundamentally different answers are given to the question: What conclusions are a group of people willing to draw from the "national sentiment" found among them? No matter how emphatic and subjectively sincere a pathos may be formed among them, what sort of specific joint action are they ready to develop? The extent to which in the diaspora a custom, more correctly, a convention is adhered to as a "national" trait varies just as much as does the importance of common conventions for the belief in the existence of a separate "nation." In the face of this value concept of the "idea of the nation," which empirically is entirely ambiguous, a sociological typology would have to analyze all the individual kinds of sentiments of group membership and solidarity in reference to their original conditions and in their consequences for the social action of the participants. This cannot be attempted here.

Instead, we shall have to look a little closer into the fact that the idea of the nation for its advocates stands in very intimate relation to "prestige" interests. The earliest and most energetic manifestations of the idea, in some form, even though it may have been veiled, have contained the legend of a providential "mission." Those to whom the representatives of the idea zealously turned were expected to shoulder this mission. Another element of the early idea was the notion that this mission was facilitated solely through the very cultivation of the peculiarity of the group set off as a nation. Therewith, in so far as its self-justification is sought in the value of its content, this mission can consistently be thought of only as a specific "culture" mission.

The significance of the "nation" is usually anchored in the superiority, or at least the irreplaceability, of the culture values that are to be preserved and developed only through the cultivation of the peculiarity of the group. It therefore goes without saying that, just as those who wield power in the polity invoke the idea of the *state*, the intellectuals, as we shall tentatively call those who usurp leadership in a *Kulturgemeinschaft* (that is, within a group of people who by virtue of their peculiarity have access to certain products that are considered "culture goods"), are specifically predestined to propagate the "*national*" idea. This happens when those culture agents . . .[2] [see also *E&S*, pp. 395–8].

## NOTES

1. Weber here seems mistakenly to have had Theodore Roosevelt in mind (see *PE*, p. 233, n. 57) instead of Grover Cleveland. See Guenther Roth, "Max Weber's Views on Jewish Integration," in *Max Weber Studies*, vol. 3, no. 1 (Nov. 2002), pp. 61ff [sk].
2. The presentation breaks off here. Notes on the margin of the manuscript indicate that Weber intended to deal with the idea and development of the nation state throughout history. The following observations were found on the margin of the sheet: Cultural prestige and power prestige are closely associated. Every *victorious* war enhances the cultural prestige (Germany [1871], Japan [1905], etc.). Whether war *furthers* the "development of culture" is another question, one which cannot be solved in a "value neutral" way. It certainly does *not* do it in an *unambiguous* way (see Germany after 1871!). Even on the basis of purely empirical criteria it would *not* seem to do so: Pure art and literature of a specifically German character did *not* develop in the political *center* of Germany [Marianne Weber].

# chapter 16

# The State, its Basic Functions, and the Economic Foundations of Imperialism

From "Political Organizations and the State," in *Wirtschaft und Gesellschaft* (*Economy and Society*), ed. Johannes Winckelmann, trans. Stephen Kalberg (Tübingen: Mohr Verlag, [1922] 1976), pp. 29–30.

A *political* organization is defined as a domination organization when and in so far as its existence and the validity of its practices within a given geographical *territory* are guaranteed on a regular basis by an administrative staff's threat – and application – of *physical* coercion. A *state* is defined as a political *organization with compulsory membership* (*Anstaltsbetrieb*) when and in so far as its administrative staff successfully claims a *monopoly over the legitimate* physical coercion necessary for the implementation of its laws and decrees. . . .

It would seem best to define the concept *state*, because it has attained its full development only in the modern period, in terms corresponding to its modern manifestation. However, . . . the state that we experience today is characterized by a changing content, and hence our concept should constitute an abstraction from the present state. Viewed in terms of its formal features, the state of today is characterized by administrative and legal orders – which can be altered through enacted procedures – and an administrative staff oriented to the flow of organized action (which in turn is ordered according to enacted procedures). This state makes a claim to possessing validity not only *vis-à-vis* those who have landed within its boundaries essentially through birth, but also, to a large extent, in regard to all action that occurs within the territory of its domination (that is, it constitutes a territorial compulsory organization). Today, furthermore, "legitimate" violence exists only to the extent that the state's laws permit or prescribe it – for example, the "right to discipline children" is permitted to the father of the family. (This right, even to the extent of allowing power over the life and death of the child or slave, is a legacy of the once legitimate violence of the household's patriarch.) This monopolization of legitimate violence constitutes a feature of the state just as essential to its contemporary situation as two other characteristics: its rational "compulsory" jurisdiction over a territory and its continuity "of operation."

From *Economy and Society: An Outline of Interpretive Sociology*, eds Guenther Roth and Claus Wittich, trans. Max Rheinstein, revised by Guenther Roth and Claus Wittich (Berkeley, CA: University of California Press, 1978), pp. 908–9.

... If the coercive apparatus is strong enough, it will suppress private violence in any form. The effectiveness of this suppression rises with the development of the coercive apparatus into a permanent from, and with the growing interest in solidarity against outsiders. Initially it is directed only against those forms of private violence which would injure directly the military interests of the political community itself. Thus in the thirteenth century the French monarchy suppressed the feuds of the royal vassals for the duration of a foreign war conducted by the king himself. Subsequently, it engenders, more generally, a form of permanent public peace, with the compulsory submission of all disputes to the arbitration of the judge, who transforms blood vengeance into rationally ordered punishment, and feuds and expiatory actions into rationally ordered legal procedures.

Whereas in early times even actions which were openly recognized as felonious were not proceeded against by the organized community except upon pressure on the part of religious or military interests, now the prosecution of an ever widening sphere of injuries to persons and property is being placed under the guaranty of the political coercive apparatus. Thus the political community monopolizes the legitimate application of violence for its coercive apparatus and is gradually transformed into an institution for the protection of rights. In so doing it obtains a powerful and decisive support from all those groups which have a direct or indirect economic interest in the expansion of the market community, as well as from the religious authorities. These latter are best able to control the masses under conditions of increasing pacification.

Economically, however, the groups most interested in pacification are those guided by market interests, especially the burghers of the towns, as well as all those who are interested in river, road, or bridge tolls and in the tax-paying capacity of their tenants and subjects. These interest groups expand with an expanding money economy. Even before the political authority imposed public peace in its own interest, it was they who, in the Middle Ages, attempted, in coöperation with the church, to limit feuds and to establish temporary, periodical, or permanent leagues for the maintenance of public peace (*Landfriedensbünde*). And as the expansion of the market disrupted the monopolistic organizations and led their members to the awareness of their interests in the market, it cut out from under them the basis of that community of interests on which the legitimacy of their violence had developed. The spread of pacification and the expansion of the market thus constitute a development which is accompanied, along parallel lines, by (1) that monopolization of legitimate violence by the political organization which finds its culmination in the modern concept of the *state* as the ultimate source of every kind of legitimacy of the use of physical force; and (2) that rationalization of the rules of its application which has come to culminate in the concept of the legitimate legal order.

# Power Prestige and the "Great Powers"

From *Economy and Society: An Outline of Interpretive Sociology*, eds Guenther Roth and Claus Wittich, trans. H. H. Gerth and C. Wright Mills, revised by Guenther Roth and Claus Wittich, slightly revised by Stephen Kalberg (Berkeley, CA: University of California Press, 1978), pp. 910–20.

All political formations use force, but they differ in the manner in which they use or threaten to use it against other political organizations. These differences play a specific role in determining the form and destiny of political communities. Not all political formations are equally "expansive." They do not all strive for an outward expansion of their power, or keep their force in readiness for acquiring political power over other territories and communities by incorporating them or making them dependent. Hence, as formations of power, political organizations vary in the extent to which they are turned outward. . . .

The power of political formations has a specific internal dynamic. On the basis of this power, the members may pretend to a special "prestige," and their pretensions may influence the external conduct of the power formations. Experience teaches that claims to prestige have always played into the origin of wars. Their part is difficult to gauge; it cannot be determined in general, but it is very obvious. The realm of "honor," which is comparable to the "status order" within a social order, pertains also to the interrelations of political formations.

Feudal lords, like modern officers or bureaucrats, are the natural and primary exponents of this desire for power-oriented prestige for one's own political formation. Power for their political community means power for themselves, as well as the prestige based on this power. For the bureaucrat and the officer, an expansion of power means more office positions, more sinecures, and better opportunities for promotion. . . .

Besides and beyond these direct economic interests, which naturally exist everywhere among strata living off the exercise of political power, the striving for prestige pertains to all specific power forms and hence to all widespread political forms. This striving is not identical simply with "national pride" – of this, more later – and it is not identical with the mere pride in the excellent qualities, actual or presumed, of one's own political community or in the mere possession of such a polity. Such pride can be highly developed, as is the case among the Swiss and the Norwegians, yet it may actually be strictly isolationist and free from pretension to political prestige.

The prestige of power means in practice the glory of power over other communities; it means the expansion of power, though not always by way of incorporation or subjection. The big political communities are the natural exponents of such pretensions to prestige.

Every political formation naturally prefers to have weak rather than strong neighbors. Furthermore, as every big political community is a potential aspirant to prestige, it is also a potential threat to all its neighbors; hence, the big political formation, simply because it is big and strong, is latently and constantly endangered. Finally, by virtue of an unavoidable "dynamic of power," wherever claims to prestige flame up – and this normally results from an acute political danger to peace – they challenge and call forth the competition of all other possible bearers of prestige. The history of the last decade [1900–1910], especially the relations between Germany and France, shows the prominent effect of this irrational element in all political foreign relations. The sentiment of prestige is able to strengthen the ardent belief in the actual existence of one's own might, and this is important for positive self-assurance in case of conflict. Therefore, all those having vested interests in the political formation tend systematically to cultivate this prestige sentiment.

Nowadays one usually refers to those polities that appear to be the bearers of power prestige as the "Great Powers." Among a plurality of co-existing polities, some, the Great Powers, usually ascribe to themselves and usurp an interest in political and economic processes over a wide orbit. Today such orbits encompass the whole surface of the planet. During Hellenic Antiquity, the "King," that is, the Persian king, despite his defeat, was the most widely recognized Great Power. Sparta turned to him in order to impose, with his sanction, the King's Peace (Peace of Antalcidas) upon the Hellenic world [387 BC]. Later on, before the establishment of an empire, the Roman polity assumed such a role. However, for general reasons of "power dynamics," the Great Powers are very often expansive powers; that is, they are organizations aiming at expanding the territories of their respective political communities by the use or the threat of force. Yet Great Powers are not necessarily and not always oriented towards expansion. Their attitude in this respect often changes, and in these changes economic factors play a weighty part. . . .

# The Economic Foundations of "Imperialism"

One might be inclined to believe that the origin as well as the expansion of Great Power formations is always and primarily determined economically. The assumption that trade, especially if it is intensive and if it already exists in an area, is the normal prerequisite and the reason for its political unification might readily be generalized. In individual cases this assumption does actually hold. The example of the *Zollverein* [customs union] lies close at hand, and there are numerous others. Closer attention, however, very often reveals that this coincidence is not a necessary one, and that the causal nexus by no means always points in a single direction.

Germany, for instance, has been made into a unified economic territory, that is one whose inhabitants seek to sell their products primarily in their own market, only through custom frontiers at her borders, which were determined in a purely political manner. Were all custom barriers eliminated, the economically determined market for the Eastern German cereal surplus, poor in gluten, would not be Western Germany but rather England. The economically determined market of the mining products and the heavy iron goods of Western Germany is by no means Eastern Germany; and Western Germany is not, in the main, the economically determined supplier of the industrial products for Eastern Germany. Above all, the interior lines of communications (railroads) of Germany would not be – and, in part, are not now – economically determined routes for transporting heavy goods between east and west. Eastern Germany, however, would be the economic location for strong industries, the economically determined market and hinterland for which would be the whole of Western Russia. Such industries are now cut off by Russian custom barriers and have been moved to Poland, directly behind the Russian custom frontier. Through this development, as is known, the political *Anschluss* of the Russian Poles to the Russian imperial idea, which seemed to be politically out of the question, has been brought into the realm of possibility. Thus, in this case, purely economically determined market relations have a politically unifying effect.

Germany, however, has been politically united *against* the economic determinants as such. It is not unusual for the frontiers of a polity to conflict with the mere geographically given conditions of economic location; the political frontiers may encompass areas that, in terms of economic factors, strive to separate. In such situations, tensions among economic interests nearly always arise. However, if the political bond is once created, it is very often, so incomparably stronger that, under otherwise favorable conditions (e.g. the existence of a common language), nobody would even think of political separation because of such economic tensions. This applies, for instance, to Germany. . . .

. . . If trade in itself is by no means the decisive factor in political expansion, the economic structure in general does co-determine the extent and manner of political expansion. Besides women, cattle, and slaves, scarce land is one of the original and foremost objects of forceful acquisition. For conquering peasant communities, the natural way is to take the land directly and to wipe out its settled population. . . . How far a land scarcity, caused by overpopulation, contributed, how far the political pressure of other tribes, or simply good opportunities, must be left open. . . .

Where the ultimate state creditors are a mass stratum of state rentiers (bondholders) such credits provide profit opportunities for bond-issuing banks, as is characteristic of our day. The interests of those who supply the materials of war point in the same direction. In all this, economic forces interested in the emergence of military conflagrations *per se*, no matter what be the outcome for their own community, are called into life.

Aristophanes distinguished between industries interested in war and industries interested in peace, although as is evident from his enumeration, the center of gravity in his time was still the self-equipped army. The individual citizen gave orders to artisans such as the sword-maker and the armorer. But even then the large private commercial storehouses, often designated as "factories," were above all stores of armaments. Today the polity as such is almost the sole agent to order war material and the engines of war. This enhances the capitalist nature of the process. Banks finance war loans, and today large sections of heavy industry are *quand même* economically interested in warfare; the direct suppliers of armor plates and guns are not the only ones so interested. A lost war, as well as a successful war, brings increased business to these banks and industries. Moreover, the powers-that-be in a polity are politically and economically interested in the existence of large home factories for war engines. This interest compels them to allow these factories to provide the whole world with their products, political opponents included.

The extent to which the interests of imperialist capitalism are counterbalanced depends above all on the profitableness of imperialism as compared with the capitalist interests of pacifist orientation, insofar as purely capitalist motives here play a direct part. And this in turn is closely connected with the extent to which economic needs are satisfied by a private or a public economy. The relation between the two is highly important for the nature of expansive eonomic tendencies backed up by political communities.

In general and at all times, imperialist capitalism, especially colonial booty capitalism based on direct force and compulsory labor, has offered by far the greatest opportunities for profit. They have been greater by far than those normally open to industrial enterprises which worked for exports and which oriented themselves to peaceful trade with members of other politics. Therefore, imperialist capitalism has always existed wherever to any relevant degree the polity *per se*, or its subdivisions (municipalities), satisfied its wants through a public economy. The stronger such an economy has been, the more important imperialist capitalism has been.

Increasing opportunities for profit abroad emerge again today, especially in territories that are opened up politically and economically, that is, brought into the specifically modern forms of public and private enterprise. These opportunities spring from public arms contracts; from railroad and other construction tasks carried out by the polity or by builders endowed with monopoly rights; from monopolist organizations for the collection of levies for trade and industry; from monopolist concessions; and from government loans.

The preponderance of such profit opportunities increases, at the expense of profits from the usual private trade, the more that public enterprises gain in economic importance as a general form of supplying needs. This tendency is directly paralleled by politically backed economic expansion and competition among individual polities, whose members can afford to invest capital. These members aim at securing for themselves such monopolies and shares in public commissions. And the importance of the mere "open door" for the private importation of goods recedes into the background.

The safest way of monopolizing for the members of one's own polity profit opportunities which are linked to the public economy of the foreign territory is to occupy it or at least to subject the foreign political power in the form of a "protectorate" or some such arrangement. Therefore, this "imperialist" tendency increasingly displaces the "pacifist" tendency of expansion, which aims merely at freedom of trade. The latter gained the upper hand only so long as the organization of supply by private capitalism shifted the optimum of capitalist profit opportunities towards pacifist trade and not towards monopolist trade, or at least trade not monopolized by political power.

The universal revival of "imperialist" capitalism, which has always been the normal form in which capitalist interests have influenced politics, and the revival of political drives for expansion are thus not accidental. For the predictable future, the prognosis will have to be made in its favor.

This situation would hardly change fundamentally if for a moment we were to make the mental experiment of assuming the individual polities to be somehow "state-socialist" communities, that is, organizations supplying a maximum amount of their needs through a collective economy. They would seek to buy as cheaply as possible indispensable goods not produced on their own territory (cotton in Germany, for instance) from others that have natural monopolies and would seek to exploit them. It is probable that force would be used where it would lead easily to favorable conditions of exchange; the weaker party would thereby be obliged to pay tribute, if not formally then at least actually. For the rest, one cannot see why the strong state-socialist communities should disdain to squeeze tribute out of the weaker communities for their own partners where they could do so, just as happened everywhere during early history. Even in a polity without state-socialism the mass of citizens need be as little interested in pacifism as is any single stratum.

The Attic *demos* – and not it alone – lived economically off war. War brought soldiers' pay and, in case of a victory, tribute from the subjects. This tribute was actually distributed among the full citizens in the hardly veiled form of attendance-fees at popular assemblies, court hearings, and public festivities. Here, every full citizen could directly grasp the interest in imperialist policy and power. Nowadays, the yields flowing from abroad to the members of a polity, including those of imperialist origin and those actually representing "tribute," do not result in a constellation of interests so comprehensible to the masses. For under the present economic order, the tribute to "creditor nations" assumes the forms of interest payments on debts or of capital profits transferred from abroad to the propertied strata of the "creditor nation." Were one to imagine these tributes abolished, it would mean for countries like England, France, and Germany a very palpable decline of purchasing power for home products. This would influence the labor market in an unfavorable manner.

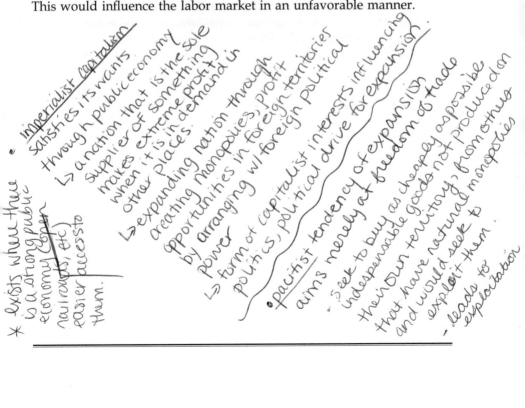

# chapter 17

# From Particularistic Law to Formal Legal Equality and the Rights of Individuals

From *Economy and Society: An Outline of Interpretive Sociology*, eds Guenther Roth and Claus Wittich, trans. Max Rheinstein, revised by Guenther Roth and Claus Wittich, and Stephen Kalberg (Berkeley, CA: University of California Press, 1978), pp. 695–6.

In the past, special law arose normally as "volitive law" (*gewillkürtes Recht*), that is, from tradition, or as the agreed enactment of consensual "status" groups (*Einverständnisgemeinschaften*) or of rational associations. It arose, in other words, in the form of autonomously created orders. The maxim that "particularistic law" (i.e., volitive law in the above sense) "breaks" (i.e., takes precedence over) the "law of the land" (i.e., the generally valid common law) was recognized almost universally, and it obtains even today in almost all legal systems outside the Occident, and in Europe, for example, to some extent for the Russian peasantry [before World War I]. But the state insisted almost everywhere, and usually with success, that the validity of these special laws, as well as the extent of their application, should be subject to its consent; and the state did this in just the same manner in which it also transformed the towns and cities into heteronomous organizations endowed by the state with powers defined by it. In both cases, however, this was not the original state of affairs. For the body of laws by which a given locality or a group were governed was largely the autonomously arrogated creation of mutually independent communities or associated groups between which the continuously necessitated adjustment was either achieved by mutual compromise or by imposition through those political or ecclesiastical authorities which would happen at the given time to have preponderant power. . . .

Prior to the emergence and triumph of the purposive contract and of freedom of contract in the modern sense, and prior to the emergence of the modern state, every consensual group or rational association which represented a special legal order and which therefore might properly be named a "law community" (*Rechtsgemeinschaft*) was either constituted in its membership by such objective characteristics as birth, political, ethnic, or religious denomination, mode of life or occupation, or arose through the process of explicit fraternization across groups of *persons*. The primitive situation, as we have seen above, was that any "lawsuit" that would correspond to our "trials" took place only in the form of reconciliation-proceedings between *different* groups (sibs) and their members. Within the group, i.e., among the members of the group, patriarchal arbitration prevailed. At the very origin of all legal history there thus prevailed, if viewed from the standpoint of the political power and its continuously growing strength, an important dualism, i.e., a dualism of the autonomously created law between groups, and the norms determinative of disputes among group members. At the same time, however, another fact intruded into this apparently simple situation: namely, that even at the earliest stages of development known to us the individual often belonged to several groups rather than to just one.

But, nevertheless, the subjection to the special law was initially a strictly personal quality, a "privilege" acquired by usurpation or grant, and thus a monopoly of its possessors who, by virtue of this fact, became "comrades in law" (*Rechtsgenossen*). Hence, in those groups which were politically integrated by a common supreme authority, like the Persian empire, the Roman empire, the kingdom of the Franks, or the Islamic states, the body of laws to be applied by the judicial officers differed in accordance with the ethnic, religious, or political characteristics of the component groups, for instance, legally or politically autonomous cities or clans. Even in the Roman empire, Roman law was at first the law for Roman citizens only, and it did not entirely apply in the relations between citizens and noncitizen subjects. The non-Moslem subjects of the Islamic states and even the adherents of the four orthodox schools of Islamic law live in accordance with their own laws; but when the former resort to the Islamic judge rather than to their own authorities, he applies Islamic law, as he is not obliged to know any other, and as in the Islamic state the non-Moslems are mere "subjects."

From "Political Groups," in *Wirtschaft und Gesellschaft. Grundriss der verstehenden Soziologie* [*Economy and Society: An Outline of Interpretive Sociology*], ed. Johannes Winckelmann, trans Stephen Kalberg. (Tübingen: Mohr Verlag, [1922] 1976), p. 516.

The modern position of political organizations rests on the prestige bestowed upon them by a specific belief held by their members in a special consecration, namely, in the "legitimacy" of that social action prescribed by these organizations. This prestige becomes greater to the extent that this social action involves physical coercion encompassing the power to dispose over life and death. A consensus regarding the actual legitimacy of this power to dispose over life and death is specific to political organizations.

This belief in the specific "legitimacy" of action oriented to a political organization can intensify – as is actually the case under modern circumstances – to the point where exclusively certain political groups (called "states") are viewed as ones, on the basis of their contracts with or permissions from some other groups, capable of "legitimately" exercising physical coercion. Accordingly, a system of casuistic statutes and rules, to which this specific "legitimacy" is imputed, exists in the fully developed political group for the purpose of exercising and threatening to exercise this coercion – namely, the "legal order." The political community, because it has in fact today normally usurped the monopoly forcefully to bestow – through physical coercion – respect for these statutes and rules, constitutes its single normal creator.

This guaranteeing of a "legal order" prominently by *political* force originated from a very long developmental process. Owing to pressures emanating from economic and organizational transformations, in this process other groups that appeared as carriers of their own coercive force lost their power over individuals. Either they disintegrated or became subjugated by action oriented to a political community. This resulted in a constriction of their coercive force or a managing of it. Yet, simultaneously, there developed constantly new interests that needed to be protected – yet found no politically guaranteed legal order to do so. A continuously expanding circle of interests, especially economic interests, would eventually find security only through those rationally ordered guarantees created by the political community. . . . In this process . . . all "legal norms" became – and are still becoming – the domain of states ("*Verstaatlichung*").

From *Economy and Society: An Outline of Interpretive Sociology*, eds Guenther Roth and Claus Wittich, trans. Max Rheinstein, revised by Guenther Roth and Claus Wittich, slightly revised by Stephen Kalberg (Berkeley, CA: University of California Press, 1978), pp. 698–9.

The ever-increasing integration of all persons and facts of the case into one compulsory institution which today, at least, rests in principle on formal "legal equality" has been achieved by two great rationalizing forces, i.e., first, by the extension of the market economy and, second, by the bureaucratization of the activities of the organs of the consensual groups. They replaced that particularist mode of creating law which was based upon the private power or the granted privileges of monopolistically closed organizations; that means, they reduced the autonomy of what were essentially organized status groups in two ways: The first is the formal, universally accessible, but closely regulated autonomy of voluntary associations which may be created by anyone wishing to do so; the other consists in the grant to everyone of the power to create law of his own by means of engaging in private legal transactions of certain kinds. The decisive factors in this transformation of the technical forms of autonomous legislation were, politically, the power-needs of the rulers and officials of the state as it was growing in strength and, economically, the interests of those segments of society that were oriented towards power in the market, i.e., those persons who were economically privileged in the formally "free" competitive struggle of the market by virtue of their position as property owners – an instance of "class position." If, by virtue of the principle of formal legal equality, everyone "without respect of person" may establish a business corporation or entail a landed estate, the *propertied* classes *as such* obtain a sort of factual "autonomy," since they alone are able to utilize or take advantage of these powers. . . .

From *Economy and Society: An Outline of Interpretive Sociology*, eds Guenther Roth and Claus Wittich, trans. Max Rheinstein, revised by Guenther Roth and Claus Wittich, slightly revised by Stephen Kalberg (Berkeley, CA: University of California Press, 1978), pp. 811–14.

Juridical formalism enables the legal system to operate like a technically rational machine. Thus it guarantees to individuals and groups within the system a relative maximum of freedom, and greatly increases for them the possibility of predicting the legal consequences of their actions. Procedure becomes a specific type of pacified contest, bound to fixed and inviolable "rules of the game." . . . The modern theory . . . binds the judge to the motions of, and the evidence offered by, the parties and, indeed, the same principle applies to the entire conduct of the suit: in accordance with the principle of adversary procedure the judge has to wait for the motions of the parties. Whatever is not introduced or put into a motion does not exist as far as the judge is concerned; the same is true of facts which remain undisclosed by the recognized methods of proof, be they rational or irrational. Thus, the judge aims at establishing only that relative truth which is attainable within the limits set by the procedural acts of the parties. . . .

. . . Formal justice guarantees the maximum freedom for the interested parties to represent their formal legal interests. But because of the unequal distribution of economic power, which the system of formal justice legalizes, this very freedom must time and again produce consequences which are contrary to the substantive postulates of religious ethics or of political expediency. Formal justice is thus repugnant to all authoritarian powers, theocratic as well as patriarchic, because it diminishes the dependency of the individual upon the grace and power of the authorities. To democracy, however, it has been repugnant because it decreases the dependency of the legal practice and therewith of the individuals upon the decisions of their fellow citizens. Furthermore, the development of the trial into a peaceful contest of conflicting interests can contribute to the further concentration of economic and social power.

In all these cases formal justice, due to its necessarily abstract character, infringes upon the ideals of substantive justice. It is precisely this abstract character which constitutes the decisive merit of formal justice to those who wield the economic power at any given time and who are therefore interested in its unhampered operation, but also to those who on ideological grounds attempt to break down authoritarian control or to restrain irrational mass emotions for the purpose of opening up individual opportunities and liberating capacities. To all these groups nonformal justice simply represents the likelihood of absolute arbitrariness and subjectivistic instability. Among those groups who favor formal justice we must include all those political and economic interest groups to whom the stability and predictability of legal procedure are of very great importance, i.e., particularly rational, economic, and political organizations intended to have a permanent character. Above all, those in possession of economic power look upon a formal rational administration of justice as a guarantee of "freedom," a value which is repudiated not only by theocratic or patriarchal-authoritarian groups but, under certain conditions, also by democratic groups. Formal justice and the "freedom" which it guarantees are indeed rejected by all groups ideologically interested in substantive justice. . . .

. . . [C]apitalistic interests will fare best under a rigorously formal system of adjudication, which applies in all cases and operates under the adversary system of procedure. In any case adjudication by honoratiores inclines to be essentially empirical, and its procedure is complicated and expensive. It may thus well stand in the way of the interests of the bourgeois classes and it may indeed be said that England achieved capitalistic supremacy among the nations not because but rather in spite of its judicial system. For these very reasons the bourgeois strata have generally tended to be intensely interested in a rational procedural system and therefore in a systematized, unambiguous, and specialized formal law which eliminates both obsolete traditions and arbitrariness and in which rights can have their source exclusively in general objective norms. Such a systematically codified law was thus demanded by the English Puritans, the Roman Plebeians, and the German bourgeoisie of the nineteenth century. . . .

From *Economy and Society: An Outline of Interpretive Sociology*, eds Guenther Roth and Claus Wittich, trans. Max Rheinstein, revised by Guenther Roth and Claus Wittich, slightly revised by Stephen Kalberg (Berkeley, CA: University of California Press, 1978), pp. 657–8.

. . . Present-day legal science, at least in those forms which have achieved the highest measure of methodological and logical rationality, i.e., those which have been produced through the legal science of the Pandectists' Civil Law, proceeds from the following five postulates: viz., first, that every concrete legal decision be the "application" of an abstract legal proposition to a concrete "fact situation"; second, that it must be possible in every concrete case to derive the decision from abstract legal propositions by means of legal logic; third, that the law must actually or virtually constitute a "gapless" system of legal propositions, or must, at least, be treated as if it were such a gapless system; fourth, that whatever cannot be "construed" rationally in legal terms is also legally irrelevant; and fifth, that every social action of human beings must always be visualized as either an "application" or "execution" of legal propositions, or as an "infringement" thereof, since the "gaplessness" of the legal system must result in a gapless "legal ordering" of all social conduct. . . .

From *Economy and Society: An Outline of Interpretive Sociology*, eds Guenther Roth and Claus Wittich, trans. Max Rheinstein, revised by Guenther Roth and Claus Wittich, and Stephen Kalberg (Berkeley, CA: University of California Press, 1978), pp. 667–8.

From the juridical point of view, modern law consists of "legal propositions," i.e., abstract norms the content of which asserts that a certain factual situation is to have certain legal consequences. The most usual classification of legal propositions distinguishes, as in the case of all orders, between prescriptive, prohibitory, and permissive ones; they respectively give rise to the rights of each person to prescribe, or prohibit, or allow, an action vis-à-vis another person. Sociologically, such legally guaranteed and limited power over the action of others corresponds to the expectation that other persons will either engage in, or refrain from, certain conduct or that one may himself engage, or fail to engage, in certain conduct without interference from a third party. The first two expectations constitute claims, the latter constitutes a privilege. Every right is thus a source of power of which even a hitherto entirely powerless person may become possessed. In this way he becomes the source of completely novel situations within the social action.

Nevertheless, we are not at present concerned with this phenomenon, but rather wish to deal with the qualitative effect of legal propositions of a *certain* type inasmuch as they expand an individual right-holder's power of control. This type with which we shall deal is constituted by the third kind of legally guaranteed expectations previously mentioned, i.e., the *privileges*. In the development of the present economic order they are of particularly great importance. Privileges are of two main kinds: The *first* is constituted by the so-called freedoms, i.e., situations of simple protection against certain types of interference by third parties, especially state officials, within the sphere of legally permitted conduct; instances are freedom of movement, freedom of conscience or freedom of disposition over property. The *second* type of privilege is that which grants to a person *autonomy to regulate* his *relations with others* by his own transactions. Freedom of contract, for example, exists exactly to the extent to which such autonomy is recognized by the legal order.

There exists, of course, an intimate connection between the expansion of the market and the expanding measure of contractual freedom or, in other words, the scope of arrangements which are guaranteed as valid by the legal order or, in again different terms, the relative significance within the total legal order of those rules which authorize such transactional dispositions. In an economy where self-sufficiency prevails and exchange is lacking, the function of the law will naturally be otherwise: it will mainly define and delimit a person's non-economic relations and privileges with regard to other persons in accordance, not with economic considerations, but with the person's origin, education, or social status.

# part 7

# The Circumscription of Ethical Action Today and Weber's Response

## Introduction

The fate of ethical action in the modern epoch constitutes a major theme for Weber. The increasing dominance of practical, formal, and theoretical rationality presents a great danger, he believes, owing to their incapacity to cultivate values. Only values, he is convinced, lend an obligatory or binding – an ethical – aspect to action, endow it with dignity, and firmly ground compassion, responsibility, and brotherhood. Moreover, values provide a foundation for initiative-taking and leadership, and uproot action from practical rationality, namely, its normal pragmatic and means–end rational flow in response to random constraints and opportunities. To him, values possess the capacity to organize and guide action in a sustained manner, and to supply *direction and continuity* – and hence unity and dignity – to life as a whole. They alone call forth autonomous individuals.

Weber's wide-ranging comparative-historical studies persuaded him that values find their origin in specific constellations of social forces. Their creation and nourishment, to the point where people understand them as binding upon action and then become ethical actors, never develop simply out of evolutionary processes. Values fade away if lacking strong carriers and if social configurations that place a pluralistic competition across values into motion are absent. They are articulated, defended, and continuously rejuvenated only within a milieu conducive to vigorous cross-value competition (see pp. 34–5).

Readings in this Part scrutinize this pivotal theme from several discrete angles. The ways in which two arenas central in the modern world – the economy and political domains, here constructed as ideal types – stand in relationships of antagonism to ethical values are first examined (Chapter 18; see also 1968a, pp. 576–601). Where today are the social carriers of values heretofore cultivated for centuries by "ethical salvation religions of brotherhood and compassion"?

Weber contends in the first selection that free market economies must not be evaluated only by reference to their demonstrated capacity to call forth high degrees of formal rationality and to produce high living standards. Once broadly in place in a given society, what general consequences do free markets imply? In what ways, he asks, does the unrestricted marketplace influence "how we live" and the fate of the ethical action cultivated originally as a "fraternal ethic" by the great world religions? To Weber, inherently anchored in interest struggles and impersonal calculations of advantage, the "rational economy is a functional organization oriented to money prices . . . [and] . . . its own immanent laws" (1946c, p. 331). Standing in radical opposition to all personal relationships, the marketplace excludes ethical action. Even the hierarchical relationship between master and slave, because personal, could be ethically regulated by appeals to conscience, he contends; however, the fluctuating relationships between stockholders who own banks and property owners issued mortgages from these banks preclude regulation in the same manner. Here the impersonal laws of the market and the search for competitive advantage govern – and must govern, at the cost of bankruptcy – decision-making (see 1946c, p. 331; 1968a, p. 1186).

Can the realm of politics cultivate and carry ethical action? In the distant past, patriarchs ruled in the political domain and rendered decisions according to the piety of the supplicant and the particular merit of the case, or "with regard to the person"; thus, an ethical appeal could be made to them even when vast power discrepancies existed. However, in Weber's ideal type, the political realm in its modern manifestation – the state – is highly bureaucratized and the *homo politicus* serves fundamentally as a manager integrated into its affairs and "rational rules." In the same sense as the modern economy, the state remains "depersonalized": it operates impartially according to laws and statutes, "without hate and therefore without love."

An "objective pragmatism" and a matter-of-fact management of affairs hold sway – a mode of operation, in other words, "in the final analysis" scarcely accessible to the ethical appeals of salvation religions of brotherhood. Indeed, the state retains, by the use of force if necessary and according to its own impersonally implemented policies, statutes, and ends ("reasons of state"), the right of life and death over its citizens. Social welfare policies and charitable programs, which may become empirically quite extensive in some states, do not alter these fundamental features of this model. The impartial administration of its "bureaucratized apparatus," and the means–end rational calculations typical of its operation on behalf of the maintenance of power, render the state "estranged from brotherliness."

Both the economy and political spheres develop in the modern era more and more freely in reference to their "own laws." Where, then, Weber asks, in light of the powerful expansion of these domains and the formal rationality their bureaucracies carry, are compassion, a brotherhood ethic, binding values, and ethical responsibility cultivated?[1] These themes are the subject of the readings in this section's second chapter (Chapter 19).

This dilemma faced by modern societies – the need for markets and states, on behalf of high standards of living and the efficient distribution of goods and justice, to become bureaucratized and to follow their own impersonal laws, yet the inaccessibility of these organizations and laws to direct ethical appeals – caused Weber enormous concern. His worries continued even though he knew that legacies of compassion, brotherhood, and charity from the ethical salvation religions *do* still exist; indeed, he remained fully aware that religions continued to cultivate these values in some countries. These values in some empirical cases penetrated even into the impersonal functioning of the economy and the state, and introduced strong limitations. Moreover, the state may, on behalf of a set of "social justice" values (substantive rationality), pass legislation that restricts the economy's formal rationality (see 1968a, pp. 880–92).[2] However, Weber sees yet a further threat to ethical action on the horizon – the bureaucratization of modern societies in an even more profound sense.

If bureaucracies become widespread throughout industrial societies, an "ossification" – a concentration of power in large organizations to such an extent that societal stagnation replaces societal dynamism – will result, he fears. Weber's concern with the background social configurations that cultivate and sustain ethical values is here again evident. Values become articulated, nourished, and defended, he argues, as noted, only when they stand in relationships of pluralistic competition – namely, in dynamic and open societies. Furthermore, he concludes that managers and functionaries, who stand at the forefront in bureaucratized societies as prestigious figures, carry a predominantly pragmatic, technical outlook and frame of mind in opposition to expansive ethical values and ideals.

Political leaders far more effectively announce and cultivate values, Weber holds. Because they are accustomed to taking responsibility and fighting for ideals, they differ distinctly from functionaries and must perform a crucial task: they must exercise control over state bureaucracies. Moreover, they must overcome "vulgar vanity," he insists, serve a cause of their own choosing, and possess three qualities: "passion, a feeling of responsibility, and a sense of proportion" (1946b, p. 115). Yet Weber fears that viable and extensive political leadership might disappear amidst encompassing bureaucratization.

Despite deep foreboding, he suggested an array of measures. They constitute "Weber's response" to the threat posed by increasing bureaucratization. Far from being a cultural pessimist who withdrew into the private realm or advocated a return to earlier, presumably more pristine epochs, Weber remained a political activist all his life. More importantly here, insights gained from his sociological research crystallized into proposals that addressed the threats to ethical action and societal dynamism in the modern epoch.

The selections in this Part convey his vigorous support for (a) strong political leaders who stand, on the basis of their values, against the formal rationality of functionaries, managers, and technocrats; (b) powerful parliaments where political positions would be aggressively articulated and, hence, leadership and an "ethic of responsibility" would be cultivated; and (c) democracy. Contesting rulership monopolies and the concentration of power, he argues, occurs more effectively in this form of governance. Moreover, he supports, despite the reservations just noted, capitalism over socialism, for the former's open competition and private enterprise call forth energetic entrepreneurs and vigorous risk-takers (see above, p. 3).

All these transformations offer hope for an injection of dynamism and openness, he contends. All contribute to the expansion of a "free space" within which citizens can debate, make responsible decisions, exercise political rights, and defend values. In this manner the stultifying effects of massive bureaucratization will be confronted and held in check. Political action, Weber argues forcefully in the selection from his famous "Politics as a Vocation" essay, can then appropriately follow an ethic of responsibility according to which people, and particularly politicians, take positions rooted in values and hold themselves accountable for the consequences that follow.

He hoped that political leaders, strong parliaments, dynamic democracies, and a vigorous capitalism would forestall the advance of bureaucratization, on the one hand, and formal and practical types of rationality, on the other. This series of forces would call forth dynamic civic arenas to oppose societal ossification. The fundamental precondition that nourished ethical values would come to the fore: a societal openness that allowed – even fostered – perpetual conflicts over values. Wherever noble values indeed oriented action, all those aspects of the West that Weber held dear, he was convinced, would be defended. Practical rationality's random push and pull of mundane interests and concerns, and the mere "sterile excitation" they give rise to, would then be counterbalanced. Life could then become *directed* on behalf of ethical ideals and a passion for "causes" would be awakened.

Within *this* context, a possibility existed for a rejuvenation of the "vocational calling" originally cultivated by ascetic Protestantism. It might expand, with strong carriers, even across both the occupational and political realms. Its ideals of service, which imply orientation to a constellation of values and, as noted, for the politician obligations and responsibilities, would circumscribe the wide-ranging thrust of practical rationality's cold and "steel-hard" instrumentalism. He argues in "Science as a Vocation" that scientists must possess a genuine dedication, enthusiasm, and commitment to their calling – "for nothing is worthy of man as man unless he can pursue it with passionate devotion" (p. 140).

These overarching concerns drove Weber's scholarly research far and wide. His many comparative investigations helped him to define clearly the ways in which the economies, laws, forms of authority, states, and religions of the West were unique, to assess possibilities regarding social change, and to better understand the social constellations that anchored meaningful action in values and ethical ideals.

## NOTES

1. Weber's famous rejection of the view that modern science can either formulate a set of guiding values or call forth ethical action is addressed in Part X. Indeed, his circumscription of its legitimate tasks seeks to protect the individual against any hegemonic claims by science. Weber also emphatically rejects the notion that two further independent domains – the aesthetic and erotic realms – are capable of formulating and cultivating either consistent ethical action or notions of brotherly love. See 1946c, pp. 340–50; 1968a, pp. 602–10.
2. It should be emphasized again that Weber's definitions of the market economy and the state constitute ideal types. He insists that his constructs are formulated according to an accentuation of the essence of the market economy and the state. The ideal type allows for – and assists, through comparison, definition of – empirical variation (see pp. 15–17).

# chapter 18

# The Antagonism of the Economy and Political Domains to Ethical Action

From *Economy and Society: An Outline of Interpretive Sociology*, eds Guenther Roth and Claus Wittich, trans. Max Rheinstein, revised by Guenther Roth and Claus Wittich, and Stephen Kalberg (Berkeley, CA: University of California Press, 1978). pp. 635–7.

... A market may be said to exist wherever there is competition, even if only unilateral, for opportunities of exchange among a plurality of potential parties. Their physical assemblage in one place, as in the local market square, the fair (the "long distance market"), or the exchange (the merchants' market), only constitutes the most consistent kind of market formation. It is, however, only this physical assemblage which allows the full emergence of the market's most distinctive feature, viz. haggling. . . . From a sociological point of view, the market represents a coexistence and sequence of rational associations, each of which is specifically ephemeral insofar as it ceases to exist with the act of exchanging the goods, unless a [legal] framework has been promulgated which imposes upon the transferors of the exchangeable goods the guaranty of their lawful acquisition as warranty of title or of quiet enjoyment. . . .

. . . Money creates a group by virtue of material interest relations between actual and potential participants in the market and its payments. . . . Within the market community every act of exchange, especially monetary exchange, is not directed, in isolation, by the action of the individual partner to the particular transaction, but the more rationally it is considered, the more it is directed by the actions of all parties potentially interested in the exchange. The market community as such is the most impersonal relationship of practical life into which humans can enter with one another. This is not due to that potentiality of struggle among the interested parties which is inherent in the market relationship. Any human relationship, even the most intimate, and even though it be marked by the most unqualified personal devotion, is in some sense relative and may involve a struggle with the partner, for instance, over the salvation of his soul.

The reason for the impersonality of the market is its matter-of-factness, its orientation to the commodity and only to that. Where the market is allowed to follow its own autonomous tendencies, its participants do not look toward the persons of each other but only toward the commodity; there are no obligations of brotherliness or reverence, and none of those spontaneous human relations that are sustained by personal unions. They all would just obstruct the free development of the bare market relationship, and its specific interests serve, in their turn, to weaken the sentiments on which these obstructions rest. Market behavior is influenced by a rational, means–end pursuit of interests. The partner to a transaction is expected to behave according to rational legality and, quite particularly, to respect the formal inviolability of a promise once given. These are the qualities which form the content of market ethics. In this latter respect the market inculcates, indeed, particularly rigorous outlooks. Violations of agreements, even though they may be concluded by mere signs, entirely unrecorded, and devoid of evidence, are almost unheard of in the annals of the stock exchange. Such absolute depersonalization is contrary to all the elementary forms of human relationship. . . .

The "free" market, that is, the market which is not bound by ethical norms, with its exploitation of constellations of interests and monopoly positions and its haggling, is an abomination to every system of fraternal ethics. In sharp contrast to all other groups which always presuppose some measure of personal fraternization or even blood kinship, the market is fundamentally alien to any type of fraternal relationship. . . .

From *Economy and Society: An Outline of Interpretive Sociology*, eds Guenther Roth and Claus Wittich, trans. Ephraim Fischoff, revised by Guenther Roth and Claus Wittich, and Stephen Kalberg (Berkeley, CA: University of California Press, 1978), p. 585.

Rational economic association always brings about depersonalization, and it is impossible to control a universe of instrumentally rational activities by charitable appeals to particular individuals. The functionalized world of capitalism certainly offers no support for any such charitable orientation. In it the claims of religious charity are vitiated not merely because of the cantankerousness and deficiency of particular persons, as it happens everywhere, but because they lose their meaning altogether. Religious ethics is confronted by a world of interpersonal relationships which, for fundamental reasons, *cannot* fit together with its basic norms.

From *Economy and Society: An Outline of Interpretive Sociology*, eds Guenther Roth and Claus Wittich, trans. Guenther Roth and Claus Wittich, slightly revised by Stephen Kalberg (Berkeley, CA: University of California Press, 1978), pp. 1186–7.

. . . Most of the time this domination appears in such an indirect form that one cannot identify any concrete master and hence cannot make any ethical demands upon him. It is possible to advance ethical postulates and to attempt the imposition of substantive norms with regard to household head and servant, master and apprentice, manorial lord and dependents or officials, master and slave, or patriarchal ruler and subject, since their relationship is personal and since the expected services result therefrom. Within wide limits, personal, flexible interests are operative here, and purely personal intent and action can decisively change the relationship and the condition of the person involved. But for the director of a joint-stock company, who is obliged to represent the interests of the stock-holders as the proper rulers, it is very difficult to relate in this manner to the factory workers; it is even more difficult for the director of the bank that finances the joint-stock company, or for the mortgage holder in relation to the owner of property on which the bank granted a loan. Decisive are the need for competitive survival and the conditions of the labor, money and commodity markets; hence matter-of-fact considerations that are neither ethical nor unethical, but simply a-ethical determine individual behavior and push impersonal forces between the persons involved.

From an ethical viewpoint, this "masterless slavery" to which capitalism subjects the worker or the mortgagee is questionable only as an institution. However, in principle, the behavior of any individual cannot be so questioned, since it is prescribed in all relevant respects by objective situations. The penalty for non-compliance is extinction, and this would not be helpful in any way. More important is that such economic behavior has the quality of a *service* toward an *impersonal* purpose.

From "Religious Rejections of the World and Their Directions," in *From Max Weber: Essays in Sociology*, eds and trans. H. H. Gerth and C. Wright Mills, slightly revised by Stephen Kalberg (New York: Oxford University Press, 1946), pp. 333–5.

. . . The problem of tensions with the political order emerged for salvation religions out of the basic demand for brotherliness. And in politics, as in economics, the more rational the political order became the sharper the problems of these tensions became.

The bureaucratic state apparatus, and the rational *homo politicus* integrated into the state, manage affairs, including the punishment of evil, when they discharge business in the most ideal sense, according to the rational rules of the state order. In this, the political man acts just like the economic man, in a matter-of-fact manner "without regard to the person," *sine ira et studio*, without hate and therefore without love. By virtue of its depersonalization, the bureaucratic state, in important points, is less accessible to substantive ethicization than were the patriarchal orders of the past, however many appearances may point to the contrary.

The patriarchal orders of the past were based upon personal obligations of piety, and the patriarchal rulers considered the merit of the concrete, single case precisely with "regard to the person." In the final analysis, in spite of all "social welfare policies," the whole course of the state's inner political functions, of justice and administration, is repeatedly and unavoidably regulated by the objective pragmatism of "reasons of state." The state's absolute end is to safeguard (or to change) the external and internal distribution of power; ultimately, this end must seem meaningless to any universalist religion of salvation. This fact has held and still holds, even more so, for foreign policy. It it absolutely essential for every political association to appeal to the naked violence of coercive means in the face of outsiders as well as in the face of internal enemies. It is only this very appeal to violence that constitutes a political association in our terminology. The state is an association that claims the monopoly of the *legitimate use of violence*, and cannot be defined in any other manner.

The Sermon on the Mount says "resist no evil." In opposition, the state asserts: "You *shall* help right to triumph by the use of *force*, otherwise you too may be responsible for injustice." Where this factor is absent, the "state" is also absent; the "anarchism" of the pacifist will have then come to life. According to the inescapable pragmatism of all action, however, force and the threat of force unavoidably breed more force. "Reasons of state" thus follow their own external and internal laws. The very success of force, or of the threat of force, depends ultimately upon power relations and not on ethical "right," even were one to believe it possible to discover objective criteria for such "right."

In contrast to naive, primitive heroism, it is typical of the rational state systems for groups or rulers to line up for violent conflict, all quite sincerely believing themselves to be "in the right." To any consistent religious rationalization, this must seem only an aping of ethics. Moreover, to draw the Lord's name into such violent political conflict must be viewed as a taking of His name in vain. In the face of this, the cleaner and only honest way may appear to be the complete elimination of ethics from political reasoning. The more matter-of-fact and calculating politics is, and the freer of passionate feelings, of wrath, and of love it becomes, the more it must appear to an ethic of brotherliness to be estranged from brotherliness.

# chapter 19

# A "Casing of Bondage" and the Rule of Functionaries

## THE CALL FOR POLITICAL LEADERSHIP, STRONG PARLIAMENTS, AND AN ETHIC OF RESPONSIBILITY

From *Economy and Society: An Outline of Interpretive Sociology*, eds Guenther Roth and Claus Wittich, trans. Claus Wittich, revised by Stephen Kalberg (Berkeley, CA: University of California Press, 1978), pp. 1401–3.

. . . [L]et us assume that some time in the future [capitalism] will be done away with. What would be the practical result? The destruction of the steel frame of modern industrial work? No! The abolition of private capitalism would simply mean that also the *top management* of the nationalized or socialized enterprises would become bureaucratic. Are the daily working conditions of the salaried employees and the workers in the state-owned Prussian mines and railroads really perceptibly different from those in big business enterprises? It is true that there is even less freedom, since every power struggle with a state bureaucracy is hopeless and since there is no appeal to an agency which as a matter of principle would be interested in limiting the employer's power, such as there is in the case of a private enterprise. *That* would be the whole difference.

State bureaucracy would rule *alone* if private capitalism were eliminated. The private and public bureaucracies, which now work next to, and potentially against, each other and hence check one another to a degree, would be merged into a single hierarchy. This would be similar to the situation in ancient Egypt, but it would occur in a much more rational – and hence unbreakable – form.

An inanimate machine is *spirit objectified*. *Only* this provides it with the power to force men into its service and to dominate their everyday working life as completely as is actually the case in the factory. *Spirit objectified* is also that *animated machine*, the bureaucratic organization, with its specialization of trained skills, its division of jurisdiction, its rules and hierarchical relations of authority. Together with the inanimate

machine it is busy fabricating the casing of bondage which men will perhaps be forced to inhabit some day, as powerless as the fellahs of ancient
Egypt. This might happen *if a technically superior administration were to
be the ultimate and sole value in the ordering of their affairs*, and that means:
a rational bureaucratic administration with the corresponding welfare
benefits. The bureaucracy accomplishes this much better than any other
structure of domination. This casing of bondage, which our unsuspect-
ing literati praise so much, might perhaps be reinforced by fettering every
individual to his job (notice the beginnings in the system of fringe
benefits), to his class (through the increasing rigidity of the property
distribution), and maybe to his occupation (through liturgic methods
of satisfying state requirements, and that means: through burdening
occupational associations with state functions). It would be made all the
more indestructible if in the social sphere a status order were then to
be imposed upon the ruled, linked to the bureaucracy and in truth
subordinate to it, as in the forced-labor states of the past. An "organic"
social stratification, similar to the Oriental-Egyptian type, would then
arise, but in contrast to the latter it would be as austerely rational as a
machine. Who would want to deny that such a *possibility* lies in the
womb of the future? In fact, this has often been said before, and the very
muddled anticipation of it also throws its shadow upon the productions
of our literati. Let us assume for the moment that this possibility were
our "inescapable" fate: Who would then not smile about the fear of
our literati that the political and social development might bring us
*too much* "individualism" or "democracy" or other such-like things, and
about their anticipation that "true freedom" will light up only when the
present "anarchy" of economic production and the "party machinations"
of our parliaments will be abolished in favor of social "order" and
"organic stratification" – that means, in favor of the pacifism of social impotence under the tutelage of the only really *inescapable* power: the bureaucracy in state and economy.

. . . Given the basic fact of the irresistible advance of bureaucratization,
the question about the future forms of political organization can only be
asked in the following way:

1.  How can one *possibly* still save *any remnants* of "individualist" free-
    dom of movement in any sense? After all, it is a gross self-deception to
    believe that without the achievements of the age of the "Rights of Man"
    any one of us, including the most conservative, can go on living his life.
    But this question shall not concern us here, for there is another one:
2.  In view of the growing indispensability of the *state* bureaucracy and
    its corresponding increase in power, how can there be *any* guarantee
    that any powers will remain which can check and effectively control

the tremendous influence of this stratum? How will democracy even in this limited sense be *at all possible*?

From *Economy and Society: An Outline of Interpretive Sociology*, eds Guenther Roth and Claus Wittich, trans. Claus Wittich, revised by Stephen Kalberg (Berkeley, CA: University of California Press, 1978), p. 1417.

Our officialdom has been brilliant wherever it had to prove its sense of duty, its impartiality and mastery of organizational problems in the face of official, clearly formulated tasks of a *specialized* nature. The present writer, who comes from a civil-service family, would be the last to let this tradition be sullied. But here we are concerned with political, not bureaucratic achievements, and the facts themselves provoke the recognition which nobody can truthfully deny: That bureaucracy *failed completely* whenever it was expected to deal with *political* problems. This is no accident; rather, it would be astonishing if capabilities inherently so alien to one another would emerge within the same political structure. . . .

*It is not the civil servant's task* to enter the political arena fighting for his own convictions, and in this sense to engage in the political struggle. On the contrary, his pride lies in maintaining impartiality, hence in disregarding his own inclinations and opinions, in order to adhere conscientiously and meaningfully to general rule as well as special directive, even and particularly if they do *not* correspond to his own political attitudes. But the heads of the bureaucracy must continuously solve political problems – problems of *Machtpolitik* [power politics] as well as of *Kulturpolitik*. Parliament's first task is the supervision of *these* policy-makers. However, not only the tasks assigned to the top ranks of the bureaucracy but also every single technicality on the lower administrative levels may become politically important and its solution may depend on political criteria. *Politicians* must be the countervailing force against bureaucratic domination. This, however, is resisted by the power interests of the administrative policy-makers, who want to have maximum freedom from supervision and to establish a monopoly on cabinet posts.

From "Politics as a Vocation," in *From Max Weber: Essays in Sociology*, eds and trans. H. H. Gerth and C. Wright Mills (New York: Oxford University Press, 1946), p. 95.

According to his proper vocation, the genuine official – and this is decisive for the evaluation of our former regime – will not engage in politics. Rather, he should engage in impartial "administration." This also holds for the so-called "political" administrator, at least officially, in so far as the *raison d'état*, that is, the vital interests of the ruling order, are not in question. *Sine ira et studio*, "without scorn and bias," he shall administer his office. Hence, he shall not do precisely what the politician, the leader as well as his following, must always and necessarily do, namely, *fight*.

To take a stand, to be passionate – *ira et studium* – is the politician's element, and above all the element of the political *leader*. His conduct is subject to quite a different, indeed, exactly the opposite, principle of responsibility from that of the civil servant. The honor of the civil servant is vested in his ability to execute conscientiously the order of the superior authorities, exactly as if the order agreed with his own conviction. This holds even if the order appears wrong to him and if, despite the civil servant's remonstrances, the authority insists on the order. Without this moral discipline and self-denial, in the highest sense, the whole apparatus would fall to pieces. The honor of the political leader, of the leading statesman, however, lies precisely in an exclusive *personal* responsibility for what he does, a responsibility he cannot and must not reject or transfer. It is in the nature of officials of high moral standing to be poor politicians, and above all, in the political sense of the word, to be irresponsible politicians. In this sense, they are politicians of low moral standing, such as we [in Germany] unfortunately have had again and again in leading positions. This is what we have called *Beamtenherrschaft* [civil-service rule]. . . .

From "Politics as a Vocation," in *From Max Weber: Essays in Sociology*, eds and trans. H. H. Gerth and C. Wright Mills (New York: Oxford University Press, 1946), pp. 114–17.

. . . [What] inner enjoyments can [a] career [in politics] offer and what personal conditions are presupposed for one who enters this avenue?

Well, first of all the career of politics grants a feeling of power. The knowledge of influencing men, of participating in power over them, and above all, the feeling of holding in one's hands a nerve fiber of historically important events can elevate the professional politician above everyday routine even when he is placed in formally modest positions. But now the question for him is: Through what qualities can I hope to do justice to this power (however narrowly circumscribed it may be in the individual case)? How can he hope to do justice to the responsibility that power imposes upon him? With this we enter the field of ethical questions, for that is where the problem belongs: What kind of a man must one be if he is to be allowed to put his hand on the wheel of history?

One can say that three pre-eminent qualities are decisive for the politician: passion, a feeling of responsibility, and a sense of proportion.

This means passion in the sense of *matter-of-factness*, of passionate devotion to a "cause," to the god or demon who is its overlord. It is not passion in the sense of that inner bearing which my late friend, Georg Simmel, used to designate as "sterile excitation," and which was peculiar especially to a certain type of Russian intellectual (by no means all of them!). It is an excitation that plays so great a part with our intellectuals in this carnival we decorate with the proud name of "revolution"

[1918 in Munich]. It is a "romanticism of the intellectually interesting," running into emptiness devoid of all feeling of objective responsibility.

To be sure, mere passion, however genuinely felt, is not enough. It does not make a politician, unless passion as devotion to a "cause" also makes responsibility to this cause the guiding star of action. And for this, a sense of proportion is needed. This is the decisive psychological quality of the politician: his ability to let realities work upon him with inner concentration and calmness. Hence his *distance* to things and men. "Lack of distance" *per se* is one of the deadly sins of every politician. It is one of those qualities the breeding of which will condemn the progeny of our intellectuals to political incapacity. For the problem is simply how can warm passion and a cool sense of proportion be forged together in one and the same soul? Politics is made with the head, not with other parts of the body or soul. And yet devotion to politics, if it is not to be frivolous intellectual play but rather genuinely human conduct, can be born and nourished from passion alone. However, that firm taming of the soul, which distinguishes the passionate politician and differentiates him from the "sterilely excited" and mere political dilettante, is possible only through habituation to detachment in every sense of the word. The "strength" of a political "personality" means, in the first place, the possession of these qualities of passion, responsibility, and proportion.

Therefore, daily and hourly, the politician inwardly has to overcome a quite trivial and all-too-human enemy: a quite vulgar vanity, the deadly enemy of all matter-of-fact devotion to a cause, and of all distance, in this case, of distance towards one's self.

Vanity is a very widespread quality and perhaps nobody is entirely free from it. In academic and scholarly circles, vanity is a sort of occupational disease, but precisely with the scholar, vanity – however disagreeably it may express itself – is relatively harmless; in the sense that as a rule it does not disturb scientific enterprise. With the politician the case is quite different. He works with the striving for power as an unavoidable means. Therefore, "power instinct," as is usually said, belongs indeed to his normal qualities. The sin against the lofty spirit of his vocation, however, begins where this striving for power ceases to be *objective* and becomes purely personal self-intoxication, instead of exclusively entering the service of "the cause." For ultimately there are only two kinds of deadly sins in the field of politics: lack of objectivity and – often but not always identical with it – irresponsibility. Vanity, the need personally to stand in the foreground as clearly as possible, strongly tempts the politician to commit one or both of these sins.

This is more truly the case as the demagogue is compelled to count upon "effect." He therefore is constantly in danger of becoming an actor as well as taking lightly the responsibility for the outcome of his actions and of being concerned merely with the "impression" he makes. His lack of objectivity tempts him to strive for the glamorous semblance of power rather than for actual power. His irresponsibility, however, suggests that he enjoy power merely for power's sake without a substantive purpose. Although, or rather just because, power is the unavoidable means, and striving for power is one of the driving forces of all politics, there is no more harmful distortion of political force than the parvenu-like braggart with power, and the vain self-reflection in the feeling of power, and in general every worship of power *per se*. The mere "power politician" may get strong effects, but actually his work leads nowhere and is senseless. (Among us, too, an ardently promoted cult seeks to glorify him.) In this, the critics of "power politics" are absolutely right. From the sudden inner collapse of typical representatives of this mentality, we can see what inner weakness and impotence hides behind this boastful but entirely empty gesture. It is a product of a shoddy and superficially blasé attitude towards the meaning of human conduct; and it has no relation whatsoever to the knowledge of tragedy with which all action, but especially political action, is truly interwoven.

The final result of political action often, no, even regularly, stands in completely inadequate and often even paradoxical relation to its original meaning. This is fundamental to all history, a point not to be proved in detail here. But because of this fact, the serving of a cause must not be absent if action is to have inner strength. Exactly what the cause, in the service of which the politician strives for power and uses power, looks like is a matter of faith. The politician may serve national, humanitarian, social, ethical, cultural, worldly, or religious ends. The politician may be sustained by a strong belief in "progress" – no matter in which sense – or he may coolly reject this kind of belief. He may claim to stand in the service of an "idea" or, rejecting this in principle, he may want to serve external ends of everyday life. However, some kind of faith must always exist. Otherwise, it is absolutely true that the curse of the creature's worthlessness overshadows even the externally strongest political successes.

With the statement above we are already engaged in discussing the last problem that concerns us tonight: the *ethos* of politics as a "cause." What calling can politics fulfil quite independently of its goals within the total ethical economy of human conduct – which is, so to speak, the ethical locus where politics is at home? Here, to be sure, ultimate *Weltanschauungen* clash, world views among which in the end one has to make a choice.

From *Economy and Society: An Outline of Interpretive Sociology*, eds Guenther Roth and Claus Wittich, trans. Claus Wittich (Berkeley, CA: University of California Press, 1978), p. 1409.

. . . Every conflict in parliament involves not only a struggle over substantive issues but also a struggle for personal power. Wherever parliament is so strong that, as a rule, the [constitutional] monarch entrusts the government to the spokesman of a clear-cut majority, the power struggle of the parties will be a contest for this highest executive position. The fight is then carried by men who have great political power instincts and highly developed qualities of political leadership, and hence the chance to take over the top positions; for the survival of the party outside parliament, and the countless ideal, and partly very material, interests bound up with it require that capable leaders get to the top. Only under such conditions can men with political temperament and talent be motivated to subject themselves to this kind of selection through competition. . . .

From *Economy and Society: An Outline of Interpretive Sociology*, eds Guenther Roth and Claus Wittich, trans. Claus Wittich (Berkeley, CA: University of California Press, 1978), p. 1420.

. . . The political preparation for [great] achievements is, of course, not acquired by making ostentatious and decorative speeches before parliament, but only through steady and strenuous work in a parliamentary career. None of the outstanding English leaders rose to pre-eminence without experience in the committees and, often, in various government agencies. Only such intensive training, through which the politician must pass in the committees of a powerful *working* parliament, turns such an assembly into a recruiting ground not for mere demagogues but for positively participating politicians. Until today the British parliament has been unparalleled in this respect (as nobody can honestly deny). Only such co-operation between civil servants and politicians can guarantee the continuous supervision of the administration and, with it, the political education of leaders and led. . . .

From *Economy and Society: An Outline of Interpretive Sociology*, eds Guenther Roth and Claus Wittich, trans. Claus Wittich (Berkeley, CA: University of California Press, 1978), pp. 1426–8.

. . . The decisive question about the future of Germany's political order must be: How can parliament be made fit to govern? Every other way of putting the question is simply wrong, and everything else is secondary.

It must be clearly understood that parliamentary reform depends . . . above all on the development of a suitable corps of professional parliamentarians.

The professional parliamentary deputy is a man for whom the *Reichstag* mandate is not a part-time job but his major vocation; for this reason he needs an efficient office with the requisite personnel and access to information. We may love or hate this figure – he is technically indispensable, and therefore we have him already. However, even the most influential pros are [in Germany] a rather subaltern species, operating behind the scenes, because of the subordinate position of parliament and the limited career opportunities. The professional politician may live merely *from* politics and its hustle and bustle, or he may live *for* politics. Only in the latter case can he become a politician of great calibre. Of course, he will succeed the more easily, the more he is financially independent and hence available – not an entrepreneur but a *rentier*. Among those dependent upon a job only the lawyers can easily take leave and are suited to be professional politicians. An exclusive dominance of lawyers would certainly be undesirable, but it is a foolish tendency of our literati to denigrate the uses of legal training for political leadership. In an age ruled by jurists the great lawyer is the only one who, in contrast to the legally trained civil servant, has been taught to fight for, and effectively represent, a given cause; we would wish that the public pronouncements of our government showed more of the lawyer's skill in the best sense of the word. However, only if parliament can offer opportunities for political leadership will any kind of independent person, not just gifted and capable lawyers, want to live for politics. Otherwise, only salaried party functionaries and representatives of interest groups will want to do so. . . .

. . . [T]he bureaucracy struggle[s] to preserve parliament's ignorance, since only skilled professional parliamentarians who have passed through the school of intensive committee work can produce from their midst responsible leaders, rather than mere demagogues and dilettantes. Parliament must be completely reorganized in order to produce such leaders and to guarantee their effectiveness; in their own way, the British parliament and its parties have long been successful in this regard. It is true that the British conventions cannot simply be taken over, but the basic structure can very well be adapted.

From "Suffrage and Democracy in Germany," (1917) in *Studienausgabe der Max Weber – Gesamtausgabe Band 1/15: Zur Politik im Weltkrieg – Schriften und Reden 1914–1918*, ed. Wolfgang Mommsen, trans. Stephen Kalberg (Tübingen: Mohr Verlag, 1988), pp. 186–9.[1]

[A] principled question should . . . be briefly addressed: what is the relationship between the development of parliaments and the development of democracy? The number of very respectable and even quite fanatical "democrats" who see the growth of parliaments as a corrupt transformation that calls forth hustlers and parasites – one that will lead to a perverting of democracy and rulership by cliques – is not at all small. "Politics," for them, is perhaps quite "interesting" for idlers, but otherwise a sterile enterprise. Particularly for broad strata throughout the nation, a good "administration" is alone important, they assert. Indeed, only this form of governance guarantees the "true" democracy, they argue, which we in Germany – the nation with the "true concept of freedom"[2] – putatively already in part possess in a superior form than elsewhere and in part can better create, without parliamentarization, than others.

It is apparent that the proponents of a bureaucracy unhindered by external controls delight in playing these two modes of democracy off each other as opposites. "True" democracy, they contend, becomes manifest in its greatest purity wherever the groups advocating parliaments prove unable to obstruct the orderly work of civil servant officials. This audacious swindle – in the case of our chattering intellectuals a self-deception deriving from an unsophisticated surrender to phrases – easily acquires supporters, indeed, in all camps, as does all that serves the interests of the bureaucracy and its allied capitalist interests. And it is obvious that a swindle exists here, for: (1) if one imagines the disappearance of parliamentary powers, the question arises of whether *democracy possesses any means to hold in check administration by officials*. To this question no answer at all is offered. Further: (2) *what can be put in place of the domination of the parliament's cliques*? Rule by still more concealed cliques and – usually – even smaller and, above all, inescapable cliques.

Viewed technically, the system of so-called direct democracy is possible only in a small state (canton). Democracy in every large state leads to bureaucratic administration and, if parliamentarization is absent, to a pure *domination* by functionaries. Certainly, wherever the rulership of a system of "Caesarism" comes into being (in the broader sense of the term) – namely, the direct, popular election of heads of cities and states, as occurs in the United States, including in some of its larger counties – a democracy *without* a parliamentary system (but not *entirely* without parliamentary power) may exist. (Its political and administrative-technical advantages and weaknesses will not be examined here.)

However, full parliamentary power is everywhere indispensable where *hereditary* heads of state – monarchs – are (formally) in charge of officialdom. Just as any member of parliament, the modern monarch is unavoidably and always a *dilettante*, and hence completely unable to monitor an administrative body and hold it in check. Nevertheless, two distinctions must be made: (1) amidst party *struggles*, the member of parliament is able to learn to weigh the *consequences of his word*, while the monarch should remain *apart* from political conflict; and (2) parliament, if given investigative *rights*, is in a position (through cross-examination of specialists and witnesses sworn by oath) to monitor and check the knowledge and activities of civil servant officials. How should a monarch and a democracy without a parliament manage to do so?

[Finally], quite generally, a nation which imagines that the leadership of a state *involves nothing more* than "administration," and that "politics" should be nothing more than an occasional activity of amateurs or a secondary task undertaken by state functionaries, should *abandon* all participation in international politics and prepare itself for the role of a small political entity, such as Denmark, Holland, a Swiss canton, or the provinces of Baden or Württemberg – all of which are administered in a fine manner. Otherwise, these polities will not be spared the experience that we [Germans] have had with this "true freedom," that is, with this unchecked officialdom when it undertakes to conduct world *politics*.

The enthusiasm for "democracy without a parliament" has naturally during [World War I] acquired sustenance, as in every difficult war, in all nations: England, France, Russia, as also in Germany. To a comprehensive degree, a political-military *dictatorship* actually replaced the earlier political form, whether it was called "monarchy" or "parliamentary republic" (and its shadows will undoubtedly be cast far into the period of peace). These wartime political arrangements everywhere operated with a specific type of mass demagoguery that turned off all acquired ventilating valves and monitoring mechanisms, including the parliamentary ones. These, as other developments conditioned by the war, blinded our dilettantish intellectuals, who were concerned to quickly produce books focussed on "relevant topics." Yet just as little as the war economy can serve as the model for the peaceful economy, so also the war constitution cannot be the pattern for the political structure during peacetime. . . .

[*This*] is the specific achievement of the parliament: through negotiation and compromise, it makes it possible for the "relatively" best position to come to the fore. This achievement is purchased with the same sacrifice the voter renders in a parliamentary election; namely, he can opt only for the political party that is *relatively* most agreeable to him. There is no substitute for this purely technical superiority of parliamentary legislation, although this is not to say that cases cannot arise in which a referendum would be the appropriate corrective mechanism. . . .

Democratization, in the sense of a levelling of status group formations with the growth of the *state administered by civil servants* (*Beamtenstaat*), is a fact. In a bureaucratic, "authoritarian state" (*Obrigkeitsstaat*) with a parliament in name only, one has only the choice either to leave the vast majority of citizens in an unfree situation without rights, and then to "administer" them like a herd of cattle, or to integrate them – as *co-rulers* – into the state. However, a nation of enfranchised and empowered citizens – and only such citizens can *and may* be engaged in "international politics" – has in this respect *no choice*. One can (for now) certainly thwart democratization, for strong interests, prejudices, and cowardice are allied against it. Yet to do so would occur at the price of the entire future of Germany, as will become soon evident. Any state that treats the masses only as objects and precludes their participation will cause all their energies to become mobilized *against* it. Certain circles would have an interest in the inevitable political consequences of such a development. But certainly not the nation as a whole.

From "Politics as a Vocation," in *From Max Weber: Essays in Sociology*, eds and trans. H. H. Gerth and C. Wright Mills, revised by Stephen Kalberg (New York: Oxford University Press, 1946), pp. 120–8.

We must be clear about the fact that all ethically oriented conduct may be guided by one of two fundamentally differing and irreconcilably opposed maxims: conduct can be oriented to an "ethic of conviction" or to an "ethic of responsibility." This is not to say that an ethic of conviction is identical with irresponsibility, or that an ethic of responsibility is identical with unprincipled opportunism. Naturally nobody says that. However, there is an abysmal contrast between conduct that follows the maxim of an ethic of conviction – that is, in religious terms, "The Christian does rightly and leaves the results with the Lord" – and conduct that follows the maxim of an ethic of responsibility, in which case one has to give an account of the foreseeable results of one's action.

You may demonstrate to a convinced syndicalist, believing in an ethic of conviction, that his action will result in increasing the opportunities of reaction, in increasing the oppression of his class, and obstructing its ascent – and you will not make the slightest impression upon him. If an action of good intent leads to bad results, then, in the actor's eyes, not he but the world, or the stupidity of other men, or God's will who made them thus, is responsible for the evil. However a man who believes in an ethic of responsibility takes account of precisely the average deficiencies of people; as Fichte has correctly said, he does not even have the right to presuppose their goodness and perfection. He does not feel in a position to burden others with the results of his own actions so far as he was able to foresee them; he will say: these results are ascribed to my action. The believer in an ethic of conviction feels "responsible" only for seeing to it that the flame of pure intentions is not quelched: for example, the flame of protesting against the injustice of the social order. To rekindle the flame ever anew is the purpose of his quite irrational deeds, judged in view of their possible success. They are acts that can and shall have only exemplary value.

But even herewith the problem is not yet exhausted. No ethics in the world can dodge the fact that in numerous instances the attainment of "good" ends is bound to the fact that one must be willing to pay the price of using morally dubious means or at least dangerous ones – and facing the possibility or even the probability of evil ramifications. From no ethics in the world can it be concluded when and to what extent the ethically good purpose "justifies" the ethically dangerous means and ramifications.

The decisive means for politics is violence. You may see the extent of the tension between means and ends, when viewed ethically, from the following: as is generally known, even during [World War I] the revolutionary socialists (Zimmerwald faction) professed a principle that one might strikingly formulate: "If we face the choice either of some more years of war and then revolution, or peace now and no revolution, we choose – some more years of war!" Upon the further question: "What can this revolution bring about?" every scientifically trained socialist would have had the answer: One cannot speak of a transition to an economy that in our sense could be called socialist; a bourgeois economy will re-emerge, merely stripped of the feudal elements and the dynastic vestiges. For this very modest result, they are willing to face "some more years of war." One may well say that even with a very robust socialist conviction one might reject a purpose that demands such means. With Bolshevism and Spartacism, and, in general, with any kind of revolutionary socialism, it is precisely the same thing. It is of course utterly ridiculous if the power politicians of the old regime are morally denounced for their use of the same means, however justified the rejection of their *aims* may be.

The ethic of conviction apparently must go to pieces on the problem of the justification of means by ends. As a matter of fact, logically it has only the possibility of rejecting all action that employs morally dangerous means – in theory! In the world of realities, as a rule, we encounter the ever-renewed experience that the adherent of an ethic of conviction suddenly turns into a chiliastic prophet. Those, for example, who have just preached "love against violence" now call for the use of force for the *last* violent deed, which would then lead to a state of affairs in which *all* violence is annihilated. In the same manner, our [World War I German] officers told the soldiers before every offensive: "This will be the last one; this one will bring victory and therewith peace." The proponent of an ethic of conviction cannot stand up under the ethical irrationality of the world. He is a cosmic-ethical "rationalist." Those of you who know Dostoievski will remember the scene of the "Grand Inquisitor" [in *the Brothers Karamazov*, BK 5, Ch. 5], where the problem is poignantly unfolded. If one makes any concessions at all to the principle that the end justifies the means, it is not possible to bring an ethic of conviction and an ethic of responsibility under one roof or to decree ethically which end should justify which means.

My colleague, Mr. F. W. Förster [the spokesman of the society for ethical Culture], whom personally I highly esteem for his undoubted sincerity, but whom I reject unreservedly as a politician, believes it is possible to get around this difficulty by the simple thesis: "from good comes only good; but from evil only evil follows." In that case this whole complex of questions would not exist. But it is rather astonishing that such a thesis could come to light two thousand five hundred years after the Upanishads. Not only the whole course of world history, but every frank examination of everyday experience points to the very opposite. The development of religions all over the world is determined by the fact that the opposite is true. The age-old problem of theodicy consists of the very

question of how it is that a power which is said to be at once omnipotent and kind could have created such an irrational world of undeserved
suffering, unpunished injustice, and hopeless stupidity. Either this power
is not omnipotent or not kind, or entirely different principles of compensation and reward govern our life – principles we may interpret
metaphysically, or even principles that forever escape our comprehension.

This problem – the experience of the irrationality of the world – has
been the driving force of all religious development. The Indian doctrine
of karma, Persian dualism, the doctrine of original sin, predestination and
the *deus absconditus* [hidden God], all these have grown out of this experience. Also the early Christians knew full well the world is governed by
demons and that he who lets himself in for politics, that is, for power
and force as means, contracts with diabolical powers and for his action
it is *not* true that good can follow only from good and evil only from
evil, but that often the opposite is true. Anyone who fails to see this is,
indeed, a political infant.

We are placed into various life-spheres, each of which is governed by
different laws. Religious ethics have settled with this fact in different ways.
Hellenic polytheism made sacrifices to Aphrodite and Hera alike, to
Dionysus and to Apollo, and knew these gods were frequently in conflict
with one another. . . .

. . . As is known in Catholic ethics – to which otherwise Professor
Förster stands close – the *consilia evangelica* [Catholic Church hierarchy]
are a special ethic for those endowed with the charisma of a holy life.
There stands the monk who must not shed blood or strive for gain, and
beside him stand the pious knight and the burgher, who are allowed to
do so, the one to shed blood, the other to pursue gain. The gradation of
ethics and its organic integration into the doctrine of salvation is less consistent than in India. According to the presuppositions of Christian faith,
this could and had to be the case. The wickedness of the world stemming
from original sin allowed with relative ease the integration of violence
into ethics as a disciplinary means against sin and against the heretics
who endangered the soul. However, the demands of the Sermon on the
Mount, an acosmic ethic of conviction, implied a natural law of absolute
imperatives based upon religion. These absolute imperatives retained their
revolutionizing force and they came upon the scene with elemental vigor
during almost all periods of social upheaval. They produced especially
the radical pacifist sects, one of which in Pennsylvania experimented in
establishing a polity that renounced violence towards the outside. This
experiment took a tragic course, inasmuch as with the outbreak of the
War of Independence the Quakers could not stand up arms-in-hand for
their ideals, which were those of the war.

Normally, Protestantism, however, absolutely legitimated the state
as a divine institution and hence violence as a means. Protestantism,

especially, legitimated the authoritarian state. Luther relieved the individual of the ethical responsibility for war and transferred it to the authorities. To obey the authorities in matters other than those of faith could never constitute guilt. Calvinism in turn knew principled violence as a means of defending the faith; thus Calvinism knew the crusade, which was for Islam an element of life from the beginning. One sees that it is by no means a modern disbelief born from the hero worship of the Renaissance which poses the problem of political ethics. All religions have wrestled with it, with highly differing success, and after what has been said it could not be otherwise. It is the specific means of legitimate violence as such in the hand of human associations which determines the peculiarity of all ethical problems of politics.

Whosoever contracts with violent means for whatever ends – and every politician does – is exposed to its specific consequences. This holds especially for the crusader, religious and revolutionary alike. Let us confidently take the present as an example. He who wants to establish absolute justice on earth by force requires a following, a human "machine." He must hold out the necessary internal and external premiums, heavenly or worldly reward, to this "machine" or else the machine will not function. Under the conditions of the modern class struggle, the internal premiums consist of the satisfying of hatred and the craving for revenge; above all, resentment and the need for pseudo-ethical self-righteousness: the opponents must be slandered and accused of heresy. The external rewards are adventure, victory, booty, power, and spoils.

The leader and his success are completely dependent upon the functioning of his machine and hence not on his own motives. Therefore he also depends upon whether or not the premiums can be *permanently* granted to the following, that is, to the Red Guard, the informers, the agitators, whom he needs. What he actually attains under the conditions of his work is therefore not in his hand, but is prescribed to him by the following's motives, which, if viewed ethically, are predominantly base. The following can be harnessed only so long as an honest belief in his person and his cause inspires at least part of the following, probably never on earth even the majority.

This belief, even when subjectively sincere, is in a very great number of cases really no more than an ethical "legitimation" of cravings for revenge, power, booty, and spoils. We shall not be deceived about this by verbiage; the materialist interpretation of history is no cab to be taken at will; it does not stop short of the promoters of revolutions. Emotional revolutionism is followed by the traditionalist routine of everyday life; the crusading leader and the faith itself fade away, or, what is even more effective, the faith becomes part of the conventional phraseology of political Philistines and banausic technicians. This development is especially rapid with struggles of faith because they are usually led or inspired by genuine leaders, that is, prophets of revolution. For here, as with every leader's machine, one of the conditions for success is a hollowing out and depersonalization, in short, a spiritual proletarianization, in the interest of discipline. After coming to power the following of a crusader usually degenerates very easily into a quite common stratum of spoilsmen.

Whoever wants to engage in politics at all, and especially in politics as a vocation, has to realize these ethical paradoxes. He must know that he is responsible for what may become of himself under the impact of these paradoxes. I repeat, he lets himself in for the diabolic forces lurking in all violence. The great *virtuosi* of acosmic love of humanity and goodness, whether stemming from Nazareth or Assisi or from Indian royal castles, have not operated with the political means of violence. Their kingdom was "not of this world" and yet they worked and still work in this world. The figures of Platon Karatajev [in Tolstoy's *War and Peace*] and the saints of Dostoievski still remain their most adequate reconstructions.

He who seeks the salvation of the soul, of his own and of others, should not seek it along the avenue of politics, for the quite different tasks of politics can only be solved by violence. The genius or demon of politics lives in an inner tension with the god of love, as well as with the Christian God as expressed by the church. This tension can at any time lead to an irreconcilable conflict. Men knew this even in the times of church rule. Time and again the papal interdict was placed upon Florence and at the time it meant a far more robust power for men and their salvation of soul than (to speak with Fichte) the "cool approbation" of the Kantian ethical judgment. The burghers, however, fought the church-state. And it is with reference to such situations that Machiavelli in a beautiful passage, if I am not mistaken, of the *History of Florence* [BK 3, Ch. 7], has one of his heroes praise those citizens who deemed the greatness of their native city higher than the salvation of their souls.

If one says "the future of socialism" or "international peace," instead of native city or "fatherland" (which at present may be a dubious value to some), then you face the problem as it stands now. Everything that is striven for through political action operating with violent means and following an ethic of responsibility endangers the "salvation of the soul." If, however, one chases after the ultimate good in a war of beliefs, following a pure ethic of conviction, then the goals may be damaged and discredited for generations, because responsibility for *consequences* is lacking, and two diabolic forces which enter the play remain unknown to the actor. These are inexorable and produce consequences for his action and even for his inner self, to which he must helplessly submit, unless he perceives them. The sentence: "The devil is old; grow old to understand him!" [Goethe, *Faust*, Part II, lines 6817–18] does not refer to age in terms of chronological years. I have never permitted myself to lose out in a discussion through a reference to a date registered on a birth certificate; but the mere fact that someone is twenty years of age and that I am over fifty is no cause for me to think that this alone is an achievement before which I am overawed. Age is not decisive; what is decisive is the trained relentlessness in viewing the realities of life, and the ability to face such realities and to measure up to them inwardly.

Surely, politics is made with the head, but it is certainly not made with the head alone. In this the proponents of an ethic of conviction are right. One cannot prescribe to anyone whether he should follow an ethic of conviction or an ethic of responsibility, or when the one and when the other. One can say only this much: If in these times, which, in your opinion, are not times of "sterile" excitation – excitation is not, after all, genuine passion – if now suddenly the *Weltanschauungs*-politicians crop up *en masse* and pass the watchword, "The world is stupid and base, not I," "The responsibility for the consequences does not fall upon me but upon the others whom I serve and whose stupidity or baseness I shall eradicate," then I declare frankly that I would first inquire into the degree of inner poise backing this ethic of ultimate ends. I am under the impression that in nine out of ten cases I deal with windbags who do not fully realize what they take upon themselves but who intoxicate themselves with romantic sensations.

From a human point of view this is not very interesting to me, nor does it move me profoundly. However, it is immensely moving when a *mature* man – no matter whether old or young in years – is aware of a responsibility for the consequences of his conduct and really feels such responsibility with heart and soul. He then acts by following an ethic of responsibility and somewhere he reaches the point where he says: "Here I stand; I can do no other" [Luther, 1521]. That is something genuinely human and moving. And every one of us who is not spiritually dead must realize the possibility of finding himself at some time in that position. In so far as this is true, an ethic of conviction and an ethic of responsibility are not absolute contrasts but rather supplements, which only in unison constitute a genuine map – a man who *can* have the "calling for politics."

Now then, ladies and gentlemen, let us debate this matter once more ten years from now. Unfortunately, for a whole series of reasons, I fear that by then the period of reaction will have long since broken over us. It is very probable that little of what many of you, and (I candidly confess) I too, have wished and hoped for will be fulfilled; little – perhaps not exactly nothing, but what to us at least seems little. This will not crush me, but surely it is an inner burden to realize it. Then, I wish I could see what has become of those of you who now feel yourselves to be genuinely "principled" politicians and who share in the intoxication signified by this revolution [1918 in Munich]. It would be nice if matters turned out in such a way that Shakespeare's Sonnet 102 should hold true:

> Our love was new, and then but in the spring,
> When I was wont to greet it with my lays;
> As Philomel in summer's front doth sing,
> And stops her pipe in growth of riper days.

But such is not the case. Not summer's bloom lies ahead of us, but rather a polar night of icy darkness and hardness, no matter which group may triumph externally now. Where there is nothing, not only the Kaiser but also the proletarian has lost his rights. When this night shall have slowly receded, who of those for whom spring apparently has bloomed so luxuriously will be alive? And what will have become of all of you by then? Will you be bitter or banausic? Will you simply and dully accept world and occupation? Or will the third and by no means the least frequent possibility be your lot: mystic flight from reality for those who are gifted for it, or – as is both frequent and unpleasant – for those who belabor themselves to follow this fashion? In every one of such cases, I shall draw the conclusion that they have not measured up to their own doings. They have not measured up to the world as it really is in its everyday routine. Objectively and actually, they have not experienced the vocation for politics in its deepest meaning, which they thought they had. They would have done better in simply cultivating plain brotherliness in personal relations. And for the rest – they should have gone diligently about their daily work.

Politics is a strong and slow boring of hard boards. It takes both passion and perspective. Certainly all historical experience confirms the truth – that man would not have attained the possible unless time and again he had reached out for the impossible. But to do that a man must be a leader, and not only a leader but a hero as well, in a very unpretentious sense of the word. And even those who are neither leaders nor heroes must arm themselves with that steadfastness of heart which can brave even the crumbling of all hopes. This is necessary right now, or else men will not be able to attain even that which is possible today. Only he has the calling for politics who is sure that he shall not crumble when the world from his point of view is too stupid or too base for what he wants to offer. Only he who in the face of all this can say "In spite of all!" has the calling for politics.

## NOTES

1. Taken from Weber's political writings, this selection includes polemical statements. The selections above from *E&S* (pp. 1401–3, 1417, 1420, 1426–8).
2. A long discussion in Germany, extending back to Kant, contrasted the German notion of freedom to the French and American ones. See Leonard Krieger, *The German Idea of Freedom* (Boston: Beacon Press, 1957) [sk].

# part 8

# The Political Culture of American Democracy

## THE INFLUENCE OF THE "SECT SPIRIT"

### Introduction

The old "sect spirit" holds sway with relentless effect in the internal character of these organizations. (p. 286)

This Part highlights a number of unique and fundamental features of American democracy. It addresses in particular its heritage in ascetic Protestantism and the original social carrier of this religion: the sect. Weber often highlights this heritage by comparing American and German political cultures. Readings in this Part render especially visible his conviction that understanding the present requires reference to the long-term past. They also address the origins of two foundational features in democratic societies: tolerance and freedom of individual conscience. Weber's sweeping explorations stress the centrality of ascetic Protestant religious beliefs, particularly in their Quaker and Baptist incarnations.

Among believers in northern America's Protestant sects, an autonomous individualism combined with its seeming opposite: a strong capacity to formulate groups. The individual stands alone in Puritanism,[1] directly responsible to God and unable to appeal – for He is too distant and wrathful – to His mercy; moreover, decisions regarding one's salvation status must be made without the compassionate assistance of mediators, such as priests. Importantly, for ascetic Protestants these decisions relate specifically to ethical conduct, which alone "proves" and "testifies to" sincere belief. Yet this devout behavior is far from asocial. Rather, it serves as a mechanism of social integration: because constituting a *sign* of one's salvation and even of God's strength within the believer, the faithful, although unrelated by blood, can gravitate together without fear or hesitation. Their visibly "respectable" and "upright" conduct identifies them as God-fearing, trustworthy, decent, and moral.

In this manner, and despite the internal isolation of believers, shared belief provides a social lubricant that knits persons together into congregations. In addition, owing to the conviction among Puritans that their energy flows from God, and hence their activity must demonstrate loyalty to Him and serve His greater glory rather than private wants and desires, the emotional components in social relationships diminished in importance and purposive elements came to the fore.[2] This impersonal aspect facilitated cooperative work on behalf of a task, particularly with similarly oriented believers, Weber contends. God's decree to construct His kingdom on earth, on the one hand, lent even more intensity to this "eminent power to form communities" and, on the other, nourished the "idea that the public good . . . is to be given preference over the 'personal' or 'private' prosperity of each person" (p. 278). Nonetheless, ascetic Protestantism's ability to pull persons into groupings never reduced the individual's obligation to practice an upright conduct – to "hold his own" within the group. The devout could do so only by adhering to the sect's – and God's – high ethical standards.

Weber emphasizes to his German audience that an attribution of an "organic mystical total essence" to social organizations and the cultivation of individualism exclusively *within* such an organic grouping, as idealized by Goethe and widespread in Germany, never appeared in the case of ascetic Protestantism. Rather, an entirely pragmatic consideration of groups – as "mechanisms for the achievement of goals" – prevails, as well as a type of individualism that accentuates goal-oriented behavior at the expense of the personality's emotional side. On the other hand, the conduct of ascetic Protestants in groups, he stresses, cannot be understood as involving only a utilitarian adaptation to the group's norms. Instead, the values decreed by God and the standards of devout behavior He demands guide behavior – even in groups oriented to markets and political advantage. Hence, in Puritan communities the market's formal rationality is *both* sustained and confronted directly. "Practical rational" activity is now replaced by a "practical-ethical" organization of life.

In this manner Weber's analysis makes a case, wherever attempts to comprehend the American political culture are undertaken, for cognizance of ascetic Protestantism's wide-ranging legacies: strong individualism *and* a proclivity to form groups oriented to tasks. Indeed, American society's "unique stamp" arose out of the innumerable sects that crystallize from Puritanism's strong capacity to build communities.

Rather than being a "sandpile" (*Sandhaufen*) of individuals lacking personal, nonmarket connections to others, as the United States was perceived throughout Germany, American society was characterized by innumerable "exclusivities," Weber insists. As the United States became more industrialized and urbanized, the "old sect spirit," rather than overwhelmed by the putatively homogenizing constraints of the modern epoch, lived on. Although secularized, it remained influential. Rather than religious communities, innumerable clubs, societies, and associations now monitored the behavior of applicants and selected, by ballot, those of integrity and "good moral character." Under the watchful eyes of fellow club members the individual must "hold his own" *vis-à-vis* the organization's behavior codes. And membership, whether in the Rotary, Kiwanis, or Lion's clubs, for example, carried the same claim to respectability, decency, and status in the community as had sect membership earlier. The club's lapel pin must be seen, Weber contends, as a "badge of association" that visibly legitimated one's membership and, thereby, social honor and integrity.[3] It "certified" one's claim to be a "gentleman"; indeed, membership proved indispensable if one hoped to be fully accepted in one's community. Although increasingly assuming secularized forms, exclusivities characterized American society rather than "the open door."

In this way, manifest as both an initiative-taking individualism and community norms of involvement and service, ascetic Protestantism contributed to the formation of diverse civic associations "between" the distant state and the individual standing alone. This achievement of the sect spirit explains American society's unique capacity to create multitudes of such associations. In turn this proclivity comprises a pivotal component in its political culture of participation and self-governance. Yet egalitarianism, commercial interests, and the interests of the individual do not explain the *origins* of these selective clubs and associations, as Alexis de Tocqueville asserted (see 1945, pp. 111–13, 116, 123–5; Kalberg, 1997b, pp. 210–12); rather, their "archetype . . . is . . . the ecclesiastical community" and they assumed in part the "functions of the religious community" (p. 288). To Weber, this "tremendous flood of social groupings" (p. 286), which accounts for the uniqueness of the American experiment, remained invisible to his highly secularized countrymen in Germany unable to imagine how religious belief earlier stamped national cultures. The "democratic traditions handed down by Puritanism [constituted] an everlasting heirloom," he contends (1946a, p. 369).

Although seeking above all to offer an analysis of the American political culture's uniqueness, the essays on the Protestant sects aimed also to unveil widespread stereotypes held by Germans and Europeans. More broadly, they sought to confront a widespread image of "modern society" Weber criticized as too monolithic. The advance of capitalism, urbanism, and industrialism, it was widely believed in Europe, would sever individuals from "community" (*Gemeinschaft*), leaving them adrift and cut off from others in "society" (*Gesellschaft*). Without viable social ties, people wandered aimlessly in society as unconnected "atoms." To Emile Durkheim, this situation led to anomie and high rates of mental illness and suicide. Others spoke of the "anonymity" of modern life.

Europeans, and Germans in particular, viewed the United States, which they considered as the nation where capitalism had developed to the farthest extent, in precisely this manner. By explaining the unusual capacity of Americans to form associations, and the particular importance – deriving from their unique religious traditions – they attributed to membership, Weber sought to confront this European stereotype directly. Moreover, as a sociologist oriented to cases rather than general "developmental laws," he wished to outline how modern nations vary, despite a common experience of capitalism, urbanism, and industrialism, as a consequence of religion-influenced historical legacies. Case-by-case analysis would reveal how each developing nation followed its own pathway, he maintained. To his German countrymen, Weber wished to convey that the origins of the nightmare scenario they associated with "the modern society" may have in part arisen out of constellations of historical and cultural forces that were specifically German.

## NOTES

1. Following Weber, "ascetic Protestantism" and "Puritanism" are used synonymously [sk].
2. According to Weber:

   All [Calvinist] social *organizations* rest internally upon "individualistic," "means–end rational," or "value-rational" motives. The individual never moves into social organizations on the basis of *feelings*. Such movement is prevented by the orientation to "God's glory" and one's *own* salvation, which continuously hovers *above* one's consciousness. Among those peoples with a Puritan past, this psychological foundation even today imprints the uniqueness of their social organization with certain characteristic traits. (2002b, pp. 194–5, n. 34)

3. And today, in a less compelling though still apparent form, the lapel pin serves the same function [sk].

# chapter 20

# The Autonomy of the Individual in the Sect and the Ability to Form Democratic Communities

## TOLERANCE AND FREEDOM OF CONSCIENCE

From *The Protestant Ethic and the Spirit of Capitalism*, 3rd edn, trans. Stephen Kalberg (Los Angeles: Roxbury Publishing, 2002), pp. 195–6, n. 39.

One might be inclined to explain the *social* character of ascetic Christianity by noting the undoubtedly large importance of the Calvinist idea of an "incorporation into the body of Christ" (Calvin, *Instituto christianae religionis*, vol. 3, sects. 11, 10). In other words, because it is necessary for salvation, there must be admission into a *community* governed by God's prescriptions. For *our* particular vantage point, however, the major issue lies elsewhere.

This dogmatic idea [the importance of an incorporation into the body of Christ] could have been formulated if the church had assumed the character of an institution with membership granted to all; indeed, this type of institution did develop [Catholicism], as is well-known. Yet such a church did not have the psychological power to awaken community-building *initiatives* and to endow them with the sheer strength that Calvinism[1] possessed to do so. In particular, the effects of Calvinism's community-building energy played themselves out *beyond* the divinely prescribed church congregation and in the "world." At this point the belief becomes central that the Christian, through activities *in majorem Dei gloriam* [in service to the greater glory of God], testifies to his state of grace. . . .

The sharp condemnation of the deification of human wants and desires and of all clinging to *personal* relationships with others must have directed this energy, imperceptibly, into this pathway of impersonal activity. The Christian, whose entire existence was burdened by the necessity of testifying to his own state of grace, now acted on behalf of *God's* aims. And these could only be *impersonal* aims. Every purely feeling-based *personal* relationship of individuals to one another – that is, relationships not determined by rational aims – now easily fell under suspicion, for Puritanism as well as for every other ascetic ethic, as involving a deification of human wants and desires. The following warning . . . indicates just this tendency clearly enough: "It is an irrational act and not fit for a rational creature to love any one farther than reason will allow us. . . . It very often taketh up men's minds so as to hinder their love of God".[2] We will confront such arguments repeatedly.

The Calvinists greeted with enthusiasm the idea that God, in creating the world and also the social order, must have wanted *impersonal and purposive activity* to constitute a means for the glorification of His reputation. He did not create, the Calvinists realized, human beings for their own sake, simply for the fulfillment of the physical needs of the body. Rather, He created a world in which the physical being would be *ordered* under His will. Liberated by the doctrine of predestination, the fervid activity of the chosen could now flow entirely into a striving to make the world rational (*Rationalisierung der Welt*). More precisely, the idea that the "public" good (or, as Baxter says, "the good of the many"; see, with its rather strained citation to Romans 9:3, . . . his *Christian Directory*, vol. 4, p. 262), which was formulated in the same manner entirely as the later liberal rationalism [Classical Economics], is to be given preference over the "personal" or "private" prosperity of each person, followed for Puritanism (even though not a new idea as such) from the rejection of all glorification of human wants and desires. The long-standing American deprecation of those who *carry out* the personal commands of others, although it must be viewed in combination with many other causes that derive from "democratic" sentiments, nonetheless goes together (in an indirect manner) with this opposition to the deification of wants and desires.

This rejection of all human glorification is likewise related to the *relatively* high degree of immunity to authoritarianism possessed by peoples influenced by Puritanism. Furthermore, this rejection is related, in general, to the internally less inhibited posture of the English *vis-à-vis* their great statesmen (and their greater capacity to criticize them). This posture contrasts to some of our experiences in Germany from 1878 to the present (both positively and negatively) in respect to our statesmen. The posture of the English is characterized by a tendency, on the one hand, to acknowledge leadership in distinguished persons. It is marked, on the other hand, despite this acknowledgment, by a further proclivity to reject all hysterical idolization of leaders.

Finally, the tendency to oppose a naive idea is also apparent in Puritanism; namely, that one can render a person duty-bound, out of a sense of "thankfulness," to obey political authorities [as in Germany]. On the sinfulness of the belief in authority, see Baxter.[3] He makes it clear that a belief in authority is permissible only if the authority is *impersonal*;

that is, the belief is oriented to the content of a written [statute or regulation in a] document. Likewise, an exaggerated respect for even the most holy and wonderful person is sinful. The great danger exists, in attributing both authority and respect, that eventually the obedience to *God* will thereby be endangered.

## NOTES

1. Calvinism is viewed by Weber as ascetic Protestantism's most characteristic case.
2. R. Baxter, *Christian Directory* (London: G. Bell & Sons, 1925 [1673]), vol. 4, p. 253.
3. Ibid. *Christian Directory*, 2nd edn (1678, vol. 1, p. 56).

From *The Protestant Ethic and the Spirit of Capitalism*, 3rd edn, trans. Stephen Kalberg (Los Angeles: Roxbury Publishing, 2002), p. 222, n. 206.

We know how this principle [reverence is owed exclusively to God] was expressed among the Quakers in the apparently unimportant external aspects of life (the refusal to remove the hat, to kneel down, to bow, to use the formal form of speech ["vous" in French]). However, the *basic* idea is indigenous to *every* asceticism to a certain degree. For this reason, in its *authentic* form, asceticism is always "hostile to authority." This hostility became manifest in Calvinism in the principle that only *Christ* should rule in the *church*. As concerns Pietism, on the other hand, one thinks of [the founder] Spener's efforts to justify, by reference to the Bible, the *use of titles*. *Catholic* asceticism, in regard to matters concerning rulership in the *church*, did not share this hostility to authority. Instead, through the oath of obedience, it interpreted *obedience* itself as ascetic.

The "inverting" of this principle by Protestant asceticism is the historical foundation for the uniqueness, even today, of the *democracy* among peoples influenced by Puritanism. It is also the foundation for the differences between this democracy and the democracies that flowed out of the "Latin spirit." This hostility to authority among Protestants is also constitutive for that "lack of respect" at the foundation of American behavior. Some view this feature of American life as offensive, while others view it as refreshing.[1]

## NOTE

1. Weber is here referring to widespread prejudices (hence the quotation marks) among many Germans who viewed Americans as rude, boisterous, and unruly, and as showing inadequate respect for high status and authority. Other Germans experienced the American "lack of respect" for authority as

relief from a German climate of widespread and unquestioned respect for authority, which they perceived as oppressive [sk].

From *Economy and Society: An Outline of Interpretive Sociology*, eds Guenther Roth and Claus Wittich, trans. Guenther Roth and Claus Wittich (Berkeley, CA: University of California Press, 1978), pp. 1207–8.

... [I]n contrast to all consistent churches, all rigorous sects adhere to the principle of lay preaching and of every member's priesthood, even if they establish regular offices for economic and pedagogic reasons. Moreover, pure sects also insist upon "direct democratic administration" by the congregation and upon treating the clerical officials as servants of the congregation. These very structural features demonstrate the elective affinity between the sect and political democracy. They also account for its peculiar and highly important relationship to the political power. The sect is a specifically antipolitical or at least apolitical group. Since it must not raise universal demands and endeavors to exist as a voluntary association of qualified believers, it cannot enter into an alliance with the political power.

From *The Protestant Ethic and the Spirit of Capitalism*, 3rd edn, trans. Stephen Kalberg (Los Angeles: Roxbury Publishing, 2002), pp. 210–12, n. 129.

Th[e] opportunity should be taken to insert a few points on the idea of *tolerance*. If we leave aside for the moment the Humanist-Enlightenment idea of *indifference*, the idea of tolerance in the West had the following major sources: (a) purely political *Staatsraison* [reasons of state] (as represented by William of Orange); (b) mercantilism (for example, as particularly apparent in the city of Amsterdam and the numerous cities, lords of manors, and monarchs who supported sect members as important social carriers of economic progress); and (c) Calvinist piety in its radical manifestation. [Before turning to a further source of the idea of tolerance in the West, several remarks must be offered regarding the manner in which Calvinist piety constituted an important source for this idea.]

The idea of predestination basically prevented the state, through its intolerance, from actually promoting religion. In light of this idea, the state's intolerance did not enable it to save a single soul; only the idea of *God's honor* induced the church to request the state's assistance in suppressing heresy. However, the more the emphasis was placed on the necessity for the minister and all participants in communion to be members of the elect, all the more unacceptable was (a) every instance of the state's intervention in processes to appoint new clergy, (b) every appointment to the ministry of students from the university made simply on the basis of completed theological training (which might include someone who perhaps did not belong among the elect), and in general (3) every intervention in the congregation's concerns by the political powers (whose conduct was often not above reproach).

Reformed Pietism strengthened this opposition to external intervention by devaluing dogmatic correctness and by gradually loosening the axiom *extra ecclesiam nulla salus* [no salvation outside the church] . . .

Cromwell's army upheld freedom of conscience, and the "parliament of saints" supported even the separation of church and state, *because* its members were devout Pietists. That is, religious reasons *were effective* in providing their motivation to uphold the freedom of conscience and, hence, the idea of tolerance.

[Now let us turn to a fourth major source of the idea of tolerance in the West.] (d) From the beginning of their existence, the *baptizing sects* . . . have continuously upheld the basic principle that only the elect can be taken into the community of the church. (They have done so more forcefully and with greater internal consistency than the other ascetic Protestant congregations.) For this reason, they (a) repudiated the idea of the church as an institution (*Anstalt*) offering salvation to all [see *E&S*, pp. 557–63], and (b) opposed every intervention by secular powers. Hence, it was an *effective religious* reason also in this case that produced the demand for unconditional tolerance.

The first who for these reasons upheld an unconditional tolerance *and* the separation of church and state was surely [the English theologian and opponent of the Anglican Church] Robert Browne [1550–1633]. He was almost a generation before the Baptists and two generations before Roger Williams [1628–80], the Puritan founder of the colony of Rhode Island and pioneer of religious liberty. The first declaration of a church community in this regard appears to have been the resolution of the English Baptists in Amsterdam in 1612 or 1613: "The magistrate is not to meddle with religion or matters of conscience . . . because Christ is the King and lawgiver of the Church and conscience." The first official document of a church community that demanded the *effective* protection of freedom of conscience from the state as *a right* was surely Article 44 of the Confession of the (Particular) Baptists of 1644.

It should once again be emphasized that the view occasionally found – that tolerance *as such* favored capitalism – is of course completely wrong. Religious tolerance is not specifically modern, nor is it unique to the West. It dominated in China, in India, in the great empires of the Near East in the Hellenic era, in the Roman Empire, and the Islamic empires. It ruled for longer epochs, circumscribed only for reasons connected to the state itself (*Staatsraison*) (and these reasons even today define the limits of its expanse). This degree of tolerance, however, was nowhere in the world to be found in the sixteenth and seventeenth centuries. It was least to be found in those regions where Puritanism *dominated*, as, for example, in Holland and Zeeland [the Dutch island province off the coast of Denmark] in the era of political-economic expansion, or in Puritan England or New England. Clearly characteristic of the West (after the Reformation, as well as prior to it, and similar to, for example, the Sassanian dynasty [of Persia, 226–651], was *religious intolerance*, as had reigned also in China, Japan, and India during particular epochs (although mostly for political reasons). It follows that tolerance as such certainly has not the slightest thing to do with capitalism. It depended on *who was favored by it*.

From *Economy and Society: An Outline of Interpretive Sociology*, eds Guenther Roth and Claus Wittich, trans. Guenther Roth and Claus Wittich, slightly revised by Stephen Kalberg (Berkeley, CA: University of California Press, 1978), pp. 1208–10.

. . . The pure sect must advocate "tolerance" and "separation of church and state" for several reasons: because it is in fact *not* a universalist redemptory institution for the repression of sin and can bear political as little as hierocratic control and reglementation; because no official power, of whatever sort, can dispense grace to unqualified persons and, hence, all use of political force in religious matters must appear senseless or outright diabolical; because the sect is simply not concerned with non-sect members; because, taking all this together, the sect just cannot be anything but an absolutely voluntary association of the religiously qualified if it wants to retain its true religious identity and its effectiveness. Therefore, consistent sects have always taken this position and have been the most genuine advocates of "freedom of conscience."

Other communities, too, have favored freedom of conscience, but in a different sense. It is possible to speak of this freedom and of tolerance under the caesaropapist regimes of Rome, China, India and Japan, since the most diverse cults of subjected or affiliated states were permitted and since no religious compulsion existed; however, in principle this is limited by the official cult of the political power, the cult of the emperor in Rome, the religious veneration of the emperor in Japan, and probably also the emperor's cult of Heaven in China. Moreover, this tolerance had political, not religious reasons, as did that of King William the Silent or, much earlier, Emperor Frederick II, or manorial lords who used sect members as skilled labor, and in the city of Amsterdam, where the sectarians were major agents of commercial life. Thus, economic motives played an important role. But the genuine sect must demand the non-intervention of the political power and freedom of conscience for specifically religious reasons – there are transitional forms, but we leave them aside deliberately.

A fully developed church – advancing universalist claims – cannot concede freedom of conscience; wherever it pleads for this freedom, it is because it finds itself in a minority position and demands something which, in principle, it cannot grant to others: "The Catholic's freedom of conscience," Mallinckrodt said in the Reichstag, "consists in being allowed to obey the pope" – in other words, to act according to one's own conscience. However, if they are strong enough, neither the Catholic nor the (old) Lutheran Church and, all the more so, the Calvinist and Baptist old church recognize freedom of conscience for *others*. These churches cannot act differently in view of their institutional commitment to safeguard the salvation of the soul or, in the case of the Calvinists, to protect the glory of God. By contrast, the consistent Quaker applies the principle of the freedom of conscience not only to himself but also to others, and rejects any attempt to compel those who are not Quakers or Baptists to act as if they belonged to his group. Thus the consistent sect gives rise to an inalienable personal right of the governed as against any power, whether political, hierocratic or patriarchal. Such freedom of conscience may be the oldest Right of Man – as Jellinek has argued convincingly;[1] at any rate, it is the most basic Right of Man because it comprises all ethically conditioned action and guarantees freedom from compulsion, especially from the power of the state. In this sense the concept was as unknown to Antiquity and the Middle Ages as it was to Rousseau's social contract with its power of religious compulsion. The other Rights of Man or civil rights were joined to this basic right, especially the right to pursue one's own economic interests, which includes the inviolability of individual property, the freedom of contract, and vocational choice. This economic right exists within the limits of a system of guaranteed abstract rules that apply to everybody alike. All of these rights find their ultimate justification in the belief of the Enlightenment in the workings of individual reason which, if unimpeded, would result in the at least relatively best of all worlds, by virtue of Divine providence and because the individual is best qualified to know his own interests. This charismatic glorification of "Reason," which found a characteristic expression in its apotheosis by Robespierre, is the last form that charisma has adopted in its fateful historical course. It is clear that these postulates of formal legal equality and economic mobility paved the way for the destruction of all patrimonial and feudal law in favor of abstract norms and hence indirectly of bureaucratization. It is also clear that they facilitated the expansion of capitalism. The basic Rights of Man made it possible for the capitalist to use things and men freely, just as the this-worldly asceticism – adopted with some dogmatic variations – and the specific discipline of the sects bred the capitalist spirit and the rational "professional" (*Berufsmensch*) who was needed by capitalism.

NOTE

1. Cf. Georg Jellinek, *The Declaration of the Rights of Man and of Citizens* (Westport, CT: Hyperion Press, 1979) [sk].

From "'Churches' and 'Sects' in North America," trans. Colin Loader, revised by Stephen Kalberg, *Sociological Theory* 3 (Spring 1985): 10.

The exclusive appraisal of a person purely in terms of the religious qualities evidenced in his conduct necessarily prunes feudal and dynastic romanticism from its roots. To be sure, the aversion to all kinds of idolatry was neither confined to the "sects" in our technical sense, nor has it been immediately characteristic of *all* communities constituted along the lines of the sect. It is much more an attribute of the religiosity whose essence is *ascetic* and, in the case of the Calvinist Puritans, is a direct consequence of the idea of predestination. Before the dreadful earnestness of this idea of predestination, all earthly institutions offering "God's grace" had to crumble into nothing but a blasphemous swindle.

To be sure, however, this frame of mind only reached its fullest expression in the naturally anti-authoritarian climate of the sects. If, by their strict avoidance of all oaths of allegiance that were courtly or stemmed from court life, the Quakers took upon themselves not only the Crown of Martyrs but also the much heavier burden of everyday derision, then this stand came from the conviction that those oaths of allegiance should be made to God alone and that it is an insult to His majesty to accord them to people. The unconditional rejection of all such demands of the state that went "against one's conscience" and the demand that the state recognize "freedom of conscience" as the inalienable right of the individual were conceivable from the position of the sect only as an overt *religious* claim. This claim reached its logical conclusion in the Quaker ethic, one of whose guiding principles was that what is duty for one can be forbidden to another, when the voice of one's own carefully explored *conscience* implied engaging in the action for the former and abstaining from it for the latter.

From "'Churches' and 'Sects' in North America," trans. Colin Loader, revised by Stephen Kalberg, *Sociological Theory* 3 (Spring 1985): 10–11.

[In the sect, the] autonomy of the individual . . . is anchored not in indifference but in religious positions; and the struggle against all types of "authoritarian" arbitrariness is elevated to the level of a religious duty. In the time of its heroic youth [in the sects], this individualism produced an eminent power to form communities. The "church's" universalism, which goes hand in hand with ethical moderation, stands in contrast to the sect's propagandism, which is coupled with ethical rigorism. Again, the latter reaches its most logical conclusion in the Quaker ethic with the idea that God can spread his "inner light" also to those upon whom the Gospel has never been urged. Not objectivized documents and traditions but rather the religiously qualified individual is seen as the bearer of revelation which continues without ever being completed. . . .

The democratic character of North America is, without doubt, dependent on the *colonial* character of its culture and so demonstrates the tendency to decline together with the latter. In addition, a part of those particular American characteristics . . . is determined by the sober, pessimistic estimation of mankind and its works which is characteristic of all forms (even those of the "church" type) of Puritanism. However, the tying together of the internal isolation of the individual (which means that a maximum of his energy is deployed externally) with his ability to form social groups having the most stable cohesion and maximum impact at first was realized most fully on the basis of the formation of the sects.

We modern, religiously "unattuned" people are hard pressed to conceptualize or even simply to *believe* what a powerful role these religious factors had in those periods when the characters of the modern national cultures were being stamped. The factors overshadowed everything at a time when people were most immediately concerned with the "hereafter." It is and remains the fate of us Germans that, due to numerous historical causes, the religious revolution at that time meant a development that favored not the energy of the individual but the aura of the "office." Hand in hand with this development, that situation arose which, on account of the religious community remaining now as ever only as a "church," i.e., an institution, had to force all individual striving for emancipation from "authority," all "liberalism" in the broadest sense of the word, along the path of *hostility* to the religious communities. At the same time, the religious community withheld from itself the development of that community-forming energy which . . . the "sects" – along with other historical factors – have imparted to an Anglo-Saxon world so completely different in these respects from the German.

From " 'Kirchen' and 'Sekten' in Nordamerika," (1906) in *Max Weber: Soziologie, Universalgeschichtliche Analysen, Politik*, ed. Johannes Winckelmann, trans. Stephen Kalberg (Stuttgart: Kröner Verlag, 1992 [6th edn]), pp. 392–4.

[The sects] . . . alone have been able, on the foundation of Protestantism, to instill an intensity of interest in religion in the broad middle class – and especially modern workers – that otherwise is found only, though in the form of a bigoted fanaticism, among traditional peasants. And here the significance of the sects expands beyond the religious realm. American democracy, for example, acquired its own dynamic form and unique imprint exclusively from them. On the one hand, the idea that the individual, on the basis of the religious qualifications bestowed upon him by God, decided on his salvation status exclusively on his own was important. That is, magical sacraments were devoid of utility for one's salvation; only the believer's practical conduct mattered: his behavior "proved and testified" to his faith and alone provided a *sign* that he stood on the road to salvation. On the other hand, this very notion – the individual could testify to his salvation through his righteous behavior – formulated the foundation for the social knitting together of the congregation. Indeed, the tremendous flood of social groupings, which penetrate all corners of American life, are constituted according to this "sect" model.

Those who imagine "democracy" to be rooted in a mass of people fragmented into atoms, such as our [German] Romantics love to do, are making a fundamental mistake – at least as concerns the American democracy. "Atomization" results far more from bureaucratic rationalism[1] than from democracy; hence it will not be eliminated by an imposition from above of "stratified formations," as the Romantics hope. American society in its genuine form – and here my remarks explicitly concern also the "middle" and "lower" strata – was never such a sandpile, nor even a building where everyone who sought to enter found open, undiscriminating doors. Rather, it was, and is, saturated with "exclusivities" of all sorts. Wherever this earlier situation still remains, the individual firmly acquires a foundation under his feet, at the university and in business, only when he succeeds in being voted into a *social organization* (earlier almost without exception a church, today an organization of a different sort) and manages, within this organization, to *hold his own*. The old "sect spirit" holds sway with relentless effect in the internal character of these organizations.

Sects are "artefacts" of "societies" (*Gesellschaften*) rather than "communities" (*Gemeinschaften*), in the terminology of Ferdinand Tönnies. In other words, they are based upon neither "tender and sentimental" feelings nor do they strive to cultivate "sentimental values" [see *PE*, pp. 194–5, n. 34]. Rather, by integrating himself into them, the individual seeks in these organizations to hold *his own*. Lacking totally is the undifferentiated "sentimentality" and companionability commonly found in a spontaneous manner among peasants – without which, as Germans believe, a sense of community cannot be cultivated. Instead, the cool *matter-of-factness* characteristic of association promotes the precise ordering of the individual into the instrumental task pursued by the group, whether a football team or a political party.

Nonetheless, this integrating of the individual in no way signifies a weakening of the necessity for the individual constantly to be concerned to hold his own. On the contrary, his task to *"prove himself"* actually becomes directly incumbent upon him only at the point when he moves *inside* the group and into the circle of his fellows. For this reason, the social organization to which the individual belongs never becomes something *organic* – that is, a mystical total essence floating above him and enveloping him. Rather, in a manner entirely conscious to the individual, social organizations *always* become mechanisms for the achievement of his own material and ideal *goals*.

NOTE

1. Weber is referring to the leveling of feudal-based status differences that occurs with bureaucratization ("passive democratization"). See above, pp. 209–11 [sk].

From *Economy and Society: An Outline of Interpretive Sociology*, eds and trans. Guenther Roth and Claus Wittich (Berkeley, CA: University of California Press, 1978), pp. 1206–7.

. . . [T]he Catholic's auricular confession . . . is uncontrolled and serves the sinner's relief but rarely aims at changing his mind. More important than any other factor is the fact that [in the sect] a man must hold his own under the watchful eyes of his peers. This basis of self-esteem spread with increasing secularization from the sects into all walks of American life, by virtue of the numerous associations and clubs, most of which recruit their members through balloting; these associations exist for all conceivable purposes and extend down to the level of the boys' clubs in the schools. Even today the middle-class "gentleman" is legitimated by the badge of some association. Even though many of these traditions are disintegrating, it is still true that American democracy is not a sand-pile of unrelated individuals but a maze of highly exclusive, yet absolutely voluntary sects, associations and clubs, which provide the center of the individual's social life. American students may even consider it a cause for committing suicide if they fail to be elected into an exclusive club. Of course, analogies can be found in many voluntary associations, for the question of being joined by other individuals is considered frequently – and in non-economic associations predominantly – not merely from the functional viewpoint of the group's manifest purpose; rather, membership in exclusive clubs is everywhere regarded as a status elevation. Nowhere was this as true as in America's classic era: The sect and its derivations are one of her unwritten but vital constitutional elements, since they shape the individual more than any other influence.

From " 'Churches' and 'Sects' in North America", trans. Colin Loader, *Sociological Theory* 3 (Spring 1985): 8.

In areas of the United States where the old relationships are still strong and where there is still minor differentiation among purposive social groups (*Zweckverbände*), the religious congregation (the initial and most universal community) still embraces almost all "social" interests in which the individual participates beyond his own doorstep. Not only instructional presentations, church suppers, Sunday school and all imaginable charitable institutions, but also the most diverse athletic activities, football practice and the like, are offered by the church congregation; and time is allotted, circumstances permitting, for announcements of these activities at the end of the church service. A man, who in earlier times was publicly excluded for dishonorable conduct or who today is quietly dropped from the rolls, suffers therewith a kind of social boycott. He who stands outside of the church has no social "connection." The guarantee of *social* qualities which is included in church membership is still important, despite the diminution which (totally apart from the development of modernity) naturally accompanies the sharp competition among denominations in the attempt to proselytize souls, and despite the general undermining of the churches' position of power.

Today, large number of "orders" and clubs of all sorts have begun to assume in part the functions of the religious community. Almost every small businessman who thinks something of himself wears some kind of badge in his lapel [e.g. Lion's, Kiwanis, Rotary Clubs]. However, the archetype of this form, which *all* use to guarantee the "honorableness" of the individual, is indeed the ecclesiastical community.

From "The Protestant Sects and the Spirit of Capitalism," in *The Protestant Ethic and the Spirit of Capitalism*, 3rd edn, trans. H. H. Gerth and C. Wright Mills (Los Angeles: Roxbury Publishing, 2002), pp. 134–5.

The entire life of a typical Yankee of the last generation led through a series of such exclusive associations, beginning with the Boys' Club in school, proceeding to the Athletic Club or the Greek Letter Society or to another student club of some nature, then onward to one of the numerous notable clubs of businessmen and the middle class or finally to the clubs of the metropolitan plutocracy. To gain admission was identical to a ticket of ascent, especially with a certificate before the forum of one's self-feeling; to gain admission meant to have "proved" oneself. A student in college who was not admitted to any club (or quasi-society) whatsoever was usually a sort of pariah. (Suicides because of failure to be admitted have come to my notice.) A businessman, clerk, technician, or doctor who had the same fate usually was of questionable ability to serve. Today, numerous clubs of this sort are bearers of those tendencies leading toward aristocratic status groups which characterize contemporary American development. These status groups develop alongside of and, what has to be well noted, partly in contrast to the naked plutocracy.

In America mere "money" in itself also purchases power, but not social honor. Of course, it is a means of acquiring social prestige. It is the same in Germany and everywhere else; except in Germany the appropriate avenue to social honor led from the purchase of a feudal estate to the foundation of an entailed estate, and acquisition of titular nobility, which in turn facilitated the reception of the grandchildren in aristocratic "society." In America, the old tradition respected the self-made man more than the heir, and the avenue to social honor consisted in affiliation with a genteel fraternity in a distinguished college, formerly with a distinguished sect (for instance, Presbyterian, in whose churches in New York one could find soft cushions and fans in the pews). At the present time, affiliation with a distinguished club is essential above all else. In addition, the kind of home is important (in "the street" which in middle-sized cities is almost never lacking) and the kind of dress and sport.

# part 9

# On "Race," the Complexity of the Concept of Ethnicity, and Heredity

## Introduction

This Part demonstrates Weber's strong aversion to the explanatory power of race, ethnicity, and "common descent."[1] The question of whether biological races exist or not never attracts his attention; rather, he focuses upon the extent to which "race membership" – or "common inherited and inheritable traits that actually derive from common descent" (p. 297) and consciousness of race – calls forth social action in a regular manner, indeed, to such an extent that it forms the foundation for a group. Is "race" influential enough to be group-forming?

Of course race *can* be "subjectively perceived as [the] common trait" of a specific group, and hence lead to group formation. Weber emphasizes, however, that highly complex issues are involved and counsels caution and circumspection. He is convinced in particular that any antipathy toward a racial group cannot be understood simply as a consequence of a dislike of inherited traits. Rather than a "natural" racial aversion, "visible differences" – such as variation in respect to power and social honor, and the extent to which political and status groups become closed – may just as likely provide an explanation for antipathy. Social forces, including general socialization differences, must be acknowledged.

Moreover, Weber stresses throughout this chapter that a variety of "historically accidental habits" have been just as important for the formation of groups as "inherited racial characteristics." Different hairstyles, beards, eating habits, and clothes, for example, may split people off one from another and serve as catalysts for a "consciousness of kind"; they do so as effectively as shared customs in political and religious communities. And shared customs, conventions, and memories may ground tendencies toward monopolistic closure, which then may be transmitted across generations.

A belief in membership of an "ethnic group" may arise from such similarities, and this belief *may* "facilitate group formation . . . particularly in the political sphere." Yet Weber sees the reverse line of causation as equally plausible: a sense of membership in a political association may give rise to beliefs in a common ethnicity. And these beliefs, and even a sense of "ethnic honor" specific to the group, may endure even if the political association disintegrates. A common language and a memory of emigration or peaceful secession may intensify the belief in a common ethnicity. A distinct physical appearance and perceptible uniqueness in the "conduct of everyday life" must be noted as further factors conducive to ethnic differentiation, as are differences in workplace gender differentiation, housing, and food. Such distinctions may become manifest in conventions and become "symbols of ethnic membership."

These forces are constituent elements in the formation of ethnic groups, Weber contends; racial qualities are only marginally effective. Moreover, wherever new groups move into regions previously sharply demarcated by grouping, the apparent sharp contrast in customs is often explained by "the idea of blood disaffinity." However, this understandable conclusion must not be readily accepted, he argues, even though "ethnically determined action," or action "determined by the belief in a blood relationship," may become widespread. History demonstrates that political action was often the source of group-forming action that later became understood as rooted in ethnicity. Although understood today as rooted in blood relationships and common descent, even tribes often came into being as "artifacts" of political associations. Common customs, which "have diverse origins," may have originated out of adaptation to environmental conditions and the "imitation of neighbors" rather than ethnicity.

If "'ethnically' determined social action" is to be explained, he concludes, a broad array of social factors must be distinguished. Indeed, because it conceals various forces and is far from uniform, the term "ethnic" would have to be abandoned. Once terms are precisely defined, he contends, the notion of "'ethnic' group . . . dissolves."

In the next selection Weber confronts Alfred Ploetz (ca 1860–1940), a prominent representative of the "race biology" school. This exchange took place at a meeting of the German Sociological Association in Frankfurt in 1910. Ploetz's lecture, "The Concepts Race and Society and Some Problems Associated with Them," had summarized his position. On the basis of a sweeping overview of Western history that combined Darwin and Nietzsche, he sought to legitimize "the necessity" for a "racial hygiene" turn – that is, for the social sciences to follow a eugenics agenda.[2]

The most modern advances in biology and genetics legitimized such a paradigm change, he argued. In its grandeur, the large collectivity – or "vital race" (*Vitalrasse*), as he prefers[3] – must take precedent over the ephemeral, miniscule and imperfect existence of individuals, for the race represents the organic unity of life. Moreover, society contains the blood of its members, according to Ploetz, and hence its health depends upon the purity of the "blood of the race." The weak and infirm, who lower the quality of the gene pool, must be prohibited from reproducing. To him, the social welfare policies of the German state, which had developed in a manner diametrically opposed to the Darwinian "survival of the fittest" axiom, threatened the vigor of the Germans. Along with his mentor, Ernst Haeckel (1834–1919), Ploetz, as "the apostle of a new race theory,"[4] would become a major early proponent of the priority given to *das Volk* by National Socialism and of the eugenics policies it adopted.[5]

Weber, who was the last commentator on Ploetz's lecture, states his opposition to all attempts to explain social occurrences and developments by reference to biological forces, or "inheritable traits," in extremely forceful terms. He offers several explanations anchored in economic and political factors that, he proposes, better explain "societal circumstances" than the "blood of a race." In respect to the fall of ancient Rome, for example, reference to economic forces provides an entirely convincing explanation, Weber holds, and any use of a hypothetical "racial theory," as Ploetz had offered, is speculative and methodologically unwarranted. And no proof exists that relationships between blacks and whites in the United States are "rooted in inherited instincts," as Ploetz had argued.[6] Similarly, social causes, rather than instinct, explain the diverging social esteem accorded to Blacks and Indians by Whites in North America. And what, in the end, is a "race"? Weber then calls attention to his own "situation of personal embarrassment, [as] I . . . am a cross-section of many races."

To him, the concept "race" possesses "a completely mystical character" and implies "subjective evaluations." At present, he contends, "innate and inherited qualities" fail to explain a "single fact relevant for Sociology." Perhaps, when research tools and methodologies have been significantly refined at some distant point in the future, an "exact proof" of the impact of inheritable qualities for social life can be acquired, he holds. For now, however, "theories of race allow one to prove and disprove whatever one wishes."[7] Moreover, Weber contends that science, given its limits for purely methodological reasons, can never determine the ultimate superiority or inferiority, as Ploetz had claimed, of races, let alone the superiority of one culture over another (see p. 331). Weber opposes vehemently all pushing to the side today of "known and accessible causes in favor of hypotheses that are speculative." Finally, his comments include a succinct criticism of all approaches that view society as an organism and all schools that ground their conclusions upon analogies across human and animal species.

The final reading is from Weber's introduction to his *Collected Essays in the Sociology of Religion*. Here he argues against the idea that, because specific types of rationalization can be discovered only in the West, heredity must be seen as playing the decisive causal role. In sum, Weber's views on ethnicity, race, and heredity conform to those held by social scientists today.

## NOTES

1. Weber arrived at this conclusion somewhere around 1900. His study of the East Elbian (Poland) farmworkers in the 1890s uses the notion of race as a causal force that explained some qualitative differences between Germans and Poles, largely to the detriment of the Poles. See Ernst Moritz Manasse, "Max Weber on Race," *Social Research* 14 (1947), pp. 191–221. That Weber no longer held this position by the time of his visit to the United States is clear from Marianne Weber's biography (1975, pp. 295–6). See also "Max Weber, Dr. Alfred Ploetz, and W. E. B. Du Bois," edited and translated by Benjamin Nelson and Jerome Gittleman (*Sociological Analysis*, 34, 4 [1973], pp. 308–12).
2. Ploetz was the main founder and editor of an influential eugenics journal, *Archiv für Rassen- und Gesellschafts-biologie* (1904–44). See Detlev J. K. Peukert, *Max Webers Diagnose der Moderne* (Göttingen: Vendenhoeck u. Ruprecht, 1989), pp. 92–101.
3. This is Ploetz's term. It refers to the entire population of a race as opposed to variations and sub-variations within a larger race population. The latter are to him "race systems" (*Systemrasse*; see pp. 306–13 below). See "Max Weber, Dr. Alfred Ploetz, and W. E. B. Du Bois" (n. 1), pp. 309–10.
4. Manasse, *op. cit.*, p. 199.
5. The historian George Mosse summarizes Ploetz's views thus:

> According to him, it was the Aryan race alone that represented the apex in racial development. He suggested that during a war it would only be fitting to send inferior members of the race to the front line as cannon fodder. Furthermore, as an added measure to insure physical fitness, Ploetz suggested that at a child's birth a consultation of doctors should judge its fitness to live or die.

   See George L. Mosse, *The Crisis of German Ideology* (New York: Grosset & Dunlap, 1964), p. 99. See also Daniel Gasman, *The Scientific Origins of National Socialism* (New York: American Elsevier Inc., 1971), pp. 149–50. For an examination of the important influence of Ploetz and his journal, see Hedwig Conrad-Martius, *Utopien der Menschenzüchtung* (Munich: Kösel Verlag, 1955), Chapter 3. See generally Hans-Günter Zmarzlik, "Der Sozialdarwinismus in Deutschland als geschichtliches Problem," *Vierteljahreshefte für Zeitgeschichte*, XI (1963), pp. 246–73.
6. See Marianne Weber, 1975, pp. 295–6 (n. 1). Weber refers to W. E. B. Du Bois, who had attended his lectures as a student in the 1890s in Germany, as "the most important sociological scholar anywhere in the Southern States"; see "Max Weber, Dr. Alfred Ploetz, and W. E. B. Du Bois"; *op. cit.*, p. 312. Upon meeting him in St Louis in 1904, Weber encouraged Du Bois to write an article for

the journal he edited (see "Die Negerfrage in den Vereinigten Staaten" [The Negro Question in the United States], *Archiv für Sozialwissenschaft und Sozialpolitik*, 22, 1906: 31–79). Weber's attempt to secure the translation into German and publication of Du Bois's "splendid work," *The Souls of Black Folk*, failed, despite Weber's plan "to write a short introduction about [the] Negro question and literature." Weber had also intended to write an article on "the recent publications [on] the race problem in America." See Weber's letter in English to Du Bois in Herbert Aptheker (ed.), *The Correspondence of W. E. B. Du Bois*, vol. 1, 1877–1934 (Amherst, MA: University of Massachusetts Press, 1973), p. 106.

7.  "Zum Vortrag von F. Oppenheimer über 'Die rassen-theoretische Geschichts-philosophie,'" in Weber, 1988b, p. 489. Weber continues, addressing here the question of whether racial factors played a role in the decline of ancient civilizations:

> It is a scientific crime to attempt the circumvention, by the uncritical use of completely unclarified racial hypotheses, of the sociological study of Antiquity, which of course is much more difficult, but by no means without hope of success; after all, we can no longer find out to what extent the qualities of the Hellenes and Romans rested on inherited dispositions. The problem of such relationships has not yet been solved by the most careful and toilsome investigations of living subjects, even if undertaken in the laboratory and with the means of exact experimentation. (1968a, p. 398, n. 1; trans. Guenther Roth)

# chapter 21

# On "Race" Membership, Common Ethnicity, the "Ethnic Group," and Heredity

From *Economy and Society: An Outline of Interpretive Sociology*, eds and trans. Guenther Roth and Claus Wittich, revised by Stephen Kalberg (Berkeley, CA: University of California Press, 1978), pp. 385–7.

A much more problematic source of social action than the sources analyzed above is "race membership": common inherited and inheritable traits that actually derive from common descent. Of course, race creates a "group" only when it is subjectively perceived as a common trait: this happens only when a neighborhood or the mere proximity of racially different persons is the basis of joint (mostly political) action, or conversely, when some common experiences of members of the same race are linked to some *antagonism* against members of an *obviously* different group. The resulting social action is usually merely negative: those who are obviously different are avoided and despised or, conversely, viewed with superstitious awe. Persons who have a different external habitus are simply despised irrespective of what they "accomplish" or what they "are," or they are venerated superstitiously if they are too powerful in the long run. In this case antipathy is the primary and normal reaction. However, this antipathy is shared not just by persons with anthropological similarities, and its extent is by no means determined by the degree of anthropological relatedness; furthermore, this antipathy is linked not only to inherited features but just as much to other visible differences.

If the degree of objective racial difference can be determined, among other things, purely physiologically by establishing whether hybrids reproduce themselves at approximately normal rates, the subjective aspects, the reciprocal racial attraction and repulsion, might be measured by finding out whether sexual relations are preferred or rare between two groups, and whether they are carried on permanently or temporarily and irregularly. In all groups with a developed "ethnic" consciousness the existence or absence of intermarriage (*connubium*) would then be a normal consequence of racial attraction or segregation. Serious research on the sexual attraction and repulsion between different ethnic groups is only incipient, but there is not the slightest doubt that racial factors, that means, common descent, influence the incidence of sexual relations and of marriage, sometimes decisively. However, the existence of several million mulattoes in the United States speaks clearly against the assumption of a "natural" racial antipathy, even among quite different races. Apart from the laws against biracial marriages in the Southern states, sexual relations between the two races are now abhorred by both sides, but this development began only with the Emancipation and resulted from the Negroes' demand for equal civil rights. Hence this abhorrence on the part of the Whites is *socially* determined by the . . . tendency toward the monopolization of social power and honor, a tendency which in this case happens to be linked to race.

The *connubium* itself, that means, the fact that the offspring from a permanent sexual relationship can share in the activities and advantages of the father's political, economic or status group, depends on many circumstances. Under undiminished patriarchal rulership, the father was free to grant equal rights to his children from slaves. Moreover, the glorification of abduction by the hero made racial mixing a normal event within the ruling strata. However, patriarchal discretion was progressively curtailed with the monopolistic closure, by now familiar to us, of political, status or other groups and with the monopolization of marriage opportunities; these tendencies restricted the *connubium* to the offspring from a permanent sexual union within the given political, religious, economic and status group. This also produced a high incidence of inbreeding. The "endogamy" of a group is probably everywhere a secondary product of such tendencies . . . "Pure" anthropological types are often a secondary consequence of such closure; examples are sects (as in India) as well as pariah peoples, that means, groups that are socially despised yet wanted as neighbors because they have monopolized indispensable skills.

Reasons other than actual racial kinship influence the degree to which blood relationship is taken into account. In the United States the smallest admixture of Negro blood disqualifies a person unconditionally, whereas very considerable admixtures of Indian blood do not. Doubtlessly, it is important that Negroes appear esthetically even more alien than Indians, but it remains very significant that Negroes were slaves and hence disqualified in the status hierarchy. The conventional *connubium* is far less impeded by anthropological differences than by status differences, that means, differences due to socialization and "upbringing" (*Bildung* in the widest sense of the word). Mere anthropological differences account for little, except in cases of extreme esthetic antipathy.

# The Origin of Common Ethnic Beliefs: The Language and Cult Community

From *Economy and Society: An Outline of Interpretive Sociology*, eds Guenther Roth and Claus Wittich, trans. Ferdinand Kolegar, revised by Stephen Kalberg (Berkeley, CA: University of California Press, 1978), pp. 387–93.

The question of whether conspicuous "racial" differences are based on "biological heredity" or on "tradition" is usually of no importance as far as their effect on mutual attraction or repulsion is concerned. This is true of the development of endogamous conjugal groups, and even more so of attraction and repulsion in other kinds of social intercourse and group formation, i.e., whether all sorts of friendly, companionable, or economic relationships between such groups are established easily and on the footing of mutual trust and respect, or whether such relationships are established with difficulty and with precautions that betray mistrust.

The more or less easy emergence of group-based social intercourse (in the broadest sense of the word) . . . may be linked to the most superficial features of historically accidental habits just as much as to inherited racial characteristics. That the different custom is not understood in its subjective meaning since the cultural key to it is lacking, is almost as decisive as the peculiarity of the custom as such. But, as we shall soon see, not all repulsion is attributable to the absence of a "consensual group." Differences in the styles of beard and hairdo, clothes, food and eating habits, division of labor between the sexes, and all kinds of other visible differences can, in a given case, give rise to repulsion and contempt, but the actual extent of these differences is irrelevant for the emotional impact, as is illustrated by primitive travel descriptions, the Histories of Herodotus or the older prescientific ethnography. Seen from their positive aspect, however, these differences may give rise to consciousness of kind, which may become as easily the bearer of group relationships as groups ranging from the household and neighborhood to political and religious communities are usually the bearers of shared customs.

All differences of "customs" can sustain a specific feeling of "honor" or "dignity" in their practitioners. The original motives or reasons for the inception of different habits of life are forgotten and the contrasts are then perpetuated as "conventions." In this manner, any group can create customs, and it can also effect, in certain circumstances very decisively, the selection of anthropological types. This it can do by providing favorable chances of survival and reproduction for certain hereditary qualities and traits. This holds both for internal assimilation and for external differentiation.

Any external feature, no matter how superficial, can serve as a starting point for the familiar tendency to monopolistic closure. However, the universal force of "imitation" has the general effect of only gradually changing the traditional customs and usages, just as anthropological types are changed only gradually by racial mixing. But if there are sharp boundaries between areas of observable styles of life, they are due to conscious monopolistic closure, which started from small differences that were then cultivated and intensified; or they are due to the peaceful or warlike migrations of groups that previously lived far from each other and had accommodated themselves to their heterogeneous conditions of existence. Similarly, strikingly different racial types, bred in isolation, may live in sharply segregated proximity to one another either because of monopolistic closure or because of migration.

We can conclude then that similarity and contrast of habitus and custom, regardless of whether they are biologically inherited or culturally transmitted, are subject to the same conditions of group life, in origin as well as in effectiveness, and identical in their potential for group formation. The difference lies partly in the differential instability of type and custom, partly in the fixed (though often unknown) limit to engendering new hereditary qualities. Compared to this, the scope for "assimilation" of new "customs" is incomparably greater, although there are considerable variations in the transmissibility of traditions.

Almost any kind of similarity or contrast of habitus and customs can induce the belief that affinity or disaffinity exists between groups that attract or repel each other. Not every belief in tribal affinity, however, is founded on the resemblance of customs or of habitus. But in spite of great variations in this area, such a belief can exist and can develop group-forming powers when it is buttressed by a memory of an actual migration, be it colonization or individual migration. The persistent effect of the old ways and of childhood reminiscences continues as a source of native-country feeling (*Heimatgefühl*) among emigrants even when they have become so thoroughly adjusted to the new country that return to their homeland would be intolerable (this being the case of most German-Americans, for example).

In colonies, the attachment to the colonists' homeland survives despite considerable mixing with the inhabitants of the colonial land and despite profound changes in tradition and hereditary type as well. In case of political colonization, the decisive factor is the need for political support. In general, the continuation of relationships created by marriage is important, and so are the market relationships, provided that the "customs" remained unchanged. These market relationships between the homeland and the colony may be very close, as long as the consumer standards remain similar, and especially when colonies are in an almost absolutely alien environment and within an alien political territory.

The belief in group affinity, regardless of whether it has any objective foundation, can have important consequences especially for the formation of a political community. We shall call "ethnic groups" those human groups that entertain a subjective belief in their common descent because of similarities of external habitus or of customs or both, or because of memories of colonization and migration; this belief must be important for the propagation of group formation; conversely, it does not matter whether or not an objective blood relationship exists. Ethnic membership (*Gemeinsamkeit*) differs from the kinship group precisely by being a (believed-in) membership, not a group defined by actual social action, like the latter. In our sense, ethnic membership does not constitute a group; it only facilitates group formation of any kind, particularly in the political sphere. On the other hand, it is primarily the political community, no matter how artificially organized, that inspires the belief in common ethnicity. This belief tends to persist even after the disintegration of the political community, unless drastic differences in the custom, physical type, or, above all, language exist among its members . . .

The belief in common "ethnicity" often delimits "group-based social intercourse," which in turn is not always identical with endogamous connubial groups, for greatly varying numbers of persons may be encompassed by both. Their similarity rests on the belief in a specific "honor" of their members, not shared by the outsiders, that is, the sense of "ethnic honor" (a phenomenon closely related to status honor . . . ). These few remarks must suffice at this point. A specialized sociological study of ethnicity would have to make a finer distinction between these concepts than we have done for our limited purposes.

Groups, in turn, can engender sentiments of likeness which will persist even after their demise and will have an "ethnic" connotation. The political community in particular can produce such an effect. But most directly, such an effect is created by the *language group*, which is the bearer of a specific "cultural possession *of the masses*" (*Massenkulturgut*) and makes mutual understanding (*Verstehen*) possible or easier.

Wherever the memory of the origin of a community by peaceful secession or emigration ("colony," *ver sacrum*, and the like) from a mother community remains for some reason alive, there undoubtedly exists a very specific and often extremely powerful sense of "ethnic" group feeling, which is determined by several factors: shared political memories or, even more importantly in early times, persistent ties with the old cult, or the strengthening of kinship and other groups, both in the old and the new community, or other persistent relationships. Where these ties are lacking, or once they cease to exist, the sense of ethnic group feeling is absent, regardless of how close the kinship may be.

Apart from the community of language, which may or may not coincide with objective, or subjectively believed, consanguinity, and apart from common religious belief, which is also independent of consanguinity, the "ethnic" differences that remain are, on the one hand, esthetically conspicuous differences of the externally-oriented habitus (as mentioned before) and, on the other hand and of equal weight, the perceptible differences in the *conduct of everyday life*. Of special importance are precisely those items which may otherwise seem to be of small social relevance, since when "ethnic" differentiation is concerned it is always the conspicuous differences that come into play.

Common language and the ritual regulation of life, as determined by shared religious beliefs, everywhere are conducive to feelings of ethnic affinity, especially since the meaningful "understandability" of the activity of others is the most fundamental presupposition of group formation. But since we shall not consider these two elements in the present context, we ask: what is it that remains? It must be admitted that palpable differences in dialect and differences of religion in themselves do not exclude feelings of common ethnicity. Next to pronounced differences in the economic way of life, the belief in ethnic affinity has at all times been affected by outward differences in clothes, in the style of housing, food and eating habits, the division of labor between the sexes and between the free and the unfree. That is to say, these things concern one's conception of what is "correct and proper" and, above all, of what affects the individual's feeling of honor and dignity. All those things are ... objects of specific differences between "status" groups. The conviction of the excellence of one's own customs and the inferiority of alien ones, a conviction which sustains the sense of "ethnic" honor, is actually quite analogous to the sense of honor of distinctive "status" groups.

The sense of "ethnic" honor is a specific honor of the masses (*Massenehre*), for it is accessible to anybody who belongs to the subjectively believed community of descent. The "poor white trash," i.e., the propertyless and, in the absence of job opportunities, very often destitute white inhabitants of the southern states of the United States of America in the period of slavery, were the actual bearers of racial antipathy, which was quite foreign to the planters. This was so because the social "honor" of the "poor whites" was dependent upon the social *déclassement* of the Negroes.

And behind all "ethnic" diversities there is somehow naturally the notion of the "chosen people," which is merely a counterpart of "status" differentiation translated into the plane of horizontal co-existence. The idea of a chosen people derives its popularity from the fact that it can be claimed to an equal degree by any and every member of the mutually despising groups, in contrast to status differentiation which always rests on subordination. Consequently, ethnic repulsion may take hold of all conceivable differences among the notions of "propriety" and transform them into "ethnic conventions."

Besides the previously mentioned elements, which were still more or less closely related to the economic order, conventionalization . . . may take hold of such things as a hairdo or style of beard and the like. The differences thereof have an "ethnically" repulsive effect, because they are thought of as symbols of ethnic membership. Of course, the repulsion is not always based merely on the "symbolic" character of the distinguishing traits. The fact that the Scythian women oiled their hair with butter, which then gave off a rancid odor, while Greek women used perfumed oil to achieve the same purpose, thwarted – according to an ancient report – all attempts at social intercourse between the aristocratic ladies of these two groups. The smell of butter certainly had a more compelling effect than even the most prominent racial differences, or – as far as I could see – the "Negro odor," of which so many fables are told. In general, "racial qualities" are effective only as limiting factors with regard to the belief in common ethnicity, such as in the case of an excessively heterogeneous and esthetically unaccepted physical type; they are not positively group-forming.

Pronounced differences of custom, which play a role equal to that of inherited physical type in the creation of feelings of common ethnicity and notions of kinship, are usually caused, in addition to linguistic and religious differences, by the diverse economic and political conditions of various social groups. If we ignore cases of clear-cut linguistic boundaries and sharply demarcated political or religious communities as a basis of differences of "custom" – and these in fact are lacking in wide areas of the African and South American continents – then there are only gradual transitions of "custom" and no immutable "ethnic borders," except those due to gross geographical differences. The sharp demarcations of areas wherein "ethnically" relevant customs predominate, which were not conditioned either by political or economic or religious factors, usually came into existence by way of migration or expansion, when groups of people that had previously lived in complete or partial isolation from each other and became accommodated to heterogeneous conditions of existence came to live side by side. The obvious contrast of ways of life that arose in this manner usually evokes, on both sides, the idea of blood incompatibility (*Blutsfremdheit*), regardless of the objective state of affairs.

It is understandably difficult to determine in general – and even in a concrete individual case – what influence specific "ethnic" factors (i.e., the belief in a blood relationship, or its opposite, which rests on similarities, or differences, of a person's physical appearance and style of life) have on the formation of a group.

There is no difference between the "ethnically" relevant "customs" and customs in general, as far as their effect is concerned. The belief in common descent, in combination with a similarity of customs, is likely to promote the spread of that part of the social action (within the larger constellation) perceived as "ethnically"-bound because the awareness of ethnic commonality furthers imitation. This is especially true of the propaganda of religious groups.

However, one cannot go beyond these vague generalizations. The content of social action that is possible on an "ethnic" basis remains indefinite. There is a corresponding ambiguity of concepts denoting "ethnically" determined action, that means, determined by the belief in blood relationship. Such concepts are *Völkerschaft, Stamm* (tribe), *Volk* (people), each of which is ordinarily used in the sense of an ethnic subdivision of the following one (although the first two may be used in reversed order). Using such terms, one usually implies either the existence of a contemporary political community, no matter how loosely organized, or memories of an extinct political community, such as they are preserved in epic tales and legends; or the existence of a linguistic or dialect group; or, finally, of a religious group. In the past, cults in particular were the typical concomitant of a "tribal" or "*Volk*" consciousness. But in the absence of the political community, contemporary or past, the external delimitation of the group was usually indistinct. The cult communities of Germanic tribes, as late as the Burgundian period [6th century AD], were probably rudiments of political communities and therefore pretty well defined. By contrast, the Delphian oracle, the undoubted cultic symbol of Hellenism as a "*Volk*," also revealed information to the barbarians and accepted their veneration, and it was an organized cult only among some Greek segments, excluding the most powerful cities.

The cult as an exponent of a "tribal feeling" is thus generally either a remnant of a largely political community which once existed but was destroyed by disunion and colonization, or it is – as in the case of the Delphian Apollo – a product of a *Kulturgemeinschaft* brought about by other than purely "ethnic" conditions, but which in turn gives rise to the belief in blood relationship. All history shows how easily social action oriented to the political arena can give rise to the belief in a blood relationship, unless gross differences of anthropological type impede it.

# "Tribe" and "People": The Relationship to the Political Community

From *Economy and Society: An Outline of Interpretive Sociology*, eds and trans. Guenther Roth and Claus Wittich, revised by Stephen Kalberg (Berkeley, CA: University of California Press, 1978), pp. 393–5.

The tribe is clearly delimited when it is a subdivision of a polity, which, in fact, often establishes it. In this case, the artificial origin is revealed by the round numbers in which tribes usually appear, for example, the previously mentioned division of the people of Israel into twelve tribes, the three Doric *phylai* and the various *phylai* of the other Hellenes. When a political community was newly established or reorganized, the population was artificially newly divided. Hence the tribe is here a political artifact, even though it soon adopts the whole symbolism of blood-relationship and particularly a tribal cult. Even today it is not rare that political artifacts develop a sense of affinity akin to that of blood relationship. Very schematic political constructs, such as those states of the United States that were made into squares according to their latitude, have a very developed special consciousness; it is also not rare that families travel from New York to Richmond to make an expected child a "Virginian."

Such artificiality does not preclude the possibility that the Hellenic *phylai*, for example, were at one time independent and that the polis used them schematically when they were merged into a political organization. However, tribes that existed before the *polis* were either identical with the corresponding political groups which were subsequently associated into a *polis*, and in this case they were called *ethnos*, not *phyle*; or, as it probably happened many times, the politically unorganized tribe, as a presumed "blood community," lived from the memory that it once engaged in joint political action, typically a single conquest or defense, and then such political memories became central in constituting the tribe. Thus, the fact that "tribal consciousness" was primarily formed by common political experiences, and not by common "descent," appears to have been a frequent source of the belief in common ethnicity.

Of course, this was not the only source: Common "customs" may have diverse origins. Ultimately, they derive largely from adaptation to natural conditions and the imitation of the circle of neighbors. In practice, however, "tribal consciousness" again signifies something specifically political: in case of military danger or opportunity, it easily provides the basis for joint political action on the part of "tribal members" (or "*Volksgenossen*") who consider one another as blood relatives. The eruption of a drive to political action is thus one of the major potentialities inherent in the rather ambiguous notions of "tribe" and "people." Such intermittent political action may easily develop into the moral duty of all members of tribe or people (*Volk*) to support one another in case of a military attack, even if there is no corresponding political association; violators of this solidarity may suffer the fate of the [Germanic, pro-Roman] sibs of Segestes and Inguiomer – expulsion from the tribal territory – even if the tribe has no common administrative mechanisms. If, however, the tribe has reached this stage, it has indeed become an enduring political community, no matter how inactive in peacetime, and hence unstable, it may be. However, even under favorable conditions the transition from the "habitual" to the customary and therefore "obligatory" is very fluid.

All in all, the notion of "ethnically" determined social action subsumes phenomena that a rigorous sociological analysis – as we do not attempt it here – would have to distinguish carefully: the actual subjective effect of those "customs" conditioned by heredity and those determined by tradition; the differential impact of the varying content of "custom"; the influence of common language, religion and political action, past and present, upon the formation of customs; the extent to which such factors create attraction and repulsion, and especially the belief in affinity or disaffinity of blood; the consequences of this belief for social action in general, and specifically for action on the basis of shared custom or blood relationship, for diverse sexual relations, etc. – all of this would have to be studied separately and in detail. It is certain that in this process the global term "ethnic" would be abandoned, for it is unsuitable for a really rigorous analysis. However, we do not pursue sociology for its own sake and therefore limit ourselves to showing briefly the diverse factors that are hidden behind this seemingly uniform phenomenon.

The concept of "ethnic" group dissolves if we define our terms exactly
. . .

# Comment on the Lecture by Alfred Ploetz on "The Concepts Race and Society"

From "Business Report and Discussion Contributions," German Sociological Association Convention (1910) in *Gesammelte Aufsätze zur Soziologie und Sozialpolitik* [*Collected Essays on Sociology and Social Policy*], ed. Marianne Weber, trans. Stephen Kalberg (Tübingen: Mohr Verlag, 1924), pp. 456–62.

*Professor Max Weber*: Dr. Ploetz began his lecture by noting that the principle of brotherly love has dominated our ethics for millennia. I would ask: When? With what consequences? And is its domination today strengthened over the view of race of the past, which was "more favorable" to a racial hygiene position?[1] Of course, the ethic of brotherly love exists in the official catechism just as in the Middle Ages. But the real problem concerns how the praxis of life related in the past and relates today to this official postulate and influences selection; that is, whether the routine of life does so in such a way that the racial hygiene position is less tenable today than earlier.

Certainly the population of the Middle Ages was subject to a sharp selection process in respect to reproduction chances. From the point of view of racial hygiene, two points surely should not be dismissed. First, childhood mortality had a particularly strong effect on the lower strata of society, as did the increasing factual – and even legal – restrictions regarding marriage for all people without their own livelihood. On the other hand, in the Middle Ages the principle of brotherly love drove many into cloisters, knight orders, and the celibacy of the priesthood. All these people were then weeded out of the population propagating the species – and none were inferior in terms of physical capacities or intelligence. The same principle of brotherly love is also manifest in the systematic support for mendicancy.

If we look at the path of development from the Middle Ages to the modern period, it appears to me that a *reversal* of this principle has made headway even on Christianity's own ground, which one never would have presumed possible in the case of a religion that once possessed certain Biblical foundations. I am reminded that Calvinism viewed poverty and unemployment as a misfortune caused by one's own failings, or as a consequence of God's unknowable decree – and it then acted accordingly; that is, to a great degree excluding the "weak" from reproduction. Hence, in the case of this religion a place for brotherly love cannot be found . . . , and I further doubt whether the modern development by and large has taken a pathway that has allowed precisely an excess spread of brotherly love in our society to become an urgent danger.

Moreover, that which one commonly calls social policy [as advocated by Dr. Ploetz] can have a very varying and a very desired significance, also in terms of racial hygiene, in keeping with the spirit of Dr. Ploetz. That is, social policy can give to the physically and intellectually stronger (although weaker in regard to *the pocket book*) – namely, stronger when viewed from the standpoint of racial hygiene – the possibility, hand in hand with the possibility of upward mobility, of a healthy propagation of the species. Yet even such a development is in no way necessarily a consequence of an indiscriminating brotherly love [as the argument of Dr. Ploetz would imply].

Dr. Ploetz also noted that . . . societal circumstances, rooted in blood, are perpetually dependent upon the blood of the race. This or something similar! Gentlemen! This is, regardless of which concept of "society" and "race" one applies, a completely unproven assertion – which I believe cannot in the least be demonstrated in light of the present state of our science and research methods. I'm quite aware of present theories that, by reference to the development of Antiquity, contend support can be found for this frequently argued theory. Excellent historians occasionally assert that the fall of ancient civilization was caused by the weeding out from the general population, as a consequence of the wars and conscription by the military, of the strongest and most capable – who then ruled the globe. In fact, it is now demonstrable that the development proceeded in exactly the opposite direction: the Roman army became increasingly composed of foreigners, and entirely so in the end. The longer this development proceeded, furthermore, ever less were demands placed upon the population of the Roman Empire for the purposes of conscription and the more defense was put in the hands of barbarians.[2] There can be no question that not the slightest bit of this theory remains valid.

In addition, we know enough today of the reasons for the great transformation of ancient civilization in order to be able to say that, in so far as issues related to ethnicity played a role here at all, not the selective *weeding* out of the Roman clans from the officer corps and administration was relevant but their conscious *exclusion* – and this development did not have any "racial" or "biological" significance recognizable to us. On the contrary, in so far as it was relevant for the destiny of the Roman Empire, the exclusion of the Roman clans involved much more an attempt to banish groups rooted in *traditional values* and to favor peoples without traditions and culture, who could then be appointed officers and administrative functionaries. Moreover, the disappearance of the ancient tastes, the old educated stratum, the Roman army's old traditions, and consequently the disappearance of the ancient administrative procedures – all these changes are so convincingly explained by changes in the administration rooted in economic forces that reference, as a complementary cause, to even a trace of this or that racial theory proves unnecessary. This having been said, perhaps racial considerations nonetheless did play a role, I freely admit, in a manner no longer knowable to us today. Yet we do not know this and never will know it. And any pushing aside of known and accessible causes in favor of hypotheses that are speculative today and will remain so in the future opposes scientific methododology.

Now, however, in general: "The blood of societal circumstances is dependent upon the blood of the race." If one understands here "race," gentlemen, in the manner commonly understood by the lay person – inheritable traits bred through reproductive communities – then I would be put in a personally embarrassing situation; namely, I feel I am a cross-section of many races, or at least of several particular ethnic heritages. Many in this circle would be in similar circumstances, I believe. I am part French, part German, and certainly on the French side somewhat infused with Celtic blood. Which of these races – for the Celts have been here referred to as a "race" – blooms then in me, or must bloom whenever the societal circumstances bloom in Germany, or ought to bloom?

*Dr. Ploetz* (interrupting): You are here referring to a race system (*Systemrasse*). That involves the variety within races! I have discussed races as large populations as "vital races" (*Vitalrasse*), which has nothing to do with this variety. All of these variations at least belong to a vital race.

*Professor Max Weber* (proceeding ahead): I must go through the different possibilities implied by the concept of race. In other words, I am now placing myself on your ground and establishing that even from this perspective a number of your statements have a completely mystical character. What does it actually mean to say: "the race blooms?" Or: "The race reacts in a specific way?" What does it mean to say that a race "is a unity," if not a unity rooted in blood? Should not, in respect to the existence of this "unity," the simple fact of a physically normal reproductive capacity (which is then, of course, viewed in the case of illegitimacy as diminished) be decisive? And does the capacity to develop certain elements of culture belong to the race's "capacity to preserve itself" – or to what else? The concept "vital race" takes us ultimately into the unbounded realm of subjective evaluations. And this realm is everywhere entered into by Dr. Ploetz whenever he decrees that connections exist between race and society.

If, of course, one assumes that certain races, identifiable in some purely empirical manner through characteristic *traits*, exist in proximity, and if one substitutes societal relationships and societal institutions for the purely conventional concept "society," then one can say that the unique features of institutions are in a certain way the rules of the game. With reference to the factual validity of these rules, specific human inheritable qualities acquire a likelihood of "winning" in the selection process – that is, of increasing their chances of survival *or* (and this is naturally not the same), on the other hand, of reproducing themselves (which in part proceeds according to entirely different laws).

That differences exist in respect to survival chances is not only the case today; it would not be otherwise in an eventual, however constituted, future socialist state. Of course, different inherited qualities would attain power, fortune, and reproductive capacities in this future state. Nonetheless, some qualities would exist more than others even in this socialist state and, regardless of how one constitutes a society, selection processes do not lie dormant. Rather, the question can be asked only of *which* inherited qualities are offered a chance in an ordering X of society as opposed to an ordering Y of society. This appears to me a purely empirical question acceptable to us [as social scientists]. And it is not otherwise if this question is reversed: which inherited qualities are the *precondition* for the possibility now or in the future for an ordering of society in a certain way? This is also a meaningful question and one that can be used to study presently existing races.

However, if one takes these ways of formulating the issues, then it becomes immediately evident that nothing can come of the concept of race as articulated by Dr. Ploetz (at least this is my belief for now; I am willing to be persuaded otherwise). His concept of race seems to me not at all to be differentiated to the necessary extent. This will be confirmed if we ask ourselves what has crystallized until now as empirical sociological research from the application of this particular concept of race. Gentlemen, extremely stimulating and interesting theories have come out of it. The journal edited by Dr. Ploetz is clearly an arsenal of boundless hypotheses, some of which have been formulated with an enviable abundance of intelligence in respect to the socializing effect of all possible institutions and processes. No one can be more thankful than I for this intellectual stimulation. However, I oppose with all forcefulness the notion that today there exists even one single fact relevant for Sociology – indeed, even one exact concrete fact related to a specific category of sociological processes – that actually, clearly and definitively, precisely and incontestably, leads back to innate and inherited qualities that one race possesses and another definitely – note well: definitely! – does not possess. And I will continue to oppose this position categorically until this fact is precisely identified to me.

For example, and although it is today often believed, it is not correct to say that the respective social situations of Whites and Negroes in North America can be traced back incontestably to racial qualities. It is possible, and to me to a high degree likely, that such inherited qualities are here present, and perhaps even considerably so. To what extent and, above all, in what way, however, is not firmly clarified. Gentlemen, it has been asserted, for example, and it is still being asserted, also in Dr. Ploetz's journal and by very prominent men, that "race instincts" are at the basis of the opposition between Whites and Negroes in the United States. Please prove to me the existence of these instincts and their content. They apparently are, among other ways, revealed in the way Negroes smell. My own nose can here be called upon; I perceived, in closest contact, nothing of the sort. It is my impression that the Negro, when unwashed, smells exactly as does the White person – and the reverse. I further note that a scene can be daily observed in the southern states in which a lady – sitting in a horse-drawn coach and holding the reins in her hands – is nestled closely shoulder to shoulder with a Negro. And apparently her nose is not suffering from this proximity. As far as I can ascertain now, the smell of the Negro is an invention of the northern states to clarify their recent [1910] turning away from the Negro cause.[3] If we today, gentlemen, had the possibility to inject black skin into babies at birth, then even these people would be continuously in a rather precarious and peculiar situation in White society. However, any proof that the specific type of racial relationships in America is rooted in innate and inherited *instincts* has not yet been reliably demonstrated, even though I will always admit that the evidence might perhaps exist someday.

Before moving in this direction, it must be noted how striking it is that these "instincts" function in an entirely different manner in respect to different races. Yet this occurs for reasons that have absolutely nothing to do with the requirements for the preservation of the race. The reason for the highly divergent evaluation by Whites in America of Negroes and Indians is repeatedly articulated by Whites thus: "They didn't submit to slavery." However, to the extent that their specific qualities played a part, the Indians were not slaves *because* they were not able (while the Negroes were) to *endure* the degree of work demanded by plantation capitalism – and it is uncertain whether this was *purely* on account of inherited qualities or also as a consequence of their traditions. Yet this circumstance clearly did not form, either consciously or unconsciously, the basis for a specific and varying "instinct" among Whites that causes a different reaction to Blacks and Indians. On the contrary, it was more so the case that the old feudal scorn for work [among upper-class Southerners] – that is, a social factor – here played a role. This being said, I will grant immediately to Dr. Ploetz . . .

*Dr. Ploetz* (interrupting): Not in the northern states. The scorn for work did not there play this role.

*Professor Max Weber* (continuing): First, that is for the present no longer entirely correct. And the scorn for the Negro appears in the northern states only in the present. Second, if you investigate the position of Negroes in unions, then you will note that they, as workers who – as a consequence of traditions – lived simply and did not expect high wages, were increasingly despised and feared. Finally, one can easily convince oneself that the middle-class American today, as everyone else, has read his Darwin, his Nietzsche and, under certain circumstances, his Dr. Ploetz, and comes, on this basis, to a certain conclusion: a man – and I'm speaking here without any hint of a mocking tone – who wishes to be an aristocrat in the modern sense of the word must possess something that he can despise, and we Americans wish to be aristocrats in the European sense. At issue here is simply a Europeanization process, one that by chance in America carries with it this residual effect.

Now, honored gentlemen, I must come to a very few concluding remarks. Dr. Ploetz has characterized "society" as an organism. He has done so by reference to the well-known argument, which he has also presented here in a compelling lecture, regarding the relationship of society to cellular organizations in particular. It may be the case that, in terms of Dr. Ploetz's aims, something fruitful has crystallized (which he himself naturally knows best); however, for the sociological approach the unification of many precise concepts into an imprecise concept never yields anything useful. And that is the case here.

We have the possibility to understand the rational action of the single human individual by intellectually re-living it. If we wish to comprehend a human association (regardless of the type) only according to the manner in which one investigates an animal society, then we would have to abandon those modes of knowing found among human beings and not found among animals. This – and no other – is the reason why, for our aims, no utility in general can be discovered from placing as the foundation of any investigation the entirely unquestionable analogy between a beehive and any human, state-oriented society.

Finally, gentlemen, Dr. Ploetz has said that the study of society is a branch in the field that studies the biological influence upon races (*Rassenbiologie*).

*Dr. Ploetz*: The biology of society (*Gesellschaftsbiologie*), not the study of society in general!

*Professor Max Weber*: Yes, then I admit that perhaps I have misunderstood. However, it is not entirely clear to me how and where societal biology distinguishes itself from race biology, unless precisely the relationships between societal institutions and the selection of specific human qualities, as I earlier discussed them, ought to be the subject matter of societal-biological research. I would like to add, on this topic, only a general comment.

It does not appear to me useful to exclude arenas and domains of knowledge *a priori* – that is, before this knowledge has congealed – and to say: this belongs to our science and this other does not. Only the most unproductive conflicts will be multiplied by doing so. Of course, we can say that all societal processes ultimately play out on Earth and that the planet Earth belongs to the solar system – and then come to the conclusion that everything occurring on Earth must actually be an object of study for astronomy. We can further conclude that it is only an accident – namely, it makes no sense to observe events on Earth with a telescope – that heuristic tools other than the telescope are used. However, would anything come out of this?

It is undoubtedly the case that the processes with which Biology is concerned – the processes of selection – are influenced by societal institutions; in turn, it is also not to be doubted that inherited racial qualities in a great many cases influence the imprint of societal institutions. However, on the basis of these observations, I would ask whether it makes sense to appropriate any object or problem and to make it a component of a science which will be created *ad hoc* just to study these influences. We expect from the race biologists exact proof that completely definable inheritable qualities are of decisive importance for practical, single occurrences of societal life. On the basis of the impression I have acquired from the reseach of Dr. Ploetz and his friends, I do not doubt that we can expect this achievement at some point from them. However, gentlemen, up until now this proof has been lacking.

This is not a reproach against a science still so young. Nonetheless, it must be stated as a fact. And doing so will perhaps serve to prevent the utopian enthusiasm which characterizes the embarkation upon such a new field from degenerating into a situation in which the practitioners of this new endeavor fail to recognize the objective limits of its own way of framing questions. We experience just this today in all fields. Some believed, as we have seen, that the entire world, including, for example, art and all that otherwise exists, could be explained by reference alone to economic forces. We have observed how modern geographers address all cultural phenomena "from the point of view of geography" – even though they fail to demonstrate that which we would like to know from them, namely, which specific and practical components of cultural production are conditioned, in the specific case, by climatic or similar purely geographical forces. Rather, they include something like the following in their "geographical" presentations: "the Russian church is intolerant." We then ask, to what extent does this conclusion belong within the realm of geography? The answer: "Russia is a region with a clear location, the Russian church expands across a defined location, and hence it constitutes an object of study in Geography."

Wherever each separate science fails to achieve that which it alone can and should achieve, it misses, I believe, its goal. I would like to express the hope that adherents of the study of societal events from the point of view of Biology will not wish to follow this route.

NOTES

1. The "racial hygiene" position advocated a complete separation, on behalf of a maintenance of purity, of the races. Weber is noting that this view stands in opposition to the ethos of universal brotherly love [sk].
2. See Weber, "The Social Causes of the Decay of Ancient Civilization," pp. 254–74 in *Max Weber*, ed. by J.E.T. Eldridge (London: Thomas Nelson and Sons, 1971) [sk].
3. Weber is referring to the rise of Jim Crow laws in the post-Reconstruction era [sk].

From "Prefatory Remarks" to Collected Essays on the Sociology of Religion, in *The Protestant Ethic and the Spirit of Capitalism*, 3rd edn, trans. Stephen Kalberg (Los Angeles: Roxbury Publishing, 2002), pp. 163–4.

. . . [T]he *anthropological* side of the problem should also be considered. If we again and again discover in the West, and *only* in the West, specific *types* of rationalizations (and also in arenas of life [such as religion, the economy, and law] that seemingly developed independently from one another), then naturally a certain assumption appears plausible: heredity is playing a decisive role. The author confesses that he is inclined, personally and subjectively, to estimate highly the importance of biological heredity. However, despite the significant achievements of anthropological research at this time, I do not see any manner of exactly comprehending, or even hinting at in terms of probabilities, the share of heredity – namely, according to its extent and, above all, type and points of impact – in the development investigated *here*.

As one of its major tasks, sociological and historical research will have to reveal as many as possible of those influences and causal chains that are satisfactorily explainable as reactions to the effect of [biological] fate on the one hand and that of social milieu on the other. Only then, and only when, in addition, the comparative study of racial neurology and psychology moves beyond its rudimentary beginnings of today [1920] (which are promising in many ways, if one examines the discrete studies), can one *perhaps* hope for satisfactory results even for the problem studied here. Yet any development in this direction appears to me for the time being not to exist and any referral to "heredity" would be, it seems to me, tantamount to both a premature abandonment of the extent of knowledge perhaps possible *today* and a displacement of the problem onto (at this time still) unknown factors.

# part 10

# The Meaning, Value, and Value-Freedom of Science

## "SCIENCE AS A VOCATION" AND OTHER WRITINGS

### Introduction

In 1917, students in a progressive student group at the University of Munich (The Bavarian Union of Free Students) invited Weber to give two lectures in their series "Intellectual Work as a Vocation." He chose to speak on "Science as a Vocation" (November 7, 1917) and "Politics as a Vocation" (January 28, 1919).[1] Published in 1919, both essays became standard readings in social science curricula throughout the world by the 1950s. The major selections in this chapter are taken from "Science as a Vocation."[2]

Approximately 80–100 students, many of whom had recently returned from the front lines of World War I, heard Weber's lecture. With defeat, the German nation, and particularly the younger generation, was searching for guidance in respect to both the future course of the nation and personal choices. Although political and military figures had been discredited, the traditionally high status of professors in German society had remained largely untouched. Students looked to them, and especially to Max Weber, for leadership.

He completely disappoints his audience in this regard. Rather than placing the social sciences high on a pedestal and charting out a lofty capacity to provide values and even a new world view, to shape a new and more just society, and to offer answers to students in the midst of major personal crises, Weber demarcates the limited tasks and modest usefulness of the social sciences. His aim is apparent in doing so; he wishes to carve out and defend an open space for individual autonomy where it would be uninfluenced by a caste of scientists pronouncing "expert opinion." He seeks, in other words, to foster individualism and a sense of personal responsibility. The essay also defines two key concepts in Weber's writings ("disenchantment" and "value-freedom") and expresses his skepticism in regard to "progress." Finally, it opposes the "meaning-lessness" of death – and hence life – in the modern epoch to their meaningfulness in past societies. People stood within an "organically prescribed cycle of natural life" in the past.

What is the nature of social science as actually practiced? Weber contends that an advanced stage has been reached in which research assumes a very specialized character. Its fate is apparent: cumulative advances ensure that conclusions will quickly become outdated. This being the case, Weber asks whether the conduct of science has any *meaning* beyond the realm of technical problems and to anyone other than its practitioners. This question becomes all the more urgent owing to his rejection, on the one hand, of the view that the history of scientific development can be understood as "progress" in a general sense, and, on the other, that the advance of science itself endows scientific activity with meaning. Why, then, "does one engage in doing something that in reality never comes, and never can come, to an end?" (p. 321).

Satisfactory answers to these questions appear less likely when one acknowledges the core "intellectualist rationalization" of science over thousands of years as following a process of "disenchantment" – an ever more wide-ranging understanding of the world's occurrences and events by reference to empirical observation, mechanical principles, and physical laws rather than to the magical and supernatural powers of spirits, demons, and gods. Today we – or engineers – can explain how the subway operates by performing calculations and acquiring technical knowledge; reference to "mysterious incalculable forces" is not required. Yet we should not conclude, Weber insists, that "we, today . . . have a greater knowledge of the conditions of life under which we exist" (p. 322). Disenchantment rather denotes a principled transformation, with important implications, in our mode of knowing. This conclusion brings Weber into a direct confrontation with "Tolstoi's question."

The "infinite progress" of knowledge – its accumulation – in the sciences implies to Tolstoi that death has no meaning. In epochs perpetually enriched by new ideas and knowledge, every individual life dies before the peak of progress has been reached. Indeed, immersed within a "march of progress," each person "catches only the most minute part of what the life of the intellect brings forth ever anew." The progressiveness itself of civilization, Tolstoi insisted, "gives death the imprint of meaninglessness." And "because death is meaningless, civilized life as such is meaningless" (p. 323).

Because it has called forth a modern era of meaninglessness, science today would seem to possess little value "within the total life of humanity." Must science, then, be condemned as a meaningless endeavor? This question poses another: should the younger generation follow scientific careers, even if some among them indeed experience a *calling* for science and others understand its pursuit as possessing viable practical and technical purposes?

Weber's sweeping argument then turns to historical examples. He situates justifications for the pursuit of scientific research within social and political contexts in Antiquity, the Italian Renaissance, and the Early Modern period. In each case he poses a particular question: what was the *meaning* of engagement in scientific activity? In each era Weber discovers that practical or technical considerations failed to encompass its full meaning; nor could it be said that the scientific endeavor comprised only an individual calling.

Science in Antiquity is given meaning in Plato's famous cave analogy because, in looking for truth, *concepts* are discovered: the good and the beautiful. Both enable not only comprehension of the true essence of the good and the beautiful, but also unveil appropriate and correct action. Once defined clearly, this action could be taught. In light of the politicized nature of Hellenic life, this right action invariably told people how to behave correctly as citizens. Hence, the scientific endeavor, located by the Greeks within a larger social and political context, became legitimate and meaningful. During the Renaissance, on the other hand, Leonardo understood science, and particularly the elevation of the rational experiment to the center of research, as "the path to *true* art [and] true *nature*." Moreover, in possession of rigorous methods, art acquired the prestige of science and the artist the social status of the physician. Finally, Early Modern scientists understood the exact measurements provided by science as offering a means of demonstrating the orderly character of the natural universe – and hence the existence of an intelligent being behind its creation. Here a larger meaning also legitimated scientific activity: it led the way to God, belief, and devoutness.

The modern age, however, stands under sets of cultural and economic presuppositions quite unlike those dominant in past epochs, Weber emphasizes. The historical configurations that earlier endowed science with meaning no longer hold. Tolstoi's conclusion – science is meaningless because it offers no answer to the question, "what shall we do and how shall we live?" – still stands.

Whether the research results of science are "worth being known" cannot be proven scientifically, Weber contends. Physicists, chemists, and astronomers cannot demonstrate that knowledge of "the ultimate laws of cosmic events" is worthwhile. And whether the world they investigate it-self possesses any meaning cannot be proven scientifically. The same conclusions must be drawn even when queries are formulated regarding the ultimate meaning of modern medicine, aesthetics, jurisprudence, and the historical and cultural sciences. Are the cultural phenomena the latter study themselves worthwhile? Is their investigation worth the effort weighed against other endeavors? Answers to these questions go beyond the capabilities of modern science, despite the unprecedented rigor of its methods.

What, in the end, is the usefulness of science today? What are its actual limits? These questions, as well as Weber's famous imperative of "value-freedom," are addressed in the next set of readings (Chapter 23).

He emphatically insists that the social sciences must be clearly and strictly separated from politics. Professors in university classrooms, in front of captive audiences, must not offer to students value-judgments, personal views, and political opinions. "So long as [they wish] to remain teacher[s] and not to become demagogue[s]" (p. 333), they must refrain from discussing the conclusions of their research as "truth." Owing to their high prestige, doing so presents a great danger: an excessive influence upon students might occur and hence a constriction of their individual autonomy. The university lecture must not be a political speech where words "become weapons" against political opponents.[3] In turn, students should not expect guidance from their professors on personal and political issues, for their science, unlike politics, excludes the activity – the clash of values – on the basis of which leaders arise.

The domain of science must be restricted in yet another fashion. Although constituting a modern "world view," the social sciences must not be perceived as empowered to prescribe ethical values, as did religious world views. They are simply incapable of doing so, according to Weber.[4] Furthermore, they *should* not do so, for an intrusion of conclusions from science into the realm of individual autonomy would thereby occur. Wherever understood as offering "objectively valid" results and wherever a caste of experts is viewed, in the name of a social science, as legitimately erecting norms for conduct, science is endowed with the capacity to elevate decision-making out of that domain where it rightfully belongs – the individual's conscience, values, and "demons." Science cannot – and *must* not – inform us how we *should* live (see 1949a, p. 54). Notions of ethical responsibility, honor, dignity, and devotion to a cause can be developed, Weber argues, only when people become aware of their own values – and this takes place alone when individuals are confronted repeatedly with the necessity of making decisions *for themselves*.

Hence, excluding in principle political views, personal opinions, and ethical prescription, the legitimate domain of social science is restricted, Weber contends. What, then, again, constitutes its purpose in the modern epoch? And is the pursuit of science a meaningful endeavor despite these restrictions? Its tasks must remain limited to "calculating external objects as well as man's activities, . . . methods of thinking, [and] the tools and the training for thought." It also seeks clarity in respect, on the one hand, to the unintended consequences of action in reference to particular ideals, and, on the other, to the suitability of the means to reach a given end (including an ethical ideal) (see also 1949a, pp. 18–19). If the means are seen to be questionable, teachers must confront students with the necessity of making choices between ends and means. The limits of science are reached with these tasks and this confrontation, Weber contends.

However, the ability of science to offer clarity in respect to ends and means is not insignificant, he argues. It forces persons to become self-aware and responsible for their own conduct. To Weber, teachers who succeed in conveying to students the necessity for such an account "stand in the service of 'moral forces.'" They will do so more effectively if they refrain from imposing their own judgments and political views on their audiences, he is convinced. In a modern world that has lost its overarching religious world view, and where multiple "gods" – now impersonal and in the form of attractive cultures, desirable products, and fashionable trends – offer irreconcilable positions and perpetually compete against each other for the loyalties of individuals, people must be confronted with the necessity of making choices. Science can assist in doing just this. Nonetheless, Weber quickly adds that this capability cannot stand as proof that science itself constitutes "an objectively valuable 'vocation.'" This chapter's final selection summarizes succinctly and in similar terms, in a lecture given at an academic conference in 1909, the tasks and limits of an empirical social science.

In the selections collected in Chapter 24, here given the title "The Opposition of Salvation Religions to Science and Modern Culture," Weber contrasts the God-ordained world of *belief* to the world of empirical knowledge. He depicts each, in the first passages from "Science as a Vocation," as a "cosmos," or an internally consistent configuration of expansive meanings that offers a comprehensive view of the universe. These "images of the world" are seen as rooted in presuppositions that place them in a relationship of principled antagonism, tension, and "unavoidable disparity." The "intellectual sacrifice" that must be made by the faithful devout can never be rendered, in respect to his research, by the modern scientist, and the "empty abstractions" of the scientist remain irrelevant for one's salvation. Religion, even though it offers "an ultimate stand . . . by virtue of a direct grasp of the world's 'meaning'" (p. 340), is more and more pushed into the realm of the irrational to the extent that the "natural causality" of modern science and its "self-sufficient intellect" advances.

However, Weber's aim here involves more than a sharp demarcation of this contrast well known to us today. Rather, he wishes above all to comment upon the implications of this monumental metamorphosis for "how we live today." First and foremost, a cosmos underpinned by a solid foundation, albeit one resting upon the intellectual sacrifice, has been replaced by an image of the world ultimately unsure of itself: science, propounding "intellectual integrity," has nonetheless "seemed unable to answer with certainty the question of its own ultimate presuppositions" and worth. Moreover, grounded exclusively in reference to empirical observation and claiming cognitive knowledge as "the highest good," the "rational culture" of science stands completely "independent of all personal ethical qualities" (p. 341). Hence, this "aristocracy of intellect is . . . an unbrotherly aristocracy" and as a consequence forever burdened with guilt. Weber then returns to Tolstoi's conclusion: Meaninglessness burdens science when evaluated by reference to its own ultimate value – the possession of knowledge and the striving for self-perfection. How does the modern person know that the knowledge selected and acquired from the overwhelming repertoire available "has reached an end . . . meaningful to him precisely at the 'accidental' time of his death" (p. 342)?

The religious axiom that proclaims the divine meaning of life here stands as direct condemnation of the modern quest for self-perfection – as fragmentary and without value for that which matters: salvation. As the modern cosmos of science extends its reach, spheres of systematically organized cultural knowledge are increasingly created that "harness" individuals into them. In turn, ethical salvation religions reassert their image of the world, reacting with repulsion and an intensification of their focus upon their "other-worldly" core and doctrinal essence. Yet this response, Weber fears, will "in the end [succumb] to the world dominion of unbrotherliness," for victorious science will be unable to call forth and cultivate, as did the great salvation religions for two millennia, a set of ethical values.

## NOTES

1. See above, pp. 257–60, 265–71.
2. In total, the selections below comprise nearly three-quarters of the original essay (see 1946d). The omitted pages (all from the beginning) compare the American and German university systems, the career routes of American and German university instructors (1946d, pp. 129–34), the specialized character of scientific research (although see the selection above at pp. 139–41), and the necessity in science (as well as art) for a complete devotion "to the work at hand." In order to highlight the essay's three remaining major themes I have placed the selections in three separate chapters.
3. The immediate political context for Weber's strong support for an ethos of value-freedom for the social sciences is important and also evident: he vehemently opposed the views of many of his colleagues who understood their lecturing and research as appropriately in service to the fatherland and its glory.
4. Owing to the formation of research questions by reference to the researcher's particular interests (see above, pp. 12–14), the social sciences do not produce general truths.

# chapter 22

# The Meaning and Value of Science

## DISENCHANTMENT, "PROGRESS," AND CIVILIZED MAN'S MEANINGLESSNESS

From "Science as a Vocation," in *From Max Weber: Essays in Sociology*, eds and trans. Hans H. Gerth and C. Wright Mills, slightly revised by Stephen Kalberg (New York: Oxford University Press, 1946), pp. 138–45.

In science, each of us knows that what he has accomplished will be antiquated in ten, twenty, fifty years. That is the fate to which science is subjected; it is the very *meaning* of scientific work, to which it is devoted in a quite specific sense, as compared with other spheres of culture for which in general the same holds. Every scientific "fulfilment" raises new "questions"; it *asks* to be "surpassed" and outdated. Whoever wishes to serve science has to resign himself to this fact. Scientific works certainly can last as "gratifications" because of their artistic quality, or they may remain important as a means of training. Yet they will be surpassed scientifically – let that be repeated – for it is our common fate and, more, our common goal. We cannot work without hoping that others will advance further than we have. In principle, this progress goes on *ad infinitum*. And with this we come to inquire into the *meaning* of science. For, after all, it is not self-evident that something subordinate to such a law is sensible and meaningful in itself. Why does one engage in doing something that in reality never comes, and never can come, to an end?

One does it, first, for purely practical, in the broader sense of the word, for technical, purposes: in order to be able to orient our practical activities to the expectations that scientific experience places at our disposal. Good. Yet this has meaning only to practitioners. What is the attitude of the academic man towards his vocation – that is, if he is at all in quest of such a personal attitude? He maintains that he engages in "science for science's sake" and not merely because others, by exploiting science, bring about commercial or technical success and can better feed, dress, illuminate, and govern. But what does he who allows himself to be integrated into this specialized organization, running on *ad infinitum*, hope to accomplish that is significant in these productions that are always destined to be outdated? This question requires a few general considerations.

Scientific progress is a fraction, the most important fraction, of the process of intellectualization which we have been undergoing for thousands of years and which nowadays is usually judged in such an extremely negative way. Let us first clarify what this intellectualist rationalization, which occurs through science and through scientifically-oriented technology, means practically.

Does it mean that we, today, for instance, everyone sitting in this hall, have a greater knowledge of the conditions of life under which we exist than has an American Indian or a Hottentot? Hardly. Unless he is a physicist, one who rides on the streetcar has no idea how the car happened to get into motion. And he does not need to know. He is satisfied that he may "count" on the behavior of the streetcar, and he orients his conduct according to this expectation; but he knows nothing about what it takes to produce such a car so that it can move. The savage knows incomparably more about his tools. When we spend money today I bet that even if there are colleagues of political economy here in the hall, almost every one of them will hold a different answer in readiness to the question: How does it happen that one can buy something for money – sometimes more and sometimes less? The savage knows what he does in order to get his daily food and which institutions serve him in this pursuit. The increasing intellectualization and rationalization do *not*, therefore, indicate an increased and general knowledge of the conditions under which one lives.

It means something else, namely, the knowledge or belief that if one but *wished* one *could* learn it at any time. Hence, it means that principally there are no mysterious incalculable powers that come into play, but rather that one can, in principle, *master* all things by *calculation*. This means, however, that the world is disenchanted. One need no longer have recourse to magical means in order to master or implore the spirits, as did the savage, for whom such mysterious powers existed. Technical means and calculations perform the service. This above all is what intellectualization means.

Now, this process of disenchantment, which has continued to exist in Western culture for millennia, and, in general, this "progress," to which science belongs as a link and motive force, do they have any meanings that go beyond the purely practical and technical? You will find this question raised in the most principled form in the works of Leo Tolstoi [see "The Death of Ivan Ilich"]. He came to raise the question in a peculiar way. All his broodings increasingly revolved around the problem of whether or not death is a meaningful phenomenon. And his answer was: for civilized man death has no meaning. It has none because the individual life of civilized man, placed into an infinite "progress," according to its own imminent meaning should never come to an end; for there is always a further step ahead of one who stands in the march of progress. And no man who comes to die stands upon the peak which lies in infinity. Abraham, or some peasant of the past, died "old and satiated with life" because he stood in the organic cycle of life; because his life, in terms of its meaning and on the eve of his days, had given to him what life had to offer; because for him there remained no puzzles he might wish to solve; and therefore he could have had "enough" of life. Whereas civilized man, placed in the midst of the continuous enrichment of culture by ideas, knowledge, and problems, may become "tired of life" but not "satiated with life." He catches only the most minute part of what the life of the mind brings forth ever anew, and what he seizes is always something provisional and not definitive, and therefore death for him is a meaningless occurrence. And because death is meaningless, civilized life as such is meaningless; by its very "progressiveness" it gives death the imprint of meaninglessness. Throughout his late novels one meets with this thought as the keynote of the Tolstoyan art.

What stand should one take? Has "progress" as such a recognizable meaning that goes beyond the technical, so that to serve it is a meaningful vocation? The question must be raised. But this is no longer merely the question of man's calling *for* science, hence, the problem of what science as a vocation means to its devoted disciples. To raise this question is to ask for the vocation of science within the total life of humanity. What is the value of science?

Here the contrast between the past and the present is tremendous. You will recall the wonderful image at the beginning of the seventh book of Plato's *Republic*: those enchained cavemen whose faces are turned toward the stone wall before them. Behind them lies the source of the light which they cannot see. They are concerned only with the shadowy images that this light throws upon the wall, and they seek to fathom their interrelations. Finally one of them succeeds in shattering his fetters, turns around, and sees the sun. Blinded, he gropes about and stammers of what he saw. The others say he is raving. But gradually he learns to behold the light, and then his task is to descend to the cavemen and to lead them to the light. He is the philosopher; the sun, however, is the truth of science, which alone seizes not upon illusions and shadows but upon the true being.

Well, who today views science in such a manner? Today youth feels rather the reverse: the intellectual constructions of science constitute an unreal realm of artificial abstractions, which with their bony hands seek to grasp the blood-and-the-sap of true life without ever catching up with it. But here in life, in what for Plato was the play of shadows on the walls of the cave, genuine reality is pulsating; and the rest are derivatives of life, lifeless ghosts, and nothing else. How did this change come about?

Plato's passionate enthusiasm in *The Republic* must, in the last analysis, be explained by the fact that for the first time the *concept*, one of the great tools of all scientific knowledge, had been consciously discovered. Socrates had discovered it in its bearing. He was not the only man in the world to discover it. In India one finds the beginnings of a logic that is quite similar to that of Aristotle's. But nowhere else do we find this realization of the significance of the concept. In Greece, for the first time, appeared a handy means by which one could put the logical screws upon somebody so that he could not come out without admitting either that he knew nothing or that this and nothing else was truth, the *eternal* truth that never would vanish as the doings of the blind men vanish. That was the tremendous experience which dawned upon the disciples of Socrates. And from this it seemed to follow that if one only found the right concept of the beautiful, the good, or, for instance, of bravery, of the soul – or whatever – that then one could also grasp its true being. And this, in turn, seemed to open the way for knowing and for teaching how to act rightly in life and, above all, how to act as a citizen of the state; for this question was everything to the Hellenic man, whose thinking was political throughout. And for these reasons one engaged in science.

The second great tool of scientific work, the rational experiment, made its appearance at the side of this discovery of the Hellenic spirit during the Renaissance period. The experiment is a means of reliably controlling experience. Without it, present-day empirical science would be impossible. There were experiments earlier; for instance, in India physiological experiments were made in the service of ascetic yoga technique; in Hellenic antiquity, mathematical experiments were made for purposes of war technology; and in the Middle Ages, for purposes of mining. But to raise the experiment to a principle of research was the achievement of the Renaissance. They were the great innovators in *art*, who were the pioneers of experiment. Leonardo and his like and, above all, the sixteenth-century experimenters in music with their experimental pianos were characteristic. From these circles the experiment entered science, especially through Galileo, and it entered theory through Bacon; and then it was taken over by the various exact disciplines of the continental universities, first of all those of Italy and then those of the Netherlands.

What did science mean to these men who stood at the threshold of modern times? To artistic experimenters of the type of Leonardo and the musical innovators, science meant the path to *true* art, and that meant for them the path to true *nature*. Art was to be raised to the rank of a science, and this meant at the same time and above all to raise the artist to the rank of the doctor, socially and with reference to the meaning of his life. This is the ambition on which, for instance, Leonardo's sketch book was based. And today? "Science as the way to nature" would sound like blasphemy to youth. Today, youth proclaims the opposite: redemption from the intellectualism of science in order to return to one's own nature and therewith to nature in general. Science as a way to art? Here no criticism is even needed.

But during the period of the rise of the exact sciences one expected a great deal more. If you recall [the eighteenth-century German anatomist] Swammerdam's statement, "Here I bring you the proof of God's providence in the anatomy of a louse," you will see what the scientific worker, influenced (indirectly) by Protestantism and Puritanism, conceived to be his task: to show the path to God. People no longer found this path among the philosophers, with their concepts and deductions. All pietist theology of the time, above all [of its founder] Spener, knew that God was not to be found along the road by which the Middle Ages had sought him. God is hidden, His ways are not our ways, His thoughts are not our thoughts. In the exact sciences, however, where one could physically grasp His works, one hoped to come upon the traces of what He planned for the world. And today? Who – aside from certain big children who are indeed found in the natural sciences – still believes that the findings of astronomy, biology, physics, or chemistry could teach us anything about the *meaning* of the world? If there is any such "meaning," along what road could one come upon its tracks? If these natural sciences lead to anything in this way, they are apt to make the belief that there is such a thing as the "meaning" of the universe die out at its very roots.

And finally, science as a way "to God"? Science, this specifically irreligious power? That science today is irreligious no one will doubt in his innermost being, even if he will not admit it to himself. Redemption from the rationalism and intellectualism of science is the fundamental presupposition of living in union with the divine. This, or something similar in meaning, is one of the fundamental watchwords one hears among German youth, whose feelings are attuned to religion or who crave religious experiences. They crave not only religious experience but experience as such. The only thing that is strange is the method that is now followed: the spheres of the irrational, the only spheres that intellectualism has not yet touched, are now raised into consciousness and put under its lens. For in practice this is where the modern intelectualist romanticism of the irrational leads. This method of emancipation from intellectualism may well bring about the very opposite of what those who take to it conceive as its goal.

After Nietzsche's devastating criticism of those "last men" who "invented happiness," I may leave aside altogether the naive optimism in which science – that is, the technique of mastering life which rests upon science – has been celebrated as the way to *happiness* [see Prologue, *Thus Spoke Zarathustra*]. Who believes in this? – aside from a few big children in university chairs or editorial offices. Let us resume our argument.

Under these internal presuppositions, what is the meaning of science as a vocation, now after all these former illusions, the "way to true being," the "way to true art," the "way to true nature," the "way to true God," the "way to true happiness," have been dispelled? Tolstoi has given the simplest answer, with the words: "Science is meaningless because it gives no answer to our question, the only question important for us: 'What shall we do and how shall we live?'" That science does not give an answer to this is indisputable. The only question that remains is the sense in which science gives "no" answer, and whether or not science might yet be of some use to the one who puts the question correctly.

Today one usually speaks of science as "free from presuppositions." Is there such a thing? It depends upon what one understands thereby. All scientific work presupposes that the rules of logic and method are valid; these are the general foundations of our orientation in the world; and, at least for our special question, these presuppositions are the least problematic aspect of science. Science further presupposes that what is yielded by scientific work is *important* in the sense that it is "worth being known." In this, obviously, are contained all our problems. For this presupposition cannot be proved by scientific means. It can only be *interpreted* with reference to its ultimate meaning, which we must reject or accept according to our ultimate position towards life.

Furthermore, the nature of the relationship of scientific work and its presuppositions varies widely according to their structure. The natural sciences, for instance, physics, chemistry, and astronomy, presuppose as self-evident that it is worth while to know the ultimate laws of cosmic events as far as science can construe them. This is the case not only because, with such knowledge, one can attain technical results, but also – for its own sake, if the quest for such knowledge is to be a "vocation." Yet this presupposition can by no means be proved. And still less can it be proved that the existence of the world which these sciences describe is worth while, that it has any "meaning," or that it makes sense to live in such a world. Science does not ask for the answers to such questions.

Consider modern medicine, a practical technology which is highly developed scientifically. The general "presupposition" of the medical enterprise is stated trivially in the assertion that medical science has the task of maintaining lift as such and of diminishing suffering as such to the greatest possible degree. Yet this is problematical. By his means the medical man preserves the life of the mortally ill man, even if the patient implores us to relieve him of life, even if his relatives, to whom his life is worthless and to whom the costs of maintaining his worthless life grow unbearable, grant his redemption from suffering. Perhaps a poor lunatic is involved, whose relatives, whether they admit it or not, wish and must wish for his death. Yet the presuppositions of medicine, and the penal code, prevent the physician from relinquishing his therapeutic efforts.

Whether life is worth while living and when – this question is not asked by medicine. Natural science gives us an answer to the question of what we must do *if* we wish to master life *technically*. It leaves quite aside, or assumes for its purposes, whether we should and do wish to master life technically and whether it ultimately makes sense to do so.

Consider a discipline such as aesthetics. The fact that there are works of art is given for aesthetics. It seeks to find out under what conditions this fact exists, but it does not raise the question whether or not the realm of art is perhaps a realm of diabolical grandeur, a realm of this world, and therefore, in its core, hostile to God and, in its innermost and aristocratic spirit, hostile to the brotherhood of man. Hence, aesthetics does not ask whether there *should* be works of art.

Consider jurisprudence. It establishes what is valid according to the rules of juristic thought, which is partly bound by logically compelling and partly by conventionally given schemata. Juridical thought holds when certain legal rules and certain methods of interpretations are recognized as binding. *Whether* there should be law and *whether* one should establish just these rules – such questions jurisprudence does not answer. It can only state: If one wishes this result, according to the norms of our legal thought, this legal rule is the appropriate means of attaining it.

Consider the historical and cultural sciences. They teach us how to understand and interpret political, artistic, literary, and social phenomena in terms of their origins. But they give us no answer to the question, whether the existence of these cultural phenomena have been and are *worth while*. And they do not answer the further question, whether it is worth the effort required to know them. They presuppose that there is an interest in partaking, through this procedure, of the community of "civilized men." But they cannot prove "scientifically" that this is the case; and that they presuppose this interest by no means proves that it goes without saying. In fact it is not at all self-evident.

# chapter 23

# Ethical Neutrality in the Classroom and the Usefulness and Limits of an Empirical Science

From "Science as a Vocation," in *From Max Weber: Essays in Sociology*, eds and trans. H. H. Gerth and C. Wright Mills, slightly revised by Stephen Kalberg (New York: Oxford University Press, 1946), pp. 145–53.

. . . It is said, and I agree, that politics is out of place in the lecture-room. It does not belong there from the point of view of the students. If, for instance, in the lecture-room of my former colleague [and German militarist] Dietrich Schäfer in Berlin, pacifist students were to surround his desk and make an uproar, I should deplore it just as much as I should deplore the uproar which anti-pacifist students are said to have made against [the pacifist]. Professor Förster, whose views in many ways are as remote as could be from mine. Neither does politics, however, belong in the lecture-room from the point of view of the docents [instructors], and when the docent is scientifically concerned with politics, it belongs there least of all.

To take a practical political stand is one thing, and to analyze political structures and party positions is another. When speaking in a political meeting about democracy, one does not hide one's personal standpoint; indeed, to come out clearly and take a stand is one's damned duty. The words one uses in such a meeting are not means of scientific analysis but means of canvassing votes and winning over others. They are not plowshares to loosen the soil of contemplative thought; they are swords against the enemies: such words are weapons. It would be an outrage, however, to use words in this fashion in a lecture or in the lecture-room. If, for instance, "democracy" is under discussion, one considers its various forms, analyzes them in the way they function, determines what results for the conditions of life the one form has as compared with the other.

Then one confronts the forms of democracy with non-democratic forms of a political order and endeavors to come to a position where the student may find the point from which, in terms of *his* ultimate ideals, *he* can take a stand. But the true teacher will beware of imposing from the platform any political position upon the student, whether it is expressed or suggested. "To let the facts speak for themselves" is the most unfair way of putting over a political position to the student.

Why should we abstain from doing this? I state in advance that some highly esteemed colleagues are of the opinion that it is not possible to carry through this self-restraint and that, even if it were possible, it would be a whim to avoid declaring oneself. Now one cannot demonstrate scientifically what the duty of an academic teacher is. One can only demand of the teacher that he have the intellectual integrity to see that it is one thing to state facts, to determine mathematical or logical relations or the internal structure of cultural values, while it is another thing to answer questions of the *value* of culture and its individual contents and the question of how one should *act* in the cultural community and in political associations. These are quite heterogeneous problems. If he asks further why he should not deal with both types of problems in the lecture-room, the answer is: because the prophet and the demagogue do not belong on the academic platform.

To the prophet and the demagogue, it is said: "Go your ways out into the streets and speak openly to the world," that is, speak where criticism is possible. In the lecture-room we stand opposite our audience, and it has to remain silent. I deem it irresponsible to exploit the circumstance that for the sake of their career the students have to attend a teacher's course while there is nobody present to oppose him with criticism. The task of the teacher is to serve the students with his knowledge and scientific experience and not to imprint upon them his personal political views. It is certainly possible that the individual teacher will not entirely succeed in eliminating his personal sympathies. He is then exposed to the sharpest criticism in the forum of his own conscience. And this deficiency does not prove anything; other errors are also possible, for instance, erroneous statements of fact, and yet they prove nothing against the duty of searching for the truth. I also reject this in the very interest of science. I am ready to prove from the works of our historians that whenever the man of science introduces his personal value judgment, a full understanding of the facts *ceases*. But this goes beyond tonight's topic and would require lengthy elucidation.

I ask only: How should a devout Catholic, on the one hand, and a Freemason, on the other, in a course on the forms of church and state or on religious history ever be brought to evaluate these subjects alike? This is out of the question. And yet the academic teacher must desire and must demand of himself to serve the one as well as the other by his knowledge and methods. Now you will rightly say that the devout Catholic will never accept the view of the factors operative in bringing about Christianity which a teacher who is free of his dogmatic presuppositions presents to him. Certainly! The difference, however, lies in the following: Science "free from presuppositions," in the sense of a rejection of religious bonds, does not know of the "miracle" and the "revelation." If it did, science would be unfaithful to its own "presuppositions." The believer knows both, miracle and revelation. And science "free from presuppositions" expects from him no less – and no more – than acknowledgment that *if* the process can be explained without those supernatural interventions, which an empirical explanation has to eliminate as causal factors, the process has to be explained the way science attempts to do. And the believer can do this without being disloyal to his faith.

But has the contribution of science no meaning at all for a man who does not care to know facts as such and to whom only the practical standpoint matters? Perhaps science nevertheless contributes something.

The primary task of a useful teacher is to teach his students to recognize "inconvenient" facts – I mean facts that are inconvenient for their party opinions. And for every party opinion there are facts that are extremely inconvenient, for my own opinion no less than for others. I believe the teacher accomplishes more than a mere intellectual task if he compels his audience to accustom itself to the existence of such facts. I would be so immodest as even to apply the expression "moral achievement," though perhaps this may sound too grandiose for something that should go without saying.

Thus far I have spoken only of *practical* reasons for avoiding the imposition of a personal point of view. But these are not the only reasons. The impossibility of "scientifically" advocating for practical stands – except in discussing the means for a firmly *given* and presupposed end – rests upon reasons that lie far deeper.

"Scientific" advocacy is meaningless in principle because the various value spheres of the world stand in irreconcilable conflict with each other. The elder Mill, whose philosophy I will not praise otherwise, was on this point right when he said: If one proceeds from pure experience, one arrives at polytheism. This is shallow in formulation and sounds paradoxical, and yet there is truth in it. If anything, we realize again today that something can be sacred not only in spite of its not being beautiful, but rather *because and in so far* as it is not beautiful. You will find this documented in the fifty-third chapter of the book of Isaiah and in the twenty-first Psalm. And, since Nietzsche, we realize that something can be beautiful, not only in spite of the aspect in which it is not good, but rather in that very aspect. You will find this expressed earlier in the *Fleurs du mal*, as Baudelaire named his volume of poems. It is commonplace to observe that something may be true although it is not beautiful and not holy and not good. Indeed it may be true in precisely those aspects. But all these are only the most elementary cases of the struggle that the gods of the various orders and values are engaged in. I do not know how one might wish to decide "scientifically" the *value* of French and German culture; for here, too, different gods struggle with one another, now and for all times to come.

We live as did the ancients when their world was not yet disenchanted of its gods and demons; only we live in a different sense. As Hellenic man at times sacrificed to Aphrodite and at other times to Apollo, and, above all, as everybody sacrificed to the gods of his city, so today our behavior also manifests an internal genuine adaptability, even though unlike for the ancients, it has become disenchanted and stripped of the mythical. Fate, and certainly not "science," holds sway over these gods and their struggles. One can only understand *what* the godhead is for the one order or for the other, or better, what godhead is in the one or in the other order. With this understanding, however, the matter has reached its limit so far as it can be discussed in a lecture-room and by a professor. Yet the great and vital problem of *life* that is contained therein is, of course, very far from being concluded. But forces other than university lecturers have their say in this matter.

What man will take upon himself the attempt to "refute scientifically" the ethic of the Sermon on the Mount? For instance, the sentence, "resist no evil," or the image of turning the other cheek? And yet it is clear, in mundane perspective, that this is an ethic of undignified conduct; one has to choose between the religious dignity which this ethic confers and the dignity of manly conduct which preaches something quite different; "resist evil – lest you be co-responsible for an overpowering evil." According to the ultimate standpoint, the one is the devil and the other the God, and the individual has to decide which is God for him and which is the devil. And so it goes throughout all the orders of life.

The grandiose rationalism of an ethical and methodical conduct of life, which flows from every religious prophecy, has dethroned this polytheism in favor of the "one thing that is needful." Faced with the realities of outer and inner life, Christianity has deemed it necessary to make those compromises and relative judgments, which we all know from its history. But today also religion is subject simply to the drift and flow of everyday life. Many old gods ascend from their graves; they are disenchanted and hence take the form of impersonal powers. They strive to acquire controlling force over our lives and again they resume their eternal struggle with one another. What is hard for modern man, and especially for the younger generation, is to measure up to *workaday* existence. The ubiquitous chase for "experience" stems from this weakness; for it is weakness not to be able to look directly at the fate of our times with its stern seriousness.

Our civilization destines us to realize more clearly these struggles again, after our eyes have been blinded for a thousand years – blinded by the allegedly or presumably exclusive orientation towards the grandiose moral fervor of Christian ethics.

But enough of these questions which lead far away. Those of our youth are in error who react to all this by saying, "Yes, but we happen to come to lectures in order to experience something more than mere analyses and statements of fact." The error is that they seek in the professor something different from what stands before them. They crave a *leader* and not a *teacher*. But we are placed upon the platform solely as *teachers*. And these are two different things, as one can readily see. Permit me to take you once more to America, because there one can often observe such matters in their most massive originality.

The American boy learns unspeakably less than the German boy. In spite of an incredible number of examinations, his school life has not had the significance of turning him into an absolute creature of examinations, such as the German. For in America, bureaucracy, which presupposes the examination diploma as a ticket of admission to the realm of office prebends, is only in its beginnings. The young American has no respect for anything or anybody, for tradition or for public office – unless it is for the personal achievement of individual men. *This* is what the American calls "democracy." This is the meaning of democracy, however distorted its intent may in reality be, and this intent is what matters here. The American's conception of the teacher who faces him is: he sells me his knowledge and his methods for my father's money, just as the greengrocer sells my mother cabbage. And that is all. To be sure, if the teacher happens to be a football coach, then, in this field, he is a leader. But if he is not this (or something similar in a different field of sports), he is simply a teacher and nothing more. And no young American would think of having the teacher sell him a *Weltanschauung* [world view] or a code of conduct. Now, when formulated in this manner, we should reject this. But the question is whether there is not a grain of truth contained in this sensibility, which I have deliberately stated in extreme with some exaggeration.

Fellow students! You come to our lectures and demand from us the qualities of leadership, and you fail to realize in advance that of a hundred professors at least ninety-nine do not and must not claim to be football masters in the vital problems of life, of even to be "leaders" in matters of conduct. Please, consider that a man's value does not depend on whether or not he has leadership qualities. And in any case, *the* qualities that make a man an excellent scholar and academic teacher are not the qualities that make him a leader to give directions in practical life or, more specifically, in politics. It is pure accident if a teacher also possesses this quality, and it is cause for concern if every teacher on the platform feels himself confronted with students expecting this quality. It is still more worrisome if it is left to every academic teacher to set himself up as a leader in the lecture hall. For those who most frequently think of themselves as leaders often qualify least as leaders. But irrespective of whether they are or are not, the university lecture simply offers no possibility of *proving* themselves to be leaders. The professor who feels called upon to act as a counselor of youth and enjoys their trust may prove himself a man in personal human relations with them. And if he feels called upon to intervene in the struggles of world views and party opinions, he may do so outside, in the market place, in the press, in meetings, in associations, wherever he wishes. But after all, it is somewhat too convenient to demonstrate one's courage in taking a stand where the audience and possible opponents are condemned to silence.

Finally, you will put the question: "If this is so, what then does science actually and positively contribute to practical and personal 'life'?" Therewith we are back again at the problem of science as a "vocation."

First, of course, science contributes to the technology of controlling life by calculating external objects as well as man's activities. Well, you will say, that, after all, amounts to no more than the greengrocer of the American boy. I fully agree.

Second, science can contribute something that the greengrocer cannot: methods of thinking, the tools and the training for thought. Perhaps you will say: well, that is no vegetable, but it amounts to no more than the means for procuring vegetables. Well and good, let us leave it at that for today.

Fortunately, however, the contribution of science does not reach its limit with this. We are in a position to help you to a third objective: to gain *clarity*. Of course, it is presupposed that we ourselves possess clarity. As far as this is the case, we can make clear to you the following:

In practice, you can take this or that position when concerned with a problem of value – for simplicity's sake, please think of social phenomena as examples. *If* you take such and such a stand, then, according to scientific experience, you have to use such and such a *means* in order to carry out your conviction practically. Now, these means are perhaps such that you believe you must reject them. Then you simply must choose between the end and the inevitable means. Does the end "justify" the means? Or does it not? The teacher can confront you with the necessity of this choice. He cannot do more, so long as he wishes to remain a teacher and not to become a demagogue. He can, of course, also tell you that if you want such and such an end, then you must take into the bargain the subsidiary consequences which according to all experience will occur. Again we find ourselves in the same situation as before. These are still problems that can also emerge for the technician, who in numerous instances has to make decisions according to the principle of the lesser evil or of the relatively best. Only to him one thing, the main thing, is usually given, namely, the *end*. But as soon as truly "ultimate" problems are at stake for us this is *not* the case. With this, at long last, we come to the final service that science as such can render to the aim of clarity, and at the same time we come to the limits of science.

Besides we can and we should state: In terms of its *meaning*, such and such a practical stand can be derived with inner consistency, and hence integrity, from this or that ultimate *weltanschauliche* position. Perhaps it can only be derived from one such fundamental position, or maybe from several, but it cannot be derived from these or those other positions. Figuratively speaking, you serve this god and you *offend the other* god when you decide to adhere to this position. And if you remain faithful to yourself, you will necessarily come to certain final meaningful *conclusions* that subjectively make sense. This much, in principle at least, can be accomplished. Philosophy, as a special discipline, and the essentially philosophical discussions of principles in the other sciences attempt to achieve this. Thus, if we are competent in our pursuit (which must be presupposed here) we can force the individual, or at least we can help him, to give himself an *account of the ultimate meaning of his own conduct*. This appears to me as not so trifling a thing to do, even for one's own personal life. Again, I am tempted to say of a teacher who succeeds in this: he stands in the service of "moral" forces; he fulfils the duty of bringing about self-clarification and a sense of responsibility. And I believe he will be the more able to accomplish this the more conscientiously he avoids the desire personally to impose upon or suggest to his audience his own stand.

This proposition, which I present here, always takes its point of departure from the one fundamental fact that, so long as life takes itself as its own resting point and is understood on its own terms, it knows only of an unceasing struggle of these gods with one another. Or, literally, the ultimately *possible* attitudes toward life are irreconcilable, and hence their struggle can never be brought to a final conclusion. Thus it is necessary to make a decisive *choice*. Whether, under such conditions, science is a worth while "vocation" for somebody, and whether science itself has an objectively valuable "vocation" – these are again value-judgments about which nothing can be said in the lecture-room. To affirm the value of science is a *presupposition* for teaching there. I personally by my very work answer in the affirmative, and I also do so from precisely the standpoint that hates intellectualism as the worst devil, as youth does today, or usually only fancies it does. In that case the word holds for these youths: "Mind you, the devil is old; grow old to understand him." This does not mean age in the sense of the birth certificate. It means that if one wishes to settle with this devil, one must not take to flight before him as so many like to do nowadays. First of all, one has to see the devil's ways to the end in order to realize his power and his limitations.

Science today is a "vocation" organized in *special disciplines* in the service of self-clarification and knowledge of interrelated facts. It is not the gift of grace of seers and prophets dispensing sacred values and revelations, nor does it partake of the contemplation of sages and philosophers about the *meaning* of the world. This, to be sure, is the inescapable condition of our historical situation. We cannot evade it so long as we remain true to ourselves. And if Tolstoi's question recurs to you: as science does not, who is to answer the question: "What shall we do, and, how shall we arrange our lives?" or, in the words used here tonight: "Which of the warring gods should we serve? Or should we serve perhaps an entirely different god, and who is he?" – then one can say that only a prophet or a savior can give the answers. If there is no such man, or if his message is no longer believed in, then you will certainly not compel him to appear on this earth by having thousands of professors, as privileged hirelings of the state, attempt as petty prophets in their lecture halls to take over his role. All they will accomplish is to show that they are unaware of the decisive state of affairs: the prophet for whom so many of our younger generation yearn simply does *not* exist. But this knowledge in its forceful significance has never become vital for them. The inward interest of a truly religiously "musical" man can never be served by veiling to him and to others the fundamental fact that he is destined to live in a godless and prophetless time by giving him the *ersatz* of armchair prophecy. The integrity of his religious belief, it seems to me, must rebel against this.

# "Is" and "Ought" in the Social Sciences

From "Debate Commentary," Association for Social Policy Convention, (1909) in *Gesammelte Aufsätze zur Soziologie und Sozialpolitik* [*Collected Essays on Sociology and Social Policy*], ed. Marianne Weber, trans. Stephen Kalberg (Tübingen: Mohr Verlag, 1924), pp. 417–18.

I agree with [the political economist] Professor [Werner] Sombart that the mixing of an "ought" dimension into scientific questions is to invite the devil. . . . This brings me to the actual problem. It is certainly true that an empirical science cannot otherwise be grounded except on the foundation of that which exists – and such a science says *nothing* about that which should be. Of course, in saying this – and Sombart will surely concede this point – I do not wish to argue that a scientific discussion touching upon the realm of that which ought to be could not at all exist. One asks, however, in what sense?

To begin, I can say to someone who confronts me with a specific value-judgment: "My dear man, you err precisely in regard to that which you actually *want*. Hear me out: I am taking your value-judgment and dissecting it for you dialectically utilizing the rules of *logic*. I do so in order to trace it back to its basic presuppositions and to demonstrate to you that several 'ultimate' *possible* value-judgments – invisible to you – lie concealed within your value-judgment. Moreover, perhaps these basic presuppositions are not to be reconciled (or, if so, only on the basis of a compromise), and hence you must choose between them." This is a conclusion arrived at through *logical* conceptualization rather than empirically.

Now, however, I can further note: "If you want to act on behalf of a certain 'ought' in accord with this particular and obvious value-judgment, *then* you must utilize, according to scientific experience, this and that *means* – that is, in order to attain the goal that corresponds to the values you uphold. And if these means are not ones agreeable to you, then you must *choose* between the means and the goal." Finally, I can say to this person: "You must keep in mind that, according to scientific experience, the means indispensable for the realization of your value-judgment will produce other – unintended – *secondary consequences*. Do you desire also these secondary consequences? Yes or no?"

*Science* can lead a person up to the boundary of this "yes" or "no." All questions lying on this side of the divide can be addressed by the information offered by an empirical discipline (or, however, logic). Yet the "yes" and "no" are *themselves no longer* questions for science. Rather, they are queries to be addressed only by the conscience or by reference to subjective taste – in any case a type of question whose answer lies on a different plane of thought. Nonetheless, for a *scientific* association to discuss practical questions of this sort is not a matter of absolute nonsense. However, such debates should be guided by a recognition that only one question can be asked in regard to these matters: which means and secondary consequences must be tolerated if one acts in conformity with this or that presupposition? An empirical science is concerned with these questions.

Yet it must be further asked: what *ultimate* positions lie concealed in the value-judgments struggling against each other? An answer to this query concerns logic – hence, similarly, a scientific debate that can be imposed upon every person who thinks theoretically can take place. The fall from grace begins at that point where the purely empirical or purely logical lines of thought are mixed together with subjective, practical value-judgments. I believe that Sombart will agree with me on this point.

# chapter 24

# The Opposition of Salvation Religions to Science and Modern Culture

From "Science as a Vocation," in *From Max Weber: Essays in Sociology*, eds and trans. H. H. Gerth and C. Wright Mills, slightly revised by Stephen Kalberg (New York: Oxford University Press, 1946), pp. 153–6.

Now you will be inclined to say: Which stand does one take towards the factual existence of "theology" and its claims to be a "science"? Let us not flinch and evade the answer. To be sure, "theology" and "dogmas" do not exist universally, but neither do they exist for Christianity alone. Rather (going backward in time), they exist in highly developed form also in Islam, in Manicheanism, in Gnosticism, in Orphism, in Parsism, in Buddhism, in the Hindu sects, in Taoism, and in the Upanishads, and, of course, in Judaism. To be sure their systematic development varies greatly. It is no accident that Occidental Christianity – in contrast to the theological possessions of Jewry – has expanded and elaborated theology more systematically, or strives to do so. In the West the development of theology has had by far the greatest historical significance. This is the product of the Hellenic spirit, and all theology of the West goes back to it, as (obviously) all theology of the East goes back to Indian thought. All theology represents an intellectual *rationalization* of the possession of sacred values. No science is absolutely free from presuppositions, and no science can prove its fundamental value to the man who rejects these presuppositions. Every theology, however, adds a few specific presuppositions for its work and thus for the justification of its existence. Their meaning and scope vary. *Every* theology, including for instance Hinduist theology, presupposes that the world must have a *meaning*, and the question is how to interpret this meaning so that it can be intellectually grasped.

It is the same as with Kant's epistemology. [In "Introduction" to *Critique of Pure Reason*] he took for his point of departure the presupposition: "Scientific truth exists and it is *valid*," and then asked: "Under which presuppositions of thought is truth possible and meaningful?" The modern aestheticians (actually or expressly, as for instance, [the Hungarian Marxist] G. v. Lukács [1885–1978]) proceed from the presupposition that "works of art *exist*," and then ask: "How is their existence meaningful and possible?"

As a rule, theologies, however, do not content themselves with this (essentially religious and philosophical) presupposition. They regularly proceed from the further presupposition that certain "revelations" are facts relevant for salvation and as such make possible a meaningful conduct of life. Hence, these revelations must be believed in. Moreover, theologies presuppose that certain subjective states and acts possess the quality of holiness, that is, they constitute a way of life, or at least elements of one, that is religiously meaningful. Then the question of theology is: How can these presuppositions, which must simply be accepted be meaningfully interpreted in a view of the universe? For theology, these presuppositions as such lie beyond the limits of "science." They are not "knowledge," in the usual sense, but rather a "possession." Whoever does not "possess" faith, or the other holy states, cannot have theology as a substitute for them, least of all any other science. On the contrary, in every "positive" theology, the devout reach the point where the Augustinian sentence holds: *credo non quod, sed quia absurdum est.* The capacity for this accomplishment of religious virtuosos – the "intellectual sacrifice" – is the decisive characteristic of the positively religious man. That this is so is shown by the fact that in spite (or rather in consequence) of theology (which unveils it) the tension between the value spheres of "science" and the sphere of religious salvation is unbridgeable.

Legitimately, only the disciple offers the "intellectual sacrifice" to the prophet, the believer to the church. Never as yet has a new prophecy emerged (and I repeat here deliberately this image which has offended some) by way of the need of some modern intellectuals to furnish their souls with, so to speak, guaranteed genuine antiques. In doing so, they happen to remember that religion has belonged among such antiques, and of all things religion is what they do not possess. By way of substitute, however, they play at decorating a sort of domestic chapel with small sacred images from all over the world, or they produce surrogates through all sorts of psychic experiences to which they ascribe the dignity of mystic holiness, which they peddle in the book market. This is plain humbug or self-deception. It is, however, no humbug but rather something very sincere and genuine if some of the youth groups who during recent years have quietly grown together give their human community the interpretation of a religious, cosmic, or mystical relation, although occasionally perhaps such interpretation rests on misunderstanding of self. True as it is that every act of genuine brotherliness may be linked with the awareness that it contributes something permanent to a transcendent realm, it seems to me dubious whether the dignity of purely human social relationships is enhanced by these religious interpretations. But that is no longer our theme.

The fate of our times is characterized by rationalization and intellectualization and, above all, by the "disenchantment of the world." Precisely the ultimate and most sublime values have retreated from public life either into the transcendental realm of mystic life or into the brotherliness of direct and personal human relations. It is not accidental that our greatest art is intimate and not monumental, nor is it accidental that today only within the smallest and intimate circles, in personal human situations, in *pianissimo*, that something is pulsating that corresponds to the prophetic frenzy, which in former times swept through the great communities like a firebrand, welding them together. If we attempt to force and to "invent" a monumental style in art, such miserable monstrosities are produced as the many monuments of the last twenty years. If one tries to construe new forms of religion, through musing and pondering, and without a new and genuine prophecy, then, in an inner sense, something similar will result, but with still worse effects. And academic prophecy, finally, will create only fanatical sects but never a genuine community.

To the person who cannot bear the fate of the times like a man, one must say: may he rather return silently, without the usual publicity build-up of renegades, but simply and plainly. The arms of the old churches are opened widely and compassionately for him. After all, they do not make it hard for him. One way or another he has to bring his "intellectual sacrifice" – that is inevitable. If he can really do it, we shall not rebuke him. For such an intellectual sacrifice in favor of an unconditional religious devotion is ethically quite a different matter than the evasion of the plain duty of intellectual integrity, which is evident if one lacks the courage to clarify one's own ultimate standpoint and instead circumvents this duty by feeble relative judgments. In my eyes, such religious devotion stands higher than academic prophecy, which does not clearly realize that in university lecture halls no other virtue holds but plain intellectual integrity. Integrity, however, compels us to state that for the many who today tarry for new prophets and saviors, the situation is the same as resounds in the beautiful Edomite watchman's song of the period of exile that has been included among Isaiah's oracles:

> He calleth to me out of Seir, Watchman, what of the night? The watchman said, The morning cometh, and also the night: if ye will enquire, enquire ye: return, come.

The people to whom this was said has enquired and tarried for far more than two millennia, and we know its shocking fate. From this we want to draw the lesson that nothing is gained by yearning and tarrying alone, and we shall act differently. We shall undertake our daily work and do justice to the "demands of the day,"[1] in human relations as well as in our vocation. This, however, is plain and simple, if each finds and obeys the demon who holds the fibers of *his* very life.

## NOTE

1.  See *PE*, p. 202, n. 74. This phrase is from Goethe. See *Maximen und Reflexionen* ed. by Max Hecker (Weimar, 1907), nos 442, 443. [sk]

From "Religious Rejections of the World and Their Directions," in *From Max Weber: Essays in Sociology*, eds and trans. H. H. Gerth and C. Wright Mills, slightly revised by Stephen Kalberg (New York: Oxford University Press, 1946), pp. 350–3.

The tension between religion and intellectual knowledge definitely comes to the fore wherever rational, empirical knowledge has consistently worked through to the disenchantment of the world and its transformation into a causal mechanism. For then science encounters the claims of the ethical postulate that the world is a God-ordained, and hence somehow *meaningfully* and ethically oriented, cosmos. In principle, the empirical as well as the mathematically-oriented view of the world develops refutations of every intellectual approach which in any way asks for a "meaning" of inner-worldly occurrences. Every increase of rationalism in empirical science increasingly pushes religion from the rational into the irrational realm; but only today does religion become *the* irrational or anti-rational supra-human power. The extent of consciousness or of consistency in the experience of this contrast, however, varies widely. . . .

. . . In effect, every religion in its psychological and intellectual substructure and in its practical conclusions has taken a different stand towards intellectualism, without however allowing the ultimate inward tension to disappear. For the tension rests on the unavoidable disparity among ultimate forms of images of the world.

There is absolutely no "unbroken" religion working as a vital force which is not compelled at *some* point to demand the *credo non quod, sed quia absurdum* – the "sacrifice of the intellect."

It is hardly necessary and it would be impossible to treat in detail the stages of the tension between religion and intellectual knowledge. Salvation religion defends itself against the attack of the self-sufficient intellect. It does so, of course, in the most principled fashion, by raising the claim that religious knowledge moves in a different sphere and that the nature and meaning of religious knowledge is entirely different from the accomplishments of the intellect. Religion claims to offer an ultimate stand toward the world by virtue of a direct grasp of the world's "meaning." It does not claim to offer intellectual knowledge concerning what is or what should be. It claims to unlock the meaning of the world not by means of the intellect but by virtue of a charisma of illumination. This charisma is said to be imparted only to those who make use of the respective technique and free themselves from the misleading and deceptive surrogates which are given out as knowledge by the confused impressions of the senses and the empty abstractions of the intellect. Religion believes that these are in truth irrelevant for salvation. By freeing himself from them, a religious man is said to make himself ready for the reception of the all-important grasp of the meaning of the world and of his own existence. In all the endeavors of philosophy to make this ultimate meaning demonstrable, as well as the (practical) stand which follows from it, salvation religion will see nothing but the intellect's desire to escape its own lawful autonomy. The same view is held of philosophical attempts to gain any intuitive knowledge, which, although concerned with the "being" of things, has a dignity which principally differs from that of religious knowledge. Above all, religion sees all this as a specific product of the very rationalism that intellectualism, by these endeavors, would very much like to escape. . . .

. . . [A]ll religions have demanded as a specific presupposition that the course of the world be somehow *meaningful*, at least in so far as it touches upon the interests of men. . . .

From "Religious Rejections of the World and Their Directions," in *From Max Weber: Essays in Sociology*, eds and trans. H. H. Gerth and C. Wright Mills, slightly revised by Stephen Kalberg (New York: Oxford University Press, 1946), pp. 355–7.

. . . [R]ational knowledge, which has followed its own autonomous and inner-worldly norms. . . . has fashioned a cosmos of truths which no longer has anything to do with the systematic postulates of a rational religious ethic – namely, that the world as a cosmos must satisfy the demands of a religious ethic or evince some "meaning." On the contrary, rational knowledge has had to reject this claim in principle. The cosmos of natural causality and the postulated [religious] cosmos of ethical, compensatory causality have stood in irreconcilable opposition.

Science has created this cosmos of natural causality and has seemed unable to answer with certainty the question of its own ultimate presuppositions. Nevertheless science, in the name of "intellectual integrity," has come forward with the claim of representing the only possible form of a reasoned view of the world. The intellect, like all culture values, has created an aristocracy based on the possession of rational culture and independent of all personal ethical qualities of man. The aristocracy of intellect is hence an unbrotherly aristocracy. Yet worldly man has regarded this possession of culture as the highest good. In addition to the burden of ethical guilt, however, something has adhered to this cultural value which was bound to depreciate it with still greater finality, namely, meaninglessness – if this cultural value is to be judged in terms of its own standards.

The purely inner-worldly perfection of self of a man of culture, hence the ultimate value to which "culture" has seemed to be reducible, is meaningless for religious thought. This follows for religious thought from the obvious meaninglessness of death, meaningless precisely when viewed from the inner-worldly standpoint. And under the very conditions of "culture," meaningless death has seemed only to put the decisive stamp upon the meaninglessness of life itself.

The peasant, like Abraham, could die "satiated with life." The feudal landlord and the warrior hero could do likewise. For both fulfilled a cycle of their existence beyond which they did not reach. Each in his way could attain an inner-worldly perfection as a result of the naive unambiguity of the substance of his life. But the "cultivated" man who strives for self-perfection, in the sense of acquiring or creating "cultural values," cannot do this. He can become "weary of life" but he cannot become "satiated with life" in the sense of completing a cycle. For the perfectibility of the man of culture in principle progresses indefinitely, as do the cultural values. And the segment which the individual and passive recipient or the active co-builder can comprise in the course of a finite life becomes the more trifling the more differentiated and multiplied the cultural values and the goals for self-perfection become. Hence the harnessing of man into this external and internal cosmos of culture can offer the less likelihood that an individual would absorb either culture as a whole or what in any sense is "essential" in culture. Moreover there exists no definitive criterion for judging the latter. It thus becomes less and less likely that "culture" and the striving for culture can have any inner-worldly meaning for the individual.

The "culture" of the individual certainly does not consist of the *quantity* of "cultural values" which he amasses; it consists of an articulated *selection* of culture values. But there is no guarantee that this selection has reached an end that would be meaningful to him precisely at the "accidental" time of his death. He might even turn his back to life with an air of distinction: "I have enough – life has offered (or denied) all that made living worth-while for *me*." This proud attitude to the religion of salvation must appear as a disdainful blasphemy of the God-ordained ways of life and destinies. No salvation religion positively *approves* of "death by one's own hand." That is a death which has been hallowed only by philosophies.

Viewed in this way, all "culture" appears as man's emancipation from the organically prescribed cycle of natural life. For this very reason culture's every step forward seems condemned to lead to an ever more devastating meaninglessness. The advancement of cultural values seems to become a senseless hustle in the service of worthless, moreover self-contradictory, and mutually antagonistic ends. The advancement of cultural values appears the more meaningless the more it is made a sacred task, a "calling."

Culture becomes ever more meaningless as a locus of imperfection, of injustice, of suffering, of sin, of futility. For it is necessarily burdened with guilt, and its deployment and differentiation thus necessarily become ever more meaningless. Viewed from a purely ethical point of view, the world has to appear fragmentary and devalued in all those instances when judged in the light of the religious postulate of a divine "meaning" of existence. This devaluation results from the conflict between the rational claim and reality, between the rational ethic and the partly rational, and partly irrational values. With every construction of the specific nature of each special sphere existing in the world [the economy, politics, scientific, aesthetic and erotic], this conflict has seemed to come to the fore ever more sharply and more insolubly. The need for "salvation" responds to this devaluation by becoming more other-worldly, more alienated from all structured forms of life, and, in exact parallel, by confining itself to the specific religious essence. This reaction is the stronger the more systematic the [religious] thinking about the "meaning" of the universe becomes, the more the external organization of the world is rationalized, and the more the conscious experience of the world's irrational content is sublimated. And not only theoretical thought, which disenchanted the world, led to this course, but also the very attempt of religious ethics practically and ethically to rationalize the world.

The specific intellectual and mystical attempts at salvation in the face of these tensions succumb in the end to the world dominion of unbrotherliness. On the one hand, the charisma of these attempts is *not* accessible to everybody. Hence, in intent, mystical salvation definitely means aristocracy; it is an aristocratic religiosity of redemption. And, in the midst of a culture that is rationally organized for a vocational workaday life, there is hardly any room for the cultivation of acosmic brotherliness, unless it is among strata that are economically carefree. Under the technical and social conditions of [modern] rational culture, an imitation of the life of Buddha, Jesus, or Francis seems condemned to failure for purely external reasons.

# part 11

# Modern Readings

## Introduction

The chapters in this Part illustrate the enduring influence of Max Weber's sociology. Many scholars across several generations have, in a variety of ways, used his insights, theories, and methodology in their own research. As noted in the general Introduction, his works have left a particular imprint upon a variety of areas within Sociology.

In Chapter 25 the distinguished American Weber scholar, Reinhard Bendix (1916–91) examines labor management problems and the different ways of organizing a workforce in nineteenth-century England and Russia. He explains these variations largely by reference to divergent religious traditions and forms of rulership. England's "ethos of work performance," Bendix notes, far more effectively prepared this nation for large-scale industrial production. He also links the Puritan heritage, which places a strong emphasis upon systematic work, to a general emotional detachment and a weakening of ties across persons.

Martin Albrow then examines the "Data Protection Act" in Chapter 26. By setting in motion a strong impetus toward the rationalization of data storage and information systems, the state, Albrow argues, is acting in accord with Weberian ideas on modernity. In Chapter 27, George Ritzer sees a parallel rationalization in the fast-food restaurant industry or, in his terms, a "McDonaldization of society." Indeed, the practices of the fast-food restaurant, particularly its efficiency, are rapidly expanding "into more and more regions of society." As evidence, Ritzer offers a series of vivid illustrations.

Two chapters follow that address Weber's notion of charisma. Luciano Cavalli in Chapter 28 evaluates the extent to which Weber's concept is useful in order to understand Hitler's appeal; he emphasizes its utility. Hans-Georg Riegl, in his intriguing examination of revolutionary movements in Chapter 29, charts the many ways in which the charisma of the *virtuoso* believer becomes, in "rituals of confession," routinized. His study examines how the disciplined revolutionaries of Lenin's party were transformed into obedient cadres in a Stalinist bureaucracy.

In the final chapter Seymour Martin Lipset identifies constituent elements of American social movements, political culture, and public education today as direct derivatives of customs and beliefs prominent in early New England Puritanism. This contribution is indebted to Weber's *Protestant Ethic* and his two essays on the Protestant sects in America (1946c, 1985).

# chapter 25

# Private Authority and Work Habits

## ENGLAND AND RUSSIA

## Reinhard Bendix

From Reinhard Bendix, "Private Authority and Work Habits: England and Russia," in *Nation-Building and Citizenship* (Berkeley, CA: University of California Press, 1977; original edition John Wiley & Sons, Inc. 1964), pp. 181–6, 189–93.

One can summarize Weber's contention by stating that he attributes to the ideas expressed in Puritan preaching the spirit of sober zeal and rationality which he finds characteristic of capitalist economic activities. He looks to the social pressure of the sectarian community for the "mechanism" of internalization; and he believes that once launched these ideas attain a momentum of their own, owing to their affinity with economic activities and to their secularized diffusion in all phases of modern culture.

Managerial ideologies . . . are a special instance of this diffusion. Their emphasis on the virtues of hard work and the systematic ordering of daily activities provides a code of conduct quite apart from religious belief. Weber refers to the significance of this code for the development of economic entrepreneurship. However, this creed acquires a new dimension when it is applied to the lower classes, as it was in England during the nineteenth century and in attenuated form in other Western societies. Prior to the industrial revolution the ancient precept of man's duty to labor had been associated with his low station in life; since then it has been associated with man's responsibility for his fate in this world – at least until the latter-day development of the welfare state. People of the lower classes are admonished with evangelical zeal to exert themselves in order to better their condition; if they fail, it is their failure and not God's inscrutable decree. . . .

For a time the early English entrepreneurs could neglect the problem of organizing their work force. There was little active interest in managerial skills or a managerial ideology, in so far as managerial responsibility and the risks of failure fell to the lot of subcontractors who frequently relied on traditional authority relationships. However, the problems of labor-management came to the fore whenever the organization of production involved the concentration of all work operations within the enterprise and depended to some extent on an *internalized* ethic of work performance on the part of unskilled as well as skilled workers. Under the conditions of factory production such an ethic involves a number of variables. Workers must be willing to do the work assigned with a steady intensity. They must have a positive interest in accuracy and exercise reasonable care in the handling of tools and machinery. And they must be willing to comply with general rules as well as specific orders in a manner which strikes a reasonable balance between the extremes of blind obedience and capricious unpredictability. Moreover, under conditions of factory production the intensity of work, its accuracy, and the careful treatment of tools and machinery cannot remain the attributes of an individual's performance. These qualities of work must be coordinated with the production schedule, and this coordination depends to some extent on the good judgment of each worker as he complies with general rules and specific instructions. Probably, this ethic of work performance developed among the masses of English workers out of the combined legacies of craftsmanship, the Puritan ethic, and the rising ideology of individual striving and success – *prior to the growth of modern large-scale industry.*

The significance and the timing of this Western European background are appreciated best by considering the contrast with the development in Tsarist and Soviet Russia. Under autocratic rule the total depravity of workers and serfs seems to have been an article of faith. An ethic of work performance is not expected of the laboring masses; it is assumed, rather, that they owe the utmost exertions to their masters and that they need to be punished severely if they fail in their obligations. An English engineer who supervised various construction projects in Russia during the early eighteenth century suggested that at least the best among the peasant serfs should be given some small monetary reward. He reports that this suggestion was rejected indignantly with the comment that the peasants would do their duty or they would be beaten until they did.[1] Workers and serfs will act as they ought to act, because they fear what will befall them if they do not. Ideological appeals in this setting exclusively stress the sacred duty of submission. In advising the police on how the peasants can be quieted, a spokesman of the Orthodox Church states in 1839:

> in their instructions to the people [the clergy] should remind them how sacred
> is the duty of submitting to the authorities, and above all to the Highest

authority; how necessary is a trusting and united respect for the government, which of course knows better than private persons what is the good of all, and cannot but wish the well-being of its subjects; and how dangerous is credulous acceptance of injudicious or ill-intentioned advice, from which proceed folly and disorders. . . .[2]

The distinctive feature of such appeals is the emphasis upon submission to the government as the principal rule of conduct. Subordination to this own lord or employer is, therefore, only a token of the worker's submission to the highest authority, an idea expressed with classic simplicity in the following address of an aristocratic landowner to his peasants:

> I am your master, and my master is the Emperor. The Emperor can issue his commands to me, and I must obey him; but he issues no commands to you. I am the Emperor upon my estate; I am your God in this world, and I have to answer for you to the God above.[3]

Thus, the exercise of private authority uses a political interpretation in order to ensure compliance with its commands, an approach which precludes ideological appeals concerned with the inculcation of work habits.

Comparison with England highlights these characteristics of autocratic rule. The assumption that the laboring poor are depraved was probably as widespread in England as in Russia in the eighteenth and early nineteenth centuries. Complete submission to the higher classes and the government is demanded there also without equivocation. A real concern with the attitudes of workers only arises as it does in Russia when the people show signs of rebelliousness. Nevertheless, these similarities are superficial. In England the depravity of the poor is rarely mentioned without reference to the good qualities which every self-respecting man can develop, and even the demands for submission are still couched in terms which make submission synonymous with ideal qualities of work and conduct.[4] Little distinction is made between submission to the authority of government and the work performance expected of the ideal laborer. Hard work is already a token of good citizenship.

In Tsarist Russia these assumptions do not apply. By relying on fear and coercion, employers fail to appeal to the conscience or self-esteem of the workers; there is little or no idealization of an internalized ethic of work performance. The demand for unquestioning submission is a duty made sacred by reference to God and Tsar, but it is not related to any other aspect of personal conduct. In this setting landowners and employers act autocratically in turn, probably because their own self-esteem depends upon an exercise of private authority patterned after that of the Tsar and his officials. And the latter are concerned with the conduct of the people only in so far as the maintenance of public order makes that concern imperative. To go beyond this concern and set a pattern for the *education* of the people lies outside the established routine of autocratic rule, for which unconditional submission to the Tsar's supreme authority is an unquestioned axiom.

Under these circumstances an ethic of work performance does not become a managerial problem in Russia until after the revolution of 1917, when industrialization has become synonymous with the development of large-scale enterprises. It is instructive to read Lenin's reflections on this problem, written in 1918:

> The Russian is a bad worker compared with workers of the advanced countries. Nor could it be otherwise under the Tsarist regime and in view of the tenacity of the remnants of serfdom. The task that the Soviet government must set the people in all its scope is – learn to work. The Taylor system, the last word of capitalism in this respect, like all capitalist progress, is a combination of subtle brutality of bourgeois exploitation and a number of its greatest scientific achievements in the field of analyzing mechanical motions during work, the elimination of superfluous and awkward motions, the working out of correct methods of work, the introduction of the best systems of accounting and control, etc. The Soviet Republic must at all costs adopt all that is valuable in the achievements of science and technology in this field. The possibility of building socialism will be determined solely by our success in combining the Soviet government and the Soviet organization of administration with the modern achievements of capitalism.[5]

When Lenin speaks of adopting the Taylor system without its capitalist abuses, or when Alexander Blok writes a poem in praise of "Communist Americanism," they are clearly borrowing techniques and ideas associated with Western industrialization and derived in part from the Puritan heritage. . . .

[However], several striking differences between the Western European and the Russian "case" must now be noted. First, there is an important difference in background. The Puritan revolution occurred in line with many correlated developments favoring sustained and systematic work habits; it was a manifestation of ethical rationalism that had its roots in the Old Testament prophets and the message of Jesus. As far as I know, the Russian revolution has no comparably favorable background. . . . Second, there is a difference in timing. In Western Europe the Puritan ethic of work developed and became diffused (in secularized form) two centuries before this ethic was utilized in rationalizing the methods of work performance and the organizational structure of the modern enterprise. In Russia an ethic of work and industrialization developed simultaneously, whether we take as the beginning date the rapid development of railroads in the 1880's or the revolution of 1917. Presumably, this difference in timing meant that at the level of work performance economic rationality was firmly established in Western Europe long before the modern requirements of industrial organization emerged; and even then more than a century intervened between Adam Smith and Frederick Taylor. In Russia, on the other hand, the development of industry coincided directly with the demand for a rational organization of work. Third, there is a major difference of ideas between a secular utopia linked to invidious contrasts between Mother Russia and a universal enemy on the one hand, and a transcendental conception of God's relationship to a community of believers on the other. The many ramifications of this point need not be considered in the present context. Fourth, there is a major difference between an inculcation of work habits which occurs through interaction among members of a religious community and diffuses from there, and a comparable inculcation which occurs throughout the nation (rather than within the community) and through the organized drive of a totalitarian party. . . .

Puritanism places major emphasis upon a double aspect of man's unremitting service to God. To prove worthy of the gifts and opportunities which God has placed at man's disposal, he must not permit anything to interfere with the productive use of his time; thus, all emotional ties are a danger to man's immortal soul for they easily divert him from God's service. This inner-worldly asceticism, as Weber calls it, results in a profound depersonalization of family and neighborhood, for it demands that man treat his next of kin and his associates with sober detachment, lest his love for them or their love for him jeopardize the work to which God has called him. And this emotional detachment within the community also reduces the emotional distance between its members and all persons who are strangers to the community For hatred is as dangerous to the soul as love, and where the relation to one's associates is detached, it becomes difficult to distinguish it from one's relations with strangers which are similarly detached. Subsequently this detachment often gave rise to a calculating approach in all human relationships, but originally this attitude had a profoundly ethical basis. Implicit in the Puritan ethic is the demand that man should order *all* his personal relationships with the same detachment so that he may be single-minded in attending to the purpose of life which transcends all mundane concerns. . . .

Thus, interpersonal reliability is buttressed by diminishing both the emotional involvement among the true believers within the community and the emotional distance between them and persons on the outside. This proved to be an essential element in economic transactions in that it furthered the development of mutual trust among men who sought and recognized in each other the same criteria of trustworthiness. The built-in secularization of the Puritan ethic (which John Wesley noted when he says that piety produces riches, and riches a decline of religion) leads on the positive side to established norms of economic conduct, albeit at the price of personal detachment and of a tendency toward calculation in human relations.

## NOTES

1. John Perry, "The State of Russia," in Peter Putnam (ed.), *Seven Britons in Imperial Russia* (Princeton, NJ: Princeton University Press, 1952), p. 61.
2. Statement of the Metropolitan Filaret of Moscow quoted in John S. Curtiss, *Church and State in Russia* (New York: Columbia University Press, 1940), p. 30.
3. Quoted in Baron von Haxthausen, *The Russian Empire, Its People, Institutions, and Resources* (London: Chapman & Hall, 1856), I, p. 335.
4. The polemical literature in this field, above all the passionate diatribes of Marx and his followers, always reserve their strongest invectives for the hypocrisy of employers, who admonish starving workers to work hard, live frugally, and be content with their lot. Yet the contrast with Tsarist Russia suggests that this moralizing approach differs significantly from a demand for submission as such.
5. V. I. Lenin, *Selected Works* (New York: International Publishers, n.d.), VII, pp. 332–33.

# chapter 26

# The Data Protection Act

## A CASE OF RATIONALIZATION

## Martin Albrow

From Martin Albrow, "The Data Protection Act: A Case of Rationalization," in *Rationalization and Modernity*, eds Scott Lash and Sam Whimster (London: Allen & Unwin, 1987), pp. 173–5, 179–80, 182.

. . . In the same spirit as Weber I am going to take a sector of social life that manifestly exhibits rationality in the Kantian sense of being guided by ideas of reason, logic, mathematics, regularity, calculability, coherence, systematic interconnectedness and so on. No attempt will be made to provide an inventory, let alone a general theoretical account of those ideas. They are all included within what Kant meant by reason, but they have been developed far beyond his own formulations. Moreover the development of reason in institutional form has gone beyond any general theory of rationality. That indeed is the justification for the approach being offered here. It is simultaneously empirical and analytical. It analyses cases to permit the gradual eliciting of a concept of rationality as already embedded in the institutional life of the modern world.

Apart from the rational organization of economic life, bureaucracy was for Weber the most pervasive expression of institutionalized rationality. It operated on the basis of both rules and knowledge, decisions being made by qualified people on the basis of systematically gathered information and legal-rational rules. In Weber's words: "the only decisive point for us is that in principle a system of rationally debatable 'reasons' stands behind every act of bureaucratic administration, namely, either subsumption under norms, or a weighing of ends and means" (*E&S*, p. 979). There could not be a better expression of the Kantian origins of Weber's thought. One facet of bureaucracy was the accumulation of knowledge, not only technical, but also in the form of a store of documentary information gathered in the course of routine administration. Factors such as the development of modern means of communication and the development of the office and files as the focus for work were also intimately connected with the rise of bureaucracy. We do not have to look far in modern bureaucracy to see the onward march of rationalization. In particular methods of processing information have developed at an astonishing rate with the development of the computer and the replacement of the filing cabinet with the disc storage of data. The first case of contemporary rationalization I wish to examine relates to data storage.

The modern computer not only makes it possible for state, commercial and other organizations to store enormously increased amounts of information about individuals. It also permits collation of data on a vastly increased scale. There has been a widespread response to this potential in the form of alarm that it could be used to supply information by the collation of data from several sources to damage individuals. Already a convention of countries within the Council of Europe has tried to set standards for the processing of data, and national legislation has been passed. In Britain this has taken the form of the Data Protection Act 1994. ... This Act sets out data protection principles, establishes a system for the registration and supervision of data users and computer bureaux, accords rights to data subjects and allows for exemptions from all or part of the Act.

By a series of preliminary definitions the Act provides for an enormously extended scope for state interest in computerized information. It defines data as "information recorded in a form in which it can be processed by equipment operating automatically in response to instructions given for that purpose". Personal data is defined as "information which relates to a living individual", the data subject, and the data user "controls the contents and use of data" that is to be processed automatically. The Act goes on to prohibit the holding of personal data unless the data user has registered with the Data Protection Registrar and has described the data, their sources and proposed use, providing for access to the data to all data subjects.

The Act is designed to enforce the implementation of a set of principles to be observed by data users. In brief these provide

(1) for the fair and lawful obtaining and processing of data;
(2) that data should be held for specific purposes only;
(3) for disclosure of data only in accord with those purposes;
(4) that data should be adequate and not excessive to the purposes;
(5) that data should be accurate and up to date;
(6) that data should not be retained longer than necessary;
(7) that data subjects should have access and rights to amend inaccuracies.

Additionally computer bureaux are obliged to take appropriate security measures against improper access, damage, or loss of data.

These principles provide an impressive instance of the development of institutionalized rationality. They enshrine specificity of purpose as a state-imposed principle on data users whether or not the data user is gathering data for the state. It is not a particular purpose or set of purposes for which legislation is being passed, but the general category of specific purposes. Principles (2)–(6) all provide at the most abstract level for the rationalization of information-gathering and -processing by anyone for any purpose, provided the data relate to individuals and are machine processed. The European Convention to which the United Kingdom is a signatory allows for the extension of the principles to data about companies and manually held data. Were these extensions implemented then the framework for a comprehensive information system for the social life of a nation state would be largely complete. As it is the state has provided a major impetus to rationalizing the information systems of all collective and individual systems of action by providing a sanctioned set of principles: specificity; relevance; adequacy; accuracy; and temporality. These were not set out explicitly by Weber as principles of rationality, but they are clearly an elaboration on the concept as he understood it. What has happened is that the technical progress represented by the modern computer, when harnessed to considerations of the rights of individuals, generates argument and reflection leading to the elaboration of the idea of rationality. In other words, rationality does not develop in the abstract as some ideal force, but is the ongoing outcome of an interplay between technical progress and reasoned argument. In the institutions of society the outcomes of that interplay are recorded and provide the premises for the next stage of the argument. . . .

## The Bounds of Rationality

In Weber's view bureaucratic organization was the animate machine that corresponded to the inanimate machine of the factory and fabricated the shell of bondage encasing the modern worker. Since his time the animate machine has been harnessed even more tightly to the inanimate through the application of the computer to administrative settings. Both kinds of machine Weber termed "objectified mind" (*geronnener Geist*). Both were constituted by human rationality and, in that, their eventual convergence was an ever present possibility. His own evaluation of this situation shared the prevailing pessimism of German intellectuals in the latter part of the nineteenth century. For Kant the growth of reason meant the enhancement of human freedom; for Weber rules meant bondage, work for purposes that the individual had not set under conditions not freely chosen.

Sometimes this is viewed as Weber taking over Marx's theory of alienation. It is fairer to see them both sharing the intellectual's distrust of the products of an intellectualized society, where rationality had been harnessed to the production of social life. . . .

Of course Weber did not ignore countervailing and contradictory factors in the rationalization process. Conflicts between groups are in part taken up in his account of the conflict of value-spheres. The rationalization of different life-spheres may on his account result in their growing contradictions, as in the classic example of the nation state and the market economy. . . . However far the rationalization of social systems proceeds, there will be material irrationalities. Population trends, resource limitations, health factors, the outcomes of market processes and of other conflicts, the shifts in public moods, all provide either the boundaries or the material for rational action but are outside the prescriptive rules of rationality. Just as at the individual level the capacities and strength that reason can mould provide limits to action, so at the societal level it is not possible for system-rationality to provide a closed and eternally predictable environment. Indeed as formal rationality grows, there is good reason to think that material irrationalities increase equivalently. Any attempt to develop the theory of rationalization will need equally to theorize the irrationalities of the modern world. It would be a fatal mistake to imagine that the one is an alternative, much less a conclusive negation, of the other. So long as human culture survives, rationality and irrationality are locked in a dialectical embrace.

# chapter 27

# The McDonaldization of Society

## George Ritzer

From George Ritzer, *The McDonaldization of Society* (Thousand Oaks, CA: Pine Forge Press, 2000), pp. 47–8, 50–6.

In Weber's view, modern society, especially the Western world, is growing increasingly rationalized. As the reader will see, Weber regarded bureaucracy as the ultimate example of rationalization. Thus, Weber can be seen as being focally concerned with the rationalization of society in general and, more specifically, its bureaucratization.

This chapter is premised on the idea that whereas the processes of rationalization and bureaucratization described by Weber have continued, if not accelerated, the bureaucracy has been supplanted by the fast-food restaurant as the best exemplification of this process. Furthermore, we will see that the rational principles that lie at the base of the fast-food restaurant are spreading throughout American society as well as the rest of the world. On the basis of Weber's ideas on the rationalization process, ... I describe the continuation and even acceleration of this process, or what I have termed the "McDonaldization" of society. ...

[B]ureaucracies ... are structured in such a way as to guide or even to force people to choose certain means to ends. Each task is broken up into a number of components, and each office is responsible for a separate portion of the larger task. Employees in each office handle only their own part of the task, usually by following rules and regulations in a predetermined sequence. The goal is attained when each incumbent has completed his or her required task in proper order. The bureaucracy thereby utilizes what its past history has shown to be optimum means to the end in question. ...

For Weber, the bureaucracy was the height of (formal) rationality, which he defined in terms of the five elements of efficiency, predictability, quantifiability (or calculability), control through substituting nonhuman technology for human judgment, and the irrationality of rationality.

Bureaucracies operate in a highly predictable manner. Incumbents in one office understand very well how the incumbents of other offices will behave. They know what they will be provided with and when they will receive it. Recipients of the service bureaucracies know with a high degree of assurance what they will receive and when they will receive it. Because bureaucracies quantify as many activities as possible, employees perform their duties as a series of specified steps at quantifiable rates of speed. As with all rationalized systems that focus exclusively on quantity, however, the handling of large numbers of things is equated with excellence, and little or no evaluation is made of the actual quality of what is done in each case. Bureaucracies control people by replacing human judgment with nonhuman technology. Indeed, bureaucracy itself may be seen as one huge nonhuman technology that functions more or less automatically. The adaptability of human decisions vanishes into the dictates of rules, regulations, and institutional structures. The work to be done is divided up so that each office is allocated a limited number of well-defined tasks. Incumbents must do those tasks and no others. The tasks must be done in the manner prescribed by the organization; idiosyncratic performance will get one demoted or even fired. The idea is to get the job done in a certain way by a certain time without mistakes. The bureaucracy's clients are also controlled. The organization provides only certain services, and not others; one must apply for the services on a specific form by a specific date, and one will receive those services only in a certain way. . . .

There is little question that the process of rationalization has spread further and become even more firmly entrenched than it was in Weber's day. The fast-food restaurant, of which McDonald's is the best-known chain, has employed all the rational principles pioneered by the bureaucracy and is part of the bureaucratic system because huge conglomerates now own many of the fast-food chains. McDonald's utilized bureaucratic principles and combined them with others, and the outcome is the process of McDonaldization. . . .

Max Weber was right about the inexorable march of formal rationality, but that his paradigm case of that type of rationality and the spearhead in its expansion, the bureaucracy, have been superseded in contemporary American society by the fast-food restaurant. It is the fast-food restaurant that today best represents and leads the process of formal rationalization and its basic components – efficiency, predictability, quantification, control through the substitution of nonhuman for human technology, and the ultimate irrationality of formal rationality. A decade after the original essay, as we had begun progressing through the 1990s, I once again examined the process of McDonaldization.

In the past decade, McDonaldization has extended its reach into more and more regions of society, and those areas are increasingly remote from the heart of the process in the fast-food business. . . . Dentistry, medicine, child care, the training of racehorses, newspapers, and television news have come to be modeled after food chains. Thus, *McDonaldization* is the process by which the principles of the fast-food restaurant are coming to dominate more and more sectors of society.

## Efficiency

The first element of McDonaldization is efficiency, or the choice of the optimum means to an end. Many aspects of the fast-food restaurant illustrate efficiency, especially from the viewpoint of the restaurant, but none better than the degree to which the customer is turned into an unpaid laborer. The fast-food restaurant did not create the idea of imposing work on the consumer, getting the consumer to be what is, in effect, an unpaid employee, but it institutionalized and expedited this development. Customers are expected to stand in line and order their own food (rather than having a waiter do it) and to "bus" their own paper, plastic, and styrofoam (rather than having it done by a busperson). Fast-food chains have also pioneered the movement toward handing the consumer little more than the basics of the meal. The consumer is expected to take the naked burger to the "fixin bar" and there turn it into the desired sandwich by adding such things as lettuce, tomatoes, and onions. We all are expected to log a few minutes a week as sandwich makers. In a recent innovation, we are now handed an empty cup and expected to go to the fountain and fill our glasses with ice and a soft drink, thereby spending a few moments as what used to be called a "soda jerk." In some ultra-modern fast-food restaurants, customers are met by a computer screen when they enter and they must punch in their own order. In these and other ways, the fast-food restaurant has grown more efficient.

The salad bar, also popularized if not pioneered by the fast-food restaurant, is a classic example of putting the consumer to work. The customer buys an empty plate and then loads up on the array of vegetables (and other foods) available. Quickly seeing the merit in all this, many supermarkets have now instituted their own salad bars with a more elaborate array of alternative foods available to the consumer. The salad lover can now work as a salad chef at lunch hour in the fast-food restaurant and then do it all over again in the evening at the supermarket by making the salad for the evening meal. All this is very efficient from the perspective of the fast-food restaurant and the supermarket because only a very small number of employees are needed to keep the various compartments well stocked.

There are many other examples of this process of imposing work on the consumer. Virtually gone are gas station attendants who filled gas tanks, checked oil, and cleaned windows. We now put in a few minutes a week as unpaid gas station attendants pumping gas, checking oil, and cleaning windows. Instead of having a readily available attendant to pay for gasoline, we must trek into the station to pay for our gas. In the latest "advance" in this realm, customers put their own credit cards in a slot, they pump the gas, their account is automatically charged the correct (we hope) amount for the gas pumped, and finally the receipt and the card are retrieved with no contact with, or work done by, anyone working in the gas station.

The latter development was pioneered in the banking industry with the advent of the cash machine, which allows us all to work for at least a few moments as unpaid bank tellers.

When calling many businesses these days, instead of dealing with a human operator who makes the desired connection for us, we must deal with "voice mail" and follow a series of instructions from a computer voice by pushing a bewildering array of numbers and codes before we get, it is hoped, to the desired extension.

Efficiency has been extended to the booming diet industry, which encompasses diet drugs, diet books, exercise videotapes, diet meals, diet drinks, weight loss clinics, and "fat farms." Diet books promising all kinds of efficient shortcuts to weight loss are often at the top of the best-seller lists. Losing weight is normally difficult and time-consuming. Hence the lure of various diet books that promise to make weight loss easier and quicker – that is, more efficient. For those on a diet – and many people are on more or less perpetual diets – the preparation of low-calorie food has been made more efficient. Instead of cooking diet foods from scratch, an array of preprepared diet foods is available in frozen or microwavable form. For those who do not wish to go through the inefficient process of eating these diet meals, there are diet shakes such as Slimfast that can be mixed and consumed in a matter of seconds.

In addition, there is the growth of diet centers such as Nutri/System and Jenny Craig. Dieters at Nutri/System are provided (at substantial cost) with prepackaged freeze-dried food. The dieter needs only to add water when it is time for the next meal. Freeze-dried foods are efficient not only for the dieter but also for Nutri/System because they can be efficiently packaged, transported, and stored. Furthermore, the dieter's periodic visit to a Nutri/System center is efficiently organized. A counselor is allotted 10 minutes with each client. During that brief time period, weight, blood pressure, and measurements are taken, routine questions are asked, a chart is filled out, and some time is devoted to "problem solving." If the session extends beyond the allotted 10 minutes, and other clients are waiting, the receptionist will buzz the room. Counselors learn their techniques at Nutri/System University (NSU), where, after a week of training (no inefficient years of matriculation here), they earn certification and an NSU diploma.

# chapter 28

# Hitler's Charisma

## Luciano Cavalli

From Luciano Cavalli, "Hitler's Charisma," in Max Weber, *Rationality and Modernity*, eds Scott Lash and Sam Whimster (London: Allen & Unwin, 1987), pp. 326–9.

As to modern tyranny (totalitarian dictatorship), it seems to me that the usefulness of the concept of charisma and the related paradigm can be tested, especially, in the case of Hitler ... [who developed] a chiliastic and messianic vision of the world. [Its] central proposition was the concept of a godlike Nature that had supposedly entrusted [him] and his people with the mission of fulfilling its designs and, by so doing, of saving humanity. Such a *Weltanschauung* goes a long way to explaining the inner strength of the dictator, his fascination, his historical project and what he did in order to accomplish it. It must be considered a necessary condition for the strict applicability of the paradigm to the case of Hitler.

The *political* history of Hitler begins with the German defeat of 1918, which he considered an utter tragedy. The ecstatic "vision" of Pasewalk, where a Hitler temporarily sightless had been hospitalized, constitutes the extraordinary experience that gives shape and credibility to the mission of saving Great Mother Germany. . . .

The relationship between Hitler and the Nazi Party is characterized by his evident vocation for leadership, ever since his first appearance at a meeting in September 1919. The surrender of the old party rulers and the grant to Hitler of the presidency of the party along with dictatorial powers in July 1921 are but the formal acknowledgement of a "called" leader, to whom complete obedience is due. Hitler becomes the unquestioned Führer and the source of norms and decisions binding all party members. He is surrounded and served by a party élite that derives its authority from him alone. . . .

. . . The relationship between Hitler and his collaborators, even the most eminent ones such as Goering, was a relationship of absolute and at times cruel domination. To these people one can very well apply Weber's concept of *Entseelung* [loss of the soul], in its full sense. At the same time the direct relationship between Hitler and the masses developed in huge meetings characterized by the almost hypnotic spell of the Führer and by the total enraptured abandon of the masses, which amazed and puzzled detached observers. That mass attitude even verged on religious worship. The appellative "Redemptor" sometimes applied to him can be taken as representative of this tendency to elevate the Führer and his mission to the dimensions of the extraordinary, that is, of the divine. All this corresponded with Hitler's psychological hold over the German masses, carrying with it more than temporary change of common values and attitudes. . . . Only a long series of defeats and the approach of the catastrophe could at last erode the spell of the Führer over his people.

Altogether the example of Hitler – together with the case of Lenin . . . – appears to corroborate the opportuneness of using the concept of charisma and its related paradigm in the study of modern dictatorships. I would even say that without this conceptual tool it is impossible to have an exact understanding of Hitler's role and the related social developments in the Nazi Party and the German state. At the same time I would underscore that the use of these conceptual instruments has no ethical implications. The point is that the same psychological and sociological processes may also develop with leaders such as Gandhi, who from an ethical point of view must be evaluated very differently. As we should remember, the paradigm does not even allow us to foresee (or explain) the historical effectiveness of a leadership. To this end we can resort instead to the criteria given by Weber in "Politics as a Vocation", and these condemn Hitler's leadership. Hitler especially lacked the psychological and cultural maturity that allows a balance between an ethic of responsibility and an ethic of conviction; he showed this clearly by adopting means, such as his concentration camps, that sharply contradicted the concept of humanity as shaped by Western culture.

# chapter 29

# The Routinization of Charisma

## RITUALS OF CONFESSION WITHIN COMMUNITIES OF *VIRTUOSI*

## Hans-Georg Riegl

From Hans-Georg Riegl, "The Routinization of Charisma: Rituals of Confession within Communities of *Virtuosi*," *Totalitarian Movements and Political Religions* 1, 1 (Winter 2000): 16–18, 22–3, 26–9.

Communities of *virtuosi* played a decisive role in Max Weber's comparative-historical studies of religion. It was particularly within the context of his theory of the rationalisation and modernisation of Western societies that Weber dramatised the Cultural Revolution accomplished by the inner-worldly, activist and instrumental asceticism of . . . Puritan Calvinism. The Puritan *virtuosi* pursued their ultimate religious ends with an astonishing single-mindedness, subjecting their daily lives to a regimen of self-control and self-discipline subordinate to their desperate search for salvation – thus also revolutionising, albeit unintentionally, the pre-industrial, magical world of their societies. The God of Calvinism demanded of his believers not single good works, but a life of good works combined into a unified system. . . .

It seems reasonable to enlarge the concept of the religious *virtuoso* to the ideological *virtuoso* in order to describe, and analyse, important components of the political religion of revolutionary movements. Crucially important to the political religions of these revolutionary movements is the fusion of religious and political spheres of their ideologies to one dominant *Weltanschauung*, and one prevailing behaviour pattern. The transfer of sacral, transcendental systems of meanings to the secular, inner-worldly horizons of revolutionary movements' ideological self-definitions leads to an inner-worldly asceticism of revolutionary action and belief. The revolutionary, inner-worldly and secular vocation (*Gesinnungsethik*) is no longer driven by the search for the other-worldly *certitudo salutis*. However, it follows the secular calling of the revolutionary commitment; that is, to realise the utopias of moral self-perfection, and the total reconstruction of societies and cultures. "Similarly, inner-worldly asceticism and the disciplined quest for salvation in a vocation" (1968a, p. 573) no longer had to "please God" but to realise the Ten Commandments of the revolutionary movements in the mundane world. In this sense, the Jacobinism of revolutionary modernity continues the salvationist legacy of the axial age. The sacralisation of politics under modern conditions takes place. . . .

Lenin's party of disciplined professional revolutionaries can be considered as a community of *virtuosi* (see 1968a, p. 539). Such communities attract only specially qualified people who are willing to subordinate their whole life to only one aim of salvation. They will totally identify with the dogmas and norms of their faith of salvation, and they are inclined to surrender themselves unconditionally to the communities' disciplinary courts. The following characteristics seem typical for these closed communities of *virtuosi*. (1) All ethical acts need be coordinated towards the ultimate ends of the believing community. Different disciplinary strategies should guarantee this uniformity of wills and acts. (2) It is intended to destroy any individual autonomy, which should manifest itself as a critical attitude of independent thinking and acting. (3) Instead of individual autonomy, an unconditional obedience is required. In order to secure the smooth running of the disciplinary machinery, all *virtuosi* have to standardise and habitualise their ethical visions, and subordinate them to the vigilant eye of the collective. . . .

Undivided commitment to the exclusive code of behaviour patterns, total identification with the doctrinal truth and unconditional surrender to the disciplinary organs of the community characterises these revolutionary communities. Their aim, to revolutionise the societies and cultures of their origin, requires an exclusive morality for the *virtuosi*. Their communities are the first social groups where the processes of moral perfection take place. The revolutionary community of *virtuosi* figures as a model of moral perfection. The whole society is to be liberated from the corrupting past and contaminated present. As a result of this utopian anticipation of future destiny, revolutionary communities develop internal mechanisms to secure this claim to moral self-perfection within the range of their disciplinary institutions. These are confronted with three structural problems of integration. First, the moulding of faithfulness of the true believers; second, the demarcation against rival communities; and third, the stabilisation of the normative identity of one's own community. . . .

Stalin transformed the Leninist community of *virtuosi* into a church-dispensed grace (*Anstaltsgnade*) which, "includes the righteous and the unrighteous and is especially concerned with subjecting the sinner to Divine law" (1968a, p. 1204). The organisational necessities of wartime communism and the revolutionary transformations of industrialisation and collectivisation in the 1930s, transformed the Leninist community of *virtuosi* to (1) a bureaucratised and hierachically organised institution of grace, with "institutionalized salvation and an office of charisma" (1968a, p. 1204). This evolved into an administrative apparatus with obedient and disciplined cadres who substituted the pneumatic enthusiasm of the early *virtuosi*. The Stalinist church was also organised as (2) an office hierarchy that dispensed grace. The correct interpretation of the store of sacral scriptures, the supervision of canonical preaching and the functioning of the missionary apparatus belonged to the duties of the office holders. The vouchsafing of grace and absolution of sins are organised as a ritual which requires little "personal ethical accomplishment" (1968a, p. 54). The structural change from the Leninist political religion of *virtuosi* to the Stalinist church institution was accompanied by (3) a selective reformulation of the Leninist legacy of sacral scriptures. The sacral experts of the Stalinist orthodoxy worked out and invented the new sacral tradition of Marxism-Leninism, with the intention of legitimising the new monocratic office holder of the church.

The most important tenet of faith in this invented sacral tradition of Marxism-Leninism was that Stalin alone qualified as the only true disciple of Lenin; the consequence thus being his monopoly of the infallible interpretation of his Holy Scriptures. Stalin's own dogmatic performances, his lectures at the Sverdlov University (1924), published as *Leninism*, can be presented in this way as an authentic interpretation of Lenin's sacral teachings. The dramatic management of the Moscow show trials (1936–38) was the last step in the formation and legitimisation of the new Stalinist monocratic rule. They brought Stalin "a monopoly of the legitimate use of hierocratic coercion" (1968a, p. 54). The means for implementing such a monopoly of hierocratic coercion consisted mainly of (4) the establishment of internal security organs, and leadership cadres who could act as representatives of the Stalinist centre. . . .

. . . [P]arty cadres had to pay the Stalinist "hierocratic domination", "pure obedience to the institution" (1968a, p. 563) (*Anstaltsgehorsam*). This "pure obedience", Weber explains, presents itself as a "formal humility of obedience" (*formale Gehorsamsdemut*) which informally deviates from the prescribed patterns of commands by formally keeping up the appearances. "Wherever the pattern of institutional grace is carried through consistently, the sole principle integrating the life pattern is a formal humility of obedience" (1968a, p. 563).

For such cadres it was sufficient to function as disciplined and obedient machines without any personal calls to revolutionary enthusiasm. The ethic of the *virtuosi* was transformed into "pure obedience to the institution, which is regarded as inherently meritorious, and not concrete, substantive ethical obligation, nor even the qualification of superior moral capacity achieved through one's own methodical ethical actions" (1968a, p. 563). The institutional grace was dispensed after the principle "extra ecclesia nulla salus" [no salvation outside the Church] (1968a, p. 560). . . .

Confessing minor and mortal sins belonged to the routine practise of an experienced cadre. Furthermore, this confession seemed to be restricted to external acts without a questioning of ideological motives. The repentance was rather conceived as an external retaliation relative to the severity of the deviant acts. Weber pointed to an analogue form of confession typical for the Catholic Church as an institution dispensing grace. He said:

> It is particularly important that the sins remain discrete actions, against which other discrete deeds may set up as compensations or penances. Hence, value is attached to concrete individual acts rather than to a total personality pattern produced by asceticism, contemplation, or eternally vigilant self-control, a pattern that must constantly be demonstrated and determined anew. A further consequence is that no need is felt to attain the *certitudo salutis* by one's own powers, and so this category, which may in other circumstances have such significant ethical consequences, recedes in importance. (1968a, p. 541)

# chapter 30

# The Political Culture of American Democracy

## THE ENDURING INFLUENCE OF RELIGION

## Seymour Martin Lipset

From Seymour Martin Lipset, "The Political Culture of American Democracy: The Enduring Influence of Religion," in *The First New Nation: The United States in Historical and Comparative Perspective* (New York: W.W. Norton & Co., 1979), pp. xxxvi–xxxviii, 153–6, 158–65, 169.

What continues to impress me . . . is how much of American behavior, after two centuries of national existence, can still be interpreted as derivative from its continued emphasis on equality and achievement. These interrelated values are linked to the formative political events which determined the national ideology, the social structure of a new society without a feudal status-bound past, and the fact the U.S. is the one country in the world dominated by the religious doctrines of Protestant "dissent" – the Methodists, Baptists and other sects. The teaching of these denominations called on people to follow their conscience, to be responsible for their own individual actions, with an unequivocal emphasis not to be found in those denominations which evolved from state churches (Catholics, Lutherans, Anglicans and Orthodox Christians). . . . The United States became the first nation in which religious groups were viewed as purely voluntary organizations, a view which served to strengthen the introduction of religious morality into politics. Although America, like other developed nations, has become more secularized, it is also still true that it remains the *most* religious nation, by far, among these countries, as reflected in the overwhelming proportion who report believing in God, in church attendance (controlling for Protestant and Catholic rates), and in taking religious beliefs seriously. Thus, the U.S. is the only country among thirteen surveyed in 1975–76 by the international

Gallup organization in which a majority, 56 percent, said that "their religious beliefs are very important" to them, while an additional 30 percent said they were "fairly important." No other country can come close to the U.S. in commitments to religious beliefs. In most other countries, close to half or more said such beliefs were "not too important" or "not at all important."[1]

The combination of an emphasis on moralism and voluntarism, derivative from our Protestant sectarianism background, has sustained social movements to enforce that moralism, as may be seen in the large variety of such movements which have characterized American history. The strength of moralistic pressures may be seen most strikingly in reactions to foreign policy issues. There have been three uniquely American stances: conscientious objection to unjust wars, nonrecognition of "evil" foreign regimes, and the insistence that wars must end with the "unconditional surrender" of the Satanic enemy. Linked to Protestant sectarianism, conscientious objection to military service was until recently largely an American phenomenon. . . .

The supporters of American wars invariably see them as moral crusades – to eliminate monarchical rule (the War of 1812) to defeat the Catholic forces of superstition (the Mexican War), to end slavery (the Civil War), to end colonialism in the Americas (the Spanish-American War), to make the world safe for democracy (World War I), and to resist totalitarian expansion (World War II, Korea, and Vietnam). Unlike other countries we rarely see ourselves as merely defending our national interests. Since each war is a battle of good versus evil, the only acceptable outcome is "unconditional surrender" by the enemy. . . .

Many . . . foreign observers [have] confessed their surprise to find that the system of competing denominations in the United States did not mean that the different groups rejected each other for adhering to "false creeds." An Italian Jesuit, Giovanni Grassi, who served for five years, 1812 to 1817, as President of Georgetown College before returning to Rome, commented in disturbed tones on these "other-directed" religious phenomena:

> Every sect there is held as good, every road as correct, and every error as the insignificant weakness of poor mortals. . . .
>
> Although how can one speak of sects? Those who describe themselves as members of one or another of the sects do not thereby profess an abiding adherence to the doctrines of the founders of the sect. . . . Thus the Anglicans of today no longer take much account of their thirty-nine articles, nor the Lutherans of the Confession of Augsburg, nor the Presbyterians of the teachings of Calvin or of Knox. . . .

Among the peculiarities of America, not the most extreme is that of finding persons who live together for several years without knowing each other's religion. And many, when asked, do not answer, "I believe," but simply, "I was brought up in such a persuasion."[2]

Timothy Smith concludes from his detailed examination of the writings of many nineteenth-century ministerial foreign travelers that visiting "Evangelicals were especially heartened to discover that the elimination of legal privilege [separation of church and state in America] seemed to lessen sectarian rivalry."[3] He cites one English visitor in the 1830's who "noted with pleasure *the numerous exchanges of pulpits, union prayer meetings and joint efforts in Bible Society, Sunday school, and mission work. . . .*

[Toqueville's] English contemporary, Harriet Martineau, who stated that almost everyone professed some form of Christian belief, perceptively added that people are not supposed to feel intensely about a particular religion:

One circumstance struck me throughout the country. Almost as often as the conversation between myself and any other person on religious subjects became intimate and earnest, I was met by the supposition that I was a convert. It was the same in other instances: wherever there was a strong interest in the Christian religion, conversion to a particular profession of it was confidentially supposed. This fact speaks volumes.[4]

In 1860 Anthony Trollope was struck by the fact that "the question of a man's religion is regarded in a free and easy way." He notes that fathers believe "that a young lad should go somewhere on a Sunday; but a sermon is a sermon. . . . Everybody is bound to have a religion, but it does not much matter what it is."[5] And in 1900, the German sociologist Max Weber was also impressed, during his visit, with the seeming secularization of religion and acceptance of religious diversity. . . .

American Protestantism has concentrated on the moral rather than the contemplative, mystical, or communal and traditional elements of religion partially because of its Puritan roots. The contemplative and the mystical have not played a significant role in Protestantism in general, and in addition "the intellectual, theological element, though prominent in Puritan Christianity came with the growth of the churches of the common man and the triumph of pietism to be neglected in American religion":

In the main drift of religion in America the theological and liturgical and mystical and contemplative move into the background; the hierarchical and communal give place to the individualistic, the traditional to the immediate, the authoritative to the freely decided, the appeal to the mind and the aesthetic sense to the appeal to the will, the awareness of the ultimate

to the concern with the practical life. The penumbra of beyondness, absolute-
ness, and mystery fades away, and leaves – as the core of what Americans
think religion to be – the moral.[6]

## Voluntarism, the Source of Religious Strength

In seeking to explain the special character of American religion many of
the foreign visitors singled out the effect of the separation of church and
state, which resulted in American churches being voluntary organizations
in which congregational self-government was the predominant form
of church government. More specifically, the special quality of American
religion has been linked to three elements in the American past: first,
New England Puritanism infused certain ascetic values into the very
concept of Protestantism – the Puritans' "Protestant ethic" lay close to the
heart of most denominations, regardless of doctrinal differences; second,
ideological emphases and institutional changes which flowed from the
American Revolution led to forms of church organization analogous to
popularly based institutions; and third, the fact that all sections of the United
States were formed out of an unsettled frontier without any traditional
class structure or significant aid or control from a central government meant
that religious institutions had to be created almost completely from
the resources of the local population, and hence closely reflected their
specific religious needs and their secular values.

It is difficult to separate out the contributions of each of these, and of
other factors. As in all complex structures, the various elements tend to
interact continually. Thus, Puritanism has been credited with supplying
much of the motivation behind the Revolution. Congregationalist pastors
overwhelmingly backed the Revolution, while the hierarchically organized
Episcopalians tended to be Tories. Congregationalism, with its stress on
self-government within the church, contributed to secular self-government
in the form of the New England town meeting. Comparative studies of
frontier settlement in Canada, Latin America, and Australia have suggested
that part of the democratic aspects of American frontier settlement
reflected the American ethos and political system, not simply the needs
of any new frontier society. In Canada . . . central authorities played a much
greater role in settling and governing the frontier than was true in the
United States. And in examining developments in American religion,
it seems obvious that the ideology which flowed from the Revolution
and the subsequent political triumph of the "left" in the early decades of
the Republic led to the decisive decision in favor of "disestablishment."
The withdrawal of government support from religion made American
Protestantism unique in the Christian world. The United States became
the first nation in which religious groups were viewed as purely voluntary

associations. To exist, American churches had to compete in the market-place for support. And conversely, membership in a given religious denomination was a voluntary act.

This emphasis on voluntary associations which struck Tocqueville and other foreign travelers as one of the distinctive American traits, and which was also supportive of political democracy, has been traced by some as essentially derivative from "voluntary religion." Sidney Mead points out that even the Episcopalians became consciously aware of the fact that with the end of the Revolution they could now exist only as "voluntary associations" (a term explicitly used in such an analysis by an Episcopalian minister). This meant they had to involve the laity in church government, and that a priest would have only as much influence as there was good opinion of his ability. As Mead says, "the acceptance of religious freedom and separation" came to mean that ministers had only "persuasive or political power."[7]

The end of religious Establishment and the growth of the sects meant that a new structure of moral authority had to be created to replace the once dominant link between Church and State. In New England, many Congregationalist ministers and laymen consciously recognized that they had to establish voluntary organizations to safeguard morality in a democratic society that deemphasized the links between Church and Government. The early organization of local and national associations for domestic missionary work, for the distribution of Bibles, for temperance, for opposition to slavery, and for peace, was invariably undertaken by well-to-do religious people, and by ministers adhering to the historic New England denominations, who felt these were the only ways they could preserve and extend a moral society. Eventually a host of voluntary groups developed around the voluntary churches.

> The separation of Church and State, and other causes, have given rise to a new species of social organization, before unknown in history.... Then opened on the American world the new era of the Religious and Benevolent Society system, and summoned into the field an immense body of superior and highly-cultivated talent....
>
> As to the right or wrong of these institutions, or as to whether they are good or bad, is not, in this place, a subject of inquiry; but simply the fact of their social importance, and their power.... And it happens, that these voluntary associations are so numerous, so great, so active and influential, that, as a whole, they now constitute the great school of public education, in the formation of those practical opinions, religious, social, and political, which lead the public mind and govern the country....[8]

American Protestantism, although Calvinist in origin, fairly early in its history became Arminian. A large majority of the Calvinist denominations, as well as most of the non-Calvinist ones, came to accept the Arminian "doctrines of free will, free grace, and unlimited hope for the conversion of all men."[9] To maintain themselves after disestablishment, practically all the Protestant groups had become proselytizing churches. And the Calvinist belief in predestination "could hardly survive amidst the evangelists' earnest entreaties to 'come to Jesus.' "[10] American Protestantism, with its emphasis on the personal achievement of grace, reinforced the stress on personal achievement which was dominant in the secular value system. Both sets of values stressed individual responsibility, both rejected hereditary status. The two dominant denominations, the Methodists and the Baptists, which contained most Protestants, stressed religious doctrines that reinforced "anti-aristocratic tendencies."[11] Here again it is possible to suggest an interacting complex. An early nineteenth-century analyst of American religion argued that the reason that these denominations outgrew others was that the "disciplinary habits, the political opinions, and ideological tenets, both of the Baptists and Wesleyans, are more congenial to American democracy, than those of the better educated and more accomplished religious sects. . . . Hence – the political opinions of America having been before determined – those forms of religion best adapted to harmonize with them, were likely to prevail most. . . ."[12] To understand the character and strength of religion in America, it is therefore important to see its fundamental links with the prevalent secular values.

The fact of disestablishment, that is, the absence of a state church, served also to enhance the application of religious morality to politics. The existence of a state Church in Europe meant that "even 'sin,' in European culture had been institutionalized."

> There, an actual place had been made for it in life's crucial experience. It had been classified from time out of mind and given specific names; the reality of "lust," "avarice," and "oppression" had given rise to the most intricate of social arrangements, not for eliminating them, but for softening their impact and limiting their scope – for protecting the weak and defining the responsibilities of the strong. . . . All this may well have been in [Henry] James's mind when he exclaimed of America: "*no church.*"
>
> What, then, might be expected to happen if *sin* should suddenly become apparent, in a nation whose every individual was, at least symbolically, expected to stand on his own two feet? The reaction was altogether destructive. The sense of outrage was personal, the sense of *personal* guilt was crushing. The gentle American of mild vices was transformed into the bloody avenger.[13]

The need to assuage the sense of personal responsibility has meant that Americans have been particularly wont to support movements for the elimination of evil by violent means if necessary. The movements for temperance and prohibition, for the abolition of slavery, for resistance to the growth of Catholicism, and most recently for the climination of Communists, have all drawn their vigor from the stress developed within American society on personal responsibility for the struggle against evil.[14]

Certainly there has been an interplay between religious and democratic values from the beginning of the nation's history. The gradual identification of Enlightenment ideals with national identity in turn affected the content of our religious values. J. Franklin Jameson explains the amazingly rapid decline of Calvinist doctrine in America after the Revolution, and its replacement by Arminian religious beliefs, not only as a reflection of the doctrinal need of evangelical revivalistic religion, but also by the assumption that, "in a period when the special privileges of individuals were being called into question or being destroyed, there would naturally be less favor for that form of theology which was dominated by the doctrine of the especial election of a part of mankind, a growing favor for forms which seemed more distinctly to be based upon the idea of the natural equality of all men."[15]

The Arminian emphasis on the personal attainment of grace, perhaps even more than the Calvinist stress on the existence of an "elect," served as a religious parallel to the secular emphasis on equality of opportunity and achievement. This parallelism, and even mutual reinforcement, was noted by many nineteenth-century foreign visitors. Unlike the situation in many European countries, in which economic materialism was viewed by the social and religious establishments – that is, the traditional aristocracy and the church – as conducive to uncouth behavior and immorality, in the United States hard work and economic ambition have been perceived as the proper activity of a devout man. Schaff commented that the "acquisition of riches is to them [the Americans] only a help toward higher spiritual and moral ends."[16] The considerable sums, as well as time, contributed to philanthropic works, which reached heights undreamed of in Europe, have also been perceived as part of the interrelationship between religious and secular activities. The emphasis on "voluntarism" in both areas has clearly been mutually reinforcing. For much of the nineteenth century many voluntary activities, such as those dealing with charity, education, and moral and social reform were closely linked to religious concerns. Men were expected to be righteous, hardworking, and ambitious. Righteousness was to be rewarded both in the present and the hereafter, and the successful had an obligation to engage in good works and to share the bounty they had attained....

... Before the Civil War, successful struggles, often led by deeply believing Protestants, were waged in many areas to eliminate any relationship between state supported education and religion. By so doing, these Protestants acknowledged the rights of all, even of the completely irreligious. In 1853, in defending a ruling that prayers "could not be required as a part of the school exercises" in New York state, a devout State Superintendent of Schools wrote as follows:

[T]he position was early, distinctly, and almost universally taken by our statesmen, legislators, and prominent friends of education – men of the warmest
religious zeal and belonging to every sect – that *religious education must be
banished from the common school and consigned to the family and church.* . . .
Accordingly, the instruction in our schools has been limited to that ordinarily included under the head of intellectual culture, and to the propagation
of those principles of morality in which all sects, and *good men belonging to
no sect*, can equally agree. . . .

Not only have the Episcopalian, the Presbyterian, the Baptist and the
Methodist met on *common* and *neutral* ground in the school room, but with
them the Unitarian, the Universalist, the Quaker and even *the denier of all
creeds*.[17]

The fact that public officials could openly advocate that the federal and
state governments must consider the rights of non-believers indicates
the extent to which many believing Protestants of the first half century
of the United States were able to tolerate religious variety. Only Catholicism, viewed by many American Protestants not as a different set of religious beliefs but as an alien conspiracy seeking to undermine the
American Way of Life, was outside the pale. . . .

The emphasis upon equality, between religions as among men, which
intensified after the American Revolution, gave the subsequent development of religious institutions in America its special character. Democratic
and religious values have grown together. The results have been that,
on the one hand, Americans see religion as essential to the support
of the democratic institutions they cherish, and therefore feel that all
Americans should profess some sort of religious faith; on the other hand,
American denominations stress the ethical side of religion which they all
have in common (and which is closely associated with other democratic
values) rather than stressing transcendental beliefs wherein they differ.
At the same time, democracy, by giving religious institutions a specific
role in American society, has allowed them to proliferate, to adjust to peculiar needs, and to have a limited influence on their members' lives.

Thus the consistency with which both secularization and widespread
adherence have distinguished American religion throughout its history
is a result of the fact that democratic values have continued to influence
the growth of religious institutions as the society has changed. In this
respect, the persistent traits in American religion resemble the constant
traits in the American character. They have continued to distinguish
America from other countries, precisely because they have stemmed
from the basic American values that have remained relatively stable as
the economy, population, and society of the country have changed.

## NOTES

1.  *Social Indicators 1976*, pp. 544, 555.
2.  Giovanni Grassi, *Notizie varie sullo stato presente della republica degli Stati Uniti dell' America* (1819), section translated in Oscar Handlin, ed., *This Was America* (Cambridge, MA: Harvard University Press, 1949), pp. 147–8.
3.  Smith, *Revivalism and Social Reform in Mid-Nineteenth Century America*, p. 37.
4.  H. Martineau, *Society in America* (New York: Saunders and Otlay, 1837), Vol. II, p. 336.
5.  A. Trollope, *North America* (New York: Alfred A. Knopf, 1951), p. 278.
6.  William Lee Miller, "American Religion and American Political Attitudes," in J. W. Smith and L. Jamison, (eds), *The Shaping of American Religion* (Princeton, NJ: Princeton University Press, 1960), p. 94.
7.  Sidney E. Mead, "The Rise of the Evangelical Conception of the Ministry in America (1607–1850)," in H. Richard Niebuhr and Daniel D. Williams, eds., *The Ministry in Historical Perspectives* (New York: Harper & Bros., 1956), pp. 214–215. An excellent, detailed analysis of the interrelationship between voluntary organizations and religious practice in the early United States may be found in Baird, *Religion in America* (New York: C. Scribner, 1855).
8.  An American Gentleman (Calvin Colton), *A Voice from America to England* (London: Henry Colburn, 1839), pp. 87–88, 97.
9.  Smith, *Revivalism and Social Reform in Mid-Nineteenth Century America* (New York: Abingdon Press, 1957), pp. 88–89.
10. *Ibid.*, p. 89.
11. *Ibid.*, pp. 24–25.
12. Calvin Colton, *A Voice from America to England*, pp. 69–70. Colton himself was an Episcopalian conservative and disliked these tendencies.
13. Stanley Elkins, *Slavery* (Chicago: University of Chicago Press, 1959), p. 35.
14. I have discussed these aspects of American political life in another publication dealing with "Religion and Politics in America," in Robert Lee, ed., *Religion and Social Conflict* (New York: Oxford University Press, 1964).
15. J. Franklin Jameson, *The American Revolution Considered as a Social Movement* (Princeton, NJ: Princeton University Press, 1926), p. 157.
16. Philip Schaff, *America: A Sketch of the Political, Social, and Religious Character of the United States of North America* (New York: S. Scribner, 1855), p. 259.
17. Cited in R. Freeman Butts, *The American Tradition in Religion and Education* (Boston: The Beacon Press, 1950), pp. 136–137. (Emphases are Butts's.)

# Bibliography

## Selected Writings of Max Weber

—— (1909) "Debattenreden auf der Tagung des Vereins für Sozialpolitik" [Debates from the Conference of the Association for Social Policy], pp. 412–23 in *Gesammelte Aufsätze zur Soziologie und Sozialpolitik*, edited by Marianne Weber. Tübingen: Mohr.

—— (1914) "Vorwort" [Introduction], pp. vii–ix in *Grundriss der Sozialökonomik, 1. Abt. Wirtschaft und Wirtschaftswissenschaft*, edited by K. Bücher, J. Schumpeter and F. Freiherr von Wieser. Tübingen: Mohr.

—— (1946a) "Capitalism and Rural Society in Germany," pp. 363–85 in *From Max Weber: Essays in Sociology*, edited and translated by H. H. Gerth and C. Wright Mills. New York: Oxford University Press.

—— (1946b) "Politics as a Vocation," pp. 77–128 in *From Max Weber: Essays in Sociology*, edited and translated by H. H. Gerth and C. Wright Mills. New York: Oxford University Press.

—— (1946c) "Religious Rejections of the World," pp. 323–59 in *From Max Weber: Essays in Sociology*, edited and translated by H. H. Gerth and C. Wright Mills. New York: Oxford University Press.

—— (1946d) "Science as a Vocation," pp. 129–56 in *From Max Weber: Essays in Sociology*, edited and translated by H. H. Gerth and C. Wright Mills. New York: Oxford University Press.

—— (1946e) "The Social Psychology of the World Religions," pp. 267–301 in *From Max Weber: Essays in Sociology*, edited and translated by H. H. Gerth and C. Wright Mills. New York: Oxford University Press.

—— (1949a) "The Meaning of 'Ethical Neutrality' in Sociology and Economics," pp. 1–49 in *The Methodology of the Social Sciences*, edited and translated by Edward A. Shils and Henry A. Finch. New York: Free Press.

—— (1949b) " 'Objectivity' in Social Science and Social Policy," pp. 50–112 in *The Methodology of the Social Sciences*, edited and translated by Edward A. Shils and Henry A. Finch. New York: Free Press.

—— (1951) *The Religion of China*, edited and translated by Hans H. Gerth. New York: Free Press.

—— (1952) *Ancient Judaism*, edited and translated by Hans H. Gerth and Don Martindale. New York: Free Press.

—— (1958) *The Religion of India*, edited and translated by Hans H. Gerth and Don Martindale. New York: Free Press.

—— (1961) *General Economic History*, translated by Frank H. Knight. New York: Free Press.

—— (1968a) *Economy and Society*, edited by Guenther Roth and Claus Wittich. New York: Bedminster Press (reprinted by the University of California Press, 1978).

—— (1968b) "Parliament and Government in a Reconstructed Germany," pp. 1381–1469 in *Economy and Society*, edited by Guenther Roth and Claus Wittich. New York: Bedminster Press.

—— (1971 [1958]) *Gesammelte Politische Schriften*, edited by Johannes Winckelmann. Tübingen: Mohr.

—— (1972 [1920]) *Gesammelte Aufsätze zur Religionssoziologie*, 3 vols. Tübingen: Mohr.

—— (1973a [1922]) *Gesammelte Aufsätze zur Wissenschaftslehre*, edited by Johannes Winckelmann. Tübingen: Mohr.

—— (1973b [1903–6]) "Roscher und Knies und die logischen Probleme der historischen Nationalökonomie," pp. 1–145 in *Gesammelte Aufsätze zur Wissenschaftslehre*, edited by Johannes Winckelmann. Tübingen: Mohr.

—— (1976a) *Agrarian Sociology of Ancient Civilizations*, translated by R. I. Frank. London: NLB.

—— (1976b [1921]) *Wirtschaft und Gesellschaft: Grundriss der verstehenden Soziologie.* Edited by Johannes Winckelmann. Tübingen: Mohr.

—— (1977) *Critique of Stammler*, translated by Guy Oakes. New York: Free Press.

—— (1978) "The Prospects for Liberal Democracy in Tsarist Russia," pp. 269–84 in *Weber: Selections in Translation*, edited by W. G. Runciman and translated by Eric Matthews. Cambridge: Cambridge University Press.

—— (1984) *Max Weber Gesamtausgabe* [Collected Works], edited by Horst Baier, M. Rainer Lepsius, Wolfgang J. Mommsen, Wolfgang Schluchter and Johannes Winckelmann. Tübingen: Mohr [in progress].

—— (1985) "'Churches' and 'Sects' in North America: An Ecclesiastical Socio-Political Sketch," translated by Colin Loader. *Sociological Theory* 3, Spring: 7–13.

—— (1988a [1929]) *Gesammelte Aufsätze zur Soziologie und Sozialpolitik*, edited by Marianne Weber. Tübingen: Mohr.

—— (1988b [1924]) "Zum Vortrag von F. Oppenheimer über 'Die rassen-theoretische Geschichtsphilosophie,'" pp. 488–91 in *Gesammelte Aufsätze zur Sociologie und Sozialpolitik*, edited by Marianne Weber. Tübingen: Mohr.

—— (1994) *Political Writings*, edited by Peter Lassman and Ronald Speirs. New York: Cambridge University Press.

—— (1995 [1908–12]) *Zur Psychophysik der industriellen Arbeit* [On the Psychological Physics of Industrial Labor], edited by Wolfgang Schluchter. Tübingen: Mohr.

—— (2001) *The Protestant Ethic Debate: Max Weber's Replies to his Critics, 1907–10*, edited by David J. Chalcraft and Austin Harrington and translated by Austin Harrington and Mary Shields. Liverpool: Liverpool University Press.

—— (2002a) "'Prefatory Remarks' to Collected Essays on the Sociology of Religion (1920)," pp. 149–64 in *The Protestant Ethic and the Spirit of Capitalism*, translated by Stephen Kalberg. Los Angeles: Roxbury Publishing Co.

—— (2002b) *The Protestant Ethic and the Spirit of Capitalism*, translated by Stephen Kalberg. Los Angeles: Roxbury Publishing Co.

—— (2002c) "The Protestant Sects and the Spirit of Capitalism," pp. 127–49 in *The Protestant Ethic and the Spirit of Capitalism*, translated by H. H. Gerth and C. Wright Mills. Los Angeles: Roxbury Publishing Co.

## Secondary Literature Cited

Beetham, David. (1974) *Max Weber and the Theory of Modern Politics*. London: Allen & Unwin.

Etzioni, Amitai. (1997) *The New Golden Rule*. New York: Basic Books.

—— (ed.) (1998) *The Essential Communitarian Reader*. New York: Rowman & Littlefield.

Evans, Peter, Skocpol, Theda and Rueschemeyer, Dietrich (eds) (1984) *Bringing the State Back In*. New York: Cambridge University Press.

Kalberg, Stephen. (1980) "Max Weber's Types of Rationality: Cornerstones for the Analysis of Rationalization Processes in History," *American Journal of Sociology* 85, 3: 1145–79.

—— (1994) *Max Weber's Comparative-Historical Sociology*. Chicago: University of Chicago Press.

—— (1997a) "Max Weber's Sociology: Research Strategies and Modes of Analysis," pp. 208–41 in *Reclaiming the Argument of the Founders*, edited by Charles Camic Cambridge, MA: Blackwell.

—— (1997b) "Tocqueville and Weber on the Sociological Origins of Citizenship: The Political Culture of American Democracy," *Citizenship Studies* 1, 2 (July): 199–222.

—— (2001a) "The Modern World as a Monolithic Iron Cage? Utilizing Max Weber to Define the Internal Dynamics of the American Political Culture Today," *Max Weber Studies* 1, 2 (May): 178–95.

—— (2001b) "Should the 'Dynamic Autonomy' of Ideas Matter to Sociologists? Max Weber on the Origin of Other-Worldly Salvation Religions and the Constitution of Groups in American Society Today," *Journal of Classical Sociology* 1, 3 (Dec.): 291–327.

—— (2002) "Introduction to *The Protestant Ethic*," pp. xi–lxxvi in *Max Weber: The Protestant Ethic and the Spirit of Capitalism*. Los Angeles: Roxbury Publishing Co.

—— (2003a) "Max Weber," pp. 132–92 in *The Blackwell Companion to Major Social Theorists*, edited by George Ritzer. Oxford: Blackwell.

—— (2003b) "The Influence of Political Culture upon Cross-Cultural Misperceptions and Foreign Policy: The United States and Germany," *German Politics and Society* 21, 3 (Fall): 1–24.

Levine, Donald N. (1985) "Rationality and Freedom, Inveterate Multivocals," pp. 142–78 in, *The Flight From Ambiguity*. Chicago: University of Chicago Press.

Mommsen, Wolfgang. (1974) "Die Vereinigten Staaten von Amerika," pp. 72–96 in Wolfgang Mommsen, *Gesellschaft, Politik und Gesellschaft*. Frankfurt: Suhrkamp.

Roth, Guenther. (1968) "Introduction," pp. xxvii–cviii in Max Weber, *Economy and Society*, edited and translated by Guenther Roth and Claus Wittich. New York: Bedminster Press.

—— (1985) "Marx and Weber on the United States – Today," pp. 215–33 in *A Marx–Weber Dialogue*, edited by Robert J. Antonio and Ronald M. Glassman. Lawrence, KS: University Press of Kansas.

Salomon, Albert. (1935) "Max Weber's Political Ideas," *Social Research* II, Feb.: 369–84.

Skocpol, Theda (1979) *States and Social Revolutions*. New York: Cambridge University Press.

Tocqueville, Alexis de. (1945) *Democracy in America*, vol. 2, translated by Henry Reeve and revised by Francis Bowen. New York: Vintage Books.

## Further Reading

### *On Weber's life and political views*

Breiner, Peter. (1996) *Max Weber and Democratic Politics*. Ithaca, NY: Cornell University Press.

Coser, Lewis A. (1971) "Max Weber: The Man," pp. 234–43 in *Masters of Sociological Thought*. New York: Harcourt Brace Jovanovich.

Gerth, Hans H. (1946) "Introduction," pp. 3–74 in *From Max Weber: Essays in Sociology*, edited by H. H. Gerth and C. Wright Mills. New York: Oxford University Press.

Honigsheim, Paul. (1968) *On Max Weber*. New York: Free Press.

Kaesler, Dirk. (1988) "Life," pp. 1–23 in *Max Weber: An Introduction to his Life and Work*, translated by Philippa Hurd. Chicago: University of Chicago Press.

Kilker, Ernst. (1993) "Weber and Plebiscitarian Democracy," *International Journal of Politics, Culture and Society* 7, Winter: 429–65.

Loewenstein, Karl. (1966) *Max Weber's Political Ideas in the Perspective of Our Time*. Amherst: University of Massachusetts Press.

Mommsen, Wolfgang J. and Osterhammel, Jürgen (eds) (1987) *Max Weber and his Contemporaries*. London: Unwin Hyman.

Roth, Guenther. (2000) "Global Capitalism and Multiethnicity: Max Weber Then and Now," pp. 117–30 in *The Cambridge Companion to Weber*, edited by Stephen Turner. New York: Cambridge University Press.

—— (2001) *Max Webers deutsch-englische Familiengeschichte, 1800–1950*. Tübingen: Mohr.

—— (2002) "Max Weber: Family History, Economic Policy, Exchange Reform," *International Journal of Politics, Culture and Society* 15, 3: 509–20.

Weber, Marianne. (1975) *Max Weber*, translated by Harry Zohn. New York: Wiley.

Whimster, Sam (ed.) (1998) *Max Weber and the Culture of Anarchy*. London: Macmillan.

### *Further interpretations of Weber's sociology*

Albrow, Martin. (1990) *Max Weber's Construction of Social Theory*. New York: St Martin's Press.

Bendix, Reinhard and Roth, Guenther (1971) *Scholarship and Partisanship: Essays on Max Weber.* Berkeley, CA: University of California Press.

Berger, Thomas. (1976) *Max Weber's Theory of Concept Formation: History, Laws, and Ideal Types.* Durham, NC: Duke University Press.

Bruun, H. H. (1972) *Science, Values and Politics in Max Weber's Methodology.* Copenhagen: Munksgaard.

Collins, Randall. (1986) *Weberian Sociological Theory.* New York: Cambridge University Press.

Eliason, Sven. (2002) *Max Weber's Methodologies.* Cambridge: Polity Press.

Habermas, Jürgen. (1984) *The Theory of Communicative Action,* vol. 1, trans. Thomas McCarthy. Boston: Beacon Press.

Hennis, Wilhelm. (1988) *Max Weber: Essays in Reconstruction.* London: Allen & Unwin.

—— (2000) *Max Weber's Central Question.* Cambridge, MA: MIT Press.

Honigsheim, Paul. (2000) *The Unknown Max Weber,* edited by Alan Sica. New Brunswick, NJ: Transaction Publishers.

Huff, Toby and Schluchter, Wolfgang (eds) (1999) *Max Weber and Islam.* New Brunswick, NJ: Transaction Press.

Kalberg, Stephen. (1994) "Max Weber's Analysis of the Rise of Monotheism: A Reconstruction," *British Journal of Sociology* 45, 4 (Dec.): 563–83.

—— (1996) "On the Neglect of Weber's *Protestant Ethic* as a Theoretical Treatise: Demarcating the Parameters of Post-War American Sociological Theory," *Sociological Theory* 14, 1 (March): 49–70.

—— (1999) "Max Weber's Critique of Recent Comparative-Historical Sociology and a Reconstruction of his Analysis of the Rise of Confucianism in China," pp. 207–46 in *Current Perspectives in Social Theory,* vol. 19, edited by Jennifer Lehmann. Stamford, CT: JAI Press.

Lehmann, Hartmut and Roth, Guenther (eds) (1993) *Weber's Protestant Ethic: Origins, Evidence, Contexts.* New York: Cambridge University Press.

Löwith, Karl. (1982) *Max Weber and Karl Marx.* London: Allen & Unwin.

Marshall, Gordon. (1980) *Presbyteries and Profits: Calvinism and the Development of Capitalism in Scotland, 1560–1707.* Oxford: Clarendon Press.

—— (1982) *In Search of the Spirit of Capitalism.* London: Hutchinson.

Mommsen, Wolfgang J. (1989) *The Political and Social Theory of Max Weber.* Chicago: University of Chicago Press.

Nelson, Benjamin. (1981) *On the Roads to Modernity: Conscience, Science, and Civilizations,* edited by Toby E. Huff. Totowa, NJ: Rowman & Littlefield.

Poggi, Gianfranco. (1983) *Calvinism and the Capitalist Spirit: Max Weber's "Protestant Ethic".* Amherst, MA: University of Massachusetts Press.

Ray, Larry and Reed, Michael (eds) (1994) *Organizing Modernity: New Weberian Perspectives on Work, Organization and Society.* London: Routledge.

Ringer, Fritz. (1997) *Max Weber's Methodology.* Cambridge, MA: Harvard University Press.

—— (2004) *Max Weber: An Intellectual Biography.* Chicago: University of Chicago Press.

Scaff, Lawrence A. (1989) *Fleeing the Iron Cage: Culture, Politics, and Modernity in the Thought of Max Weber.* Berkeley, CA: University of California Press.

—— (1998) "The 'Cool Subjectivity of Sociation': Max Weber and Marianne Weber in America," *History of the Human Sciences* 11: 61–82.

Schluchter, Wolfgang. (1989) *Rationalism, Religion, and Domination: A Weberian Perspective.* Berkeley, CA: University of California Press.

—— (1996) *Paradoxes of Modernity*, translated by Neil Solomon. Stanford, CA: Stanford University Press.

Schroeder, Ralph (ed.) (1998) *Max Weber, Democratization and Modernization.* New York: St Martin's Press.

Swedberg, Richard (1998) *Max Weber and the Idea of Economic Sociology.* Princeton, NJ: Princeton University Press.

Tenbruck, F. H. (1980) "The Problem of Thematic Unity in the Works of Max Weber," *British Journal of Sociology* 31, 2: 313–51.

Turner, Bryan S. (1992) *Max Weber: From History to Modernity.* London: Routledge.

Whimster, Sam and Lash, Scott (eds) (1987) *Max Weber, Rationality and Modernity.* London: Allen & Unwin.

## Weber Bibliographies

Kaesler, Dirk. (1988) "Weber's Works in German," pp. 242–75 in *Max Weber: An Introduction to his Life and Work.* Chicago: University of Chicago Press.

Sica, Alan (ed.) (2004) *Max Weber: A Comprehensive Bibliography.* New Brunswick, NJ: Transaction Publishers. (Weber's works available in English and commentary on Weber; 5,000 items listed.)

# Author Index

Note: Information in notes is signified by n after the page number.

Aptheker, Herbert 295n6

Baird, Robert 375n7
Butts, R. Freeman 375n17

Colton, Calvin 375n8, n12
Conrad-Martius, Hedwig 294n5
Curtiss, John 352n2

Eldridge, J. E. T. 313n2
Elkins, Stanley 375n13
Etzioni, Amitai 46n33
Evans, Peter 224n1

Gasman, Daniel 294n5
Gittleman, Jerome 294n1

Handlin, Oscar 375n2
Haxthausen, Baron von 352n3
Hecker, Max 340n1
Honigsheim, Paul 8

Jamison, L. 375n6

Kalberg, Stephen 9, 17, 19, 21–2, 24, 37,
    41n1, 42n5, 44n13–17, n19–21, n24,
    46n31, 47n39, 51, 63n3, 64n15, 73, 74n2,
    275
Krieger, Leonard 271n1

Lee, Robert 375n1
Levine, Donald N. 45n29

Manasse, Ernst 294n1
Miller, William Lee 375n6
Mommsen, Wolfgang 32, 208n1
Mosse, George 294n5

Nelson, Benjamin 294n1
Niebuhr, H. Richard 375n7

Perry, John 352n1
Peukert, Detlev 294n2
Putnam, Peter 352n1

Roth, Guenther 45n27, 47n39, 208n2,
    229n2, 295n7

Salomon, Albert 35
Schluchter, Wolfgang 44n16
Skocpol, Theda 224n1
Smith, J. W. 375n6
Smith, T. L. 375n3, n9

Tocqueville, Alexis de 74n5, 275

Weber, Marianne 229n2, 294n1
Williams, Daniel D. 375n7

Zmarzlik, Hans-Günter 294n5

# Subject Index

accounting
  formal rationality of 127, 129
  in Western capitalism 59, 61
action *see* ethical action; social action
administration
  accumulation of knowledge 353–4
  bureaucratization of 137–8
  democratic 186–8
  domination and 186–8
  expansion of 211–14
  by *honoratiores* 198–201
  mass 188
  monocratic 188
  required by modern capitalism 49, 61–2,
    65–6, 122, 127, 129
adventure capitalism 58, 92–3
aesthetics 317
  presuppositions 327
  *see also* art
affectual social action 11
affinity
  elective 83
  ethnic 300–1, 302
agency: bureaucratic 194–5
agriculture: Protestant ethic and 98
  *see also* land; rural social structure
allegiance, oaths of 284
Alsatians 226
American Revolution 370
anomie 275–6
anonymity: of modern life 275–6
antipathy: towards racial groups 291,
  297–8
Antiquity *see* Greece, Ancient; Rome,
  Ancient
Apocrypha 91
appearance, physical *see* differences, visible
Aquinas, Thomas 89
  on work 88

architecture: Western 54
aristocracy
  England 165
  Germany 163
  US 145, 150, 166–7
  *see also honoratiores*
Aristophanes 235
Aristotle 54, 324
army: bureaucracy 212
art
  inspiration in 141
  intimacy of 339
  Puritan position toward 94–5
  Renaissance 317, 324
  by status groups 159
  Western 54–5
  *see also* aesthetics
ascetic Protestantism 24–6
  influence on American democracy
    367–75
  US 8, 31–2, 273
  work ethic 69–74, 347–52
asceticism
  inner-worldly 25, 31, 117–18, 351,
    363–4
  other-worldly 25
  spirit of capitalism and 85–107
  testifying belief through 84–5
Asia
  administration 66
  protection against Western individual
    self 64–5
  *see also* specific countries
associations
  political: source of ethnic groups 292
  US civic 73, 276, 371
    economic help through 113–14
    ethical actions 31–2
    exclusive 274–5, 286, 287, 288

astronomy
  presuppositions 326
  Western 53
atomization 286
attraction: racial differences and 299
Austria: as nation 225
Australia: frontier settlement 370
authority 38
  attitude to formal justice 241–2
  bureaucratic (rational-legal) 173, 175–6,
    190, 192–3, 219
  charismatic 22, 175, 176–7, 191,
    192–3
    administration 218–19, 220
    Hitler 361–2
    irrationality of 217, 219
    legitimacy 217, 219
    notion of 345
    routinization of 219–20, 268–9, 345,
      363–6
    succession 220
  in groups 162
  hostility to 278–9, 284
  labor management and 347–52
  legitimate 174–5
  modern 173–8
  traditional 22, 175, 190, 192–3, 219
  United States 371
  Weber's formulation 174
  *see also* domination
autonomy *see* individual, autonomy of

Bacon, Francis 324
Bakuninism 215
banks 58, 360
  economic interest in war 235
Baptists 112–13, 114, 115
  freedom of conscience 281, 283
  US 372
Barclay, Robert 86, 96
bargaining: status groups 161
Baudelaire, Charles 330
Baumgarten, Ida 8
Baxter, Richard 72, 91, 92, 93, 98, 103
  on authority 278–9
  *Christian Directory* 86
  on vocational calling 86–90
Belgium: rural social structures 143
belief
  as basis for authority 174–5, 192
  testifying 25, 84–5, 117, 118
Bernstein, Eduard 115–16
Besant, Walter 56
biology: race and 312–13

Bismarck, Otto von: bureaucracy 215
Black people, in United States 226
  relationship with whites 293
  smell of 310
  status of 298, 311
Blok, Alexander 350
blood
  disaffinity 292
  of the race 307–8
*Book of Sports* 93
bourgeoisie: concept of 60
  *see also* middle classes
Britain
  Data Protection Act 353–6
  parliament 262
  *see also* England
brotherliness 338–9
Browne, Robert 281
Buddha 343
Buddhism 158
Bunyan, John 99–100
bureaucracy 3, 355
  authority of 173–8
  controlled by politicians 255–71
  difficulty of destroying 214–16
  discipline of 122–3, 215
  domination of 34–5
  ethical action and 247–8
  ethos of office 201–4
  expansion of 211–14
  external form 194–7
  impact upon society 209–16
  inequality and 204–7
  in modern economies 130–1
  patrimonial 216
  political problems 257
  power of 205–7
    checks to 4
  rationality and 353–4
  right to the office 202
  superiority over administration by
    *honoratiores* 198–201
  *see also* officials
bureaucratization
  of administration 137–8
  fast-food restaurants and 357–60
  law and 223, 240–1
Butler, Samuel 94

Caesarism 263
calculation 140, 322
  in capitalism 56–7, 61, 65
  in formal rationality 125, 127
Calderon de la Barca, Pedro 160

calling, vocational 101
  Hitler 361
  notion of 81–2, 84, 102–3, 321–2, 323
  Old Testament 91–2
  politics 271
  Puritans 84, 86, 88, 89–91
  rejuvenation of 248–9
  science as 123, 139–40, 249, 326, 333,
    334–5
  striving for profit as 79–82, 128
Calvin, John 92, 100
  on wealth 87
Calvinism 95
  community 277–8
  ethical action 268
  freedom of conscience 283
  hostility to authority 279
  on poverty 307
Canada: frontier settlement 370
capitalism 57
  adventure 58, 92–3
  compared with modern capitalism 49
  imperialist 222–3, 235–7
  modern
    control over state bureaucracies 248,
      255
    facilitated by rights of man 283
    Germany and United States compared
      123–4
    law and administration in 49, 61–2,
      65–7, 122, 127, 129
    rural social structures and 142–6
    severing from community 275–6
    uniqueness of 49–51
    Weber on 2–5
    of West 55–63
  tolerance and 281–2
  *see also* spirit of capitalism
capitalist form 77–8
carriers, social: described 23–4
cartels 169–70
castes 149, 157, 161
Catholic church, Roman
  bureaucracy 210–11
  charisma of 177
  power of 143
Catholicism, Roman
  American views of 374
  attitude to authority 279
  confession 287, 366
  ethical action 267
  freedom of conscience 282–3
  Puritan sects as antithesis to 117–18
  work 87–8
causes: politicians 260

certificates, education 123, 138
change, social: proposals for 36
charisma *see* authority, charismatic
charity 252
Charles I 93
chemistry
  presuppositions 326
  Western 53
China
  bureaucracy 210
  examinations 138
  freedom of conscience 282
  as nation 227
  obstacles to economic development
    50–1, 62
  printing 55
  rationalism 27, 51
  social carriers 24
  writing of history 54
chosen people 25, 302
Christ, Jesus 176, 343
Christianity: theology 337
churches
  disciplinary powers 116–17
  lack of community-forming energy
    285
  membership of 113
  separation from state 280–2
    in United States 369, 370–1
  social interests within 287–8
  support for peasants 143
  *see also* specific names
citizen: concept of 60
civic values
  Germany 33
  US 31–2
civil servants *see* officials
class struggles 153–4
  myth of superiority in 190
  types of 154–5
classes, social
  social action and 153–4
  status groups and 147–9, 158, 161
  Western 60–1
  *see also* aristocracy; bourgeoisie;
    *honoratiores*; Junkers; middle classes;
    proletariat; working class
clergy
  influence of 85–6
  leadership in rural districts 143
colonies: ethnicity and 300
commercialization 59
communication, speed of 199
communism 60
  substantive rationality 126

communities
  charismatic 218, 219
  effect of capitalism on 275–6
  formed by sects 277–89
  law 223, 238–9
  tribes 305–6
  US 287–8
companies, industrial: organization of
    58–9
  *see also* large-scale enterprises
compliance: to authority 174
computers: Data Protection Act 353–6
concepts: discovery of 317, 324
conduct: ascetic Protestants 273–4
confession 366
  Catholicism 287, 366
Congregationalists: American Revolution
    370
conscience, freedom of 273, 281, 282–3, 284
consciousness
  of kind 291, 299
  tribal 305
consecration 220
consumers: as workers 359–60
contract, freedom of 129
conventions: status groups 159
conviction, ethic of 265–6, 269–70, 362
cottage industries 56, 78
*coups d'état* 215
Court, Peter de la 100
craftsmen 130–1
credit ratings
  churches 116–17
  Protestant sects and 111–13, 114
Cromwell, Oliver 135
cultivated man
  meaninglessness of death 342
  replaced by specialist 123, 137–41
cults 304
  tribal 305
cultural sciences 317–18
culture
  meaninglessness of 341–3
  Puritan position toward 93–5
customs
  ethnicity and 299–300, 303–4
  formation of groups 291–2
  tribes 305, 306

data 354
  personal 354
Data Protection Act 345, 353–6
data users: principles for 354–5
death: meaninglessness of 316, 322–3, 342
Defoe, Daniel 102

democracy
  attitude to formal justice 241–2
  bureaucracy and 205, 209
  direct 263
  ethical action and 248
  influence of sects 280, 285–6
  mass 209
  parliaments and 262–4
  political concept of 210
  status groups 156
  true 262–3
  United States 332, 367–75
    political culture of 273–6
democratization 209–10
  Germany 165–7
  passive 211
  political and social 150, 166–7
devotion, religious 339
dictatorships
  charisma 361–2
  wartime 264
diet industry 360
differences, visible
  antipathy toward 291, 299–300
  ethnicity and 292, 302
dignity
  ethnic 299, 302
  Germany 167
  of status groups 149, 158
discipline
  concept of 179
  ethical 111–19
  in modern economies 122–3, 131, 132,
    135–6
  sects 116–19
disciplines, academic: Western 55
disenchantment of the world 36, 316, 322,
    339, 340
domains, societal
  autonomy of 22–3
  described 18–19
  interweaving of past and present in
    21
domination
  administration and 186–8
  advantage of the small number 188–9
  characteristics 189
  concept of 179
  definition 181, 184–5
  legitimacy 189–91, 192–3
  power and 180–6
  relationships of 185–6
  types of 181–4
  valid bases of 188–91
  *see also* authority

Dostoievski, Fyodor 266, 269
Dowden, Edward 99–100
dress, Puritan 95
Durkheim, Emile 4, 11
  anomie 275–6
  capitalism 2–3
dynamism, societal 3

Early Modern: science 317
East: protection against Western individual
  self 64–5
economic ethics 26, 101–2, 121–2
  modern *see* spirit of capitalism
  of religion 50
  traditional 25–6, 121–2
economic factors
  multicausality and 22–3
  status stratification and 159–61
economic form 26
economic foundations: of imperialism
  222–3, 234–7
economic materialism: United States 373
economic power 151–3, 180–1
  of bureaucracies 204–7
economy
  ethical action and 245–7, 251–3
  market 122, 125–9
  planned 122, 125–9
  universal suffrage and 169–70
education
  capitalism and 144
  certificates and examinations in 123,
    137–8, 332
  privilege and 168–9
  religion and in United States 373–4
efficiency 359–60
emigration: ethnicity and 292, 300, 301,
  303
emotional detachment: Puritans 351
England
  aristocracy 165
  attitude to authority 278
  examinations 137–8
  farmers 142
  guilds 119
  industries 101
  justice 242
  labor management 345, 347–8
  law 66, 81
  national character 98
  parliament 261
  political parties 213
  political party donors 205
  Puritans 94
  work ethic 70

Enlightenment 81, 283
enterprise, bureaucratic 194
*Entseelung*, concept of 361
Episcopalians: American Revolution
  370
equality: United States 374
  *see also* inequality
esteem, social *see* honor
ethical action 245–9
  economy and 251–3
  politics and 253–4
ethics
  market 252
  religious 252, 267
  *see also* conviction, ethic of; economic
    ethics; responsibility, ethic of;
    Protestant
ethnic groups
  dissolution of concept 306
  as status groups 149, 157–8
ethnicity
  concept of 291–2, 299–304
  concept of nation and 226
  group formation 292
  sexual relations and 297–8
  symbols of 292, 303
eugenics 292–3, 307
Europe: rural social structures 142–6
  *see also* specific countries
examinations 123, 137–8, 332
  in bureaucracies 202
exclusivities: United States 274–5, 286, 287,
  288
experiments
  appearance of 324
  controlled 61
experts: in bureaucracies 200, 206,
  207

factories
  discipline in 135–6
  labor management 348
  *see also* large-scale enterprises
farmers 142
Fichte, Johann 265, 269
Florence 79
formal rationality *see* rationality
Förster, F. W. 266, 328
frame of mind 24
France
  bureaucracy 210
  guilds 119
  political parties 213
  practical rationalism 81
Francis of Assisi 343

Franklin, Benjamin 79, 80, 87
  spirit of capitalism 70, 75–7, 78, 102
fraternities, student
  Germany 164, 165
  United States 289
Frederick II, Emperor 282
freedoms: legal guarantees of 223, 242,
  243–4
frenzy, prophetic 339
frontier settlement 370
Fugger, Jakob 77
future: fears for 34–6

Galileo 324
Gandhi, Mahatma 176, 362
gas stations 359–60
geography 313
Germany
  attitude to authority 278
  bureaucracy 176, 215
  eugenics 292–3
  examinations 137, 332
  individualism 274, 285
  inequality 150
  language 180
  modern capitalism 124
  modernity 32–3
  officials 143
  parliament 261–2
  political parties 213
  political party donors 205
  politics 8, 36
  rural social structures 142–6
  social honor 288
  social stratification 163–7
  status groups 156
  unified economic territory 234–5
  universal suffrage 150, 168–71
Goering, Hermann 361
Goethe, Johann Wolfgang von 3, 7, 269, 274
  asceticism 102
Goldschmidt, Levin 7
grace, state of 90
Grassi, Giovanni 368–9
Great Powers
  expansion 234–7
  power prestige 233
  see also specific countries
Greece, Ancient: science in 317, 323–4
Gregory VII 210
groups 284–5, 286
  foundation of 18–19
  inequality in 147–50, 151–62
  race and ethnicity and 291–2
  United States 273–5

guilds
  ethics 118–19
  as status groups 148

Haeckel, Ernst 293
Hansa League 205
Hebraism: English 92
Hegel, G. W. F. 7
Helmholtz, Hermann von 140, 141
heredity 293–4, 309–10
hierarchy
  bureaucracies 195
  not with charismatic authority 218
history
  course of 149
  interweaving of past and present in
    20–1
Hitler, Adolf 176
  charisma 345, 361–2
holism, positivist and organic: Weber on
  19–20
Holland
  asceticism 97
  language 180
  Protestant ethic 101
  Puritans 94–5
  tolerance 281–2
homogeneity: concept of nation and
  226
honor 288–9
  ethnic 292, 299, 301, 302
  groups 147, 151–2
  power and 151–2
  status groups 155–7, 157–8, 160–1
  United States 275
  see also prestige
*honoratiores*
  administration by 198–201
  definition 187–8
household: separation from industry 59

ideal types
  authority 174–5, 176
  autonomy of 22–3
  of class and status 149
  described 15–16
  interweaving of past and present in
    20–1
  as models 16–17
ideas 140–1
Ihering, Rudolph von 141
imitation: ethnicity and 300
imperialism
  economic foundations of 234–7
  states 222–3

India
  calculation 61
  castes 149, 161
  experiments 324
  freedom of conscience 282
  logic 324
  obstacles to economic development
    50–1, 62
  rationalism 27, 51
  social carriers 24
  state theorizing 54
Indians, in United States: social esteem of
    293, 298, 311
individual, autonomy of 8, 244
  destruction in revolutionary movements
    364
  science and 318
  in sects 118, 277–89
  uninfluenced by science 315–16
  United States 273–5, 285–6
industrialization: Russia 350–1
inequality
  bureaucracy and 204–7
  social stratification and 147–50,
    151–62
  universal suffrage and 168–71
inspiration 141
instincts: race 310–11
intellectual sacrifice see sacrifice
intellectualization 322–3, 339
interpretative understanding see
    understanding
Italy
  practical rationalism 81
  rural social structures 143

James I 93
James, William 114
Jameson, J. Franklin 373
Japan
  freedom of conscience 282
  social carriers 24
Jellinek, Georg 283
Jews
  as nation 226
  as status group 157, 158
Job, Book of 91–2
Judaism 92–3
Junkers 150, 163–7
jurisprudence 317
  presuppositions 327
  see also law
justice
  administration and 200–1
  formal 223, 241–2

kadi-justice 66, 200
  nonformal 242

kadi-justice 200
  definition 66
Kant, Immanuel 7, 337, 353, 355
King, Martin Luther 176
knowledge 320
  in bureaucracies 204, 207, 353–4
  progress of 316
  religion and 319, 340–1
  religious 340–1
Kürnberger, Ferdinand 76, 77
Kürung 220

labor
  coerced 58, 132
    see also slaves
  division of 89
  free 49, 58–9, 60–1, 129
    see also work
labor management: England and Russia
    345, 347–52
land
  forceful acquisition of 235
  Protestant ethic and 97–8
language
  concept of nation and 225–6
  domination and 180
  ethnicity and 292, 301–2
large-scale enterprises 129
  bureaucracy 212
  labor management 348, 350–1
  in modern economies 134
  separation of workers from tools of
    trade 122
Latin America: frontier settlement 370
Laud, William 101
law 327
  bureaucratization 213–14, 223, 240–1
  Islamic 239
  modern 223–4
  natural 66–7
  private 213
  propositions 243
  public 213
  rationalization of 81
  required by modern capitalism 49, 50–1,
    61–2, 65–7, 129
  Roman 239
  special 223, 238–9
  status groups and 149
  Western 54
  see also jurisprudence
lawyers: as politicians 262

leadership: teachers 332–3
Lenin 176, 345, 350, 362
 revolutionary movement 364–5
Leonardo da Vinci 317, 324
Liebig, Justus 212
life
 everyday, and ethnicity 292, 302
 knowledge of conditions of 322
 meaninglessness of 316, 323
 organization of 70, 79–80, 93–6
life styles
 ethnicity and 300
 status groups 156, 159, 161
location 17–19
love, brotherly 306–7
Lukács, Georg von 338
Luther, Martin 268, 270
 on status groups 89
Lutheran Church 143
 freedom of conscience 283
Luxembourg: as nation 227

Machiavelli, Niccolò 269
management *see* labor management
markets
 class situation and 152–3
 colonies and 300
 free
  consequences of 246
  ethics and 252
  impersonality of 251–2
  law and 223, 240–1
  open 121, 129
  planned 121
  public administration and 199
  Puritan attitude to 274
  state and 231–2
  status groups and 148, 155, 159–61
marriage
 colonies 300
 ethnicity and 297–8
 Middle Ages 307
 Puritan 88
 status groups 156, 159
Martineau, Harriet 369
Marx, Karl 4, 11, 122
 alienation 356
 capitalism 2, 3
 inequality 147
Marxism-Leninism 365
mass behavior 148, 154
mathematics
 inspiration in 141
 Western 61
Mayer, Robert 140

McDonalization 345, 357–60
Mead, Sidney 371
meaning, subjective 18, 71
 of social action 10–12
means and ends: science 318–19, 333–4
means–end rational social action 10–11
mechanics: Western 53
medicine 317
 presuppositions 326–7
 Western 53
Methodists 99
 business ethics 116
 United States 372
middle classes
 capitalism 60–1, 72, 78
 Germany 163–4
 membership of civic associations 113–14
 Protestant ethic and 91, 98, 100, 101–2, 115, 118
 religion 285
 *see also* bourgeoisie
migration: ethnicity and 292, 300, 301, 303
Mill, James 330
ministers: United States 371
miracles 330
mission, culture 221–2, 228
model-building: Weber 16–17
models: open-ended 20, 21
modernity: Weber on 37
 *see also* rationalism, modern Western
Mommsen, Theodor 7
monarchs: need for parliaments with 263
monasticism
 asceticism 84–5
 wealth 98–9
monopolies
 domination and 181–4
 status groups 149, 158–9, 160
morality
 in American Protestantism 369–70
 revolutionary movements 364
 United States 371
Moses: law of 92
motives: pluralism of 11–12
movements, social: United States 346, 368, 372–3
multicausality: Weber 6, 22–7
music 324
 Western 54

nation: concept of 221–2, 225–9
national character 86
 England 98
national sentiments 221, 227–8

natural law: Western 66–7
natural sciences 326
  presuppositions 327
  Western 53, 61
nature: science and 324–5
Negroes *see* Black people
neutrality, ethical: of teachers 328–35
New England 94, 346
  asceticism 97
  morality 371
New York 184
Nietzsche, Friedrich 35, 36, 158, 325
notables *see* honoratiores

obedience
  to authority 174
  duty to 181–4
  to institution 365–6
  in revolutionary movements 364
objectivity 12–14
  business 199–200
occupations
  specialization of 89, 91, 102
  stratification of 89
officials
  in charismatic authority 218, 220
  election of 196–7
  fixed position of 214
  Germany 166
  impartiality of 257
  in modern economies 130
  power of 122, 133, 143
  salaries and career 197
  Western 55
officers: Germany 163–4
Old Testament 93
  vocational calling 91–2
organization of life 70, 79–80, 93–6
ossification 3, 34, 35, 247, 248
other, the 12
ownership
  influence on social class 147
  in modern economies 122, 133
  social stratification and 152–3

Pandectist Civil Law 223, 242–3
pariah peoples 157, 158
Parker, Matthew 101
parliaments
  control of heads of bureaucracy 257
  Germany 150
  need for powerful 248
  role of strong 260–4
  universal suffrage 169, 170
  Western 55

parties 149–50, 161–2
  political: bureaucracy 213
passion: politicians 258–9
patriarchalism 191
  ethical action 246, 254
  race and 298
Paul, St 88
peace, public 231
peasants 142
  completion of life cycle 342
  religion 285
  sentimentality 286
  supported by churches 143
Petty, William 101
philanthropic works: United States 373
philosophy 334
physics
  presuppositions 326
  Western 53, 61
Pietism 100, 281, 325
  attitude to authority 279
Pius X 210
Plato: cave analogy 317, 323–4
Ploetz, Alfred
  on race 292–3
  Weber's comments on 306–14
politicians
  control over state bureaucracies 247–8,
    255–71
  ethos of office 203–4
  power 259–60
  qualities of 258–9
  responsibility 258, 259–60
  training 261
politics
  ethical action and 245–7, 253–4
  influence of ascetic Protestantism
    367–75
  neutrality of teachers 318, 328–33
  Weber 3–4, 8, 36
poverty 91, 100
  Calvinist views on 307
power
  concept of 179
  definition 174
  distinct from authority 174
  distribution in groups 147–50
  domination and 180–6
  economic 180–1
  parliaments 170, 248
  political organizations 232–3
  politicians 258, 259–60
  states 222
power politics 260
practical rationality 27–8

predestination, doctrine of 278, 280–1,
    284
  described 24
  United States 372
prestige: states 222, 232–3
  *see also* honor
presuppositions 319–20, 326–7, 330,
    337–8
price policy: Quakers 115–16
pride, national 233
printing: Western 55
private sphere *see* public
privileges
  legal 243–4
  status groups 158–9
professors *see* teachers
profit
  Protestant ethic and 90–1
  pursuit of 56–7, 79–80
progress
  cultural 342
  scientific 316, 322–3
proletariat 3
  concept of 60
  indifference to concept of nation 227
  *see also* working class
proof, rational: Western 53
property
  social stratification and 152–3
  status groups and 147, 155–6
proportion, sense of: politicians 259
Protestant ethic 12, 24–6
  religious origins of 69–74, 75–110
  spirit of capitalism and 111–19
Protestantism
  Arminian in United States 371–2, 373
  ethical action 267–8
  *see also* ascetic Protestantism; specific
    churches and sects
providential 25
Prussia 184
  bureaucracy 176
Prynne, William 101, 102
public good 274, 278
public sphere: separation from private 195,
    213–14
Puritanism
  American Revolution 370
  inner-worldly asceticism 351
  organization of life 93–6, 118
  persecution of 101–2
  United States 346
  vocational calling 84, 86, 88, 89–91
  wealth 98–100
  work ethic 70–3, 92–3, 345, 350

Quakers 90, 96, 98
  ethical action 267
  freedom of conscience 283
  hostility to authority 279, 284
  price policy 115–16
quality: rationalization and 358
quantity: rationalization and 358

race
  concept of 291–5
  consciousness of 291
  vital 292–3, 309
race membership 291, 297–314
race system 309
rationalism
  Chinese 27
  economic: spirit of capitalism in 79–82
  India 27
  modern Western: Weber's model 27–34
  practical 81
  Western 49–51, 53–67
rationality
  formal 27, 223, 357, 358
    of accounting 127, 129
    concept of 125–6
    practical 27–8
    substantive, concept of 125–6
    theoretical 28
rationalization 339
  Data Protection Act and 353–6
  fast-food restaurants 357–60
  science 316, 322–3
reason 353
  Enlightenment 283
referendum 264
Reformation: influence of 82–3
religion
  communities of *virtuosi* 363
  concept of nation and 226
  economic ethics of 50
  education and 373–4
  ethical action 247, 266–8
  ethics 252
  ethnicity and 301–2
  influence on United States democracy
    367–75
  rationalism and 28–9
  science and 319–20, 329–32, 337–43
  *see also* churches; clergy; Reformation;
    sects; specific groups
Rembrandt 95
Renaissance: science 317, 324
reproduction: Middle Ages 307
repulsion: racial differences and 299
respect, lack of: United States 279

responsibility
  ethic of 3, 248, 265–71, 362
  politicians 258, 259–60
restaurants, fast-food 345, 357–60
revelations 330, 338
revolution 215
  American 370
revolutionary movements: routinization
  268–9, 345, 363–6
revolutionary socialism 265–6
rights 355
  economic 283
  freedom of conscience 283
  individual 223
  protection by state 231
Robespierre, Maximilien 283
Rodbertus, Karl Johann 59
Roman Catholic *see* Catholic
Rome, Ancient
  ethnicity 308
  fall of 293
  freedom of conscience 282
Rousseau, Jean-Jacques 283
routinization of charisma 219–20, 268–9,
  363–6
  in revolutionary movements 345
rules: bureaucracies 196
rural social structures: in Germany and
  United
  States 142–6
  *see also* agriculture; land
Russia
  bureaucracy 210
  labor management 345

sacrifice, intellectual 319, 338, 339, 340
salvation 319, 320, 338, 341, 342, 343
  revolutionary movements 364
  social action and 26–7
savings: with asceticism 97
Schäfer, Dietrich 328
Schaff, Philip 373
Schiller, Johann von 3
Schopenhauer, Artur 7
Schulte, Aloys 117
science
  bureaucracy 212
  against charisma 177
  limits of 335–6
  meaninglessness of 320, 326
  presuppositions 330
  race 293
  religion and 319–20, 329–32, 337–43
  specialization in 123, 139–41
  theoretical rationality 28

value of 316–18, 321–7, 333–5
vocational calling 249
Western 53, 61
  *see also* natural sciences; social sciences
sciences: historical and cultural 317–18, 327
secession: ethnicity and 301
secrecy
  bureaucracy 206–7
  official 189
sect spirit: United States 275, 286
sects 273, 368–9
  autonomy of individuals in 277–89
  baptizing 281
  democracy and 280
  freedom of conscience 282
  hostility to authority 284
  influence on work ethic 71–3
  spirit of capitalism and 111–19
  United States 274
  *see also* specific names
self, individual: Western search for 64–5
  *see also* individual, autonomy of
sentimentality: peasants 286
serfs 348
service providers: social stratification and
  153
sexual relations
  Puritan 88
  race and 297–8
Shakespeare, William 160, 270–1
Simmel, Georg 36, 258
slaves and slavery 132, 183, 205
  Indians and 311
  as status group 153
Smith, Adam 89
Smith, Timothy 369
social action
  centrality of 10–12
  ethnicity and 292, 303–4
  locating 17–19
  parties 161–2
  race and 297
  regularities of 14
  social class and 148, 153–4, 155
  status groups and 148
  types of 10–11
social movements: United States 346, 368,
  372–3
social policy: racial hygiene 307
social sciences
  domain of 318–19
  limited usefulness of 315–16
  meaning of 316
social welfare policies 246, 254
  Germany 293

socialism 60, 122, 128
  modern economies 132–3
  substantive rationality 126
societal domains *see* domains
society
  dynamic and open 34
  proposals for change in 36
  Weber's vision 19–22
sociology
  race 293, 310
  research strategies and procedures
    Weber 14–19, 345
    assessment of 37–9
    foundational features of 8–14
    impact of 5
Socrates 324
solidarity: sentiment of 225–6
Sombart, Werner 80, 335
specialists: replacing cultivated man 123,
    137–41
specialization
  in modern economies 130
  of office management 196
  in science 123, 139–41
  of work 89, 91, 102, 121, 122
Spener, Philipp 86, 279, 325
Spinoza, Baruch 7
spirit of capitalism 24–6
  asceticism and 85–107
  capitalist form and 77–8
  development of economic rationalism
    and 79–82
  Franklin 70, 75–7, 78, 102
  Protestant sects and 111–19
sports: Puritan aversion to 93–4
Stalin 345
  transformation of revolutionary
    movement 365–6
state
  advantages of universal suffrage 169–70
  basic functions 230–7
  bureaucratization 213–14
  capitalism and 101
  data protection 355
  definition 222
  ethical action 246–7
  Germany 33, 124
  law 238
  legitimacy 239–40
  monopoly of legitimate physical coercion
    222, 230–1, 239–40, 246, 254
  religion and 280–1
  separation from church 280–2
  in United States 369, 370–1

Western 55
  *see also* specific names
state-socialism: imperialist capitalism
    236–7
status
  ethnicity and 302
  race and 298
status groups
  bureaucracy 202
  ethnic groups as 157–8
  honor 155–7
  market principle and 155
  occupational 161
  origins of 149
  privileges 158–9
  social class and 147–9
  United States civic associations as 287,
    288
stratification, social: inequality and 147–50,
    151–62
  *see also* classes
students: ethical neutrality of teachers 318,
    319, 328–33
  *see also* fraternities
subjective meaning *see* meaning
submission: duty of 348–9
substantive rationality 125–6
succession: of charismatic authority 220
suffrage, universal: Germany 150, 168–71
suicide 342
superiority, myth of 190
supermarkets 359
Swammerdam, Jan 325

Taylor system 350
teachers: ethical neutrality of 318, 319,
    328–33
technology: Western 61
telephones 360
testifying to belief 25, 84–5, 117, 118
theaters 95
theology 337–8
  Western 53
theoretical rationality 28
Thucydides 54
time
  capitalism and 75
  productive use of 75, 87, 351
Tocqueville, Alexis de 371
tolerance 273, 280–2
Tolstoi, Leo 269, 317, 320, 335
  on death 316, 322–3
  on science 326
Tönnies, Ferdinand 286

tools of trade: separation from workers 122, 130–2
tradition: power in rural social structures 142
traditional social action 11
traditionalism
economic *see* economic ethic
follows revolutionism 268–9, 345, 363–6
training: officials 201–2
tribes 292
relationship to political community 305–6
Trollope, Anthony 369
trust: development of 351

understanding
interpretative 71
of social action 10–12
intuitive and empathic 10
rational 10
unions: Negroes in 311
United States
American Revolution 370
Caesarism 263
democracy 273–6, 332, 367–75
examinations 137
foreign policy 368
modern capitalism 124
modernity 31–2
new aristocracy 150, 166–7
New York's position in 184
political culture of democracy 273–6
political parties 213
political party donors 205
poor white trash 302
Protestant ethic 25–6, 111–13
Protestant sects 71–3
pursuit of gain 103
race 298, 310
relationships between blacks and whites 293
rural social structures 142–6
status groups 156–7
tribal cult 305
Weber visits 7–8
universities
academic disciplines in 55
bureaucracy 212
examinations 137
neutrality of teachers 318
workers in 131

value-freedom 12–14, 318
value ideal 13
value-judgments 335–6

value-rational social action 10–11
value-relevance 12–14
value-spheres 356
values 12–14, 245, 247
civic 31–2, 33
ethical: neutrality of teachers 328–33
origin 245
Protestant ethic 24–6
weakening of 34–5
vanity: politicians 247, 259
violence
ethical action and 254, 265–9
monopoly of physical by states 222, 230–1, 239–40, 246, 254
private 231
vocation: office as 201–2
*see also* calling, vocational
Voltaire 81
voluntarism: United States 370–4

wars
economic interests and 235, 237
origins of 222, 232
United States attitudes to 368
wealth
production of 25
Protestant ethic and 70–1, 72, 86–7, 91, 96–7
secularizing effects of 98–100
separation of public and private 59, 129, 195
United States 373
wealthy *see honoratiores*
Weber, Helene 8
Weber, Marianne 7, 8
Weber, Max (father) 7, 8
Weber, Max
biography 7–8
comments on Ploetz 306–14
comparative concepts 4–5
*Economic Ethics of the World Religions* 50, 51
*Economy and Society* 14, 16, 17–19, 21
influence of 345
modern Western rationalism 27–34
multicausality 22–7
politics 3–4
"Politics as a Vocation" 315
*Prefatory Remarks* 49–50
*Protestant Ethic and the Spirit of Capitalism, The* 8, 23–4, 69–71
*Protestant Sects in North America, The* 71
research procedures and strategies 14–19

Weber, Max (*cont'd*)
 "Science as a Vocation" 315
 sociology 5, 8–19, 37–9
 texts 40–1
 themes 2
 vision of society 19–22
 works 1–5
welfare *see* social welfare
Wesley, John 99
West: rationalism of 49–51, 53–67
White people in the United States
 poor white trash 302
 relationship with Black 293
William of Orange 280
William the Silent 282
Williams, Roger 281
work
 capitalist organization of 59–61
 poor status of physical 159
 scorn for 311

specialization of 121, 122
 *see also* labor
work ethic 87–90
 England and Russia 347–52
 religious origins of 75–110
 *see also* Protestant ethic
workers
 consumers as 359–60
 depravity of poor 348, 349
 mass behavior 148, 154
 Negroes as 311
 separation from tools of trade 122, 130–2
working class 144
 separation from tools of trade 122
 *see also* proletariat
world views 38
 absence of religious 28–9

Zeeland: tolerance 281–2
Zinzendorf, Nicolaus 100